**Praise for *Fundamentals of H...***

"...parents will appreciate the book's wealth of wisdom on child development, learning and family life... in the tradition of David Elkind (*The Hurried Child*) and Neil Postman (*The Disappearance of Childhood*) ... reminds readers of the benefits of living a life that celebrates the simple things: play, conversation, togetherness, and growing up..."
— JANUARY 12, 2004 REVIEW, *Publishers Weekly*

"...yours is the only homeschooling book I actually bought ..."
— HOMESCHOOLING MOM

"...This book bursts with creative ideas and resources that every homeschooling parent will find valuable."
— JULY 2003 REVIEW, *Mothering Magazine*

"If you've been looking for a book that respects parents' common sense and wisdom, that honors children and their amazing power to learn, and that tackles its subject with thoughtfulness and insight, this is the book for you."
— ELIZABETH McCULLOUGH REVIEW, *Home Education Magazine*

"... an extensive, 'parent friendly' guide to the techniques, pitfalls, and advantages of homeschooling... strongly recommended primer...an invaluable supplementary resource ... a balanced homeschooling teaching plan, as well as a wealth of tips, tricks, and techniques to creating the best home learning environment possible."
— MIDWEST BOOK REVIEW

"If you're having a hard time mastering the idea that learning is about life... [this is] a great resource... a rich and eloquently personal look at how children learn in families... well organized and easy to dip into whenever the need arises."
— JANUARY/FEBRUARY 2003 REVIEW, *Life Learning Magazine*

"Many books make such a clear distinction between school and life. This books helps us see how these can be beautifully intertwined.... Our goals are to educate the kids while building a strong family. It is possible to do both! This book shows us how to accomplish these goals with love and togetherness."
— CHRISTINE FIELD, *The Old Schoolhouse Magazine*

"...Every parent should read this book... an outstanding learning plan for families..."
— CHILDREN'S LIBRARIAN, Newport, Oregon

# More Praise for *Fundamentals of Homeschooling* —

"Finally! A homeschooling book that puts first things first! Ann Lahrson-Fisher has unlocked the simple yet fundamental notion that children's learning is best rooted in successful family living.

"I've often told anxious parents that schools are nothing more than poor substitutes for good families. By focusing on what really matters — play, conversation, togetherness, exploration, and providing living examples of lifelong learning — *Fundamentals of Homeschooling* will both reassure and equip homeschooling families for the chaotic and sublime journey that education should be all about."
— DAVID H. ALBERT, author, *Homeschooling and the Voyage of Self-Discovery: A Journey of Original Seeking*, and columnist, *Home Education Magazine*

"Many years of homeschooling experience and wisdom shine bright and clear through the pages of this book. It goes far beyond the basics to get at the heart of how homeschooling families succeed, and offers a multitude of great ideas for all ages and stages."
— LAURA DERRICK, homeschooling mom of two; president, *National Home Education Network*

"…Bravo! …Comprehensive doesn't say enough…forty-five chapters divided into six parts, plus a helpful appendix – all in an easily readable 430 pages!"
— SHARI HENRY, *Homeschooling Today*

"Ann Lahrson-Fisher has written a thorough and friendly handbook about how to live comfortably with your children as you homeschool them. What separates this book from similar titles is Lahrson-Fisher's passion and insight about how to help parents 'give their children freedom to discover their heart's desire in their own time and way.'"
— PATRICK FARENGA, author, *Teach Your Own: The John Holt Book of Homeschooling*

"…a work of great good sense that will enlarge your imagination as it holds your hand. This is a potent package, a sword and shield against the demons of doubt. Mrs. Fisher deserves a medal."
— JOHN TAYLOR GATTO, author, *Dumbing Us Down*; *The Underground History of American Education*

"Ann's subtitle hints at the underlying thesis she works from, which is that homeschooling works because families work. Ann's writing portrays a sense of wonder and discovery at the simple truth of how people who live together also learn together.

"...Through page after page I found myself nodding in recognition and agreement with her perceptive observations. She writes, "The Main Event of growing up is the process of gaining control, balancing freedom with responsibility." Of course! This makes so much sense — I am reminded of the clear, common-sense observations of another great homeschooling writer: John Holt. This is a book that will...empower anyone seeking to homeschool."

— HELEN HEGENER, publisher, *Home Education Magazine*


"...does for homeschoolers what *The Joy of Cooking* does for cooks — offers a guide to the novice and a handy reference tool for the experienced. Whether you need ideas for a new approach, or want help resolving a problem, you'll find the information in here. Ann adeptly offers both reassurance for what you're doing, and new ideas if you're looking for a change. The chapters offer food for thought for working with toddlers through teens. Even after seven years of homeschooling, I had never considered using a talking belly button alter ego to create a joyful disruption to help point my child in a more desirable direction!
...at the top of my list of recommended resources for all homeschoolers.

— AMY GRANT, president, *Oregon Home Education Network*


"Parents can sometimes get so wrapped up in educational expectations and worries, that they forget just how easy it is for a child to learn...This book gets them back on track, and not just by inspiring them, but by offering time honored detailed suggestions.

"*Fundamentals* is a new gem that could easily become a classic. It has been written for all homeschoolers from beginners to old timers, but I'd urge that it be placed in the hands of new parents as well because it's such an outstanding book on how to help children learn.

"This is a wonderful book — don't miss reading it, and don't forget to give it to new parents so their new family has a successful start!"

— KAREN TAYLOR, editor, *The California Homeschool Guide*

# Fundamentals of

# HOME-

# SCHOOLING

## By
## Ann Lahrson-Fisher

Foreword by Linda Dobson
author of the classic
Homeschooling Book of Answers

Nettlepatch Press
Carson, Washington

Fundamentals of Homeschooling:
*Notes on Successful Family Living*
By Ann Lahrson-Fisher

2 4 6 8 10 9 7 5 3

Prior publication:"Against the Flow: Handling Criticism" first appeared in 1991 in *Home Education Magazine* edited by Mark and Helen Hegener, and later in *Growing Without Schooling*, edited by Susannah Sheffer. Early versions of "Learning Clubs" and "Learning by Computer" were included in the book *Creating Learning Communities*, edited by Ron Miller, in 2000. Some chapters have been adapted from *Homeschooling in Oregon*, including material that has been made available on the Internet for one-time inclusion in local homeschooling newsletters.

**ISBN 0-9640813-6-9**
Library of Congress Control Number: 2002105271

Publisher's Cataloging in Publication Data
Lahrson-Fisher, Ann
    fundamentals of homeschooling: notes on successful family living/
    by Ann Lahrson-Fisher
    Included index and bibliographical references.
    ISBN 0-9640813-6-9 (pbk.)
    1. Homeschooling — United States. 2. Homeschooling — Resources. 3.
    Education — Home-based. 4. Home Instruction. 5. Home Schooling.
    I. Lahrson-Fisher, Ann.  II. Title.    LC 37-44.3        371.042

Cover design by Riverside Graphics, Stevenson, Washington www.riverside-graphics.net
Photo by Kay Caldwell, Gresham, Oregon 503/667.4644
Printed in the United States of America by McNaughton & Gunn, Inc., Saline, Michigan

Published by
Nettlepatch Press, PO Box 1279-C, Carson, Washington 98610 U.S.A.
509/427.4771  fax: 509/427.7473
    ann@nettlepatch.net     www.nettlepatch.net/homeschool
    To purchase additional copies of this book, contact the publisher
    or your favorite bookseller. Bulk discounts available upon written request.

IN GRATEFUL MEMORY


This book is dedicated to the memories
of two steadfast advocates for learning, children, and families,
of two unique people who opened very different doors
to the way of homeschooling,
of two who left us before we were ready.


John Holt
Boston, Massachusetts
1923-1985

Dorothy Moore
Camas, Washington
1915-2002

# TABLE OF CONTENTS

## PART ONE   PLAY

# PART TWO   CONVERSATIONS

# PART THREE    TOGETHERNESS

# PART FOUR    GROWING UP

# PART FIVE EXPLORATIONS I - THE BIG PICTURE

# PART SIX EXPLORATIONS II - SUBJECTS

# FOREWORD

*by Linda Dobson*

Can an act seemingly as complex as educating one's children at home really be reduced to the four remarkably simple elements outlined in this book — play, conversation, togetherness, and growing up? Like the author of this book I, too, can look back at the homeschooling experience and offer an unequivocal *yes!*

Believe me, I know the concept is hard to grasp. It goes against everything we were programmed to believe during our years in traditional school settings. The concept begins to make sense, however, when we take a moment to look at what the word "educate" really means. Despite our many shared school experiences, such as sitting in a classroom where, like a pitcher, a teacher dispensed knowledge into all of the little cups sitting in rows before her and they later poured out the acquired knowledge on to test papers, the intent of the word "educate" isn't "to put in." In fact, it means just the opposite. *Educere*, the Latin root of educate, means "to lead out."

If we consider education in this perspective, the perspective much truer to education's purpose, what better opportunities exist for parents "to lead out," or educate their children, than play, conversation, togetherness, and growing up?

Also contrary to what we were programmed to believe during school attendance, learning can happen without bells and whistles, teachers and administrators, tests and diplomas. Many experienced home educators will happily testify that learning happens *better* in direct proportion to the degree that it unfolds without these things; in other words, much more naturally. And what is more natural in the context of family life — where homeschooling is conceived, born, and nurtured — than play, conversation, togetherness, and inevitable growing up?

Most of today's parents, compliments of our own school experience, were hoodwinked, bamboozled, and occasionally outright lied to when it came to the benefits of learning. We were told that if we sat still and soaked up that which was being poured into us we would get good grades that would get us into a good college that would get us a good job that would get us good money that would get us a good house in a good neighborhood filled with good things to which we would drive after work, exhausted, in a good car. (During all of those formative years we spent inside school, how often did the adults placed in charge of our time say things to us like "Learning is its own reward," or "Mistakes are learning opportunities" or "He who knows much about others may be learned, but he who understands himself is more intelligent"?)

If the schooling experience left you wondering, "Is that all there is?" don't worry. You're in good company — and you've got lots of it. Thankfully, that *isn't* all there is, and today it's easier than ever for growing numbers of parents to offer more — much more — to their children.

In her opening note, Ann Lahrson-Fisher describes successful homeschooling's simple foundation as "living a satisfying learning lifestyle." Education characterized as a learning lifestyle instead of an ordeal to survive until you make it to the welcome reprieve of summer vacation. Success defined in terms of satisfaction instead of things. A family that plays, converses, and grows up together. Ah, yes, homeschooling is so different from — and so much more than — schooling at home.

Forget about the "schooling" you received and focus instead on learning. Learning happens in a natural fashion when a child with curiosity even mildly intact sets off on an educational journey guided by a parent who is observant, caring, and "thinks out loud." (You'll find out more about this wonderful — and fun and effective — way to "teach" as you get into this book.)

Lucky are the families newly turning to homeschooling, not only to have access to the wisdom of one who has "been there and done that," but also to receive that wisdom so neatly presented in a down-to-earth, common sense package as the one *Fundamentals of Homeschooling* has grown to be. Some of the ideas will leave you wondering, "Now, why didn't I think of that?" Others will be revelations that because of your own schooling you wouldn't have considered in a million years. All of the ideas are born of the author's experience, remembrances of the good *and* the bad, the personal successes, and lessons learned from the failures.

And that, dear reader, is what learning is all about.

---

*Linda Dobson began homeschooling her three children in New York in 1985. A nationally respected conference speaker, article and book author, she was Home Education Magazine news editor and columnist for eight years, and currently writes the "Notes from the Road Less Traveled" column. Linda is "early years" advisor for Homeschool.com, and editor for the Prima Publishing Home Learning Library.*

ACKNOWLEDGMENTS

Of the many people who have contributed to this book with support, ideas, or information, my husband Don has been my greatest strength. He believed in this project for years before I let him read even *one* word. His love, willingness to listen, patience, and support have bolstered me every time I wailed that I could not possibly go on. Thank you and I love you.

My children: Alice and Erin, wonderful daughters now grown, graciously allow me to tell their stories. Without them, I have nothing to write about, for they taught me most of what I know. Chad and Lenor, Don's terrific kids, homeschooled long before the word was coined, have let me peek at their experiences as vigorous adult learners. Thanks, kids.

I am grateful to Rick Lahrson for being a sounding board for many years, for being a good dad to his children, and for his great contribution to my appreciation of play and puzzle solving.

Three editors, dear friends all, have been pivotal in helping me put my thoughts in presentable order: Kim Gordon, Jeanne Biggerstaff, and Christine Webb. You let the editorial red ink flow, ladies, and you improved my work with every stroke. Thank you and your families for the irreplaceable gift of your time.

Rick Lahrson, Alice Cone, and Erin Lahrson willingly proofread when I needed extra sets of eyes. How I appreciate your time and effort! (All errors were added *after* their proofing.)

Among the many others who have contributed to this book: Rebecca Severeide, thanks for the portfolio work that inspired parts of "Family Friendly Evaluations." I owe an huge debt of gratitude to many members and attendees of Oregon Home Education Network, Oregon Chautauqua, ORsig e-mail list, Greater Portland Homeschoolers (and its previous incarnations), and National Home Education Network, who have contributed enormously to my understanding of homeschooling and the homeschooling way of life.

Finally, thank you to the parents and children I have known over the years. You invited me into your lives, and I am honored by your trust. While we worked together, you allowed me to glimpse your real lives, and thus gather the bits of understanding that confirmed my ideas again, and again, and again.

## A NOTE FROM THE AUTHOR

Any attempt to examine an "unstudy-able" topic such as homeschooling is a walk on the wild side. Twenty-some years of homeschooling experience, head-scratching and serendipitous research have led me to first ask, and then answer, these questions, "How does homeschooling work so successfully for so many decidedly different families, all of whom use unique plans, materials, values, and theories of learning?" "Just how do homeschooling families succeed so reliably, so independently, and so joyfully?" Perhaps more to the point, I had to ask myself, "Why do successful homeschooling parents, students, and graduates walk around with big ol' grins on their faces?"

In time I realized that I was seeking the underlying foundations of successful homeschooling. I found those foundations deeply rooted in the familiar: the natural and age-old practices of successful families. Parents have successfully guided and directed their children's education throughout human history. What better assurance of success could a family want than to live and learn together in the same satisfying lifestyle that has been in place from time immemorial?

## Habits of Successful Family Living

Homeschooling success builds on this simple foundation: living a satisfying learning lifestyle. Say it to yourself: "Living a satisfying learning lifestyle." Can you feel the tension leave your limbs? Do you feel a grin coming on? Are you surprised to discover that successful homeschooling is not founded on parental heroics but on family satisfaction?

Invariably, this satisfying learning lifestyle interweaves fundamental and natural themes. Families learn how to live together effectively. Families enjoy play of all kinds. Family members delight in conversations among themselves and with others. Families fully support their individual children in the process of growing up and finding a satisfying niche in the community. Families immerse themselves in exploring the world around them, actively pursuing all manner of interests.

When seen in the light of these common themes, we can readily see why homeschooling works so well in so many different kinds of families. Those diverse families really have a great deal in common. Variations of beliefs, politics, finances, location, social position, academics, and talent fade in significance and slip properly into the background.

These age-old themes are easily thought of as habits. According to Webster, a *habit* is "1) a thing done often and hence, usually done easily; 2) a pattern of action that is acquired and has become so automatic that it is difficult to break."

It has been said that everyday habits and patterns of behavior are the true fabric of success. That concept rings especially true for the homeschooling family. Everyday habits — habits of togetherness, play, conversation, growing up together, and exploring the world — build a foundation for homeschooling success.

## This Book is About Habits

In this book, I explore many aspects of homeschooling from the perspective these habits of success. Each habit is presented as a section theme. A keynote chapter introduces each section, discussing some broader implications of the habits/themes in family life. Other chapters in each section dig into nitty gritty issues of the homeschooling family life.

Here is a thumbnail sketch of the contents of this book.

## Play

Parents who homeschool with the greatest success love to play with their children. They learn to protect children's playtime. They appreciate how much learning results from many kinds of play. *Play* allows the spark of creative insight to flame — a most powerful learning tool.

## Conversation

Parents who homeschool love to talk and listen to their kids. Conversation includes all communications — oral, written, and mathematical. Parents encourage and guide their children to love learning through daily conversation. *Conversation* builds strong families through the oral tradition of passing culture and information from one generation to the next.

## Togetherness

Parents who homeschool love to hang out, go places, and do things with their children — together. This section explores several important family togetherness issues, including challenges, social concerns, homeschooling management issues, and tips for coping with differing ages and stages. *Togetherness* suggests a process of staying connected with family and loved ones, building community, and learning to live with others in the wider world.

## Growing Up

Parents who homeschool find ways to celebrate or otherwise note the myriad steps of growing up in a way that is consistent with a homeschooling lifestyle. Accomplishments, culminating events, rites of passage, and celebrations memorialize the path to maturity and independence. In this section, we'll discuss some of the issues of concern that are often part of our modern coming-of-age experience, such as test-taking, college, and decisions about work. *Growing Up*, including ordinary family activities and those activities that others hand over to schools, are those activities that celebrate the seasons of their lives.

Exploration I — The Big Picture
Exploration II — Subjects

Finally, dig into *Exploration*, a storehouse of practical tips, suggestions, and resources — ample grist for the learning mill of the mind.

The first part of this two-pronged resource section features general approaches to acquiring information. Suggestions for successful field trips and group learning activities are included.

The second part covers typical subjects and topics individually, exploring knowledge systematically through details, deeper study, acquiring skills, and learning facts, topic by topic by topic. You'll find straightforward approaches and a sampling of resources to get you started throughout.

Finally, the bibliography, curriculum resources, and the legal compliance/support resources listed in the appendix will expand your understanding of key issues and help you access the many materials available.

That's it, homeschooling success in its shortest form.
And now the long form …

# PART 1
## Play

Featuring:

## chapter one

# KEYNOTE
# PLAY, THE ROOT OF LEARNING
*learning to play, playing to learn*

Pssst! Wanna hear a secret? Kids love to play. Not only do they love to play, but the better they are at playing, the better they are at learning. How can that be?

It is easy to forget that the rudiments of play begin to develop in the earliest days of life, so we'll begin with a look at babyhood to see the basic connection between play and learning. Once you recall the importance of play in your child's early learning life, you can better appreciate how learning occurs through play.

No, I will not tell you to teach your children to play. No need to do that, for *they* will teach you how they play. I just want to trigger your own memories of how your children learned to play so that you will better understand how they play to learn. Remember those precious years when your child first learned to play? Did you notice what was going on?

## Before Play

Belly blows and giggles. Rattles and teething rings. From diaper changes to baths, feedings to naps, loving parents interact with their babies all day long. We couldn't wait for that first smile, could we? We just kept on playing and interacting with our newborn children. *To be able to **play**, a child first discovers the pleasure of interaction* with people and things, not just to meet needs, but to occupy time and just for fun.

Did you go as gaga over your newborn as I did? I gazed into the eyes of my newborn child for hours, responding to every gurgle and coo. Chattering about the daily routine, reading adult materials aloud as the baby plays, singing lullabies, talking through the tears and sleepless nights you and your child share: these are the earliest of social activities. Before long, children understand words such as Mama, Dada, siblings' names, pets, drink, down and up. First efforts at speech follow soon thereafter. *To be able to **play**, a child first observes that people interact with one another to share information, to stay connected, and for personal enjoyment.*

Do you remember that you were the most perfect first playmate for your child? That is what *she* thought. She valiantly reached for the toy keys you dangled because she was encouraged by your smiles and urging. He may have let you put that green goo in his mouth because you entertained him in so many ways before — what little delight might you have for him this time? Perhaps he swallowed the mashed peas and perhaps he spewed them with a grimace. In either case, he continued exploring the world with all its surprises — because of you. *To be able to **play**, a child must feel safe and supported by the people in his world.*

"V-room v-room." Were you thrilled when you could get down on the floor for a playful romp with your crawling baby? Most parents can't wait to drive toy cars and feed baby dolls. They play with the building blocks and dolls and stack, knock down, build, rock, cuddle — whatever the activity, the parent is there exploring and encouraging, helping when necessary, and offering occasional new ideas. Splash in the bath, sit on the grass, or pet the cat with soft strokes. *To be able to **play**, a child first discovers that the world is an interesting place and worth exploring.*

Any activity that brought my children to peels of laughter was my greatest joy. I loved it all — peek-a-boo games, starring the incredible disappearing parent; knee-bouncing horsey rides; taking piggies to market; airplane spoons delivering food to baby-mouth hangars; nursery rhymes, stories, poems. I sang all the children's songs and lullabies I could remember, in or out of tune. I kept at it. These small joyful activities are the first tiny steps towards literacy. You keep at it too, Mom and Dad. Children love the repetition, the flow, and the sound of baby games. *To be able to **play**, a child first develops a rudimentary knowledge of the passage of time, as demonstrated by his desire to repeat pleasurable events.*

And then there is silliness. Goofy incongruities crack kids up. Did you try to comb your hair with your coffee cup? If so, you probably elicited fits of glee from your young child. A child who knows a cup is for drinking will see the inconsistency at once. You may have talked about what you were doing, saying things like, "No, I can't comb my hair with a cup. A cup is for what? Yes, it is for drinking juice. What can I use to comb my hair?" And the tot may scoot off to the bathroom to find a comb or brush. Mom plays by making a big joke of her "mistake" and letting her tot show her how to fix it. *To be able to **play**, a child finds ways to handle mistakes and surprises.*

All well and good, you might say, but what do these "playing with baby" tasks have to do with learning? Hang on. First, read the sentences that follow — the sentences that follow — I copied the italicized sentences from the previous paragraphs.

*To be able to **learn**, a child first discovers the pleasure of interaction with people and things, not just to meet needs, but to occupy time and just for fun.*

*To be able to **learn**, a child first observes that people interact with one another to share information, to stay connected, and for personal enjoyment.*

*To be able to **learn**, a child must feel safe and supported by the people in his world.*

*To be able to **learn**, a child first discovers that the world is an interesting place and worth exploring.*

*To be able to **learn**, a child first develops a rudimentary knowledge of the passage of time, as demonstrated by his desire to repeat pleasurable memories.*

*To be able to **learn**, a child finds ways to handle mistakes and surprises.*

Did you notice that in each sentence, I substituted the word *learn* for the word *play*? What does play have to do with learning? Play is so much more than a critically important element of learning. Play *IS* learning! If play is learning in the early years, learning can be play in the later years. Learning *IS* play!

## Creating a Play-Friendly Environment

As a child launches into the playful years, how can you as a parent best support a healthy play environment? Generally, the best support is to be fully accessible, supporting your child's play development as you take on roles in addition to the role of favorite playmate. These are some ways that parents support the processes that allow their children to *learn to play* and *play to learn*.

### Social Consultant

What? You don't think of yourself as the Emily Post of the diaper set? Well, you are! When the baby is old enough to enjoy the company of other children, Mom or Dad stays close to the child and supplies guidance when it is needed. "Wait until Billy has finished playing with the toy bear. Here is a floppy-eared rabbit." "Tell Suzie thank-you for the cookie." "Can you share the blocks or shall we put them away?" How could our children ever learn appropriate social behavior without the services of a social consultant?

### Playtime General Manager

Children need parent *availability* whether they play alone or with other children. Parents may find they are both the most and the least important person when they have created an environment that supports free play.

An atmosphere of safety allows the child carefree play. Choosing a few compatible playmates reduces the chance of playtime disagreements that are beyond each child's ability to handle. Skinned knees and bumped heads are inevitable, quickly healed with a kiss, a hug, or a colorful bandage. Busy nearby with their own tasks, parents still observe the play from the corner of the eye.

Occasionally, the parent takes on a different role. Supply sergeant or wardrobe supervisor might describe it best. "Mommy, I need a spoon!" "Tie this ribbon in my hair, please, Daddy." By being readily available, you can easily redirect your child to the desired props as the request comes up. If she wants a pretend feather in her hair, you might offer a real feather if you have one. If he takes a real knife out of the drawer, perhaps you'll need to do some cutting for him, suggest a pair of scissors for his project, or help him make a play knife to cut imaginary ropes!

## Playtime Protector

Children need protected time for uninterrupted play. Playtime must be long enough, often enough, and without responsibility or care. Chores interrupt. Reminders to put away his socks or put away his toys interrupt. Simply set aside different times for chores and for playtime.

If you protect playtime, your whole schedule may run smoother. If you need to have your child watch the baby while you take an emergency phone call, no problem. Just remember that watching younger siblings is a different kind of playtime for him. Make certain that he has other times to play freely and without responsibility.

## Activities Scheduler

One way to protect your child's playtime is to help him find closure to the play activity when you must load him into the van for some reason. Many children learn to make a smooth transition to the next activity if they have a reminder of what is next. "We need to get ready for your swimming lesson." "It is time for your dolls to take a nap so that we can go to play group." "You have five minutes to find a stopping place and finish building your space shuttle later." Or try a subtle message of activity change. "Lunch will be ready in ten minutes. Do you want orange wheels or apple slices with your sandwich?" A small chore sometimes works as a transition. "You can play five more minutes. When your cars are lined up on the toy shelf, it will be time for a snack and a story." You might even help your child set a timer so that he can take charge of keeping track of time for himself.

## The Right Amount of Free Play

Once your baby has crawled off your lap to explore on her own, how do you know if she is getting a good balance of structured activities and free play?

Happily for parents, children give clear signs when their lives are out of balance. Watch for excessive whining, irritability, clinging, tantrums, aggressiveness with playmates, siblings, pets, or toys, or excessive-for-this-child emotionalism or crying. These are typical behaviors to watch for when *anything* goes wrong in your child's life. Such childish communications can mean anything from "I am ill" to "I am bored" to "I am overstimulated." Parents have the added joy of learning how to be emotional and intellectual detectives!

Use the techniques you drew upon when the child was an infant. Something was wrong, but you didn't know what. You know the drill: Hungry? Tired? Too hot? Too cold? Lonely? Coming down with a cold? Whatever was wrong, you kept looking until you discovered the problem. Your older child may still use some communication methods left over from babyhood when she feels out of sorts for any reason. Some children will give clear verbal hints, such as "Daddy, I want to play with a friend," or "I don't WANT to go to Bobby's house today." Remember that children have widely varied and different social needs. A schedule that satisfies one child perfectly (e.g., time with many friends daily; seeing one or two friends rarely) can be crazy-making to another.

You can't count on young children to use words to tell you that something is amiss. Some children give only subtle and easily missed clues. Take a careful look at how your child uses playtime. Does he lose himself in play, throwing himself into the pleasure of the moment? Perhaps he talks or sings to himself. Behaviors such as running, skipping, making motor or animal sounds, talking to dolls, all suggest that the child is fully engaged in play. If his play is listless or self-conscious, or he seems not to be his usual self at play, something may not be right in his world.

Your child may have too much free play or too little, or too many friends or too few. Chances are good that the clues you get will be the same not matter what. You will have to discover how to best adjust your daily routines.

Are you scheduling too much? If you get into the car every day to go somewhere, even for the most wonderful educational activities, you might be overloading your child. You can't do it all and you shouldn't try.

Are you scheduling too little? Perhaps you have been engrossed in your own projects for too many days. If she becomes more clingy or demanding every day she may be asking for more attention or something new in her life.

Sometimes a different mix of stimulating activities and playmates is all that is needed. Adjust the mix all you want, but don't skimp on playtime.

## Imagination Blooms

Did you notice the rudiments of imagination beginning to develop in your little one? Imagination is satisfying to children in the same way that creative thinking is satisfying to adults — a significant contributor to the learning process, to boot. Let's consider the fascinating quality of imagination in slow motion for a moment.

First, we know that the human brain constantly seeks patterns or meaning. Newborns are highly responsive and take in a great deal of information rapidly. Attempts at imitation, communication, and interpretation occur soon after birth.

Second, in that constant search for meaning, at some point each individual uses brain power to put unrelated ideas together in unusual or unique ways. Combing the hair with a cup is one such example. Exploring early incongruities are the beginnings of creative thought.

Finally, for imaginative thought to fully bloom, the child must be able to hold an *image* in his mind, whether that image is a picture, a sequence of actions or sound, or some mental construct. He must be able to think of an object, action, or experience when it is not present.

When all of these capabilities work together to create little scenarios and stories, we say that the child begins to pretend. Pretending is a way of acting out the images in her mind.

When people become adults, they don't use the word *pretend* anymore. Instead, they say *create, envision, think, conceive, foresee, originate, write* — all mature and adult-sounding words rooted in that early childhood act of play — pretending.

## Finally

Learning. Play. One and the same. Knowing that play and learning are two sides of the same coin should encourage you to fan the flame of play at every stage. Introduce stimulating materials and ideas and let the child at play do the rest: search for meaning, create connections from one notion to the next, and build a mental construct on which to hang future learning.

The chapters in this section include ideas for free play and for structured play — games, materials, and adaptations that will help you incorporate learning with play and play with learning.

Playtime for your young child is money in the bank of family relationships while it builds a solid love of learning. Don't sacrifice the accruing interest. Now go find your kids and play.

## chapter two

# WHY CHILDREN PLAY

*and learn to love the work of learning*

"Mommy, look at me, I'm Hooper-man!" Alice, a towel pinned around her neck as her cape, sped around the yard saving the world from bad guys. Her mispronunciation of Superman was cute, her pleasure unfettered, and I was more determined than ever that her joyous love of play should remain intact.

What I knew in my bones then was that playtime in childhood was a key fundamental for growing to a healthy adulthood. Today, now that I've spent years reflecting on how that play supports a healthy and creative adult life, I am more certain than ever. Although the capacity for carefree play arises spontaneously, that ability is not wholly resistant to assault. Children who lose the ability to play at an early age lose a powerful tool for learning.

Some aspects of why children play that are discussed in this chapter show how the ability to play can support later learning. Also included are some concerns about threats to the older child's playtime that parents should watch for.

## Elements of Free Play

Take yourself back to your childhood and identify a play experience of your own. Recall a time when you played with water and dirt, sand and mud, sticks and rocks. Perhaps you took the idea of mud pies quite literally, packing mud into old kitchen pans and setting it in the sun to "bake." Maybe you later frosted your mudpie with chocolate mud icing and decorated it with garden flowers to present to your grandmother on her birthday. Did it look so tasty that your mouth watered?

Did you dig a hole to China, and then, tired of digging, filled the hole with water and squeezed mud between your toes? Did you and your cousins bring out all your toy cars and trucks to drive up and down the super highway that you "paved" with water? Did you scoop a mound of damp sand into a cup, a cup that became an ice cream cone so real that you actually took a lick?

If mud was not your interest, possibly you played with stuffed animals or dolls, construction sets, toy cars, blocks, dress-up clothes, or a doll house. Did you have a playhouse, tree house, or a garden swing you loved? Maybe you rode your bike for hours on end. Whatever activity you recall with satisfying fondness was probably a perfect playtime activity for you. When you have a clear picture of your playtime in mind, see if you had these experiences.

## A Sublime Sense of Timelessness

So engrossed were we in our play that Mother's call to dinner startled us out of our reverie. Catapulted from our imaginary play world, jolted back to reality, we arrived at the dinner table, where clocks and other people's schedules controlled our lives. See if you can recapture the sense of timelessness and the pleasure of that feeling. If you can, you know firsthand what I mean by a sublime sense of timelessness, the experience of time standing still.

Just how does that "sublime sense of timelessness" help your child's development? That ability to get lost in play is a keystone for self-immersion in enjoyable activities of all kinds, including, of course, learning. If a student can immerse herself in enjoyable play — which is actually a child's work — a firm foundation is laid for the enjoyment of meaningful work in adulthood.

The benefits of play are little studied, but by using common sense we can speculate on other benefits of the sense of timelessness. Perhaps that shimmering illusion of endless playtime helps a child manage the difficulties of childhood. Many children struggle with transitions between activities, a feeling of powerlessness and lack of control over their own lives. The freedom to pretend to be a baby today and an astronaut tomorrow gives a child a fulfilling sense of power.

As they mature, youngsters begin to transfer that sense of timelessness to other life activities such as playing music, building a model or woodworking, game playing, riding a bike, stamp collecting, sports, reading or writing, gardening, cooking, computer games, painting or sculpture, knitting and so on. The child learns that he can regularly take a break from the trials of daily life and do something that is enjoyable and satisfying.

For some, play may lead, directly or indirectly, to a hobby, job, or lifelong interest. Although a child may not become the next Edison, Bach, or O'Keefe, he may find work that he loves. What better legacy can parents hope to give?

Children who are charging rapidly into adulthood may seek refuge from the emotionality and confusion of the teen years. The urge to find a sense of timelessness or escape is stronger than ever. Young people who have well-established "escape" routes — play opportunities and activities they enjoy — may find the path through the teen years both safer and more bearable. We may well speculate that, if a child is allowed ample healthful playtime throughout childhood, upon reaching adulthood, that same child may be able to find healthy outlets for stress. Is it possible that harmful escape activities — including addictions — are sometimes chosen by people who struggle to satisfy an unfulfilled need for play?

## A Sense of Power and Control

Now, go back to your childhood moment of play once again. Notice that you may have felt a similar feeling, closely related to your sense of timelessness: a sense of power and control over your experience. This was not your parents' project. It was yours and yours alone. Can you remember your feelings?

The child's sense of control over her play universe — whatever size it may be — is enormously satisfying to her. The control and power that children hold over their playtime universe are both serious and real even as we parents smile indulgently at those imaginary worlds. Free play allows a child time to process new or scary experiences from daily life. Your child may clue you in on what is bothering her if you keep an ear open to the play activity.

In her own world, she can create actions and props out of whatever and whoever is handy. "This desk is a hotel desk because I say it is, and I will be the clerk that helps people." A few minutes later, the game changes. "That doorway is a drive-up window where I can buy french fries because that is what I want it to be. I can buy the fries because I have imaginary money right here in this bag, which I pretend is my purse. The store person puts the money in this shoe box because it is the cash register. Daddy, will you take my order?"

Control is usually shared when two or more children play together. The rules are made up to meet the needs of the moment. Listen and you will hear, "Let's pretend that you are the Mommy." "But I want to be the big sister, not the Mommy!" "Okay, you can be the big sister, and I will be her best friend." "I'll drive the big fire truck." "Okay, you can drive the fire truck, and I'll drive the ambulance, but then I get to drive the fire truck to the next fire." Only when there is a conflict does the parent need to become involved in directing any part of this kind of play.

The perfect world of play that children create is a universe they can control, separate from the real world over which they have little control. You may discover that children need to experience power and control through play when they feel the most helpless. Times of stress, such as family problems, illness, or what have you, are times when you should make especially sure your child has a safe playtime. Sometimes little things, such as getting into the car to drive a sibling to band practice, are the most upsetting. Finding a way to assure adequate playtime puts the child back in charge within the safety of her own world.

As children grow older, they usually become involved in other kinds of activities that serve as their "play." The transition doesn't happen overnight and it can happen at various ages, depending on the child's personality, independence, and interests. Soon enough, though, you will rev up your minivan and haul students around to all those interesting activities. Your children give strident clues when they are ready for something new, so you will know when it is time for free play to give way to other activities.

During the middle years, most children begin the transition to adult types of play activities. Now they begin playing in the larger sandbox of community activities, still under adult guidance. In this way, youth prepare for the power and accompanying responsibility that looms a short distance around the corner in adulthood. By the teen years, activities of interest provide helpful boundaries that give teens more freedom and power to make their own decisions, choices, mistakes and misjudgments.

Allow your child ample appropriate opportunities to practice managing herself (control) and to take charge of her life (power). From an early age, your child can practice making mistakes in the small and safe arena of play under your protective wing, at home and with friends. Learning to accept one's errors and finding ways to correct them is a lifetime process. The sooner a child becomes comfortable with his fallibility, the sooner he discovers ways of making lemonade from life's lemons.

The Main Event of growing up is the process of gaining control, of balancing freedom with responsibility. Taking a first step, managing a spoonful of food, riding a bike, reading, doing tricky math, controlling impulses, driving a car, getting a job — all are among the endless small steps that all children take to full adult responsibility. Feeling in control of her imaginary world creates a firm base for her to launch those bigger challenges as she grows.

## Creative Outlet and Self Expression

Consult your personal childhood memory bank again. Do you recall times when you felt fully expressive? You, alone or with pals, were able to create a fantasy world that was fully satisfying. You had an absolute ability to express yourself clearly and completely and with satisfaction, remember? Reflect on the power you felt.

Children are born expressing themselves, sometimes loudly! As the infant grows into a young child, he begins to put different ideas together in his own creative ways. He may even try to invent a memory to tell you. And why not? You probably tell him "before you were born" and "while I was away" stories all the time. How is he to understand that you did not invent your story? The clumsy mixing and matching he attempts results in wonderfully amusing incidents and many messes, messes that we as parents often struggle to appreciate. A good sense of humor is a must! Parents who provide a time and place for self-expression activities, who listen to all the chatter and stories, and who keep an ear turned to the child's activities provide an optimal creative opportunity.

Play is the perfect creative outlet. During play, he can create whatever he wants to create in whatever way suits his fancy. Smile all you want at those cute little sayings and interpretations. If blending corn and cottage cheese will make mustard "because it is yellow," who are you to argue? Just smile and recognize that your child is brilliantly creative.

Creative outlets such as arts, crafts, and music are great for the earliest explorations. Some children use art materials as a type of storyboard. The child may redraw and retell the story until the picture is a muddy mess!

Role playing is another favorite form of creative free play. Toys, dress up items, odds and ends used for props need not be complex to provide the realism the child needs. Some children prefer to build or construct as they play. Pay close attention and you will discover the types of activity that are most satisfying.

Try to empower your children's use of creative play as long they are interested. Children usually learn to express themselves through other creative outlets. As children approach the teen years, for example, creative expression might expand to include technical aspects of music, art, dramatics, crafts — building abstract knowledge on the foundation of free play and exploration.

Remember, too, that free play is a dynamic and effective way of calming chaotic feelings of their lives. Let your child know that many adult artists also use their art as an outlet for strong inner emotion.

## Life Skill Practice and Imitation

Hark back one more time to a playtime memory. Remember how intently you sometimes pretended to be in another time or to be someone else? That pretending was practice — practice at being grown up. With ample time and just a few props, most children will practice the skills they need to develop through the natural course of their lives. Life skills — skills such as cleaning, cooking, nurturing, communicating, creating — take practice.

Nor is play merely an exercise for future skills. The physical skills that children need at this stage, such as holding a crayon, running, jumping, pedaling, and throwing are important to healthy development. You may notice that play activities often reflect recent life experiences. If we observe a child lost in play, it is not too difficult to discover what his recent life experiences have been. New discoveries are practiced in play.

What the child is practicing (read that *learning*) and how they use materials might surprise you. At age three, one of my daughters had watched older children jump rope. She was fascinated. When she finally got her hands on a jump rope, she jumped up and down while bouncing the rope on the ground in front of her. She had no interest whatever in learning to jump over the rope. She was not a rope jumping prodigy after all — she just wanted to flip the rope around!

Children love to explore the fascinating world of adulthood through their play. To do so, they need time with adults who are busy living their lives. That includes time with parents, as well as older siblings and friends, relatives, and favorite care givers. It doesn't matter whether you are brushing your teeth, scrambling eggs, playing your flute, planting radishes, or driving the car. What matters is that your child will imitate the activities of your life. Imitating you and practicing your daily routines and habits is how he learns who he is. And yes, it is sometimes embarrassing when we as parents find our children repeating behaviors that we wish we had not demonstrated. You'll want to practice a new behavior — together!

As children grow up, play activities sometimes turn serious. For example, fooling around on the piano often leads to a desire to know more. Some parents choose to pay for lessons from experts at that point, while others encourage the child to continue to explore the activity on their own. Is she interested in astronomy? Build a telescope together, and you will be committed to learning how to use it. Does she want to learn to ride horses? Help your child find a stable where she can exchange stall mucking for riding lessons.

As you see, play doesn't always look like play. In fact, it might look like hard work to the untrained eye. Those teens who become computer whizzes — are they "just playing," or are they working?

## Essential Time for Processing New Knowledge

Does your child have adequate play time to process his new knowledge? We know that children's brains grow rapidly during the early years of life. What a lucky coincidence — speedy brain growth at a time when everything is new knowledge!

Yes, kids are bombarded with information of all kinds every day, intended or otherwise, and intellectual knowledge expands at the same time. Did he learn to write his name, or count to ten or twenty or one hundred? Did you show him how to make his "s" forwards rather than backwards? Did you visit a river or shore where he built a dam and skipped rocks?

Trips of every kind power that high speed learning engine of her mind. If you go to the post office or fire station, science museum or zoo, she may come back brimming with new information. Did you take a train, boat, or airplane trip? Perhaps she will retell, draw, or play-act the experience to process what she learned.

Be a fly-on-the-wall during playtime and see how often he incorporates new knowledge into play. Watch him re-enact the event with his stuffed animals, dolls, or even his cars! In our home, little families of marbles acted out the day's events. Other times our cats played mysterious roles beyond adult understanding.

Finally, play is an important way for your child to process new social, physical and emotional knowledge. Did you scold her for yanking the baby's arm? Did he have an illness, accident, or other physical trauma? Has she had to take turns with playmates to play with a special toy? Did you move to a new home? Did a favorite relative die or move away?

Play helps your child process experiences for which he has no prior frame of reference. Playtime is a safe time and place for expressing unfamiliar feelings such as envy, loss, and sadness. Often the best thing you can do is offer a good mix of play and talk time with Mom or Dad and give him time to sort out feelings that are stirred by big events.

Older children and teens also need free time to process new knowledge, just as they needed playtime when they were small. Engaging in recreational activities gives the young person an escape, a place to figure out how to navigate the indignities of growth and social pressure. Usually, children have already transferred their playtime enjoyment to activities such as sports, music, art, or drama. For some youth, writing, hobbies, or even political involvement, can offer youth play-like opportunities.

Developing the habit of play early in life teaches youngsters to work hard at whatever they choose to do. Could you ask for a better work ethic?

## Protecting Playtime

Yes, older children need to have their playtime protected every bit as much as growing tots. While parents usually agree that older children need to play, subtle forces sometimes undermine parental confidence and pressure them to sacrifice playtime for myriad other activities. I've noticed five anti-play forces that work subtly to undermine a child's opportunities for play.

The most common anti-play force is the busy-ness of modern lives. Even in play-friendly families, parents and older family members can easily get caught up in activities and forget to preserve playtime for the younger set. It is paradoxical, too, that the more activities we try to jam into our days, the more free play time the young child actually needs.

A second insidious anti-play force is an emphasis on academic achievement, causing knowledgeable parents who want to do the right thing to willingly sacrifice their child's playtime for premature academics. Kindergarten and preschool programs, formerly safe havens for children's play, have fallen prey to the rush to force academics at the earliest age possible. Beginning homeschooling parents are just as easily seduced by"earlier is better" hype.

A third anti-play force for some families is early emphasis on activities that build up to sports skills. Sports are great when children are older, of course, but very few young children benefit from competitive sports activities. Remember too that trucking a young child around to activities that teach sports is not a play activity, but training. He may enjoy it, of course, but do not substitute this type of activity for the kind of play in which a child can freely express. Young children need free play experiences first. Later, sports training activities can build on the base of skills learned during free play.

The fourth anti-play force is the temptation to let "screen time" activities such as television, videos, and computer games lull parents into thinking that these games and activities might serve the child's need to play in the same way that fantasy play does. It is certainly hard to resist the appeal of these activities, but to allow screen based play to replace physical play and interaction with real things is hardly an ideal.

The fifth anti-play force is a tough one for parents to notice or acknowledge. Sometimes parents choose play activities for their children that they themselves enjoy rather than allowing wide access to free play choices. How torn and confused a child must feel if he is limited to choices that do not interest him, limited by the very parent he loves and adores and wants to please more than anything! He will rarely be able to tell you what is bothering him. Instead of telling you with words, though, he may tell you with behaviors or attitudes. If your child's actions and attitudes are inconsistent with joyful and carefree play, you may want to explore this possibility.

Remember that culturally, today's parents are pressured to fill a child's every waking moment with structured activity. If you suspect that too many activities or the wrong activities undermine the true play needs of your child, it may be time to start eliminating the excess and let your child choose for himself.

## Finally

The sense of timelessness, the sense of power, the creative outlet, practice time, and the processing time afforded by ample free play-time are important habits of living and learning.

Play is an essential and efficient learning activity for young children. During the middle years children begin to enjoy more structured play, such as games and sports. By the time children fly off into the world as young adults, time spent in free play has built a basis of enthusiasm for interests and a willingness to work hard.

Fiercely protect playtime as a priceless jewel of childhood.

## chapter three

# ENHANCING EARLY LEARNING

*through play, the learning workhorse of childhood*

How will you include those all-important enriching activities that help children maximize their learning / play? Luckily, daily living is the best way for children to learn, if the child has ample free play, loving parents, and an environment rich in material resources and human interaction.

Do you wonder how you can help your children stay busy and learning without constantly hovering or nagging? Are you unsure which learning materials might enhance learning? This is the chapter for you! We'll talk about things parents can do and ways to optimize your home for learning. Then we'll list some materials and resources that are known to stimulate both learning and play.

## General Tips

Use the following suggestions to help you choose activities that best suit your child's needs. Remember, these activities are the basis for much more than play, and, to a great extent, they are a better use of time than direct instruction in specific facts for young children. To put it another way, sitting a young child down to hours of curriculum every day is a drab substitute for the learning available through a rich family life.

- Read aloud every single day. Read aloud for hours every day, as I did, if that suits your lifestyle, your fancy, and the interests of your child. Children will build their play around stories and ideas of interest. It is your job to keep the ideas flowing and to introduce new and appropriate ideas. Books and stories serve that purpose nicely. (And all this time you thought reading aloud was for helping kids learn to read.)

- Extend the ideas of your life and the ideas in stories. Tell family stories and invent new ones. Use puppets, finger plays, and songs to engage your child's imagination and ability to visualize. Try role playing and dramatics by acting out stories. Animate all of the numbers in drawings. "Pretend." While you play with your child, extend vocabulary by using new words and synonyms.

- Focus on your child's uniqueness to find ideas that appeal to your child. Your child's favorite playtime activities can be a springboard to new learning. If the child wants to play dolls all the time, plan an imaginary doll trip to Grandma's house, or the beach, or Mexico, or the moon. Introduce new ideas through play, if the child is willing, of course. Teach the dolls to read their names, or have the cars park themselves in two-by-four arrays, for example. Have a tea party and speak French. Teach the stuffed animals Russian.

- Learn more about the favorite toy that is the focus of your child's play. For example, if your child loves to build with LEGO's, get some books and learn all you can about LEGO's. Maybe you can go to a LEGO show or form a LEGO learning club. Use the building blocks in math activities, in the bathtub, or for art explorations. Perhaps you could learn where they are made and more about that company. You are in LEGO Land now!

- Deselect materials that frustrate or cause problems by putting them away. Children can tire of the most wonderful materials. Don't take it personally, but do give them a break. Rotating materials makes everything new some of the time.

- Introduce real games (for example, board games card games) when your child is ready. Modify as needed. See "Modifying Classic Games" (chapter 5) for suggestions. Save instructional games for structured lesson time unless he selects the game on his own.

- Directed Activities — Shameless interference! Of course you will balance free play with directed activities. Children love to do arts and crafts, play games, have friends over, help with cooking and other chores, take walks, go on outings, and so on. These are the activities that expose your child to ideas that she can further explore during her free play time.

## Sample Activity Centers

See if you can use some of these ideas in your home.

### Housekeeping Center

Place a child-sized broom and dustpan and a spray bottle of diluted vinegar water (for cleaning windows and mirrors) in the closet alongside your cleaning materials. Other items your child may enjoy include a little tub for washing, a toy iron and ironing board, a play kitchen, and a play workbench. Nothing has to be fancy. A chair can be used as a workbench. You can make play appliances, cars, and much more with cardboard boxes, tape, and imagination.

### Dress-up Corner

A corner of the sewing room, laundry room, bedroom, or family room may be perfect. Ours was often in a corner of the living room, the bedroom, or the project room. Used clothing of any kind is always enjoyed. Include hats, belts, gloves, jewelry and bags if you can find them. Hats typical of certain occupations are popular. A train engineer's hat, a fireman's hat, and a cowboy hat are well recognized and make the beginning of a costume.

### Reading Center

Children's books and magazines should be right alongside your books on the family bookshelf. Comfy chairs or cushions and good lighting are about all you need besides books. It is nice to have paper and pencil handy in case someone wants to make a quick note or drawing. A small chalk or white board might be appealing.

### Writing Center

Where do *you* spend time composing letters, writing checks, or making shopping lists? Set up your child's writing and drawing center nearby. Get a laminated alphabet strip for the print and cursive alphabets and for the numbers. Writing and art centers coexist peacefully since both require similar materials. Crayons, markers, paper, scissors, glue, watercolor or other paints, and a variety of papers make a good beginning. Don't forget some project books or coloring books. Just include whatever you happen to find on sale, or what interests you or your child.

## Art Center

The art center builds on the basic materials of the writing center — paper, markers, pencils, crayons, scissors, and glue. An easel makes kids feel cool when they paint, but it is not necessary if you don't have the space. Try clay, play dough, craft supplies, art books, paints, and mixed media materials. Flip through your favorite children's art books for extensive supply lists. Include the materials needed for the projects and the materials for cleanup, smocks, and table coverings in your art space.

## Play Center

Is your child's play centered in the family room, your child's own room, or outdoors? Maybe the whole house is a play center! Toys, such as dolls, cars and trucks, building blocks, as well as many other learning materials, can be well-used in a room apart. From time to time, help your child set up a special play center, such as a post office or a store. Our puppet stage found extra lives as a bank, a post office, a drive-thru for hamburgers, and I don't know what else. Refrigerator or packing boxes can be used in many ways. Just get out a craft knife, some duct tape, and your imagination!

## Science Center

Science centers often depend on the current activities and interests of your family. Do you keep animals, grow houseplants, or plant a garden? Most science projects do best in a location that suits its unique qualities. A plant project needs a location with adequate light, for example.

## Math Center

The concepts of math can be easily taught through the use of everyday items. Nearly everything can be counted or measured. Children need access to the tools of counting and measurement: rulers, tapes, scales, measuring cups and spoons, thermometers, weather instruments, calendars, clocks, stop watches, and timers of all types. Fill a drawer or cupboard with some of these and make sure that your children have a chance to learn to use them. If they don't, pull items out yourself and start using them with your child. Rather than keeping math items in centers, some people prefer to keep them at the site of use. Measuring tapes kept with sewing kits or in tool boxes, and cups and spoons located in the kitchen, bath, or sandbox; and so on.

## School-Type Centers

You may have admired learning centers that school teachers have created for their classrooms. If you want to use some of those ideas be cautious about duplicating the assignment cards, worksheets, or suggested activity lists. Activities that seem interesting and challenging in a classroom environment often feel like busywork in the home environment. If your child turns off to an idea, who will you take your cue from, the classroom teacher's dazzling plan or your child? (In my family, the overzealous teacher in me doused the light of learning more than once.)

## **Finally**

Did you ever drop a pebble into a pond to watch the ripple pattern? You may have noticed how long it takes for the ripple to reach the farthest shore. Living in a learning environment with children is like that pond: everything in and about our homes and lives has a ripple effect that may not be obvious at first glance. Books, magazines, TV, video, audio, software, tools, toys, educational materials, games, projects, materials, the foods we eat, the furnishings we choose — all are a part of the learning environment. Everything we have and do goes into the pond of the culture our children soak in. Parents can choose which pebbles are best for their pond.

The lists that follows can be used as starting points for stocking activity centers. These ideas are by no means the final word, but merely ideas to get you going. I've tried to organize materials into categories that made sense to me, but I found many ways to categorize these items. For example, is play money a role-playing activity or is it mathematical learning? Feel free to reorganize and add to these lists to meet your needs. A few quality resources can help you and your child re-engage in learning, if either of you should run dry.

## Natural World Exploration – Science

sand box and sand toys —
  sifters, spoons, cups, bowls,
  scoops, pails, and shovels
a corner of the yard to dig in
  and make mud pies
indoor alternative — a dishpan
  half full of rice, beans, or
  cornmeal
water play — bath time, sink
  play, dishwashing,
  swimming, hose and
  sprinkler, wading pool,
  bucket, siphon, water wheel,
  toy pump
toys for water play, including
  dolls for washing
plastic containers
toys that float
ice
soap bubble pipes, wire loops
nature specimens — fish,
  turtles, salamanders, snails,
  birds, plants, animals
butterfly net
bug house
plant press
baskets and boxes

rope, cord, string, colored yarns
pulleys
interlocking gears
PVC pipe
small and large boards with a
  cleat at each end for inclines,
  ramps, balancing, sliding
collections — buttons, stones,
  spools, small blocks,
  marbles, feathers, shells,
  pine and fir cones, old keys,
  checkers, poker chips, coins,
  small toys
magnifying glasses
microscopes
telescopes
compass
magnets
containers that nest
un-spun wool and cotton
packing boxes of different sizes
refrigerator boxes
chemistry sets
science kits
weather station
camera
 tape recorder

## Building Toys

Baby blocks
Lincoln logs
Legos, Duplos, Knex
Tinker toys
dominoes
wooden blocks of any kind
parquetry and pattern blocks
geometric shaped blocks

geometric solids
light hollow blocks for large
  constructions, small boards
  for connecting
homemade blocks — milk
  cartons, cereal boxes, book
  shipping cartons

## ROLE PLAY MATERIALS

dolls and doll accessories
toy animal collections — farm,
    mammals, reptiles, birds, and
    fish
vehicle collections — cars,
    trucks, boats, planes, trains,
    toy tractors, dump trucks,
    loaders, backhoes, fire truck
nurse and doctor kits
stuffed animals
child size furniture — table,
    chairs, cupboard, stove
dishes, pots and pans
broom, dustpan, mop, dustcloth
toy ironing board and iron
real clothes pins and clothesline
suitcases, purses, wallets
bags of various sizes
play money
materials for playing store (or
    bank, post office, hotel)
telephone, toy computer

cash register
obsolete business forms
carbonless paper
manual or electric typewriter
adding machine or calculator
colorful fabric of many textures
    — silk, satin, velvet,
    corduroy, fur, cotton, moire,
    leather, lame
costume box or corner —
    gloves, scarves, jewelry, lab
    coat, hats, wigs
garden tools
workbench, hammer, saw, nails,
boards
puppets and puppet stage
"pretend" school — easy
    workbooks, old school
    books, small slates and
    chalk, school-type writing
    tablets

## LARGE MOTOR DEVELOPMENT

climbing apparatus — jungle
    gym, ladders, boxes
small and large boards for
ramps
climbing ropes
fire pole
slide, seesaw
jump ropes and hula hoops
trampoline
balls - all kinds and sizes

swing, trapeze, rings
wheelbarrow, wagon
riding toys or tricycles
bikes with training wheels
skates
balance beam
chinning bar
tin can or real stilts
basketball hoop

## CREATIVE EXPRESSION, EYE-HAND COORDINATION

clay, modeling wax, play dough

crayons, markers, colored pencils

easel and brushes

paint - tempera, water color, fingerpaint, oils, acrylic

large brushes to "water paint" on hot sidewalks

beads for stringing

variety of paper in many colors and sizes — construction, tissue, origami, tracing, butcher block, lined and unlined

scissors, tape, and staplers

office supplies

paste or glue

craft project scraps and recyclables, such as fabric, paper, yarn

beads and buttons

foil and glitter

paper tubes

wallpaper samples

bottle caps

colored pipe cleaners

feathers

googly eyes

popsicle sticks

Styrofoam trays

cartons, cans, jugs

different kinds of tape

chalkboard and chalk

sidewalk chalk

whiteboard and markers

## MUSIC AND RHYTHM

musical rhythm instruments: wrist bells, drums, triangle, gong, xylophone, cymbal, rattle

music tapes or CDs — marches, children's songs and stories, and sing-along tapes, oldies and modern favorites that both children and parents enjoy

toy or beginner instruments — flutophone, whistle, drum

pitch pipe

metronome

tape recorder for recording compositions

tuning fork

kitchen kettle drums

homemade musical instruments — rubber band / cardboard box guitars, musical water glasses, tissue paper / comb kazoos, gourd rattles

real instruments — keyboard or piano, recorder, ocarina, flute, ukelele, guitar, violin, other instrument of choice

Music books or sheet music

Composition paper

songs and musical games (London Bridges, etc.)

## INTELLECTUAL GROWTH

thousands of conversations
thousands of questions
answered
millions of questions puzzled
over
easy, sturdy puzzles
harder puzzles too
sticker books, dot to dot, mazes
games — see subsequent
    chapters for ideas
puzzlers — physical, word,
mental
Cuisenaire rods and Unifix
cubes
counting collections
magnetic refrigerator alphabets,
    words, and numbers
anagrams
clocks, stopwatches, timers
hour glass, sundial

calendars
scales and balances
rulers and yardstick
measuring tape
measuring cups and spoons
volume containers
    (liters, quarts, pints)
magazines and books
activity and puzzle books
alphabet strip - print and script
number strip
counting chart
multiplication chart
teaching posters and photos,
    purchased or of your design
selected computer software and
    videos — to provide a
    needed "time out" for a
    pooped Pop or a weary Mom

## Selected Resources

### 200+ Games and Fun Activities for Teaching Preschoolers

By Kathryn Kizer, 1997.
New Hope, PO Box 12065, Birmingham, AL 35202-2065.
A selection of classic games and activities for young children.

### Entertaining and Educating Your Preschool Child

By Robyn Gee and Susan Meridith. An Usborne book.
Many useful activities and ideas, in the typical Usborne book style.

### Playful Learning: An Alternate Approach to Preschool

By Anne Engelhardt and Cheryl Sullivan. La Leche League International, PO Box 4079, Schaumburg, IL 60168-4079.
Enjoyable games, activities, and crafts which can easily be used by one child or a group.

### Ring A Ring O' Roses. Finger Plays for Preschool Children

Eleventh Edition. Flint Public Library, 2000.
Flint Public Library, 1026 East Kearsley, Flint MI 48502-1994. 800/232.7111
Many popular and less familiar fingerplay poems and chants, with fingerplays explained. Many fingerplays are in Spanish. Baby through preschool.

### Don't Push Your Preschooler

By Louise Bates Ames, 1980. New York: Harper and Row, Inc.
For parents who feel pressure to start early academics with young children. Helps parents understand the importance of developmentally appropriate activities for their kids and that *pushing* is ineffective in the long term at best or damaging at worst.

### Games for Learning

By Peggy Kaye. The Noonday Press, Farrar Straus and Giroux.
Eighty-five games. You will regularly pull this book off the shelf for ideas for years to come.

## chapter four

# ENHANCE LEARNING
# WITH GAMES AND PUZZLES
*the multiple vitamins of learning interest: fun and motivation*

My daughters were perhaps two and five when we first began to play *Yahtzee*. My older daughter fell in love with *Yahtzee* as soon as she learned it. I adapted the game very little — I just helped with strategies and scoring. Within a year, my younger daughter, forever trying to keep up with her sister, played with us. She and I often played as a team. We all had a ball!

And what learning from that simple game! Both children soon honed basic math skills playing this dice game. They developed skills in strategy and logic, as well as a basic understanding of probability. Arithmetic skills grew as well. Before I knew it, adding up scores with carrying and multiplication facts through six came effortlessly for both.

*Yahtzee* taught me an important lesson, too: seek out games whenever possible. Not only do children learn skills and develop mental agility through games, but they continue to associate learning with pleasure, just as they did as tiny tots.

In this chapter we'll look at several types of structured games that are particularly strong in learning opportunities. A structured game usually implies a set of predefined rules, and as such, is played pretty much the same way anywhere. Soccer, chess, *Monopoly*, *Scrabble*, pinochle, and golf are examples of structured games. Examples of common games that are passed down through the culture include tic tac toe, musical chairs, and Simon says.

Whether for distraction, entertainment or learning, we enjoy board, card, and dice games; computer and video games; group and party games, races, and competitions; organized sports; solitaire games and puzzles. Some games are full of factual knowledge, some are silly, and other games challenge our logical and thinking skills.

Following are some of the benefits of some types of games that I've loved to play.

## Card Games

Very young children can learn simple card games. Try playing your favorite solitaire game with your child sitting in your lap. She will enjoy turning the cards for you, and will begin to learn the numbers, suits, and rules of the solitaire game as you play. Answer all her questions! Give her a worn deck to play with.

*Slapjack* is a good first game that requires only that a child be able to discriminate a jack from other cards. *Crazy Eights* teaches number identification and suit discrimination. Knowing that one card has special powers in the game appeals to children!

*War* is a popular children's game that helps children learn inequalities and equalities. If your children love playing war, as many do, remember that as they get older and more skilled, you can change the game to help math skills develop. Ask them to play two cards at a time and add their values to determine who takes the trick. When the adding version is mastered, have children subtract the value of one card from another. Later ask your child to find the product of his two cards to see who has the highest score.

*Go Fish* develops memory skills and is a perennial favorite. Specialty card games based on *Go Fish*, such as *Authors*, increase or introduce factual knowledge in a fun way. Since children naturally strive to remember the information on the cards in order to play the game well, they are likely to build their factual knowledge. Cards that teach gemstones, ocean life, animal families, and states and capitals, are among the many types available. Can't find what you want? Help your children create personal decks that match their interests.

As children get a little older you might try these favorites. *Twenty-one* teaches adding, strategy, and probability. *Rummy* requires scoring skills including adding and subtracting by fives and tens. *Hearts* and *Casino* are strategy and memory games that can be enjoyed by people of all ages. Each is a good introduction to more complex games.

*Concentration* and other memory/matching games often provide young children an equal playing field for competing against their parents. Many children have better short term memory skills than adults. Peals of laughter ring out as young children trounce Mom, who hates this game anyway!

Card playing offers practice with arithmetic skills such as counting, sorting, order, pairs, equalities, multiples through four, adding, and subtracting. Logic, strategy and probability are other mathematical skills learned through card games.

## Board Games

Most of the benefits derived from board game playing won't be announced on the box cover. Your children may learn far more than you expect, including the generic game-playing skills intrinsic to most games: following directions, taking turns, experiencing setbacks and success, and interacting with others for amusement. Other skills that you might not think of include the hand-eye coordination that develops in the handling of cards, dice, and game pieces. Spinners, dice, and card draws create background experiences for understanding probability. Children may take the plunge into learning to read so they can play a favorite board game without assistance.

Many games that younger children enjoy do not require reading skills. Games such as *Candyland* and *Chutes and Ladders* teach sequence, numeration, probability, one-to-one relationship (count the die spots or read the number on the spinner, move that many spaces), and penalty moves introduce the concept of negative numbers. Others, such as *Memory* or *Lotto* and other *Bingo* type games may teach simple concepts, such as colors, numbers, letters, initial sounds, and animal families.

Often young children can learn the moves for sophisticated strategy games such as *checkers* and *chess*. *Mancala* is another game

## Money Games

*Money* has a special attraction: it is fun for children to handle and gives them a chance to use one of the powerful symbols of adulthood. You can use money to teach so many things. Making change and calculating sums for pretend or real purchases is a good start. You can help students learn the decimal system using pennies, dimes, and dollars. Money has a history that entices many reluctant junior historians. Create your own set of coins as part of your art study. Collect a can of coins and a few bills to have on hand. Play money can be an attractive tool for some children, particularly if they need large bills for their purchases!

With a coin collection and a few dice, try **Change Up,** a coin value game, similar to *Poison* (p. 45). Taking turns, children roll the dice to determine how much money they draw from the can. Each child must *change up* to the fewest high value coins or bills possible. The first person to reach one or five dollars wins. Another approach is for each player to begin with a dollar bill, then subtracting the roll on the dice to see who runs out of money first.

of strategy that very young children can learn and enjoy, a game that is also a challenge for people of all ages. Youngsters will learn one-to-one relationships and they may invent playing strategies that do not occur to you. If children of varying ages and abilities want to play, try to adapt the game in some of the ways suggested in the next chapter.

You may decide to skip the simpler preschool games in favor of family games that everyone can play. Children who have not yet developed reading skills can enjoy many games if someone will read for them. Some families deliberately skip right to higher level games, such as *Monopoly*, with their younger children joining in as they are ready. Simply plan to assist them until they have the skill and maturity to play for themselves.

Some board games offer very interesting content besides being fun. Our favorite, an unusual game called *Nectar Collector*, was based on interesting facts about honey bees. The information was printed on the board. Children too young to read the game were delighted to hear the words read over and over by their just-learning-to-read older siblings and friends. (What a nice way to listen to an older child's oral reading!)

If you want to find useful board games to teach content, look for games that focus on *topics* rather than games that teach *subjects*. Farming, whales, allowances, life, foreign language, maps, travel — just some game topics to whet your appetite.

## Trivia Games

This type of game may be played on a board or with cards alone. You can also easily develop your own trivia games based on a special interest, family facts, or any topic of your choosing. Both general knowledge and specific knowledge can be explored, studied, and tested with these games. History, states and capitals, the sciences, foreign language, are typical examples. If your family loves this type of game, try to find versions that have easier cards for young children and harder cards for more sophisticated players so everyone can play together.

My family enjoyed trivia type games most when we disregarded the rules and scoring, and simply tested our knowledge. It really doesn't matter how you choose to play. If your child finds trivia games interesting, factual knowledge will be gained in the process of the play.

## Mental Games

Many parents use guessing games and other mental games with their children every day without even thinking about it. Just think of what children learn from these activities!

Mental games are with you all the time — whether you are stuck in traffic, stuck on a math concept, or stuck on spelling, you can pause for a mental game as a pastime or pick-me-up. Try quick paper and pencil games such as *tic tac toe* or *hangman*, or other classics such as *twenty questions*, license plate and other travel games. Guessing games of every stripe fit this category.

The portability and instant readiness of mental games are admittedly a big part of the appeal, but mental games can be much more than simple time fillers. Mental games are thinking games, games that are interesting, fun, and stimulating. Isn't that what learning is all about?

Use your child's current level of knowledge to develop ideas for games. Is she learning to count to ten? Play "I am thinking of a number between one and ten." Does he grasp the concept of numbers through 100? Try "I am thinking of a number between 1 and 100." Is she learning about inequalities? Extend the number guessing game with every guess your child makes, indicating, "No, the number is not 15. It is greater." After playing this game for a time, your child will figure out how to best use the information you give. You might eventually ask, "What are the best first and second guesses?" Watch those deductive reasoning skills develop as your childdevelops a system to guess your number.

Guessing games can make reading, phonics, and spelling fun. "I am thinking of a word that begins with 'a' and has five letters. Give other clues as needed. A variation that my children loved was, "*I am packing my suitcase for a trip to Hawaii*, and I will take an alligator. What will you bring?" You (the leader) have a hidden rule in mind that they must discover. You give clues to the hidden rule as you approve or veto their guesses. Start with a simple rule: each item must begin with the succeeding letter of the alphabet, i.e., alligator, banana, couch, etc. Younger children will enjoy playing the game with the same rule again and again. See if they can remember and repeat each item that has been mentioned, until you have used the entire alphabet. See if *you* can remember!

*Hangman* is an enjoyable game for spelling practice even for very young children. Start with simple words that you know they know, such as family and pet names.

Guessing games are enormously flexible and there are dozens of variations. You can play for a minute or an hour. Many ages can enjoy themselves together. They are wonderful car games that can be made easier or harder. I regularly invented guessing games out of desperation while standing in long checkout lines with restless children.

Mental games develop visualization, listening, audio discrimination, and higher order thinking skills. They are highly interactive and require conversational skill. When children are playing mental games their minds are in overdrive!

## The Rhyming Guessing Game

"I am thinking of a word that rhymes with..." This game was a favorite car game for our family for years. There are two versions.

In the simplest game, say, "I am thinking of a word that rhymes with *shoe*." Let children take turns guessing words until they guess what your word is. Guessing naturally appeals to most children. If they miss the rhyme, simply explain why their word doesn't rhyme and let them guess again. This game really helps children who have not yet sorted out similar sounds such as *m* and *n*; *t, p,* and *k; b* and *d*. What a fun way for children to refine their listening and speaking skills.

When children are older, try the advanced game. The *Rhyming Guessing Game* becomes a vocabulary game by requiring guessers to give the meaning of the word they want to guess without pronouncing it.

Here is a sample advanced game: Leader: "I am thinking of a word that rhymes with *can*." Guess: "Is it something to cook in?" Answer: "No, it is not a *pan*." Guess: "Is it a light brown color?" Answer: "No, I am not thinking of the word *tan*." Guess: "Is it a kind of truck to haul stuff around?" Answer: "Yes, I am thinking of the word *van*." Rhyming skills are perfected, and kids really have to think to come up with a meaning rather than blurting out the word.

The person who guesses correctly gets to think up the next word and then figure out what words the guessers are trying to define. Another good challenge!

Younger children can play the simple version at the same time older kids and adults play the advanced version with good results.

## Simulation Games

Simulation games hardly need discussing. Simulation is a way of life for many children, as they re-enact the activities of their days. Given enough play time and real life experiences, they will relive their experiences again and again. What powerful activities for deep understanding!

You can expand on the natural desire to create simulations with the slightest encouragement. After a visit to the zoo, a favorite simple game for very young children is to role-play animals. "Can you be the tiger? What does the tiger say? How does he walk? How many tigers did you see today?" An elephant? A kitty? The child's imagination goes to work as he recalls his experiences and memories and acts them out.

After reading a favorite fairy tale or story, use a simple prop to encourage your child to act out the story. Most children enjoy re-enacting stories and plays. Some children can hardly be stopped from role-playing activities once they begin.

If you have visited a community center such as the fire station or the post office, find some simple props to help your children act out their experiences. A box with a slot in it can be decorated to look like a mailbox, for example.

More formal simulation games, such as *Monopoly* and *Clue*, are exciting for older children. You may also want to look for quality computer and video simulation games.

## Video and Computer Games

These games are rolling off the production line as fast as the clever young game experts can make them up. Many of them are actually electronic chase or hide and seek games. Many are wonderful adventures that are thought-provoking and exciting. Some are highly educational.

How will you choose video and computer games? How many hours of each day will you allow your child to use TV, computer, and video games? Will you be able to see beyond the attractive colors, clever sounds, and flashy characters to decide which games stimulate thinking?

Playing strategy games on the computer is a superb way to enjoyably learn logic and strategy. Games such as *chess*, *Mancala*, *hearts, solitaire* and *checkers* are widely available as computer software. These games pit the player against the computer, giving the player the chance to try many wrong options as effective strategies are sought out. The computer never tires of beating you while you learn! Seek games that offer varied setups so that you can practice. For example, I was able to learn strategies for playing *Mancala* by playing a computer version in which I could limit the number of stones in play. By watching the computer's moves, I soon learned some winning strategies. You might enjoy *IQ Booster*, a free software game that provides nearly unlimited variations for the beginning player to quickly learn strategies.

During the early and most formative years, being conservatively selective in allowing children to play video and computer games may be the wisest choice. Keep in mind all the many important activities your child is not able to participate in while he is at the TV or computer. Your child won't lose out if he isn't playing computer games at age three! Remember too that there will be plenty of time, as your child grows older, to take advantage of all the knowledge that can be accessed by video and computer.

One family chose not to allow their child access to computer games until he was school age, and then only as a way to play games with friends. Not long ago, I saw the same boy, a young man of fourteen, packing an advanced computer book under one arm, and enthusing about his various computer projects.

One strategy that has proven popular with families is to select one or two games or videos that the child enjoys and then take advantage of the electronic babysitter for a few hours a week! Children can enjoy a few games and you can enjoy time for your own projects.

Other families choose games that are educational and/or entertaining and include them in their homeschooling program. Children may still be restricted to a certain number of hours playing the game each day or week.

The computer and video worlds are just now developing. Classic games are yet to be decided. Parents should make their software decisions carefully. Maybe you will find games that withstand the test of time.

## Homemade Games, value added

Give special consideration to games you and your children make. A make-it-yourself game we used was a photocopy that was passed out on a field trip. A simple board game, the kids cut out and colored the game board, spinner, and playing pieces. The "value added" by their crayoned efforts made the game a priceless favorite!

Get your ideas for homemade games anywhere. One parent bought several inexpensive board games at garage sales and let the kids invent their own games from the bits and pieces. Will they need to write down the rules? Help them as needed, but try to let the game-making process evolve from their interests and play.

Don't forget to make games together. One family made simple board games where they had to answer made-up questions (regarding whatever they were currently studying) in order to progress (first one to the finish line won).

You can create simple games from the slimmest resources. Using only your recycling bin, see what your family can create. Let children decorate, help create the game, or write the numbers. Maybe deciding the penalty or the bonus scores should be up to your children. Children often create more challenging activities than we do.

One parent created card games on the computer. She made different sets of cards based on *Fish* or *Authors* type games. In one game players matched inventions to inventors. The variations on this idea are endless: you could match composers to their music, scientists and explorers to their discoveries, or try matching different kinds of word families (gaggle to geese, mob to kangaroos).

## Self-testing Games

Sometimes the best games aren't games, but opportunities to compete against yourself. "How high can you jump?" "How long can you hop on one foot?" "Can you say the alphabet?" "Wow! I wonder if you can say the alphabet backwards?" "How high can you count by twos before we get to Mary's house?" "How many animals can you name that begin with the *mmm* sound?" The ideas are endless. Only your imagination can slow you down.

If you have a hard time thinking of these kinds of questions on the fly, sit down with a pad of paper and jot down your ideas as they come to you. Keep your list in your purse or on the fridge, handy for when you need them.

For a time I carried a stopwatch in my purse, just in case we met

---

## Poison

This is a homemade dice game that children love! You can use regular dice, but the game is the most fun when homemade dice are used. I have used small wooden cubes, foam cubes cut from packing material (silent when tossed!!), and oven-hardened clay dice that the children made. Students practice addition, multiplication, or subtraction.

On two dice, write five different digits on five faces. I often included zero, since normal dice games do not give practice with zero. On the sixth face of each die draw a little skull and crossbones — or other symbol — to stand for Poison.

To play the game, set a goal, say 100. Each player tosses the dice in turn, recording his score, and adding it up to keep a running total. If a player throws a single Poison, he loses that turn. If a player rolls two Poison dice, he loses his entire score and starts again from zero. Oh no! *Variations:* The game can be varied endlessly. Digits 0-4 on two cubes are the perfect beginning adding game. Play to a score of twenty or forty or so. Make several sets of dice with different numbers so you can mix and match to practice different facts. One child who loved this game used all the dice she could find — dozens! — and set her goals in the thousands.

As children learn to total their scores they become grounded in the concepts that underlie borrowing and carrying, even if they still use fingers or objects to help them count. When they get tired of finger-counting, take a short break and teach re-grouping, then get right back to the game and practice this wonderful shortcut.

Tired of addition? To practice subtraction at the same time that you practice multiplication, subtract the product of each roll of the dice from a pre-selected number. The first person to land squarely on zero wins.

delays while running around on errands. I could count on happily busy and learning children as long as I was willing to time them while we waited and they tried new stunts.

Self-testing activities are a boon to homeschooling parents whose children are rarely the same age. Use a stopwatch to measure their speed at completing some activity. The children all do the activity at the same time, but they compete against themselves. So if six-year-old Billy can run to the corner and back in 12 seconds and it takes little Susie 23 seconds, Billy didn't "beat" Susie. Billy beats Billy when he bests his own effort.

## Puzzles

Some people feel that puzzles are akin to magic tricks, requiring special prior knowledge or sleight of hand for success. Some may think of puzzles as physical riddles. I tend to think of puzzles as a solitaire game played against a master gamesman who happens to be the inventor of the puzzle.

Puzzles offer many of the advantages of game play. Puzzles help children hone mental agility, creative thinking, problem solving, strategic thinking, certain mathematical concepts, as well as fine motor dexterity.

People who like mathematics usually like to solve challenging puzzles. Can we assume that those who learn to solve puzzles can also learn mathematical thinking? Maybe!

Puzzles challenge children's mental capacities in engaging processes that are both compelling and noncompetitive. Some children who do not usually enjoy competition are often willing to be competitive with themselves and will push hard to solve difficult puzzles.

Most puzzles require little explanation. The problem to be solved is usually apparent in the nature of the puzzle. Naturally quiet children will enjoy the nonverbal process. Children who like to talk have a chance to reflect and do something quietly.

Be sure to work puzzles with your child sometimes, whether you are an avid puzzler or a bare beginner. Your child will learn from you and with you. Remember to talk aloud about your strategies. I have learned a great deal by listening to and watching other puzzle fans solve puzzles that have stumped me. Your children can watch you with the same result.

Try making your own puzzles. Not only can you save money, but the child learns the crafting skills, and may learn important clues about how puzzles are created, and therefore, solved. Simple jigsaw puzzles can be made from paper or cardstock. Try cutting up a photograph of your child that you have laminated and he will enjoy piecing it back together. Most of the other puzzles mentioned here may be made from paper, cardboard, or wood.

## Jigsaw Puzzles

Jigsaw puzzles fall into a category of their own. Families who work jigsaw puzzles may do so without even thinking about why they choose them. Very young children can begin with simple puzzles of only a few big pieces. As physical coordination, dexterity, patience, visualization skill, and interest develop, puzzles with a greater number of smaller pieces become enjoyable. Working puzzles together with your child develops both interest and skill. Perhaps yours will become a family for whom puzzles are a lifelong fascination!

## Problem Solving Puzzles To Try With Your Child

A variation on the jigsaw puzzle asks you to simply put the pieces back once you take them out. Whether two- or three-dimensional, these puzzles promise to challenge and amuse.

*Piet Hein's Soma Cube* is a good example of a three dimensional puzzle that asks you to build something. It is rumored that Hein invented the puzzle while listening to a lecture on Quantum mechanics. Twenty-seven cubes glued together into seven different shapes can build a cube that is 3x3x3, but not always easily! Younger children naturally use the pieces to build with, exploring the interesting shapes that two or more pieces form together. Older puzzlers can try to reconstruct the cube or create other symmetrical constructions. Purchase a *Soma Cube* or make your own. The puzzle explores geometry, spatial relationships, and perspective, while developing finger dexterity.

*Topology puzzles* are challenging twice — taking them apart, and later, putting them back together. The puzzles are based on the mathematics of topology (a doughnut and a coffee mug have the same shape in topology). Rings, cords, and beads are some of the items that must be removed or untangled, when it is clearly impossible! These puzzles are tantalizingly hard until you figure out the solution, when they become forehead-slapping simple. Physical dexterity is needed, but the most important skill is being able to think in new ways about how to solve the problem.

*Towers of Hanoi* is a classic puzzle that asks you to move pieces from one of three pegs to another, according to a set of rules. The problem solver must discover the correct sequences and repeat them until the goal is reached. The goal of this particular puzzle is to move a set of disks from one peg to a third peg, one piece at a time, never placing a larger piece on a smaller piece. The puzzle can be simplified for even the youngest players. Children can try the puzzle with two, then three, pieces until they unlock the strategy. Then try the puzzle with all of the disks. You can usually find this puzzle where games are sold.

A classic puzzle that you shouldn't overlook is the Chinese *tangram*, drawn here for you to copy. The tale is told that a tile

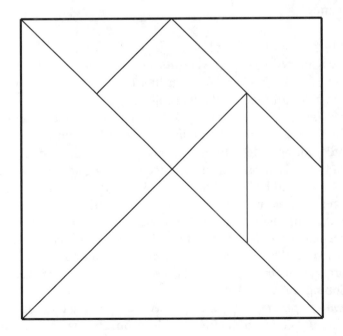

maker created a beautiful tile for the emperor. The tile maker accidentally dropped it, and the tile broke into the seven pieces of the puzzle. The emperor was fascinated at the many different shapes that could be made in the attempt to put the tile back together.

Make your own *tangram* from a square of paper. Try it! You will be challenged to put the puzzle back into its original square shape! Many versions of the puzzle can be purchased. Our favorite is *Tango*, a game version of the *tangram* that can be played either cooperatively or competitively.

Young children enjoy using the tangram puzzle pieces creatively, perhaps drawing and naming their pictures. Children who explore this puzzle develop geometric knowledge, mental agility, creativity, and dexterity.

## Other

Many wonderful games defy my categories. Party games and other group games — kick the can, all the variations on relay races, musical chairs, and pin the tail on the donkey — are fun to play. *Charades* encourages creativity and a playful approach. These kinds of games offer fun social learning experiences.

*Pictionary* is another great game that doesn't categorize well — challenging, fun, a great ice breaker, good for all ages, and requires no drawing skill. Drawing interest or skill may develop, as can creative thought and vocabulary skills.

*Password* and its variations build vocabulary and imagination. Dice games, such as *Perudo*, involve skills such as counting, learning multiples, exploring probability and scoring. *Darts* are fun for accuracy and scoring. Nearly all *sports* offer some math practice in the scoring. Get the idea?

## Finally

Most of the games discussed in this chapter can be found in stores everywhere or in the resources in the chapter *Game List*. If you include games in your homeschooling program, I believe you'll find, as I did, that well-chosen games can sidestep dozens of workbooks. The benefits of regular family game days cannot be overemphasized. I'll tell you once again — go play!

## chapter five

# MODIFYING CLASSIC GAMES
*so everyone can play*

So your youngest wants to play *Monopoly*, chess, *Scrabble*, and checkers? Your older children don't want to be bothered? What now, Mom?

Finding ways to modify games can provide the best possible experience with the game materials while children learn the elements of the game. You'll want her to have fun while learning so she'll be willing to give you a good game later on! For some children, learning the rules of a given game may be within their ability, but the competitive elements are too intense for their developmental level. Here are some ways to adapt your favorite games so everyone can play.

## Tips for Modifying Games

### Cooperate, Don't Compete

We could spend hours discussing the pros and cons of competition among children and the lessons children learn when they compete in games. We would probably never agree on, or solve, the common problems of competitiveness. Most of us would agree, however, that young children are not developmentally ready to handle serious competition. So why not wait?

Some of our family's favorite early games were cooperative games in which all players worked together for a common goal. Choosing cooperative games can provide hours of family fun and learning without the complications of competitiveness. If you prefer, adapt other games so they can be played cooperatively.

Generally, if you can invent a way to play the game alone, you can use that model as your cooperative system. *Scrabble* can be easily made cooperative — the game is won or lost by cooperating players who attempt to make a certain number of points before a given time limit. Most games played for scores can be played this way. The goal is the same with any number of players. *Monopoly* can also be played cooperatively against the clock. I have watched children enjoy playing checkers against themselves, first black, then red, moving around the board to play each turn.

## Play as Teams

Parents can team up with their children for play experience. Children get a great vicarious learning experience and a chance to identify with each parent, as well as practice at winning or losing just the way mom and dad model it. I will not even mention all the social benefits that come from this type of team play, such as developing empathy and a code of fair play or ethics.

## Moral Support Team Play

Play the traditional way, but have all players work together for each person as his turn comes up. If the person has bad luck, commiserate with him and encourage him to keep trying. If he is winning, help him enjoy his fleeting good fortune with grace, and then help him move on to cheer for the next player.

## Surrogate Play

Sometimes it is easier to play for someone else. If you lose, you do not face the loss alone. One way to do this is to play for the dog or your pet goldfish. Or you and your child might have favorite dolls or stuffed animals placed around the playing area to play the game, with the child and you playing for each in turn. Another approach would be to have your child play *your turn* in a game with Dad while you fix dinner.

## Modify the Rules

Many board games come with modified rules for shorter or easier versions of the game. Use those rules to get ideas. *Monopoly* lends itself to perpetual modification to meet the needs of players. Get really creative and turn chess and checker boards at an angle, inventing new starting setups — see what that does for your game! If two checkers make a king, what do three checkers make — an empress? What special powers might that include? Try your hand at modifying games. A dose of silliness can make many serious games more palatable for young children.

Game modifications that worked for our family: reduce or eliminate certain penalties; allow dice re-rolls; no one left the game until everyone had completed the game; instead of winners and losers, we had first winners, second winners, third winners, and even last winners. Looking back on the idea of winner levels, this seems a bit silly, but what a difference it made in how games ended! We all enjoyed it at the time.

## Reduce the Game

You can sometimes create a new challenge for all by making the game smaller. Try playing checkers with only five or six checkers, perhaps making them all kings; use the *Scrabble* pieces to play *Anagrams* and forget the scoring; try playing chess with only selected pieces or you may want to purchase one of the modified chess games that are now on the market. Instead of playing the card game 21, play 11 and leave out all the cards above six.

## **About Competitiveness**

Should children be taught to compete? If so, how and when? Much has been written to either extol the virtues or revile the pitfalls of competitiveness. Arguing the pros and cons of competitive activities for older children makes some sense. Competition doesn't sit well with many young children, though, and the effort may backfire.

I found myself squarely on the fence and undecided about the merits of competition versus cooperation when my children were young. Providing opportunities for the children to both cooperate and compete seemed to work best for us. I softened the games when needed and adhered closer to the rules as they grew older.

We wisely modify sports equipment into toys for young children — plastic bats and wiffle balls, low basketball hoops, tiny bicycles, and shortened golf clubs, hockey sticks, and skis. Use the same premise with board and card games. The idea is to help children enjoy the activity. Younger children often enjoy the simple processes of the game — moving the pieces, throwing the dice, shuffling and dealing, drawing the cards, taking turns. Why spoil their enjoyment with premature introduction of competitive rules?

## About Thinking Skills

Do you want to teach higher order thinking skills? Like walking, talking, and reading, these skills bloom in the proper environment.

However, direct teaching of thinking skills is about as practical as giving talking lessons. What children benefit from is practice with materials that are challenging, interesting, and rewarding — games and puzzles.

Buy your children interesting puzzles, puzzles that challenge just enough to engage their interest. Engage them in strategy games as they get older. Give them games and puzzles with which to practice, someone to talk to when challenged.

Offer tips about strategy, logic, or divergent thinking as opportunities arise. Commiserate with them over their failed attempts and frustration. Be a "game buddy" when invited, someone else who can admit that they too are stuck on a puzzle or game strategy.

Thinking skills develop without thinking about them. *Let the games begin.*

## chapter six

# GAME LIST, THE TRIED AND TRUE
*homeschooler approved games*

This list follows a slight hesitation: what if someone thinks these are the ONLY or the BEST games? Because they are not. They are simply a sampling of games that have been used successfully by families who homeschool. Choose your own favorites. Most of these games carry trademarks and are capitalized to indicate such.

One more note — many of these games are rich learning tools and hard to classify accurately. For example, *Scrabble* is primarily a word game, but the scoring provides math practice. Nearly every game includes reading or reading related skills. Try many to really explore their richness.

## READING, WRITING, GRAMMAR, LANGUAGE

| | |
|---|---|
| *Word Yahtzee* | *Scrabble Junior* |
| *Mad Libs* | *Anagrams* |
| *Charades* | *hangman* |
| *Boggle* | most board games |
| *Scrabble* | spelling bees |

## MATH — STRATEGY, LOGIC, SKILL PRACTICE

| | |
|---|---|
| *24* - linear algebra | *Perudo* |
| 21 | *Presto-Change-O* |
| *Backgammon* | *Quarto* |
| *Blisters* | *Racko* |
| *Boggle Jr. Numbers* | *Rat-A-Tat Cat* |
| *Canasta* | *Risk* |
| *Candyland* | *Rummikub* |
| *Checkers* | rummy |
| *Chutes and Ladders* | *Mancala* |
| *Concentration* | *Scotland Yard* |
| *Crazy Eights* | *Sequence* |
| *Cribbage* | *Set* |
| chess | *Six Cubes* |
| dominos | *S'math* |
| *Equate* | *Star Wars* |
| *Euchre* | *Stratego* |
| go | *Tango* |
| hearts | tic tac toe |
| *Hi Ho Cherrio* | *Triology* |
| *IQ Booster* | *Traffic Jam* |
| *Lotto* | *Uno* |
| *Mastermind* | *Yahtzee* |
| *Monopoly* and variations | *Wake Up Giants* |
| *Muggins* | war |
| *Pente* | |

## MISCELLANEOUS

| | |
|---|---|
| *Memory* | *Earthsearch* |
| *Concentration* | Shanghai rummy |
| *Monopoly* | *5 Crowns* |
| *Clue* | *Herd Your Horses* |
| *Vacation* and other travel games | *Secret Door* |
| *Trivia* | *Constellation Station* |
| *Hail to the Chief* | *Knights & Castles* |
| *Marbleworks* | *Moneywise Kids* |
| *Mosaic Mysteries* | *The Sleeping Grump* |
| *Pit* | *Flying High* |
| *Made for Trade* | |

## Selected Game Resources

### Ampersand Press

750 Lake Street, Port Townsend, WA 98368
800/624.4263  fax: 360/379.0324  www.ampersandpress.com
Publishers of games and rubber stamp kits. *The Garden Game* and *The Bug Game* are among the nature games that children enjoy.

### Animal Town Game Company

PO Box 757, Greenland, NH 03840-0757
800/445.8642    fax: 800/603.430.0334    www.animaltown.com
Quality cooperative and non-competitive games, books, videos and CDs, and other play things. Family oriented. If your family likes to learn through play, this catalog is for you. *Nectar Collector* is our favorite.

### Aristoplay

8122 Main Street, Dexter, MI 48130
800/634.7738    fax: 734/424.0124  www.aristoplay.com
info@aristoplay.com
Excellent collection of games for fun and learning; many homeschool favorites can be found here.

### Bits and Pieces

One Puzzle Place B8016, Stevens Point, WI 54481-7199
800/JIGSAWS  fax: 715/341.5958  www.bitsandpieces.com
Free, fun catalog of quality puzzles, brain teasers, children's games and more.

### Catalog of Co-operative Games

Family Pastimes, RR 4, Perth, Ontario Canada K7H 3C6
613/267.4819    fax: 613/264.0696    Fp@superaje.com
Play together not against each other. Young children often want to play games, but may not be ready to handle competitive games. Our favorite was *The Sleeping Grump*. We all won together! Ages three and up. Many games.

### Exploring Math Through Puzzles

By Wei Zhang. Key Curriculum Press, 1150 65$^{th}$ St., Emeryville, CA 94608
800/995.MATH  fax: 800/541.2442
customer.service@keypress.com  www.keypress.com
An exciting book full of puzzles of all difficulty levels that you can make and solve with your children. Topology puzzles of string and beads, interlocking wire puzzles, *Soma* type wood block puzzles and more. A materials kit for making all 54 puzzles is also available.

### Games

Ivan Bulloch. New York: Thomson Learning. 2000. Colorful and simple instructions for making and playing simple games. Make your own cards, dice, spinners, board games and more. Instructions for playing the games are included.

## The Games We Used to Play

By Ron Bullock.

VideoTrend Associates,744 Wisconsin Street, Oshkosh, WI 54901
414/231.9218

Video of kids playing traditional games — marbles, jacks, kick-the-can. Rules and history are discussed. Worth finding.

## I. Q. Booster

www.supsof.com/sampprog.html

A free computer game that will, well, boost your intellectual capacity. Fun for all ages. Read the online help.

## MindWare Catalog

Jeanne Voigt, 121 5ᵗʰ Ave. NW, New Brighton, MN 55112
800/999.0398  fax:  888/299.9273  www.mindwareonline.com

"Brainy toys for kids of all ages." Puzzles and games that broaden your horizons. A carefully selected collection of puzzles and games to tease your mind.

## Provoking Thoughts

IDEA, PO Box 1004, Austin, MN 55912
800/828.1231    www.ccjournal.com/publications.shtml
info@ccjournal.com  Devoted to the thinker in all of us. Twenty-four page booklets, available separately, of math puzzlers and problems that encourage people of all ages and abilities to think creatively and independently.

## Puzzlemania or Mathmania

PO Box 269, Columbus, OH 43216  800/603.0591
www.highlights.com/bookAndActivitySeries/offer/puzzlemania.html

A book club for puzzle loving children. *Puzzlemania* is for 5 and up, or *Mathmania*, puzzles for ages 7-12. Color illustrations, widely varied puzzles that build skills while being appealing and fun.

## Rex Games, Inc.

530 Howard St., San Francisco, CA 94105-3007
800/542.6375  fax: 415/777.1013    folks@tangoes.com
www.rexgames.com

Logic and thinking games such as *Tangoes* and *Word Trek*.

## Set Enterprises, Inc.

15402 E. Verbena Dr., Fountain Hills, AZ 85268
800/351.7765  fax: 480/837.5644
setgame@setgame.com      www.setgame.com/

*Set* is a game of perceptual thinking. *Five Crowns*, *Quiddler*, and *Triology* also challenge right and left brain thinking. Card/ computer versions; try them online.

# PART 2
## Conversations

Featuring:

## chapter seven

# KEYNOTE
# CONVERSATIONS
*optimal learning through family chitchat*

Besides play, what else do successful parents do with their children? Well, for one thing, they talk, and they talk, and they talk!

This constant stream of interaction is one reason successful home-schooling parents love homeschooling. They love listening to the arguments, the debates, the rambling stories, the wheedling, the screams and shouts, the silly jokes, the budding sarcasm, and the battles of will.

Don't be misled by the occasional parent who complains, tongue-in-cheek, that their children talk all day long. Deep down parents love it. Daddies delight in telling and reading stories, singing silly songs, and making up goofy games. The flubs of children tackling tricky new words trigger fits of mommy-glee.

Talk permeates every activity and parents constantly demonstrate conversational interaction to their children. If not for the fact that parents listen so carefully, you might think they loved the sound of their own voices!

For whatever reason, we learn through conversation, and increased conversational skill is essential to successful learning. To make sure you know where I am coming from on this point, let's assume for a moment that all knowledge can be thought of as conversation.

## Knowledge as Conversation

In this conversational model of learning, the bubbling stream of family chatter allows knowledge to flow. I sometimes think of speaking and listening as a delivery system for knowledge. However you hold the idea, let's expand a bit on the notion of knowledge as conversation.

The conversations that define the collected knowledge of humanity are recorded in widely varied media. Ancient tales of prehistory are told through fossil remains, artifacts, and engraved stone. Books, letters and original documents are the modern versions of collecting and preserving information. Photographs further expand the availability of history's more recent conversations to a wide audience. Rapidly increasing access to technology brings conversations through electronic media such as radio, television, audio and video, fax, computer software and Internet access. The types of media through which we access knowledge also grow at an astonishing rate.

Usually, we think of conversations as verbal interchanges that take place right here and right now. It is not a big stretch, though, to see that books and relics can be thought of as conversations that take place between the writer (creator) and the reader (learner) over time and space.

For example:

- **Fiction or literary books record the art of the storyteller.** The author may use storytelling as a way to convey more than an interesting story. He may include a metaphorical message or a timeless truth of the human condition. When the stories are recorded on tape by a favorite author, we step closer to an actual conversation with that person. A play is a more complex conversation, written by one speaker/writer, then interpreted by others — actors, directors, and producers — for an audience of listeners.

- **Music is a complex conversation of high emotional content.** Consider Beethoven's Ninth Symphony. Already deaf, Beethoven translated the music he heard in his head into a written musical code. The musical notes are then read from sheet music by skilled instrumentalists whose interpretation is directed by a conductor. Upon hearing a performance of the Symphony, we share a conversation with

Beethoven as interpreted by the orchestra. What a miraculous conversation!

- **A work of art can be thought of as a conversation.** The artist's ideas are captured in physical and visual form that viewers can interpret according to their own level of understanding. Whether in paint, sculpture, or other form, a gifted artist tells a story with power and beauty.

- **Architecture, the styling of buildings and homes, tells a story.** A gifted builder's understanding and use of materials speak powerfully and wordlessly. Steeply sloped roofs speak of snow and ice, wind and cold. Adobe homes bring visions of hot deserts and cool interiors tucked behind thick walls. Tepees, tents, and yurts bring nomadic living to the mind. A builder's values may be captured in his or her work. Synagogues, churches, mosques, temples, and cathedrals echo, in the eye and ear of the mind, of ritual, music, faith, and the grandeur of the world's great religions.

- **Museums are vast collections of past conversations.** Collections of specimens, such as stamps, insects, rocks, and art, are physical demonstrations of patterns of knowledge. Think of the conversation between the collector and the viewer, again, across space and time. The collector presents knowledge in such a way that a viewer can learn from it.

More examples you might want to explore:

- Archaeology is a conversation with/about the past.
- Biology is a conversation with/about living things, past or present.
- Astronomy is a conversation with/about space.
- Theology is a conversation about spiritual belief.
- Mathematics is a conversation, using a specialized language, about the nature of the universe.

Books of nonfiction are perhaps the most familiar repository of information. These resources retell factual knowledge or opinion, creating a conversation between the author and reader in another time or place. Published journals and diaries are the self-talk of individuals. Some books are collections of a broad range of standard information, such as dictionaries and encyclopedias. Magazines, newspapers, Internet sites, video, and audiotapes record recent contemporary conversations.

To stretch the metaphor even more, common items have a story to tell. What does a yellow Dixon Ticonderoga soft lead pencil have to say? A highlighter pen, chewing gum, bicycle, and rice cooker all tell a story if we care to seek it out. No matter how far we take the metaphor, the best access to knowledge is available through conversation. Parents are the perfect ones to teach conversational skill.

## Bridging Conversations

Parents rarely think about the fact that knowledge is shared through conversation — they just do what works. Parents rarely think about how children learn to speak and listen — they just do what works. And why not, when what works best is such a powerful tool — the tool of common family conversation?

Everyday talk is so natural and normal that it rarely recognized as the incredible and respectable tool it is. When we as parents begin to notice family conversations, though, we discover that nothing draws a child out more powerfully than daily conversations with his parents.

With very little effort on anyone's part, conversations between parent and children fling open the head gates of curiosity. Parents develop *bridging conversations* to help their children move from baby babble to sophisticated communication skills.

Parents know how to create effective bridging conversations — but how? Their children teach them! Step-by-step and day-by-day, conversational skill grows through practice and through all those delicious little lisps, goofs, and mispronunciations that make parenting a young child such a hoot.

You don't need me to tell you how to talk to your kids. As long as you enjoy talking and interacting with your children, they are learning. Here are some of the basic conversational patterns that I have noticed again and again in successful homeschooling families.

### Interpersonal Conversations

Interpersonal conversation — dialogue — is a most effective method of learning.

"Did you put your toys away?" "No, I forgot!" The clearest and simplest conversations of daily life clarify understanding. On the foundation of such basic interactions, children build their ability to understand and interpret meaning. In time skill develops so they can grasp the complex communications that explore the nature of the universe.

As children build their skills, interpersonal conversations can be enjoyed through varied media — written correspondence, e-mail, photos, videotape, audio recordings, drawings, and cartoons. These have the advantage of taking place over time and space, allowing each participant time to think out his comments and to record them carefully. Reading and writing — the processes of translating ideas into and out of print — hone communication skills.

Dialogue is efficient: there are two minds to bounce ideas around; you are both there to check and double check the information. Error correction can be instantaneous when one person questions and the other has knowledge to share. Dialogues between individuals who care about one another make the exchange satisfying on several levels.

Dialogues, besides being the usual conversations in families, are the basis of efficient and effective tutoring. Even if your child doesn't care that much about learning to subtract, at least she gets to have some fun with her dad. That is often enough to motivate learning.

## Family-Sized Group Conversations

As children grow older, they benefit from learning experiences outside the family with a social group, class, or learning circle.

Workshops, study circles, and book clubs are examples of groups where students learn from some different kinds of two-way dialogues. In this type of setting, conversations between each child and the teacher/leader are most common. While students interact with a variety of others, group dynamics usually require that some listen more while others speak. Students increase their conversational skills by listening to others speak.

Learning through group conversations often seems time consuming, as time is taken for individuals to make and explain points. That extra time is counterbalanced, though, by the benefits of learning from ideas of others, learning patience, and formulating one's own ideas before speaking.

Group learning does suffer a drawback when the group grows too large. While some individuals thrive in the spotlight that a larger group offers, speaking more frequently and/or longer, perhaps dominating the conversation, that advantage may come at the expense of others. Quieter students often fade into the background, content to listen without engaging. And depending on who is in the group, even a group of three can be too large!

The conversational pattern that develops in groups needs to be well understood. If you are to assure that your child develops conversational skills, she needs the chance to participate frequently and fully.

Most children learn to converse best either in one-to-one conversation or in very small groups. And wouldn't you know it? When a child pulls back in a group, the size of the group has usually swelled beyond "family-sized." If you wonder whether the size of a group works for your child, sit in once or twice and you will easily be able to see if your child is learning speaking skills or simply being an audience for others.

A flaw of crowded classroom schooling is its inevitable failure to help all children develop strong interpersonal conversational skills. Classroom schooling pushes too many children into too-large groups too early in their lives for too many hours in the day. Conversational skill development is stopped cold. Children learn to sit and listen to the teacher at the very time they should be developing their own one-on-one conversational skills. The teacher talks and silent, stifled students listen. Self-stifling, as taught to children in group settings, is at once damaging and wrong-headed.

Homeschooling offers the extraordinary advantage of allowing children to develop conversational skills naturally through their daily experiences — talking and listening — with parents, family, and friends.

## Inner Conversations or Self-talk

The conversations and thoughts we have in our own minds are powerful tools for processing information. It is helpful to think of self-talk as a two-way conversation. The student is both the speaker and the listener when inwardly reflective. Pose a question; seek an answer. People who learn to use quiet moments to think, to reflect, to speculate, or to create also sharpen their ability to process and use information effectively.

Try this: think of journals, diaries, and other self-talk notes as two-way conversations with ourselves, over time. Writing down a rant or a rave for later review gives inward conversations a second perspective. If your child writes a heated letter to the editor of the local paper, allowing the letter to languish in a drawer for a week gives him a fresh and calmer perspective for editing. If your student drags out an old journal to read, he can reflect on the changes made and goals accomplished. He benefits first from the writing of the original journal, and again from rereading it to gain more insight. He can even put today's reflections about the old journal in a fresh entry for future review.

## The Skilled Listener

How do parents teach children to be skilled listeners? First, you listen and respond to your child's communications from birth on. Your child learns how much she is valued and that her needs are important. Secondly, parents talk with the child from birth on. The child begins to solve the amazing puzzle of discovering the meaning of the parents' chatter. Taken together, early demonstrations of listening to and speaking with your child show that listening is what we humans do.

The listener's life experiences influence her perception of the message. When your child is ill or tired, for example, her ability to listen may be reduced. As she matures, she learns to set external distractions aside and focus more intently. You can most easily observe how well your child listens when she is fascinated by the subject at hand.

The listener's task in conversation is sometimes thought of as easier than that of the speaker. Good listeners, though, do not just sit passively. Sometimes the listener's task is to learn or follow directions; other times it is to relax, enjoy or laugh. Listeners may need to work and question to fully understand the message. A skilled listener creates an inner conversation with the speaker or with the ideas themselves.

## The Skilled Reader

The tasks of oral communication — speaking and listening — become tasks of written communication — writing and reading — when information is transmitted through time or space through print.

The reader's job is to grasp the intended meaning. The reader brings her reading skill and life experiences to the task without ever thinking about it. Active reading involves thinking ideas through, agreeing, disagreeing, raising questions, and drawing one's own conclusions about the information. The tasks are similar to listener's tasks in conversation, and similarly, the reader's task is easier if the writer has written clearly.

Stretch a little further into the model and you'll return to the original idea: plays, scripts, poetry, movies, music, art, science, architecture — all works of man and nature — are conversations to be heard. We participate fully when we know how to listen, whether with our ears or visually as we interpret print.

## Finally

Parents should exude great confidence in their ability to teach their own child how to read and write, as they are the very best qualified people in the world to guide this particular child to acquire these skills. After all, they have their child's absolute attention, a strong foundation of communication during the early years upon which to build, and a huge commitment to help the child succeed.

The following chapters explore some of the bridging conversations and activities that parents may employ, including rudimentary reading, writing, and math. I will also remind you that the time you spend keeping the child's love of learning kindled through conversations is an investment you cannot afford *not* to make.

## chapter eight

# EARLY READING AND WRITING

*learning written conversation — conversationally*

Your baby's babbles, early crayon scribbles, pointing at objects for you to name, looking at picture books with you: these are the kinds of activities that demonstrate your child's natural desire to communicate just as you do — speaking, listening, writing, and reading.

Parents build the underlying skills of reading and writing in the course of daily conversations. Children learn from the smallest of experiences that we read from left to right, turn pages from right to left, and that reading and writing start at the top left of the page. To master the many skills of written and spoken language, to proficiently *read* and *write*, we begin with tiny steps.

The first step you may want to take toward your child's fluency is to plan a home environment in which it is *impossible not to learn reading and writing*. Although some children will bloom as readers early or later than others, children raised in homes that teem with reading and writing have the easiest time become fluent readers.

## A Reading and Writing Environment

Children learn about the skills of reading and writing by observing. The following foundations can help you create your own language-rich home environment.

## Models – Parents and Others Who Read and Write

Without a doubt, the most important influence on your child's ability to read is — You! How do the models in your home — each older child and adult — spend their time? Is reading and writing a daily activity? Can each family member be routinely observed reading and writing?

## Materials for Reading and Writing

Scan each room of your home for materials that tell your child that reading and writing are done here. You may not read in every room in the home, but make sure that reading and writing happen where the children are.

Here are some of the materials that our family and friends used. Try these or your own favorites.

- **Writing materials** that develop small motor coordination, drawing, scribble-writing, and creative expression. Include colored paper, big paper, little paper, lined or unlined paper, pencils, paint, colored pencils, crayons, markers, chalk and chalkboard, scissors, paste, tape, and other desk supplies such as staplers and hole punches.

- **A selection of books, magazines, and newspapers**, for both adults and children, that are readily available.

- **Letter sets**, such as refrigerator magnets, anagrams, letter blocks, or *Scrabble* tiles. Some early writing activities might involve moving letters into words. Other ways to help your child learn letters include using a sand tray for tracing letters and learning the Alphabet Song.

- **Alphabet and number strips** taped to the child's work table. Choose a strip that teaches letter forms that you want your child to learn. Or make your own strip, either by hand or using a computer.

- **Other aids** that you might find useful: an old electric or manual typewriter, a computer, dress-up materials and props for acting out stories, stamping kits, calligraphy sets, labels, posters, bulletin boards, marker board, a play store, stickers, activity and coloring books, play dough and clay to form letters, beginner puzzles, craft kits, magnetic poetry sets, blank books, wood, fabric, string, homemade paper, diaries, and charcoal from your campfire to write on bark. You can "paint" words with water on a sidewalk. Once you get started, you'll never run out of ideas!

- **A place for writing activities**. Your child needs a workplace of his own. It can be as big as a table or a desk, or he can use a small child's table if that is more comfortable. In our home, we had a small table that lived for years between the kitchen and family room. Some families provide a small portable desk that can be taken where you need to go. One boy turned the back seat of the family car into his "office."

## Read Aloud Together

Read with your child at least once a day. Find times that work for both you and the child. After breakfast, after lunch, and bedtime were favorites for our family. Make read-aloud time a *protected* time and avoid interruptions. Don't answer the phone and do let household tasks wait. Read while the baby is napping. In our family, my younger daughter was often an eager listener when her older sister was busy learning to read with me. At other times, she was happy to play by herself. If your toddler flips out when you spend time reading with older children, seek creative ways to entertain him until he is old enough to join in.

Get comfortable for reading time. If your child loves to sit in your lap for stories, great. Some families prefer to sit side by side on the couch or at a table. Sit side by side at a table, not across from each other. Learning is easiest for some children when taken as a joint venture, heads together, one person learning while another aids and supports the process.

Other children need to move while they listen. A wad of play dough to squeeze may be the perfect calming activity. Some families keep a basket of quiet activities for busy hands to use just during reading time. Active children may work best on the floor where they can move their whole bodies while listening. Short poems, nursery rhymes, and brief books are a good beginning for very active children. Enjoy finger-play stories, such as The Eensy-Weensy Spider. Act out fairy tales such as The Three Bears. You could even act out a story with dolls or puppets to keep those hands busy.

Choose materials that you both enjoy. In addition to choosing children's books that you both enjoy, occasionally look through your own books and magazines with your child. Search for the alphabet letters, interesting pictures, favorite animals, or toys. Maybe you'll find an ad for his favorite breakfast cereal. Alice learned the letter "B" from a license plate. Both Alice and Erin learned about farm animals while looking at farm magazines at Grandpa's house. These activities remind us how much fun reading is!

## Point Out Print Wherever You Are

I learned my first French word, before I could read, from the dashboard of my parents' car: Chevrolet. I wonder how many children's first reading word is McDonald's! Print is everywhere — in our cars, on road signs, on stores and malls, and on billboards as we drive. There is literature at the post office. Toys have labels, brand names, price tags, and directions. Cereal boxes are covered with print. Your child's new jacket has a tag with laundering instructions. Are you going to a sports event, play or performance? Read the program. Movies? Read your ticket stub. And is there a room in your house that doesn't have *something* to read?

## Think Out Loud About Reading

Have you ever watched toddlers look at a magazine or book, often holding it upside down, pointing and chattering away? They are "play reading." They learn to do this from watching us — it is what reading looks like to them! They sit and look at a book and vocalize in imitation of our reading to them. In time, the child discovers that there is meaning attached to the pages through pictures and words.

We demystify the process of interpreting print by letting them know how it works. When we think our processes through aloud, we help children understand that there is a systematic process to reading and writing. "You want to read this book? Hmmm. Let's turn it right side up so we can read it together." Or "Here is the title of the story. It says...." Or "Look at this big word on your shoes. The letters are …" "Oh, do you want to write your name? Let's find the letters of your name on these blocks. Can you find a 'k' block? Here is one. Let's trace the 'k' together. Can you find another 'k' block?"

## Parent Patience — Wait and Observe

Some parents enjoy spending time reading with their children so much that they gently teach from the earliest signs of possible readiness. Why not, if both parent and child enjoy the activity?

If you are busy, though, you may want to wait until more signs of readiness are in place so that both you and your child will feel successful. Waiting doesn't mean you stop doing all the good things you have always done to prepare your child for literacy — reading aloud, talking, involving him in writing activities whenever you can.

# Reading Readiness Mileposts to Watch For

## Can your child attend to a task?

- Can she listen to a story for ten minutes or more?

- Can he play intently for twenty minutes or more?

## Does she have small motor coordination?

- Can he turn the pages when you read to him?

- Can she use a crayon or pencil to draw or color?

- Does he "scribble-write?"

- Can he build with blocks, do puzzles, or string beads?

## Does your child show interest in reading and writing?

- Does she recognize the relationship between print and meaning?

- Does he grasp the meaning of stories you read to him?

- Can he retell a favorite story?

- Has she memorized a favorite story or tale?

- Does she act out, draw, or build, favorite stories?

- Does he enjoy "reading" the pictures in a book?

- Can she dictate short sentences for you to write down?

- Can he tell you the story of a picture he is making?

- Can she "scribble-write" a story and then tell it to you?

- Does he ask you what print says?

It just means that, in your own mind, reading instruction has not yet begun! You can relax and enjoy watching your child pursue his many other interests, knowing that reading will fall into place in its own time. Just keep reading aloud together and watching for signs that your child is ready.

Use "Reading Readiness Mileposts to Watch For" if it helps, but please be prepared to ignore this and similar lists! Strict adherence to a checklist can squelch you or your child and keep you from enjoying the process before you.

The truth is, you don't need this list, really. If all items in the list are true for your child, she is probably already well launched as a beginning reader. If none of them are true, you already know she is not yet ready to read and the list gives you nothing new, except possibly an unhelpful feeling of guilt.

## Special Concerns

I know you are wondering what methods you should you use to teach reading. In two chapters that follow, "The Laptop Approach to Reading" and "Writing Toward Reading" (chapters 9 and 10), I'll show you two effective approaches for teaching reading and writing, parent- and child-friendly approaches that reinforce one another. These approaches are practical and do not require the use of a specific program. Always be skeptical if someone tells you *their* way is the only way or the best way to teach reading skill. Don't shortchange your child by teaching him only one approach to reading. Shouldn't you teach him *all* the skills that lead to success? I hope you'll be patient for a bit longer, though. You need to know about a couple of special situations first.

### Children Who are Inclined Toward Literacy From Birth

In the big picture of a child's life there is no advantage to early reading. Younger readers do not read faster or with better comprehension when they reach adulthood. Reading should not be pushed at the expense of other normal developmental activities. There is no advantage, although there could be considerable loss.

On the other hand, there is no sense in delaying reading and writing when a child is chomping at the bit to learn. If reading blooms early for your child, just enjoy the process. Focus on helping her discover reading and writing at her rate, naturally and joyfully.

If she asks for reading lessons at some point, that might be a good time to try formal instruction if you are inclined. The methods described in the following chapters work for beginning readers and writers of all ages. Make sure that the method and timing of instruction match the interests and abilities of the child.

Here is one more note regarding early reading. Some vision experts believe that excessive early reading can lead to or aggravate myopia. Young children who do read early are discouraged by these experts from reading for more than twenty minutes at a sitting. If you have concerns, check with your vision specialist.

For reasons unknown, my daughters both read earlier than "school normal." Each had her own approach.

### Alice learns to read.

Alice took an interest in print at eighteen months — who knows why? It was just her way. At age two, she read letters, a few sight words, and was interested in discovering the meaning in print. A thousand times she asked how to make an "s," how to spell "cat," and how to write "I love you, Mommy." She spent hours looking at books and being read to every day. She had favorite books read again and again, memorized them, and even recorded them on tape.

Alice's early interest excited the "teacher" in me. When she was three or so, and enthusiastic about language and print, I devised little lessons that I thought would help. But no matter how clever and cute I made my lessons, they were met with a resounding thud. Nursing my bruised "teacher's ego," I tossed my lesson plans out the window and followed my daughter's lead. I knew that I did not want to risk having her hate reading just because I loved teaching! We had plenty of time for reading to bloom.

Instead of giving her lessons that dulled the light in her eyes, I followed her clues and built on her enjoyment of the printed word. Road signs, store signs, food packaging, and newspaper or magazine headlines were our primers. We had dozens of the *Dr. Seuss* type of books which she delighted in, some favorite alphabet books, fairy tales, nursery rhymes, poetry, and of course many books of children's literature. We went to library story time. We put up a chalkboard and wrote and drew. I labeled her drawings for her, or helped her label them. She acted out her favorite stories and tales. She read fluently at an early age.

### Erin learns to read.

Erin's process of learning to read was usually an inner experience, an experience she often kept to herself. Occasionally, long before she could officially read, she would write or read something that absolutely astounded me. I had no idea that she knew this stuff. However, pushing her only brought resistance. I learned to trust the process with this daughter, too, and let her develop at her own pace. I continued to read with her, though, every day. Eventually, a computer game and Winnie the Pooh forced her to discover her reading skills.

Long before Erin made the discovery for herself, though, the rest of the family knew that Erin could read. We also knew that Erin did not yet know that she could read. She put a good deal of energy into getting other people to read for her, particularly that Winnie the Pooh computer game. Finally, a day came when no one had the time or interest in reading the story along with her. "Erin, try it by yourself." She was reluctant, but Winnie the Pooh was calling!

"I can read! I can read!" Her joyful shout was followed by the whole family dropping everything to celebrate with her. What a moment! Erin transformed in that instant from being a non-reader to being a reader. Had her skills improved greatly? Of course not — what had changed was her image of herself. She now saw herself as a reader.

The following day, brimming with confidence in her new found self-knowledge, she took up one of Laura Ingalls Wilder's books. Her image of herself as a reader changed so drastically that she just assumed that all text would now be available to her. She struggled for hours to read just a few paragraphs, and patiently worked her way through the text. As hard a struggle as those hours were, she never faltered. She knew the most important thing — she could read! — and the rest was petty detail.

Learning to read is not an overnight process, though new readers often claim, as Erin did, "I learned to read yesterday!" The transition to being a reader will occur when your child is ready, with or without direct instruction, somewhere between the preschool years and late childhood.

Oops, did I say children usually learn to read somewhere between preschool and late childhood? I did? Then it is time for the next topic.

## Older Blooming Readers

Yes, children may make the transition from non-reader to reader at any time within an eight to ten year range. For some children, either extreme is their own personal "normal." Are you shocked? Don't be. Students who learn to read at age two and those who read at age twelve or thirteen are generally indistinguishable from each other as adults. They all read!

If you find it difficult to accept such a broad age range for reading development, you are probably basing your opinion on a classroom model of group reading instruction. With a classroom approach to instruction, same-age children are taught basic reading skills in groups on a pre-planned schedule. By third grade or so, many of those students are readers. Those older-bloomers who are not yet reading are taken aside for special instruction. That experience frequently creates within the older-blooming reader an image of herself as a non-reader, learning disabled, or worse. Such a "shotgun" model doesn't fit many children and, unfortunately, many in the classroom environment don't learn to read very well, even with extra instruction.

Homeschooling families can individualize and assure that the tools of reading are there for the child when the child is ready to read. Why race to reach an artificial goal when you can set your own goal and learn at your own pace and interest?

And then there is Jimmy. The little guy was covered with mud from his nose to his toes. His pockets were full of dirt, rocks, and bugs, and his face beamed when he shared each treasure with his mom. His Big Wheel trike was his favorite toy, and he buzzed around the yard for hours each day. He loved to eat, his bath was a daily joy, he slept like a log all night long, and each day was as fresh and exciting as the one before. He could curl up for a story or book for just a few minutes before he was off to ride his trike.

Although Jimmy bloomed in reading by age eight, many active youngsters like Jimmy are not yet ready to read at that age. Would it be sensible to force such a child to sit quietly for reading lessons when he was three? Of course not. By the same logic, it makes no sense to force reading on children who still have their pockets full of bugs at age eight or nine. Should you give them bites and tastes of reading? Of course. But there is little point in wasting their time and yours until they acquire both motivation and readiness.

If your child shows little interest in learning to read on her own, she may be an older-blooming reader. I'll tell you not to worry, that your child will learn to read in her own good time. Not worrying is not so easy, though, particularly when siblings, sometimes younger siblings, or the public school children across the street, are reading chapter books and your child hasn't mastered a primer such as the *Bob Books*, and worse yet, doesn't appear to have any desire to read. Try to avoid panicking, and don't let your child know that you are worried.

Homeschooling families can avoid the biggest disadvantage to late reading — feeling stupid. If your child is an older blooming reader, be happy he is homeschooling and not in school being labeled learning disabled (because he is not) or feeling humiliated by teachers and peers. Reassure your child (if he is concerned) that he will find his own time and way of learning to read. Meanwhile, keep the love of reading alive. Tell him over and over that you know he loves reading because he enjoys being read to. Remind him that everyone is unique. Try to find an adult — someone your child knows and who now enjoys reading — who was also a delayed reader. It can give you (and your child) some perspective.

You should also remind him that there are many other important skills to know and many ways to learn besides reading. Isn't he learning all the time? Many older-blooming readers are very active physically and learn many difficult sports and skills. Help him make a list of all the things he knows how to do and subjects he has learned without the benefit of reading. Remind him that everyone learns different skills when they are ready, and reading is no different.

Some parents opt to impose reading lessons on their older-bloomers for their own peace of mind. Sometimes the lessons help and sometimes they don't. In either case, you'll want to keep on doing all the good things you've been doing with your child. You may want to take time to reflect and see if there is some way that you could be more supportive. The "Reading Environment Checklist" on the following page suggests areas that might bear further scrutiny.

## Finally

If you've tried everything you can think of and you realize that he is a late reader, you may sweat blood and agonize daily, but when reading does kick in, you will be amazed. One young friend went from struggling with the easy reader *One Fish, Two Fish* to reading three or four chapter books a week in a matter of months. Another became interested in reading in March, and read fluently by December. Remember, older-blooming readers quickly catch up with peers. As a matter of fact, many late readers may have more interest in reading, once they learn, than some early readers. Be patient and have confidence in your child.

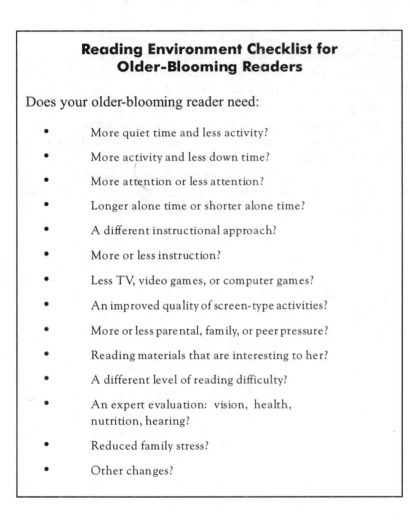

**Reading Environment Checklist for
Older-Blooming Readers**

Does your older-blooming reader need:

- More quiet time and less activity?
- More activity and less down time?
- More attention or less attention?
- Longer alone time or shorter alone time?
- A different instructional approach?
- More or less instruction?
- Less TV, video games, or computer games?
- An improved quality of screen-type activities?
- More or less parental, family, or peer pressure?
- Reading materials that are interesting to her?
- A different level of reading difficulty?
- An expert evaluation: vision, health, nutrition, hearing?
- Reduced family stress?
- Other changes?

## chapter nine

# THE LAPTOP APPROACH TO READING

*or on the floor, across the room, or in the car — together*

Have you read aloud to your child regularly for as long as you can remember? Teaching your child to read is a continuation of the same, and just as enjoyable. Most families slide into an incremental approach without realizing it, teaching reading in tasty nibbles that fit their child's appetite for learning perfectly. Parents and children just assume slightly different roles, and the reading continues pretty much as before.

## Choice of Materials

Beginning reading materials that both parent and child enjoy make reading time a happy time. Some families have used *Dr. Seuss* type limited-vocabulary books very successfully. Many are tickled by the *Bob* books. Limited-vocabulary books are especially useful for those children who want to be able to read *all* the words in a book before they become fluent.

While limited-vocabulary books are popular, they are not at all necessary. Many families prefer children's literature, or favorite versions of traditional tales. Poems and nursery rhyme books also make terrific first readers. You can always fill in the harder words your child cannot yet read. Families who choose literature for reading instruction may first focus on finding meaning in print. Of course, many parents feel confident using both types of books.

Sometimes a child chooses a "personal reading primer," a book that he wants to know how to read for himself. If so, it is usually a well-loved book, one that you have already spent hours reading and re-reading with your child. Yes, you face more hours with the same book! If you can't enjoy it any more, at least try to appreciate that this book has special meaning to your child. Parents are often surprised at the extent of the need for repetition. Remember, when the skills are solid, he will no longer need the repetition.

When you select books, toss out books you or your children don't enjoy. There are millions of books out there. Who has time to read books they don't like?

## When Your Child Reads to You

As a general rule, keep the reading moving, no matter who is reading. If the material is interesting, yet too difficult for your child, just hand him the words he needs so he can get the meaning and enjoy the book. Who cares if a reading lesson becomes a read-aloud session? The basic principle is still the same: developing a love of reading.

You will want to find an effective balance between telling a child a difficult word and letting him attack it on his own. Don't insist that the child sound out every word that she struggles with. On the other hand, don't tell her every word that gives her pause. Allow enough time to work it out on her own if she wants. You may want to wait until she asks for the word or shows frustration.

Use your detective skills to spot flaws in your child's reading strategies. If he always pronounces a certain word incorrectly, ask yourself why. You may need to offer a brief phonics lesson to support the correct pronunciation.

Don't stop an interesting story for phonics lessons, except for quick mini-lessons that give clues to the word such as, "This word rhymes with *bat*." "In this word (*cough*), *ough* sounds like *off*."

Nor should you give pop quizzes on content. Minimize interruptions of the flow of reading. Think about how you react to interruptions when you are reading for pleasure or information. Your child is probably wired like you are. Respect his style. On the other hand, don't hesitate to stop an interesting story to answer questions, to explain an unfamiliar word, or for your child to talk about a related experience of his own. Reading "side trips" enhance interest and understanding if used sparingly. I know this advice sounds contradictory — so when in you are in doubt, listen to your child's clues.

Pay close attention to the stops, pauses, questions and comments your child makes as reading progresses. These are the generous clues your child gives you about what he already knows and what he is ready to learn. Usually you will know what to do to help him next. If you are really stuck, take a break and pick up a book on reading instruction or phonics *for yourself, not for your child.* If you read up on how children typically learn to read, you can usually figure out what the next step should be.

## Teach Skills with Mini-Lessons

Sometimes the best strategy is to allow your child to struggle with the information on the page in her own way, just as she learned to walk and talk; other times she clearly needs help.

Mini-lessons are the little tips and suggestions you give your child when he is stuck on a word. Mini-lessons rarely take more than a minute, usually just a few seconds, but they are the ideal tools to deliver the information to the child quickly and without fuss. Why must the lessons be short? Because reading is really about meaning, not lessons or word analysis. If you keep the mini-lessons brief — your goal being to move on with the story, i.e., *read* — your child will stay focused on the meaning with you. For most students, mini-lessons are exactly what they need to bring their skill level to fluency.

### Semantics

The use of semantics, using words in their intended context, is a valuable skill that all fluent readers use constantly. Just what did the author intend to say here? You have probably introduced the idea of semantics many times while reading stories aloud.

Using semantics to figure out meaning is a useful reading strategy. If a student cannot decode a word, or if he can read it but doesn't know what it means, perhaps the rest of the sentence or paragraph can be used to find clues to the word's meaning.

Many gifted children's writers carefully introduce new ideas and unfamiliar words in just this way. Suppose a sentence reads, "The

Smiths moved all of their boxes to their new abode." If the writer does not expect the child to know *abode*, the next sentence might read, "The new home was just one mile down the road from the house they had lived in for so long." The context is clear and there is little doubt about the meaning of *abode*.

Some children will seek the context through the pictures in a book. We all do this, looking at maps and illustrations to help us grasp the writer's intent. The only thing to be wary of is those books, such as some graded readers, that give too many picture clues. Children may learn to read the pictures and ignore the print!

If your child is reading aloud to you and reads *home* instead of *house*, his understanding of semantics will usually allow him to overlook the minor error. The meaning is what counts, he will tell you. You should probably let it go as well. We all make these kinds of mistakes in our reading. What's the difference? If you later find that he writes *house* and still reads it as *home*, that's a good time to discuss the two different words.

Children who can learn new words from the context in which they are written are well on their way to developing a large reading vocabulary.

## Syntax

Syntax helps to answer the question: Does this make sense? Technically, syntax tells how and why a part of speech functions as it does in a sentence. One rich demonstration of syntax is found in this sentence fragment: "That that that the man used, ..." Three "thats" are used in sequence, yet we understand the fragment because we intuitively know each "that" is used as a different part of speech.

We might say that syntax is the *way* we talk. However, ordinary speech is often sloppy, whereas writing — what we read — must be more precise if the author is to convey her meaning to the reader. As a result of that carefulness, readers can use what they know about syntax to understand a written passage.

Even beginning readers use syntax clues to make sense of their reading. For a simple example, consider these sentences. "The dog jumps." "The dogs jump." To read either sentence precisely, your child will use what he already knows about how we put sentences together. On the other hand, if you ask your child to read, "The dogs jumps," he will laugh and tell you that it "sounds funny." If you don't believe me, try it!

## Correct Word Choice

Correct usage of words can also help a child read. Suppose, for example, a sentence reads, "Bobby has taken his cat to his room." If your child reads "token" instead of "taken" the sentence loses its meaning. Coach your child to think about the word he actually sees on the page. You might ask him to read the sentence again. Most beginning readers will quickly correct their errors. If not, point it out and move on.

## Phonics

Phonics is a term we use to describe the system of sound-symbols that we use to decode words, or as children often say, "to sound them out." Most English words are spelled phonetically and technically speaking, learning to read should be simple. That is, each spoken sound can be represented by a letter or group of letters. Unfortunately, some sounds have multiple spellings and no easy way to tell which is needed where.

In helping children learn to read English, we have another dilemma. Although the majority of English words do follow phonetic rules, many common words — particularly those that children like to use and want to write — do not follow those rules. Learning to read phonetically helps with most words, but it may not help beginning readers with the words and ideas that interest them most.

Phonics is best taught in small bits, such as those mini-lessons that come up in the process of reading. Parents must decide whether a word or concept merits a more extensive lesson later.

For example, if the child needs to know the word *the* or *of*, just tell him the word and go on. (Hang on — we'll talk about sight words in a minute.) Maybe he'll remember and maybe he won't, but phonetic explanations are needlessly confusing. In time, we all learn *the* and *of*, don't we?

If he is stuck on the word *scrape* and you know that he's already read the word *tape*, you might point out the pattern, or note that the word rhymes with *tape*, or remind him briefly of what he may know about *vowel-consonant-silent e*. Then go on with the reading.

Many beginning readers move quickly through the phonics stage of reading. These youngsters easily learn to decode — sound out — words and soon move on to identifying words as wholes without using phonic techniques. They move rapidly from an early reader stage of a handful of memorized words and sound-symbol methods to full fluency.

Some students need to spend more time on phonics, figuring out the relationships of printed letters to the sounds they hear. If you believe your child needs the extra time, you may want to work with limited vocabulary books so that he can have success with reading. If you were not taught phonics yourself, but feel it could help your child if you knew more, get a book for yourself and learn the basics.

Some parents like having the safety net of a phonics program. You may choose a simple phonics program or a phonics game. Avoid phonics programs that *over-teach*. More is not better and can be mind-numbing. Look for a program that has a light approach and don't feel obligated to belabor any of the points. Just touch on them and go on. Don't dwell on a point. When the system of sound-symbols begins to make sense to your child, he can move on to fluent reading. You can always review later.

Remember that phonics instruction is not a substitute for reading readiness. To the contrary, premature instruction can be unhelpful and confusing to a child who needs more time to develop language skills through listening and speaking. Just because he is five or six, and a neighbor child of that age already reads, is not a good enough reason to sit him down for lessons. Nor is he doomed because you read in an "authoritative" magazine or newspaper that he must read by a certain age or be considered a non-reader forever. Don't believe it for a minute!

Buck up and just keep doing the wonderful things you are doing to help him know that he loves reading, and that, although he doesn't know how to read yet, he can be proud to be an emerging reader!

## The Rhythm and Flow of Language

Ah, reading is so much more than decoding symbols, isn't it? The ebb and flow of well-constructed sentences, the poetic images that rise from precise word choices, and the underlying themes that create a meaning much larger than the words themselves — these draw us to engage again and again with the printed page.

We know that fluent adults rarely sound out words phonetically, except for the occasional unknown or scientific word they meet. They read words and phrases in wholes and in chunks of meaning. We also know that well-written material has a rhythmic, sometimes musical, quality, a quality that helps us interpret those squiggles on paper into the vivid speeches and stories of Shakespeare, poetry, and other great literature.

Why am I telling you this? It is my backhanded way of suggesting that you not get overly caught up in the phonics versus whole word versus whole language arguments about how to teach reading. Each is good, and each has drawbacks. Reading is far too important for you to put all of your reading eggs in one or another basket of belief.

Do it all, with moderation! Most words can be decoded phonetically, so it makes sense to know the phonetic system, even if the child does move quickly past phonics to adult type fluency. And since children learn about reading from being read to, hearing whole sentences and learning to love the flow of language and a good story, it makes good sense to use syntax and semantic skills to unlock meaning at any stage of reading development.

## Sight Words

What about sight words, a list of memorized words? This is certainly the least effective approach for teaching children to read. The secrets of phonics and meaning are rarely unlocked from such lists. When lists of memorized words are separated from both meaning and decoding skills, (as in the Dick and Jane era) an unexpected death blow to the desire to read may befall your child. Don't risk it.

Still, what child doesn't memorize a few favorite words before really learning how reading works? Some children memorize entire books as part of their personal learning process! When the memorized words are of the child's choosing, selected from his own interests and experience, a word list can be a fun adjunct to the learning process. Make sure the list includes favorite student-selected and possibly a few highly meaningful words — love, mom, dad, family, friends, pet names, favorite foods, and toys, for example, that you choose. You might include those ornery words kids love to use that are not phonetic such as *of, love,* and *the.*

A personalized sight word list can be a useful springboard that supports reading growth. Some children may want to write the words they know in a handmade book. Others like to write the words on three by five cards. Just hole-punch one corner and slip the word cards on a ring. "Just look at the words I already know how to read!"

## Advanced Reading Skills

Before you know it, your beginning reader will pick up chapter books! Make sure she has some of the skills that mature readers use every day, and your reader will be well launched. You might start with these.

### Reading for Information

Reading for information is important enough that you will want to make sure your child has the skills to do it.

One important skill is *skimming,* scanning a page for a specific idea or information. Many children learn this skill on their own. They've watched parents do it for years. "Right here on the top of that page you'll find out how to spell your word," says a busy parent. You could make a game of it with a book the child has not read before. "Look through this book and find the name of the city where Grandma lives."

### Critical Thinking

Do you want your children to develop critical reading and thinking skills. One sure way to accomplish the task is to continue to read aloud to them. (Don't mind if I repeat myself on this important point!) You can read more complex literature or books with ideas that are a bit out of their grasp. Take time to discuss and probe into the author's meaning. What are the themes of the story? What bigger idea is the author trying to get you to think about? What do you think about those ideas? Another strategy is to read the same books separately, for later discussion. Ask provocative questions about the reading. I would only caution you not to focus too heavily on analyzing literature — the main thing is to enjoy it!

## Finally

There are many ways to learn to read, and many ways to help a child learn to read. Choose what works for you and your child. In addition to the selections below, take a look at the resources listed in "Exploring Literature and Books" (chapter 39).

### SELECTED READING RESOURCES

*Games for Reading*

By Peggy Kaye. Pantheon Books, 1984. Designed for early elementary age students, the book may provide some parents helpful ideas for use during the preschool years. If not, you can always put it on the shelf for a year or two. This book will provide structure for the parent and enjoyable learning activities for the young child who is ready for reading. An excellent option.

*Glad Rags: Stories and Activities Featuring Clothes for Children*

By Jan Irving and Robin Currie. CO: Libraries Unlimited, Inc. 1990. A happy blend of fingerplays, rhythms, rhymes, songs, stories, activities, props to make and much more. Language enrichment activities include colorful expressions such as "walk in my shoes," "pass the hat," "too big for your britches." A very rich resource book.

*Give Your Child a Head Start In Reading,*

By Fitzhugh Dodson. New York: Simon and Schuster, 1981. A quick read for those who want to make sure they have the reading bases covered. Worth a look for the simple nursery rhyme ideas and for the rich children's reading and "read to" lists.

*The New Read-Aloud Handbook*

By Jim Trelease. Penguin Books
Tips on reading aloud, as well as selected books to read aloud, from picture books to novels, with interesting and helpful commentary. A valuable resource.

*Predictable Books*

Strategies and Activities for Teaching with More than 75 Favorite Children's Activities
By Michael F. Opitz. Scholastic Professional Books. 1995. Does your child love books with repeating themes? This book may bring some variety to your life and teach your child some concepts not found in that dog-eared favorite! 800 books are listed.

### Reading Reflex / Phono Graphix
PO Box 1246, Mount Dora, FL 32756
352/735.9292    orders: 800/732.3868
fax: 352/735.9294 www.readamerica.net
A phonetic reading program that uses games for instruction. This twelve-week program is for use with students age 5-8, or remedially through adult.

### Reading Without Nonsense
3rd Ed., by Frank Smith. Columbia University Teachers College Press, 1997. A look at reading as a natural and joyous event that takes place easily within the context of daily living.

### Sing, Spell, Read & Write
International Learning Systems of North America, Inc.
800/321.8322    www.pearsonlearning.com/singspell
Multi-sensory kits — includes songs, videos, games, readers, student books, teacher materials. Free information.

### Teach a Child to Read with Children's Books:
Combining story reading, phonics, and writing to promote reading success
By Mark B. Thogmartin. 3rd edition, 1999.
EDINFO Press, PO Box 5247, Bloomington, IN 47407
If you still doubt your ability to teach your children to read, invest in this book! You will learn that you already have what it takes. Put the book on the shelf after you read it, save it for reference, and then go read with your child with confidence.

### Teach Your Child to Read in 100 Easy Lessons
By Siegfried Engelmann, Phyllis Haddox and Elaine C. Bruner.
Phyllis Haddox, Dept. TYC, PO Box 10459, Eugene, OR 97440
541/485.1163  www.startreading.com  Phyllis@darkwing.uoregon.edu
Proven easy-to-use and affordable phonetic reading method for up to second grade. Many homeschooled students have learned to read using this material.

## chapter ten

# WRITING TOWARD READING

*learning to read by learning to write*

Some young children, as soon as they can pick up a crayon, want to make words or letters. They've made a connection between print and ideas. Parents who want their children to read, write, and spell well have an opportunity they should not pass up. Children who learn to write also learn to read.

## Spelling Words and Reading Words

"Mommy, how do you spell *cats*?"

"Let me think," says Mom. "You want to write CATS. 'K-k-k' is the first sound. In this word we spell that sound with the letter 'c.' Write 'c' just like you always do. 'A-a-a' comes next. Write the letter 'a.' Here is how you make 'a' — you copy mine. 'T-t-t' is spelled with the letter 't.' Now, do you remember how to write 's'? There, you have written CATS. Can you read the word you wrote?" In this example Mom is thinking out loud and the child learns from observing the process.

Even if your child does not instigate the writing process, opportunities to help him with writing are endless. "Your name is James, and I'll help you write it. 'J-J-J' we write this way. 'A-a-a' looks like this."

Other examples: "That sign reads STOP. Let's make a stop sign when we get home. I'll help you write the letters." "We are out of milk. I will help you write MILK on the shopping list. Listen to the sound 'm-m-m.' Can you remember how to write that sound?"

Is he having a birthday party? Invitations must be written. If he is a beginner, let him write his friends' names on the envelopes. Help him write and spell their names correctly. If he is a more skilled writer, perhaps he can write the whole invitation.

With little effort, you can teach the basics of phonics through this natural process of helping your child write whatever he wants or needs to write.

## But First, Handwriting

Handwriting comes hand in glove, if you'll excuse the expression, with writing, so let's talk about it now.

### Forming Letters, Making Words

At the beginning, if the child is just learning to write letters, you may need to hold her hand and help form that ornery 'S.' When she is ready, she'll try it on her own. But what if she isn't ready?

To help fine motor skill development, offer activities that give practice. Putting together puzzles with large pieces is a favorite activity for developing finger coordination, as is building with blocks. Encourage large-scale freehand drawing and scribbling on a chalkboard, a whiteboard, large pieces of newsprint or butcher block paper. Use markers or paints regularly.

Some very young children delight in writing squiggles on lined paper that they call "cursive" and will gladly tell you the story of what they have written. Encourage this wonderfully rich activity — using and controlling those tiny finger muscles while organizing, memorizing, and retelling ideas!

Pre-handwriting stages are a good time to work on the concepts of left and right. Our culture's written material has both pattern and form and children need that information.

There are many ideas about the best way to teach children to print. You might purchase a handwriting program so that you are consistent. Many people skip the structured program, instead teaching their children to write when they ask for help. For young children, uppercase letters are easier to make, as many can be constructed with straight lines and large strokes. Teach the letters, both upper and lowercase, as the child has the need to write them. Some people prefer to teach letters of the alphabet systematically. Some set aside a special day for each letter, days when you eat foods that start with the day's letter, find the letters in books and magazines and newspapers, cut your food into letter shapes, paint the letter, and similar activities.

When children are ready to write more than just the occasional word, an alphabet strip of both upper and lowercase letters is handy. Just tape it to a table or writing desk.

## Writing Without Handwriting

The physical act of using the pencil can be a daunting challenge to the young child, but need not limit her writing experience. Until a child's fine motor skills are developed and controlled enough that writing is comfortable, parents can write ideas down for her. Some parents write words for the child on cards that she can arrange into "sentences."

You may also use refrigerator magnet letters, anagrams, or *Scrabble* tiles and let him write words with those. Refrigerator magnets are especially nice because messages can be left up to be read later. You might put the magnetic letters on a metal bake pan for word building. Magnetic poetry word sets can expand the vocabulary for this type of writing.

Children may enjoy using a tape recorder for "writing" stories. Some parents buy the child a word processor or computer. Even those students who delay the physical "handwriting" process eventually find a system of handwriting that works for them. It is important for children to realize that writing is about recording ideas, not just moving a pencil across paper.

## Fluent Handwriting

Your child may beg you to teach her cursive writing. You might approach cursive writing by teaching the letters of the words she needs to know first, and then add in the others later.

As children grow older and become fluent in their writing, expect them to go through several legibility stages. When they first begin to write, they actually draw the letters. As students pick up speed, sloppiness kicks in. Dismayed, I watched both of my daughters trade neat writing skill for speedy sloppiness. I was much relieved to discover that it really was just a stage.

Other writing stages are fun, too, such as when many girls and some boys dot their i's with little circles, or even cuter, little hearts. Sometimes students take great delight in writing as small as they can, or even as lightly as possible, rendering their work unreadable. Let it pass, but be sure to save a couple of those pages for your nostalgia scrapbook!

## Left-handed Writers

A word about your left-handed child. As a left-handed writer myself, I'll tell you this: leave her alone, and she will figure out writing for herself. I grew up to be a left-handed teacher and had no trouble teaching children how to write, regardless of handedness. The same principles apply to righthanders teaching lefthanders.

The challenges of writing are a little different for the lefty, but very doable. A left-handed writer generally moves the writing tool somewhat toward the body, assuming the paper is placed on the table at a slant, while the right-handed person usually moves the hand away from the body. Young lefties may try variations, such as mirroring you or writing upside down and backwards. Encourage your child to try to make the writing looks like yours.

Try to discourage a style of writing that unnaturally cramps the hand. Most handwriting programs give a few positioning instructions for the left-handed writer, and you might want to review those if your child has trouble with positioning.

When teaching letter formation, right-handed parents should sit to the left of the child at a table to demonstrate. Left-handed parents should stay to the right for all students. Try it, and you'll see how much easier the learning task becomes for your child, no matter who uses which hand.

Later on, when you try to teach your older southpaw a complex skill such as knitting or crocheting, righthanders might try sitting across the table and let her work in mirror image with you. You can use this method now to demonstrate, in mirror image, how to position the paper and to hold a pencil, but unless you can write upside down and backwards, don't try to demonstrate letter forms this way!

## Encourage Writing Activities

**Write with your children regularly.** Even as tiny children, my daughters crawled up next to me as I wrote in my journal and made their own special scribble entries along with mine. How I treasure those scrawls today — I just wish I could remember the stories that go with each scribble! Letter writing, thank-you notes, holiday cards, and E-mail are also meaningful places for writing to take place as part of family life. We did "car poetry." Pass time in a traffic jam by making up poems or limericks with the kids. Later your child can write down the ones he remembers.

**The best early writing instruction does not send a child off to write by himself.** There is so much that he doesn't know yet! Although writing is often a solitary activity for adults, many students enjoy learning all these skills with their parent close at hand. Learning sizzles when parent and child put their heads together to write.

**Continue regular writing activities together as skill grows.** Some days you may write out the day's schedule, a recipe, or a *To Do* list with your children. Other times try journal-writing, in shared journals or private ones. Write short stories together. Record events, such as field trips, birthdays, visits from relatives, a new puppy, a new project, or an old project completed. Make up stories together and then write them down so children can see their stories on paper, just like a storybook. You can introduce all kinds of writing this way — descriptions, comparisons, narratives, poems, reviews, and so on. You might read an example first. Discuss what you want to say, then put the ideas on paper.

**When reading aloud, occasionally talk about the materials as written-down talk or conversation.** That is not the whole story of writing, of course, but it helps youngsters to realize that writing originates with speech and ideas. Even favorite information books come from the ideas in the writer's mind. Extend these ideas by discussing books and literature and by trying to figure out what the author was trying to convey. Movies and cartoons can be discussed as drawn or acted stories and ideas. You might try writing a screenplay or storyboard if youngsters are really into a TV show.

**Turn favorite family stories into books as a way to develop a love for writing and to learn editing skills**. Whether you write down a familiar fairy tale, a made-up wild adventure story, Dad's family ghost story, or Mom's snake-on-the-bridge story, the process can be quite enjoyable. Two books titled *Spring,* my children's first handmade and hand-bound books, hold a very special place on my bookshelf and in my heart.

## Write, Edit, and Publish

The writing life is easier if we remember to identify the separate tasks of writing, editing, and publishing.

Writing is that creative, free-flowing process of getting ideas down on paper. Most writing never hits the editing desk, and we shouldn't expect children to edit every single piece they write. Decide for your family just how frequently children should polish up a piece of their writing. Then encourage children to journal or write stories or poems for their own pleasure.

Editing is the process of preparing the work so that it means what the writer wants it to mean to readers. Tell your child to try to make the meaning so clear that a reader will understand when no one is there to explain.

Go lightly with the red pen as you edit your child's work. Editing is important, but it is not the only important writing skill. Very young children should not be required to edit much, if any, of their work. They will usually let you know if you are demanding too much. Excessive editing can erode the desire to write.

Publishing is the process of getting your writing out to the public of your choice. Example: Johnny sits down and writes a letter to Grandma. The next day he sits down with his "editor," Mom, and makes sure that what he wrote makes sense and says what he wants to say. He might try reading it aloud or Mom might read it to him. Next the spelling, capitalization, and paragraphing are corrected. Finally, he sits down with a special piece of stationery and recopies (publishes) the letter and mails it off to Grandma.

Other examples of publishing children's writing include writing out birthday invitations, sending the work to a newsletter or magazine or contest, making a book, and collecting different types of writing for a portfolio.

## Learning to Write by Reading

Successful writers will tell you that one key to skillful writing is extensive reading. Reading may give beginning writers a place to start. If you have a favorite family author, try to imitate that writer's style and type of story. Younger children can join in the fun and work on illustrations that imitate their favorite storybook illustrators. Even the most reluctant writer, a child who writes very little, will develop *some* of the skills used in writing if he reads.

You can save time by talking about the use of punctuation and grammar with your children as they read. If they understand what punctuation and capitalization mean when they read, they will probably acquire those skills without too much extra instruction.

## Finally

Oh, dear. We've circled back, haven't we? I started out suggesting ways that children learn reading through writing, and I've ended up with tips for launching enthusiastic writers. You can be sure, though, that enthusiastic writers will improve their reading skill. I would only add that reading improves writing skill. But then, it is all just conversation, isn't it?

## SELECTED EARLY WRITING RESOURCES

*Refer to "Exploring Writing" (chapter 4o) for more ideas.*

### ELP - Essential Learning Products

PO Box 2590, Columbus, OH 43216-2590
800/357.3570  fax: 614/487.2272  www.elp-web.com
A variety of handwriting paper and journals, alphabet strips, finger-fitting pens. The print catalog offers much more than is available online.

### Hajek House

Ellen Hajek, 12750 W. 6th Pl., Golden, CO 80401
303/237.3471      800/570.1386
Grammar, writing, and sentence diagraming workbooks for young children that take a light approach.

### Italic Handwriting Series

Continuing Education Press/PSU, PO Box 1394, Portland, OR 97207
800/547.8887 fax: 503/725.4840  www.cep.pdx.edu/  press@pdx.edu
A comprehensive pencil (as opposed to a calligraphy pen) italic handwriting program for Grades K-6 and Adult Learners. Teaching aids available.

## chapter eleven

# EARLY MATH CONVERSATIONS
*that jump start math understanding*

"Let's cut the cookies in triangles."
"Can you wait for five minutes?"
"Your birthday is in 12 days."
"The scales say that the dog weighs 47 pounds."
"Four eggs plus eight eggs equal one dozen eggs."

Our homes and lives swim in number and math concepts if we but stop to notice. It is easy and fun to take advantage of that fact by establishing a strong mathematical understanding when a child is still quite young. First, explore math concepts in your day-to-day conversations. Second, use oral language and written symbols to express the mathematical concepts that fill the child's world.

When we talk about math ideas with young children, we explore simple relationships among objects, space, shapes, and time, beginning with the most basic of experiences.

Is your child a math natural, one who thrives on all the mathematical activities parents can dream up for her to do and inventing other ideas of her own? Perhaps she will take on little arithmetic or math projects for fun — counting to one million, sorting and arranging toys, measuring, weighing, comparing, and so on. Children who love math sometimes invent a system for regrouping before you even get a chance to teach them.

Most children, though, do not especially notice the numerical concepts in their lives unless we take the time to point them out, using the language of math in daily conversation. Parents can easily lead conversations toward mathematical ideas — matching, sorting, comparing, adding, subtracting, multiplying and dividing — all accompanied by discussion and enjoyable interaction. Below are several strategies that parents use to embark on math talks.

## Use Collections

Your home is loaded with collections, sets of similar objects, that can be used for many math learning activities. You may not want to bring out Grandma's antique silver for your child's creative math exploration, but her collection of buttons might be perfect.

Even the most reluctant mathematician likes to handle pretty marbles, smooth stones, tickle-y feathers, shiny toy cars, or fuzzy bears. It is quite natural for children to sort and arrange the items in a way that interests them. My daughters loved marbles: the Mommy marbles, Daddy marbles, the baby marbles, sister and brother marbles were all counted. Talk and play with your child, using math vocabulary to describe her activities, then ask leading questions that make her think. Try unusual collections from time to time to rekindle interest.

Many mathematical concepts, such as counting, one-to-one matching, sorting by various qualities, groupings and remainders (adding and subtracting), sizing, multiple groups (multiplying and dividing), making groups of ten and then counting the groups (decimal system), can be explored using collections.

Respect your child's need to explore the materials in his own way. If she resists your direction, she may be working on a different concept. Just watch her with the materials and you may discover which math ideas she grasps and which ones you'll want to work on.

Collection questions could include: "Can you find different types of keys? How many of each type can you find? How many groups are there? Which group is greater? Which group has less? Are there equal groups?" Follow your child's lead and talk together about what each of you is doing with the materials. Once the child understands words we use to describe these very basic concepts, move on!

## Use Measurement Tools

Use authentic tools of measurement when you can. Tools will stimulate questions and conversations, a perfect lead-in to mathematical conversations.

As much as possible, let your child use the tools with you. Talk with him about how they work, and then let him explore independently. Or he may enjoy a little project that you devise. A list of suggested measurement tools is given at the end of this chapter.

### Measurement Tools Children Enjoy

| | | |
|---|---|---|
| one-inch tiles for exploring area | plastic containers for volume play in water, sand, or rice | one-inch cubes for exploring volume |
| rulers and tapes | food scale | money, real or play |
| scales | food thermometer | calendars |
| weather station | desk tools | analog clock |
| thermometer | geometric shapes for tracing | digital clock |
| anemometer | abacus | "Judy" clock with moveable hands |
| rain gauge | dice and spinners | stopwatch |
| blood pressure cuff | computer | timer or hourglass |
| stethoscope | calculator | metronome |
| measuring cups and spoons | old adding machine | carpentry tools, such as levels, tapes, and squares |
| | *Cuisenaire* rods or *Unifix* cubes | |

## What About the Calculator?

Go right ahead and teach your child whatever he wants to know about using a calculator. If he tires of using counting collections to keep game scores, letting him use a calculator to keep score teaches him yet another math skill. It seems unlikely that a child who is adept at using a calculator will have difficulty understanding the process he is performing. Watch how he uses the calculator for hints about his understanding. Of course, if you suspect your child is growing dependent on the calculator instead of using his mind, you can always shelve it for a while.

## Ask Provocative Questions

Even if you use collections and measuring tools for directed math discussions, you can provoke math thinking throughout the day. Try these:

- Are there more fuzzy bears or dolls on your bed?
- Can you get enough spoons from the drawer so everyone in the room can have one?
- How many toys do you want in the bathtub with you, three or four?
- Are there more rabbits or more animals in the world?
- Can you put three olives on each plate?
- Shall I cut your sandwich into halves or fourths?
- Please arrange the books in order from tallest to smallest. Which book is first? Second? Last?

There is no end to the kinds of direct questions that require a child to express her mathematical knowledge. A more difficult type of question or request is the kind that causes the child to think her way through a new idea without being told. Try to ask the kind of question that empowers the child to do the most thinking for herself.

For example: Instead of asking, "Will you please bring three cups for our juice?" say instead, "Bring enough cups for everyone to have juice." The child must match up people to cups or count in order to carry out the task. You can make the request more complex by saying, "Bring enough cups for everyone but me to have juice." This simple change in language introduces basic subtraction. Some common relationship questions to try:

- Can you make sure everyone has the same number of cookies?
- Will you please check the clock and see if it is time to go to Barbie's house?

As your child's math understanding builds, you too will stretch your questions so that you pose more complex problems using many math concepts.

## Point Out Math Ideas Wherever You Are

With just a little forethought, you can encourage alertness and active thinking in your child as you go through daily life activities together. Real life experiences such as measuring flour, counting spoons, and weighing fruit, help children understand math concepts in a concrete way.

If you are not used to noticing math concepts in your everyday surroundings, take a tour of your home after you read this chapter and look for examples. Your house really is full of math. Notice the simple arithmetic in the daily routine of your life — home, grocery store, car, yard, and so forth — and include it in your conversations with your child. You will be amazed!

Much math learning takes place in the kitchen. "Help me count the forks while we set the table." "Get three eggs from the carton." "Let's see if we can figure out how to double this recipe." "Measure three cups of water into this pan."

In the laundry: "How many pairs of socks do you have in the laundry pile? Let's count together. What is a pair anyway?"

In the living room: "Help me count these videotapes before we put them away." If you own a piano or keyboard, be sure to find the key sets of two, three, five, eight, and thirteen keys (a full octave). And count the keys. Children who learn to read written musical notation also build a foundation for understanding fractions.

In the car: "Help me find the gas station with the lowest price." Or "Let's see who can find a car with a two on the license plate."

In the restaurant: "Let's look at the bill and see if we can estimate how much it will cost. Can you estimate the tip, too?"

In the bathroom: "Use the scale to find out how much you weigh."

In the garage or shop: "Find a board that is twice as long as this one." "I'll need eight nails for each of these chairs. Can you get them for me and put them into piles, one pile for each chair? Hmm. I wonder how many nails that will be all together."

The yard: "We will plant half of these flowers in the front and half in the back. How many will that be in each flowerbed?"

## Think Out Loud

Thinking aloud as you perform simple mathematical tasks lets your child into your inner world and gives him clues about the ways people think. Most adults do many calculations mentally and without thinking about them, but to the child, it is all hocus pocus. By counting your change slowly and aloud, for example, you can help your child attach meaning to a part of the world that can be very mysterious. Or try: "We need one cup of flour, and all I have is a ½ cup measure. Hmm. What could we do?"

When Alice asked, "How many cups should I bring?" my response was, "Let's see, you'll have juice, and Tina will, and ...." In other words, I gave her a start on a strategy to solve the problem she presented, but sneaky Mom left it for her to solve.

As children get older, you can think aloud through problems that involve adding and subtracting larger numbers. There are little mental tricks that we all use, such as grouping tens, that can launch your child's mathematical thinking to new levels of understanding. Thinking through math ideas out loud first leads up to, and then goes hand in hand with, writing math on paper.

## Write Math Stories Together

Even before children have developed fine motor skills well enough to manage pencil and paper, you can help them explore the elements of written arithmetic and symbols.

Why not sit down for Math Stories once in a while? These can be stories you make up, or they can be descriptions of math ideas or problems that you've worked on with your child during the day. Make it as simple or as complex a process as you like. Use a chalkboard, the backs of old envelopes, your journal, or create a formal math journal — whatever suits your style.

In the beginning, you may do all or most of the writing. When you are finished writing the story together, give your child a chance to read the page back to you.

"Remember how you cracked all those eggs for breakfast this morning? Let's write that story." He may draw it in his own way, and you should encourage him to do that. Perhaps he will make a picture of each egg, then count up the total. You "read" his picture story to him. "First, you cracked four eggs. Later you cracked five more. I see how you are writing the story. Here is how I will write the story." On your paper, use an appropriate combination of symbols, pictures, and words to expand the mathematical story, and perhaps his understanding.

Read the problems you've written together. If your child made a separate drawing, be sure to read it and admire it. If you begin to write stories and simple math sentences for your child to read with you, he will be able to write about math using digits and symbols himself before long.

## Read or Make Children's Math Books

Popular books about math, especially if well illustrated or humorous, have a far greater appeal to children than textbooks. Many families enjoy counting books, for example. Check out a couple at the library, or find a favorite or two at your neighborhood bookstore.

If your child really enjoys books, you may want to help her make a handmade book for math. How about a counting book or a greater than/ less than concept book for a baby brother? Find a book you like and imitate the style, or let your child use her own ideas.

## Use Math Symbols

Believe it or not, learning to read and write math symbols is exciting for many children, especially those who are struggling with writing skills. All those complicated math words have fancy symbols that are much easier to write than the words! You might use the symbols of basic operations ($=$, $\neq$, $+$, $\times$, $<$, $>$, $\div$ or $/$), symbols for fractions ($\frac{1}{2}$, $\frac{1}{4}$, $\frac{3}{4}$), money symbols ($\$$, $\textcent$), or abbreviations for inches, feet, yards, pounds (in., ft., yds., lbs. or $\#$). Some families put up a poster of these kinds of symbols for reference.

When talking about a math concept, don't limit your conversations to the simplest language; instead, use and explain the correct words. If your child shows no interest, move on and bring it up again later.

If you are working with a collection and your child's portion is *greater than* your portion, you could show her the symbol $>$ and write a descriptive number sentence. (How do you keep $<$ and $>$ straight? The "alligator's mouth" opens wide toward the larger quantity.)

## Worksheets Are Optional

Worksheets, when available as a free choice activity, are sometimes a beneficial way for young children to practice some math skills and facts.

Some of our family's best worksheets were actually "worknapkins." For some reason, math was a frequent dinner table discussion. Paper napkins were always handy, so we regularly created math problems to occupy active young minds.

Other times, either daughter could be found poring over pages and pages of problems in workbooks, only to abandon the practice for weeks or months on end. I never pushed them to finish a book or page, assuming that they had gotten what they could from the activity. Interestingly, only some of the time did they want to know, "Did I get the answers right?" Other times, they did the work for the pleasure of doing the work!

Your child may love to work on problems that you create for him. Some parents prefer to purchase inexpensive workbooks instead. And for the price of a few minutes and a simple search, a lifetime supply of worksheets can be downloaded from the Internet for free.

## What About Drill?

It depends on the student, but be careful about math burn-out.

Some students think there is nothing more thrilling than discovering how fast they can perform a new skill. They might even beg you to pull out your stop watch or kitchen timer to see how fast they can do a page of multiplication problems or fill in the facts on a blank multiplication table. She might be delighted to discover how fast she can speed through a set of flash cards and then try to improve upon that speed. Student-chosen drill can be effective and fun.

Suppose, though, that your child doesn't care about how fast she solves problems. She is perfectly content to take out a basket of stones and work out a fact, even if it takes all morning, even if it is the same fact she struggled with yesterday and the day before. Tell the truth now: doesn't that drive you nuts? You have seen her do this dozens of times and inside you may be thinking, if she would simply *memorize* that fact, it would be hers forever and she wouldn't have to count stones or make lines on a piece of paper to count. Aren't you tempted to pull out the flash cards and *make* her learn that fact?

Please, resist the urge. Don't make the mistake of imposing premature drill activities on your child because *you* are uncomfortable with her approach. Math teachers call it "drill and kill." The price of excessive or at-too-early-an-age drill activities can be high. You might short-change your child forever, trading her delight in number concepts (contentment in using the basket of stones to leisurely handle and count) for an "I hate math" attitude that can last a lifetime.

If you believe your young child needs more practice with his math skills, playing games that require him to use his math skills is a superior use of his time that carries little risk of him becoming a math-hater.

When your child is ready to benefit from drill activities, you'll be able to tell. Suppose your child has been pulling away from math activities that he used to enjoy. Perhaps he resists getting out the basket of stones to solve a problem, but shows frustration that the facts don't roll off the tip of his pencil as they do for you. That is a good sign that you could introduce your own favorite drill activities, activities taken from "Math Whiz Basics" (chapter 12), or from "Exploring Math" (chapter 35).

The bottom line with drill is this: some drill activities can be fun, too much drill is deadening, and you will be surprised at how little drill is needed if you wait until your child is ready.

## When Your Young Child Wants to Know More . . .

How will you know when your child is ready for more advanced concepts? If the foundation is well established, you will know from your child's conversations with you. Perhaps he'll be able to calculate the restaurant tab mentally, or skip count by nine to nine hundred, or count backward by three from 71, or figure out six weeks' allowance in his head. You can't push big concepts during the early years, nor should you try to prevent them.

If your young child shows he is ready for more, go with it. Explore difficult concepts. Just remember: use a hands-on and playful approach. Even if he is ready for algebra and calculus, find hands-on materials to demonstrate and to practice with. Remember that you are building a conversational foundation. There is plenty of time for abstract paper-and-pencil type thinking as he matures.

## Finally

The most useful math activities for young children are part of the natural conversations they have with their parents in daily activities. If you are stuck for ideas, try some of the selected resources below or  those listed in"Games and Puzzles," "Math Whiz Basics," and "Exploring Math" (chapters 4, 12, and 35).

## SELECTED RESOURCES

### Games for Math:
Playful ways to help your child learn math from K to grade 3
By Peggy Kaye. Equals/UC Berkeley, Lawrence Hall of Science, Berkeley,
CA 94720    510/542.1910 fax: 510/643.5757
equals@maillink.berkeley.edu      Interesting and effective materials. Catalog
also includes *Family Math*; *Family Math for Young Children*.

### Hands-On Math: Manipulative Math for Young Children
By Janet Stone. Good Year Books, 1900 East Lake Ave., Glenview, IL
60025. 1990. 121 activities and ideas adaptable to the home environment,
especially for those who want a more structured format.

### MathArts
By Mary Ann F. Kohl and Cindy Gainer, Bright Ring Publishing, PO Box
31338, Bellingham, WA 98228-3338. www.brightring.com 200 art projects
that explore many math concepts including counting, order, measuring,
patterns, sequence, symmetry, fractions, graphing, money, and more. 3-6.

### Miquon Math
Available from FUN Books, 1688 Belhaven Woods Court, Pasadena MD
21122-3727  888/386.7020 MD only: 410/360.7330
FUN@FUN-Books.com   www.fun-books.com
Popular elementary math workbooks that use manipulative materials,
including Cuisenaire rods, which can be purchased from FUN Books.

### Number in Preschool & Kindergarten
By Constance Kamii.      Washington, DC: NAEYC. 1992.
Identifies math-based games to try, including directions for old favorites such
as *Candyland, Chutes and Ladders, Hi-Ho! Cherry-O*, war, etc.

### Patterns; Shapes; Measure
Three books by Ivan Bulloch. E-book or traditional format. *Patterns* —
exploration of patterns in nature; weaving; cut paper; making tiles and
mosaics; potato print patterns and more. *Shapes* — stand-up zoo and
stretchy jewelry. *Measure* — finger puppets, a bottle band, sand timer.

### Play and Find Out About Math: Easy Activities for Young Children
By Janice Van Cleave. NY: John Wiley and Sons, Inc. 1998.
Fifty simple activities that will give your child a better understanding of math
concepts than any stack of workbooks could, and fun too!

### Young Children Reinvent Arithmetic
By Constance Kazuko Kamii and Leslie Baker Houseman. 2000.
Does your child insist on finding solutions to problems "my way" but you
can't figure out what he's doing? Reassurance for parents whose children
reinvent arithmetic concepts. Games included.

## chapter twelve

# MATH WHIZ BASICS

*essential math through everyday life*

Basic math skills and concepts are readily learned through conversation and ordinary life activities. What? You say you have forgotten what those basic skills and concepts are? Or you remember the concepts but can't remember how you learned them? You are in the right place, then!

If your math skills are rusty, use this chapter as your oilcan. You may discover that you are already solidly on the path to helping your child grasp the rudiments of math through daily interactions.

A few readers may feel that some of these concepts are too obvious to bother with. It is true that, once a person understands these ideas, they seem trivial. Regardless of any personal "post-understanding" view you may hold, remember that these are huge concepts, concepts that are the building blocks of all future mathematical understanding. If the concepts should fall into place at a very early age, parents can move to other concepts.

Even very smart children sometimes misunderstand the most basic mathematical concept. If you have ever met a bright ten- or twelve-year-old who is confused about even one basic concept, you might understand why the basics are so important. If uncorrected, those errors trickle up and weaken the child's understanding, eventually making even a bright child "math stupid" or a "math hater." Correcting misconceptions at a later age is far tougher than taking a few moments to assure the concepts are well understood in the first place.

One of the great advantages of conversational math with young children is that you will detect your child's misunderstandings through the course of conversation and use errors as a springboard to help him build his foundational knowledge. Here we go, then, with a look at the basic mathematic concepts your young child needs.

## Counting and 1-1 Correspondence

Alice first showed interest in math in an Amtrak car. "One two fee five!" "One two fee five six seben!" She enthusiastically counted cows and horses, and I dutifully stuck in the "four" when I could. Alice's counting was rote, but she loved the rhythm and repetition of the sounds. Clearly, Alice did not yet understand the meaning of the one-to-one correspondence of counting objects.

Include simple counting and matching in your daily routines from toddler-hood on. Don't worry too much about accuracy at first. Instead notice your child's process. When he has figured out how counting works, you will notice that this concept is firmly in his grasp, and that will be that. When five cookies on a plate await five hungry children, the concept can become very clear.

When your child begins to count beyond twenty, you might post a 100 counting chart to help her learn the multiples of ten. Board games such as *Candyland* are useful for counting to 100.

Children may also enjoy counting by multiples of any number as they gain skill. Count by threes, fives, 30, 90, 700, 8000, or whatever seems interesting to your child.

## Number — Seeing Numerals As Symbols

Counting to ten and knowing how to read the individual numbers is an early milestone. But can he recognize that the numeral *6* stands for six cookies, six puppies, six bell chimes, or six jumps? Try some simple labeling or matching activities to find out. "Show me which numeral tells us how many blocks are in this stack." "Look at this number on the fridge. Can you get that many forks from the drawer?"

Watch for creative confusion. The terms "bigger number" or "smaller number" often confuse young children. They may think you mean the size of the numerals, convinced that **8** is bigger than ๑. We commonly use the word *number* when we mean *numeral*. When the concept of numerals as symbols for numbers is clear, your child's confusion will vanish.

## Sequences and Ordinal Numbers

Ordinals are the numbers that we use to indicate order: first, second, twenty-fifth, and so on. We can use these in conversation in many ways. Some children connect best using their favorite belongings. "Put your dolls in a row on the bed. Which doll is third from you?" "Line up the vehicles. What position does the fire truck hold, fourth or fifth?" "Who was born first, you or your brother?" Opportunities to learn this concept abound in daily life. Whose turn is it to help set the table? Try using the calendar as skill with ordinal numbers increases — the first day of the week, the twentieth day of the month, and so on.

Don't forget counting by twos, threes, fours, nines, and more. Skip counting is fun and leads to a increased understanding of multiplication. For a challenge, count backwards by ones, twos, threes, or forty-nines.

Sequence can be explored in many ways. Tell the story in the order things happened. Play or sing a sequence of notes or rhythms. Number events in a list in the order they happened or list items in alphabetical order, by size, by age, or by cost.

## Spatial Relationships

Just where is everything, anyway?

Above, below, close, far, up, down, inside, outside, behind, in front, higher, lower, greater, less than — all tell us where things are. Again, these concepts are learned best through conversations with parents. Use these types of words in your earliest conversations from babyhood on.

Don't worry if he doesn't understand you, because he will let you know! "Johnny, bring me the book that is *under* the coffee table, please." If Johnny brings the correct book, you can be quite sure he understands *under*. If he brings something else, or shows frustration, you have a so-called teachable moment — Yay! "That book was *on top of* the coffee table. Here is the book that is *under* the coffee table." Then play an *under* and *on top* of game until you fall over in giggles.

If you are not sure whether your child knows the meanings of the words, plan to play some guessing games with him. "I am thinking of something in this room that is *above* the floor and *below* the chair. Can you guess what it is?" You'll know right away if he understands the concept, and he will delight in the game.

Move on to comparatives, such as *closer, farther, higher,* and *lower.* Other related concepts include ideas such as *big* and *little, right* and *left, map directions, opposites,* or *balance.* As they grow up, advanced students explore spatial relationships without even thinking about it through projects, measurement, estimation, travel, sports, and other daily life activities.

## Patterns

You will find patterns everywhere: buildings, cars, signs, books, nature, gardens, art, fabric. Help your child notice the patterns around him, and then help him to create patterns of his own. Is there a pattern in the fabric of your child's favorite jammies? Can the little O's in his breakfast cereal form a pattern? Can he make new or similar patterns? Discovering and making patterns can be explored with construction toys for those who enjoy it.

Math concepts, art, and hand-eye coordination are just some of the benefits of honing your child's pattern awareness. Use all kinds of materials: blocks, paint, crayons, even favorite toys can be arranged in a repeating pattern. Make your own gift wrap or greeting cards using potato prints.

Rhythms — patterns in time — are everywhere too: drum cadences, clocks ticking, the sound of a shoe thumping in the dryer. Create musical patterns that repeat tones or rhythms; discover the patterns in poetry. Seasons, hours, and day and night sequences are patterns too.

Are you working with a counting collection? Try making repeating patterns. Start simply, then build more complex patterns. Blocks of varying shapes can be used to create tile patterns or tessellations — a $3 word your child will love! Not only can your child learn geometric shapes and patterns, you are laying the groundwork for an understanding of area and perimeter.

## Shapes

Help your child find geometric shapes in the world around him. Our homes, towns, and cities are abound with shapes such as circles, spheres, squares, cones, rectangles, triangles, cubes, lines, and points. Don't forget to look in the natural world for many shapes, including spirals. When you play ball, use a synonym for the ball such as sphere, orb, or globe. "Get the basket sphere and let's go out and shoot some hoops." Aren't we supposed to have some goofy fun while we stretch children's thinking?

Many children enjoy making geometric constructions using a straight edge and compass. Why not learn the vocabulary at the same time? Another nifty tool for exploring shapes, particularly the unique traits of right triangles, is the geoboard. A geoboard can be purchased or made by nailing a grid of nails to a board, perhaps 5" x 5" or 8" x 8", or you could make a larger one. Only the size and stretch of your rubber bands limits the size of the geoboard. Children love to stretch rubber bands on these boards, creating all kinds of designs and patterns. Help your children discover the principle of the Pythagorean Theorem with a geoboard. Very cool.

## Measurement

Measurement is easy to teach when there are projects around the home. You can start by helping even a very young child measure and weigh anything she can think of: socks, apples, the dog, coins, safety pins, toys, or herself. Use a ruler, tape, or yardstick to measure the height and length of objects. Then move to more complicated ideas when ready.

Try to let your children hang out with you, even when the math for your projects may be beyond them, and think the steps through aloud. Let them participate in a step that is within their ability.

Calculate the volume of the kitchen sink, the bathtub, the swimming pool, your hat, or a thimble. Use a variety of units. How many thimblefuls of water will fit in the sink? How many sinks full will fill the wading pool? Could you figure out how many gallons of chocolate milk it would take to fill your house? How many pints in a five-gallon bucket? Calculate the area of the sidewalk that you are pouring. What volume of cement will you need?

Make a guessing game of estimation and estimate distance, time, quantities, expense, and volume. Calculate miles per hour, steps per mile for walkers, and other rate problems.

Divide and double measurements: food and drink, floor space, time, and money. Build a bird feeder, birdhouse, or play space. Take apart anything, such as old clocks or cars or office machines, and sort or count the parts; calculate how much fertilizer you need for your garden.

Concepts and terms you might use include the English terms: inches, feet, yards, miles; square units of area, including acres and sections, even townships; teaspoons, tablespoons, cups, pints, gallons; ounces, pounds, tons.

Or put away the English units and measure everything in the metric system, using meters, square meters, liters, and grams. Don't worry about converting from one system to another— post a conversion chart if you want. Instead, focus on familiarity with the units of each system.

## Symmetry

Symmetry, the mirror image idea that the two halves of a design or shape are identical, and divided along a *line of symmetry* can be explored in so many ways. Children don't need the fancy words, though many will enjoy trying the big words out!

Most children don't have much trouble with the concept. Our bodies and faces, animals, butterflies and other insects, all have some symmetry to them if we don't examine them too closely. It is fun to find the line of symmetry on the back of a skunk! Find asymmetrical objects for contrast.

Use mirrors to play with symmetrical images. Art projects, sewing projects, building blocks, pattern blocks, the Tangram puzzle, and parquetry blocks are all good for exploring symmetry.

Advanced activities could include finding symmetry in two dimensional representations of three-dimensional objects. Create puzzles for one another to solve.

## Fractional Parts and the Whole

The concept of the whole and its fractional parts are so easily explored in the kitchen. Scored graham crackers and soda crackers are there to help. Whole apples need to be sliced into eighths, and whole sandwiches must be quartered or divided into fourths (use both terms when you think of it). Musical notation is actually a system of noting fractions of duration and intervals between pitches. Reading music and playing musical keyboards and piano are all great for exploring fractions. Recipes require careful fractional measurement with special spoons and cups. Make spoons and cups available for sand and water play as well.

Use your collections to explore fractional concepts. Can the whole collection be divided into equal halves? Fourths? Thirds? Can you make a grouping of items that cannot be divided into two equal parts?

Egg cartons provide a basic model for equivalent fractions, i.e., $1/2 = 3/6 = 6/12$, and learning about denominators and numerators. Multiples, odd and even numbers, prime numbers, greatest common multiple, least common factor, all types of fractional, decimal and percentage work will build on basics of egg carton fractions.

## Estimation

Learning to take your "best educated guess" takes practice but it can be tons of fun too. Oh, how I remember the day that Erin became restless in a long grocery checkout line. Desperate for ideas to entertain her, I asked, "How many holes do you think there are in this ceiling?" I thought she might say a billion, but she began to count! Estimate, Erin, estimate!

Estimating games are a great time filler when all you can do is wait. "How many times do you think you can jump in one minute?" Let him make his guess, and then get out your watch with a second hand and tell him to start jumping. When he is rested, let him try again, and see if his estimate improves.

Knowing how it fascinated my kids, I often carried a stopwatch in my purse just for such odd moments. The contests varied with the circumstances. How long will it take you to run to the end of that sidewalk and back? Backwards? On one foot? Don't fall!

Invent estimation games for concepts such as distance, volume, and number. Estimate the number of seeds in a packet; crackers in a box; grapes in a clump; or pickles in a jar. Then count to see how close their estimate came. Liquid volume estimations can be surprising. Can you estimate the volume of water in the bathtub or wading pool? How much water does the garden hose hold? How could you check your estimation for accuracy?

Guessing is interchangeable with estimating at first. With practice, estimates become more accurate. Estimate people in a city, trees in a forest, bricks in a building, or gallons of water in a lake. Then devise a system for checking your estimate. Students learn to manage very large numbers and can be introduced to scientific notation.

## Telling Time

For many children, all you need to do is answer their questions about time and they will learn to read clocks in their own way. "When will Billy be here to play? Yes, at three o'clock. Show me three o'clock." Worry about minutes after hours are firmly understood. To help your child learn to read an analog clock, make sure you have one or two around the house. Novelty clocks can make telling time a bit more fun. My children enjoyed our cat clock that had a swinging tail. *Judy* clocks are hands-on teaching clocks with knobs that turn the hands. Wearing their own wristwatch inspires many children.

Digital clocks, for all their convenience, make it harder for many children to even care about reading analog clock faces. Digital clocks are easy to read; analog clocks are complex. Learning to read an analog clock is important for several reasons. Telling time on an analog clock builds a base for understanding other math concepts, such as the degrees in a circle, longitude and latitude, counting by fives, and even negative numbers. Reading a clock is also a foundation for understanding number bases other than ten.

More advanced time related ideas include using 24-hour clocks, daylight savings time, time zones, Greenwich mean time, the International Date Line, and light years. You can even explore the idea of time travel.

## Calendars

Calendars extend the concept of tracking time, providing us with a way of counting and grouping days. Days of the week, months, and seasons of the year are all numbered and listed for our use. Help your child mark special events on the calendar. Wednesday is the day your best friend comes over to play. Friday we go to the dentist.

Making a twelve-month calendar for a year can be a satisfying experience for some students. Try using a marking pen to make a notched stick calendar, one stripe for each day, and every seventh day is a longer stripe to denote a week. How will you mark a month or a year? It can get tricky!

A delicious form of torture that children often love to impose on themselves is to make countdown paper chains marking the number of days till the next special day — whether that is a birthday or holiday, the day Grandma comes to visit, or the day swimming lessons start. One link for each day remaining, and each day they tear off the next link.

Calendar activities and paper countdown chains also reinforce the one-to-one correspondence of number to days, counting backwards is explored, and ordinal numbers are used.

Advanced ideas: Compare the modern calendar with ancient calendars or religious calendars. Investigate Leap Year. Invent a calendar for the moon, Jupiter, or Mercury.

## Money

What child doesn't enjoy learning more about money?! Empty your pockets and make a coin collection for your child, or purchase some play money. First, help your child identify the coins by name and recognize both heads and tails for each coin.

The next step is equivalent value — finding out what each coin is worth. Five pennies to a nickel, ten pennies to a dime, 100 pennies or 10 dimes to a dollar, and so forth. Demonstrate with stacks of coins. Make exchanges. Set up a play store to practice spending and giving change.

You might deliberately leave nickels and quarters out to emphasize how the decimal system is learned with money. Understanding the relationship between one cent, one dime, and one dollar gives your child a real life model of the decimal system and place value. If she understands money and can make change accurately, regrouping (you know — borrowing and carrying) in addition and subtraction will fall into place more easily.

Use all the coins to teach fractions and to lay a groundwork for understanding percentages. *Whole, half, quarter or fourth, tenth, twentieth, hundredth* portions of one dollar are right there in your pocket for you and your child to explore.

Do you want your children to learn decimals, percentages, or compound interest? Let them earn some money to manage. Open bank accounts. Invest in penny stocks. Or you might give your child a single share of stock and show him how to track it on the Internet or in the newspaper. Let him cash his dividend checks and buy ice cream if he wants.

He can study the economy through actual practice. Help your child set up a lemonade stand or other small business. Let him help with the shopping, or even take over the shopping at some point. Play games such as *Monopoly*. Teach him about taxes, interest rates, and how insurance works. Amortization and actuarial tables need not be treacherous territory to be discovered in adulthood. Parents don't need to have a great deal of money to teach students a sound understanding of finance.

Other money ideas: Are you studying pirates? Don't overlook pieces of eight and two bits, four bits, etc. Learning a foreign language? Acquire the basic coin set for an appropriate country and learn how to make change.

## Basic Operations: Add, Subtract, Multiply, Divide

Young children learn to perform these operations easily when using real objects, perhaps food or toys. You can also use your counting collection, or money, or figure out scores for games or sports. When opportunities arise, don't pass them up.

When you and your child are sorting clean laundry, for example, you may match his socks. One pair, two socks; two pair, four socks. What is going on here? Really, it is both adding and multiplying, isn't it? First the socks are counted, 1, 2. Then the *pairs* are counted. When a child begins to understand multiplying, he'll be able to tell you how many socks all together. Teach him that the big kids' word for the clever way he understands how many socks are going into the drawer is multiplication.

Or maybe you've baked dozens of cookies that are to be put in three boxes. First the cookies will need to be counted. Are they lying on cooling racks in an array? Terrific. They are easily counted by groups, another way to look at multiplication. Help your child understand the array approach to multiplication by letting her count the cookies, either individually or by repeated addition of the rows. And when you fill the cookie boxes, let your daughter help you solve that division problem!

## The Multiplication Table

The best way to make sure that a child knows the facts of the multiplication table is to give him a copy of it to study. The multiplication table is a rich mathematical tool that will reinforce his understanding of skip counting, grids, arrays, graphs, number patterns, common multiples, square numbers, the commutative property, the special qualities of zero and one, symmetry, and more. Or have you forgotten?

Take the time to study the table together. Before insisting that your child start learning the table, though, remind her of how much of it she already knows. Most children delight in realizing they already know the zeros, ones, and twos of the table. The tens are almost as easy as the ones. The fives come easily to children who understand coins and money. Threes are easy to learn by skip counting, and the fours build on the twos. Children who have played *Yahtzee* and other dice games know the facts through six. The eights build on the twos and fours, and the nines build on the threes. The nines family has patterns to be explored, patterns that mystify many children until they grasp the underlying concepts of multiplication and the decimal system. (Jot down the nines facts to remind yourself how interesting they are.) Most of the table is well understood when your child reaches this point, with very few slippery facts left to work out. "Just think, you already know most of the multiplication table and you've only just begun!"

Give your child many hands on experiences so he can own the concepts of multiplication from many different perspectives. Build arrays of the difficult facts using collections, and seek out clever tricks for learning tough facts. Work with square numbers. Studying the chart has helped many children learn the nines facts.

Maybe you can post a blank table on the fridge and see what he does with it. He might fill it out on his own. If he fills that one, post another blank one! My experience teaching the multiplication table to many, many children tells me that 6 x 9, 6 x 7, 7 x 8, 7 x 9, and 8 x 9 are the worst gremlins, and usually the last facts children commit to memory.

Game play reinforces the commitment of those facts to memory. Judicious use of flash cards or other drill activities may help commit those final facts to memory when the child is finally ready to nail the whole table to memory.

Until the facts are well memorized, be sure to keep a complete and correct multiplication table or a calculator handy when he works on math problems. You won't want a few ornery facts to stop him from learning and enjoying more advanced math skills.

## Finally

When your child is ready, fill in any gaps — perhaps long division or fractions — that may be too complex for conversational approaches. A later chapter, "Exploring Math" (chapter 35) includes more information and selected resources.

But for now, have you discovered that you really do know much of the math your child needs to know? Did you realize that you can help her discover math concepts and principles through daily living? If your child has been well immersed in the kind of activities and concepts discussed in this chapter, a sound understanding of basic math principles will follow. You will be amazed at how much your child has learned through daily life.

## chapter thirteen

# FOR THE LOVE OF LEARNING

*rousing curiosity through talk and example*

The best tools you have for keeping your child's love of learning afire are your own natural communication skills. And truthfully, there is little I can tell you about how conversation works that you don't already know.

Still, those natural family conversational skills cannot be over-emphasized, especially when those skills are little valued by popular culture. I am saddened when I realize that the important work parents have always done to help their children learn is undermined or poorly appreciated. In the face of that popular criticism, parents may need some backing so they are not tempted to abandon those effective practices for watered-down substitutes. Hence, this chapter.

## Listening

Are you listening to your child at full tilt?

Do you want your child to be a rapt listener, an able speaker, a skilled learner? To fan the flame of learning through conversations, the parent demonstrates what it means to be a skilled listener. Children naturally attend to their parents, and they will listen with the same listening habits and intent to understand that their parents use to listen to them. The intent to imitate parents is so strong that, if you wanted to, you could easily teach your child to listen poorly, by ignoring him or listening inconsistently.

*Children imitate their parents.*

Learn to listen to your children, not just with ears, but with all your senses, focusing until intended communication is unlocked. *Then, reflect the child's communication back to her, rephrasing it as best you can, to verify whether you've heard correctly.*

Some parents fear that they won't respond correctly to their child's communications. If you are such a parent, abandon that fear because the right response is the response you make, even if it is the "wrong" one. That is, if you get it wrong, your child will let you know and you can try again. When toddler Erin asked for "raw toast," it took more than a few tries for me to realize what she really wanted was plain, untoasted bread. She persisted until I really heard her request. Really simple, huh?

Now, let's look at some of the different ways parents interact with their children.

## Demonstrating

The most powerful conversations you can have with your child are examples such as this simple one my father set for me.

I remember the smell of those rawhide shoestrings as if it were yesterday. We sat side by side, my father with one work boot, I with the other. Using slow and broad motions, he tied the laces slowly, waiting at each step to see if I was following. He said little, but provided brief directions as needed. He repeated. And again. When I finally created big loopy ties just once, he left me to practice with those big boots by myself. The lesson was over.

How simple the task seemed when Dad took the time to go slowly and make sure that I was duplicating his actions! How glad I was to be learning from him and not my older brothers, brothers whose fingers flew like the wind as they showed off their superior tying skill to their annoying little sister!

Nonverbal communication is a potent teacher.

### Thinking Out Loud — Mental Demonstration

It is one thing to give an effective — wordless or not — demonstration to teach a physical skill. It is quite another task to demonstrate mental agility and reasoning power. How is a child to know that we use step by step processes to figure things out if we do not tell them? "Thinking out loud" demonstrations help children understand the inner workings of their own minds.

"Do we have enough change in our pockets to buy ice cream? Let's see. Ice cream costs $ .75. You have a quarter and a penny. Here is my change. How many more quarters do we need? Here is one, and we still need another. A quarter is worth $ .25. Let's see if we can make that value with these dimes and pennies." You let your child know that there is no big mystery to the process of counting change and making purchases. Later, when he begins to grasp these ideas, he can take them over for you when you haul out your fistful of change.

## Demonstrating Self Control

Parents show ways to manage emotions by describing their own interior state of feelings. State your feeling and how you manage it. "I feel angry right now. When I feel angry, I need a cooling off period. I feel more in control after I shoot some hoops or work in the yard for a while." Give other examples as needed.

Kids may show frustration when learning something new. Sometimes that frustration drives them harder, but oftentimes they need to reduce the stress so the brain can get back to work. To help your child along that path, try *active listening*.

Active listening statements reflect the child's possible inner state. This type of statement is especially useful for perfectionists who are easily frustrated. Don't worry if you guess the feeling wrong. Your child will let you know just what he is feeling. Here is the format and a few examples:

- "When you [name the exact behavior], you must feel [take your best guess at what the child may be feeling]."

- "When you pour milk and some spills, you are frustrated because the milk jug is too heavy."

- "When you solve a whole page of problems wrong because you added when the signs said to subtract, you are furious."

- "When you and I take the car to practice driving, you feel annoyed and distracted when I point out every possible hazard two blocks before we get to it."

# Responding to Mistakes

Is your child making enough mistakes? Adults often forget that the greatest learning happens when students make 20-30 percent errors. In fact, they learn best when they are free to make innumerable errors during exploration, delaying concerns about accuracy until the skills begin to feel natural. Unless errors discourage their efforts, they are probably learning well.

Some children are born perfectionists who respond sharply to the slightest nudge or correction. Other students blunder their way gaily through life, oblivious to both results and errors, but relishing the process. If you listen carefully and "read" your children, you will learn from each child's mistakes how best to guide that particular child. You can take cues from your child's mistakes to redirect or re-frame the problem, causing the child to use his resources in a different way, and perhaps resolving the error in the process.

## Learning through Trial and Error

Have you ever tried picking out a tune on an unfamiliar musical instrument? As you blunder toward the tune you hear in your head, you learn from each error what not to repeat, and decide what to try next. Exploratory mistakes give your child feedback when she tries to learn a new task. Legible handwriting is achieved through *trial and error*. Sewing crooked seams, dropping stitches when knitting, throwing wild balls when playing catch, falling while skating — these errors self-correct with practice.

## Learning from Factual Errors

Suppose your child tells you the moon is made of green cheese because he read it in a book. This kind of error usually self-corrects if you allow enough time.

Although *errors of fact* catch our attention, the best strategy may be to help him toward the correct fact with as little fuss as possible. Is he reading and stuck at a difficult word? Tell him the word and move on. Other times, as in the case of the moon being made of green cheese, you may smile and let it go for the time being, ready to boost him toward the truth when he is ready.

## Learning from Process Errors

Suppose your child has gotten confused about regrouping in addition or subtraction. That would be a common example of a process error. The best way to catch those *process errors* is to be attentive to the work as your child is doing it. If the process is the correct one and a fact is incorrect, you may let that slide sometimes. If the process is wrong, though, it doesn't matter how right the facts are. Take steps to correct his process. Go back to the basics and use manipulative materials, or whatever else you feel will help him understand and remember.

Did your child make an error in long division? Encourage her to discover where she went wrong on her own. Have her retrace the steps with you so you can point out what she doesn't understand. Or hand her a calculator to check it herself. If you both work the problem again, you might comment, "Hmm, one of us got this wrong. Show me how you solved it and we'll compare." Usually, the child will discover her error with a big "Aha!" of insight. If not, do the problem again yourself, showing all your work, and demonstrating your thought process by talking aloud "to yourself" about each step.

Helping your student learn the process correctly in the early stages will save her a world of frustration and help her avoid developing an incorrect "process" habit.

## Learning from Careless Errors

Careless errors, when you are certain that the errors stem from inattention, can be approached differently. Sometimes greater attention to detail develops with greater maturity. Suppose she miscues a word while reading, yet continues to read on, grasping the storyline. You can let it go — reading carelessness often self-corrects. She will read the word correctly the next time she sees it.

Another common carelessness error — and one that usually bothers parents — is deteriorating handwriting. Why does a child who has developed good cursive writing suddenly lose legibility without seeming to care? Frequently, the cause is the child's desire to write faster, regardless of control so she gives it a whirl. As yet, she cannot manage both control and speed. Ask her what's up with the sloppy writing, or give it some time to self-correct.

Sometimes, carelessness is a sign of disinterest. Is the assignment too long? Is he tired or stressed? Does he need a change of pace or a different activity? If he has lost interest in the topic, it might be time to move on to another task or take a break.

## Learning from Safety Errors

Of course, some errors are safety errors and require prompt attention. For example: "You tied your shoes together. Let's retie them so it is safe to walk." Or: "Tell me the rule about using the tools and wearing safety glasses. Your actions tell me you have forgotten." "You weren't wearing your safety belt. Your driving privileges are suspended."

## Conversing to Stimulate Thinking

Here are samples of common conversational responses that parents use to stimulate their child to think. Are there others that you use with your child?

## Saying Nothing at All

"I do it myself." Isn't that is a wonderfully clear message from a young child? When you notice that your child is productively engaged in a self-directed activity, resist the temptation to offer guidance — just let it happen. All that is really needed is for you to step back and stay available.

As she gets older, you may have a tougher time knowing when your child is self-directing. Often, self-direction looks like goofing off. The most profound learning might be taking place deep within a child who is doing something as meaningless as flipping a deck of cards against a wall, one by one. Sometimes, students who prefer self-directed activities are misunderstood by their parents as being defiant or rebellious. Take the time to discover what is going on with your older child. That is simple enough — just ask. Then keep her safe, keep the lines of communication wide open, and watch your student thrive.

If you can't stand the suspense and end up rudely interrupting your daughter's line of thinking as she counts silently to one million, causing her lose her place, apologize profusely! Then help her get back on track. Taking out the garbage may just have to wait.

Should you interrupt your child's processes to give her praise? We generally think of praise as a good thing, but too much praise feels insincere to the child and can actually discourage learning if over-used. Think of praise as the salt in the stew of your child's learning: a little salt is needed for health, a bit extra once in a while adds flavor and interest, and too much salt makes the meal inedible. Saying nothing at all is often the seasoning of choice.

## Storytelling

Parents can set an intriguing stage for conversation with their children by telling stories. Perhaps you will tell stories of your own youth or stories of family lore, relating a wild tale about Aunt Marge. Some families tell traditional stories — myths, allegories, fables, religious texts, or historical events. Don't forget to retell classic anecdotes and stories with a point — riddles, poems, jokes, fables, fairy tales, parables, comic strips, and the like. Storytelling may engage older students when you want to approach difficult subjects, convey ideas, or stimulate discussion.

Most stories are told for the simple pleasure of time spent spinning a yarn together. Children learn the rudiments of storytelling by retelling known stories. Encourage your children to retell their experiences and activities to you. Here are some tips to help them become better storytellers.

- If your child likes to make up stories, the stories may ramble on and on. Find ways to listen attentively for a short period. "I'll set the timer for five minutes, and I'll listen hard to your story. When the timer dings, you can tell the rest of the story to Bo the dog."

- Help your child organize her story. "I'm confused. What did you do first, pet the snake or count the bears?" "I got lost." "What did Scottie say when you dropped the monkey wrench?"

- Paraphrasing, telling a known story in your own words, is good speaking practice and a useful pre-writing activity for written compositions.

## Using Words and Language

Learning more about language — the ways that speaking, listening, writing, and reading convey meaning — helps students use and understand conversations. Here is a sampler of ways to study language conversationally.

## Literature

Controversial ideas are perfect discussion starters for older children. One way to introduce those ideas is by reading a book and discussing it. Try the classics, contemporary books, movies, TV programs, news stories, plays, and poetry. Explore works of philosophy, religion, spirituality, politics, or history. Bring up discussion points about the content, of course, and be prepared for a lively conversation!

From the earliest days of reading with your children, discuss the author's techniques and methods, which might include foreshadowing, point of view, themes, the author's intent, characters, the plot, dialogue, actions, description, word choices, and time line. Look for analogies, similes, and metaphors. You might be surprised at where some of these discussions take you, even when you are reading picture books with the very young.

Then, when you share more advanced literature when they are older, they will have the skills and framework in mind for evaluating literature on their own. You also give them a head start at being able to create these devices on their own. If your skills feel a bit rusty, find a high school or college level literature textbook and start from there.

## Logic Puzzles and Brain Teasers

Mental games — conundrums, paradoxes (see below) — are fun ways to get the brain working. "All things in moderation, including moderation." Thought-provoking statements like this one can help your student think critically. Or consider this classic from Alexander Dumas: "Most general statements are false, including this one."

Front of a 3x5 card:
The sentence on the other side of this card is true.

Back of a 3x5 card:
The sentence on the other side of this card is false.

Have you explored deductive reasoning and logical syllogisms? (Remember these? A sample syllogism: Mammals are warm-blooded animals. Whales are mammals. Therefore, whales are warm-blooded animals.) Students also enjoy extending the idea by considering false syllogisms. A false syllogism is a similar set of statements that appear by their structure to be true, but which we know to be false. My personal favorite: "Hard work is honorable. Stealing refrigerators is hard work. Therefore ..."

## Arguing, Debating, Negotiating

Has your teen taken up a new form of conversation — snarling at the parents who have tenderly reared him? Some may whine, complain, beg, or threaten, trying all the failed tricks of the past. Those annoying conversations might be an essential part of maturation. Under the protective parental umbrella your child finds a safe environment to practice saying no, to practice developing conversational skills, and to practice independence.

Your young adult needs this practice every bit as much as he needed to say "NO!" a thousand times at age two. After all, saying no and defending one's position are skills parents want their children to have, eventually. Why shouldn't he practice on the most powerful influence in his life, his parent?

Since some parents are going to be in this stage for a while, consider introducing your student to formal debate, argument, and negotiation. You might like it too.

## Chocolate or Vanilla — Making Decisions

What a shame it is when parents don't discuss and practice decision-making skills. A child faces decisions at every stage of his life: whether to wear the red shirt or the green shirt, whether to play basketball or join a wrestling team, or whether to attend college or join the military. Help him develop decision-making skills at each stage through family life activities.

## Questioning Strategies

Asking questions can keep your child's curiosity engaged.

### Direct Questions

*Direct questions* form the underlying structure of journalistic conversations: who, where, what, when, and why. Just the facts, Ma'am. Among these, questions that ask how and why are somewhat less direct because they require interpretation by the respondent.

Young children ask direct questions by the hundreds, for they depend on direct answers to their questions to acquire knowledge. Some things are best taught directly: safety, naming, labeling, learning symbols such as numerals, the alphabet, and mathematical signs are examples. Sometimes we need facts: How much does this cost? What time is it? Did you feed the dog? Where are your shoes? Whom are you going with? When shall I pick you up? When was the War of 1812?

Children who love factual knowledge cannot get enough of these quiz type questions. *Trivial Pursuit* types of games, not to mention television game shows, depend on minor facts and details to delight and challenge fact lovers. These detail oriented kids often excel in geography and spelling bees and other competitions that rely on rote memory.

Direct questions do have a few limitations — limitations that more complex questioning strategies gracefully sidestep.

### Open-ended Questions

I discovered that my children's eyes glazed over if I asked too many direct questions, so I switched to open-ended questions to stimulate thought or imagination. Open-ended questions lead to the connections and meaning behind the facts, causing the child to *use* facts and dates to show connections and relationships. Open-ended questions are very helpful for students who need to see the big picture.

Open-ended questions are also less likely to create opposition or confrontation. Questions for which there can be no "right" answer cause the student to look beyond the actual facts and toward the circumstances, reasons, and meaning that surround the factual details, even when the details alone bring on a yawn.

Examples:

- How much can you find out?

- How did that happen?

- How did you solve the problem?

- How do you feel about that?

- How is this different from (or the same as) that?

- What do you think might happen next?

- Are there other ways to think about this?

- How else could we do this?

- I wonder why?

- Why do you think....?

- What do you think is the meaning of....?

Open-ended questions do not have to be framed as questions. Framing questions as statements leaves it up to the child to decide whether to engage with the question you have posed. When in doubt about what kind of open-ended question to ask, try a how or why question.

Examples:

- I'd really like to help you with that. Help me understand.

- I wonder what would happen if ....

- I heard there are five other ways to do this.

- Tell me how you figured this out.

- Show me how you solved the problem

- Tell me how you are thinking about this problem.

## Leading and Speculative Questions

Sometimes questions can be used to lead students to explore ideas they haven't considered, or to expand existing knowledge.

Leading questions, questions where the expected answer is obvious from the format of the question, are asked to draw out a particular response. These questions should lead the student to think about a topic, much the same way that the sentence "Try not to think about pink elephants" immediately forces a pink elephant into the mind's eye.

Examples:

- Have you ever told a lie?

- Did you ever think about what it is like to be deaf?

- Did you ever wonder why the sky is blue?

- Can you imagine what it would feel like to ....?

- Did you ever wonder where babies come from?

- If the Civil War hadn't happened, would African-Americans still be slaves?

Be careful — asking too many leading questions can easily degenerate a good discussion into a game of "guess what I am thinking." If you are unsure whether your leading question will stimulate further thought, it is time to listen instead. At their best use, leading questions can introduce tough topics that might not come up in day-to-day life.

## Finally

Parents certainly have the skills to keep the love of learning alive — we just need to remember to use them. Use any of these conversational strategies that interest you when your brain feels dull. It is fun and easy to keep the light bulbs of discovery flashing above your child's head — and your own!

# PART 3
## Togetherness

Featuring:

## chapter fourteen

# KEYNOTE
# HOMESCHOOL = TOGETHERNESS
*family learning as family living*

Have you noticed that *togetherness* is a nearly perfect synonym for homeschooling? My *Webster's New World College Dictionary* defines *togetherness* thus: "The spending of time together, as in social and leisure-time activities by the members of a family, especially when regarded as resulting in a more unified, stable relationship." That means homeschooling and togetherness can be one and the same.

But wait.

Stop the music, the dancing, and the unbridled celebration.

Do I hear a grumbling, a disgruntled and sour note? "Family togetherness isn't all sunshine and roses, lady. How do I manage endless days of cranky kids with no relief in sight, ever?"

You are so right. I've painted a glistening picture of the home-schooling life so far — joyful kids learning through play, families in rapt discussions, parents wisely guiding their lovely cooperative children. While those joys and successes absolutely are at the core of a successful homeschooling and family life, it is also true that the intense togetherness of homeschooling can wear thin, even in the most patient and gentle of families.

But before we pause and look at some nitty gritty details of how families manage the homeschooling lifestyle, you should set up a personal watch for homeschool burnout. We all have bad days, and homeschooler bad days can be tough. How well I remember the day a frantic and crying mom called me, desperate to know if there was room for one more person in my homeschooling workshop. Toward the end of the workshop — her personal challenge long over and homeschooling once again ticking along for her — the mom confided the depth of the crisis she had been in when she called. While her daughter sobbed in her bedroom, the sobbing mom had chosen to call me — that is, she chose to seek support — as a last-ditch effort before abandoning homeschooling and registering her child for school.

Homeschooling burnout can happen suddenly, with devastating effects, if the family doesn't prepare for the possibility.   Burnout is a bit like coming down with the flu. You do what you can to avoid catching the bugs, but when you do, it is best if you have made a few preparations ahead of time. Who wants to run out to the store when you feel rotten? Better to have something on hand to sooth the scratchy throat, wipe the runny nose, cool the fevered brow. Burnout prevention begins with you by taking regular personal breaks — hobbies, time with your spouse, nights-out — or whatever recharges your battery. What else can you do to hedge against a very bad, miserably awful homeschooling day? What is the "long hot bath" of burnout recovery?

You might try this. Prepare yourself , on your very next bad day, to call the schedule to a halt and retire to your favorite chair for a personal support session. Have some alternative activities on hand for your kids to do that do not involve much supervision. Maybe watching favorite videos or looking through family albums would be perfect. You might try game day, play-dough day, play-in-your-own-room day, or cook-your-own-meals day. Select activities that you know will engage your children constructively, but that will give you some real time off.

Once the kids are busy, grab a pencil and pad and jot down the advantages of homeschooling togetherness that you've enjoyed on your good days. If you are really stuck and cannot think of even one, flip through the pages of this book for clues that call to mind the uncommon advantages of togetherness. Call a friend, read a magazine, go online, do what you need to do to remind yourself that bad days are part of a normal life.

You may discover advantages of homeschooling that you have not noticed before. For example, the "together" lifestyle builds a strong set of values. Building a strong family foundation may be the most valuable benefit of homeschooling.

Parents teach, by personal example, values, and children naturally learn by their example. As children begin to stretch their wings, they play at friends' homes, have overnights, join group and club activities. They eventually notice that other families have different values and rules from their own.

What opportunities families have to learn about diversity and respect for differences! In fact, children may learn more about their own family's values by spending time with families with different values than they do spending time with families of identical values — especially if they can talk about the differences openly at home. Openly discussing differences reinforces the strength of their own family. Children learn that the family value system doesn't collapse or change simply because others display a different set of values.

As older children explore their community, that indelible print of the family's value system gives them a basis for comparing the values and moral codes of other families, groups, cultures, and countries. When children encounter greatly conflicting moral codes as they often do during adolescence, the strong home base lends strength to the family code, even as it is challenged. *Family togetherness reinforces the family's values.*

Has your family faced hard times while homeschooling? Hard times may strike your family at one time or another. No matter what life throws you, you can work around it or learn from it while continuing to homeschool. Even in the darkest days of your life, the flexibility and family strength of a homeschooling lifestyle can help your family move forward.

On the most basic level, activities can be packed up and taken along when a family emergency arises. Sometimes activities can be delayed until later. Sometimes a family crisis can set off a flurry of research and new learning. If a family member suffers a serious illness, for example, siblings may get less attention for a time.

However, they may instead learn important lessons about empathy, cooperation, helping, and sharing. Family solidarity grows as the rest of the family works together.

The twofold message to your child is profound. First, she realizes that she is such an important part of this family that there is no thought to leave her on the outside looking in. Second, she realizes she is such an important member of this family that her individual needs are still being met, although perhaps differently.

When homeschooling activities are adapted to meet the family's current situation, children are encompassed by the closeness of the family unit. ***Family togetherness strengthens family integrity and loyalty during challenges and hard times.***

Don't even think of getting out of that chair until you plan three activities that support you personally and that give you a break: a short daily activity such as journaling or meditation, a weekly activity for you and your spouse such as dinner out, and a future big break, such as a weekend retreat. ***Family togetherness supports the personal and private needs of its members.***

Now, while you are still curled up there in your chair, think about why you decided to homeschool in the first place, and what new reasons you have added as time has passed. Maybe you like the way your kids play together on good days. Maybe you see a stronger attachment between siblings than existed before.

Homeschooling is not always easy. You can expect some hard work, occasional sacrifice, and a need for flexibility, yes, but always remember that there is a payoff — a lifestyle that is often relaxed, seamless, and joyous. Find the effects of family togetherness that you value and dwell on those, and try not to think about the tough days-of-ten-thousand screeches.

## Finally

Homeschooling and togetherness — one and the same. Now, where were we? Oh, yes, some how-to's. Take what works for you; ignore the rest.

## chapter fifteen

# SOCIAL LEARNING
*getting along with others*

Trust me on this — if you hear it once, you'll hear it a thousand times: "What about socialization?"

You'd think I'd be used to those comments by now, but I am always amazed when I hear that someone's friends or family members cast doubt on the ability of homeschooling parents — their own loved ones! — to teach their children social skills. Of course homeschooled students learn social skills — they live in families with their socially skilled parents, don't they? They go into the community, don't they? They make friends, learn how to get along, take turns — the whole gamut of social skill — don't they? Eventually, I realized that "doubt casters" were overlaying a school-based template of socialization on homeschool social learning. Of course it was a poor fit! Family-based social learning is tailor-made, not one-size-fits-all.

To truly see how easily and naturally homeschooled students learn social skills, try this. Think of socialization in school as a social tumbler, something like a rock tumbler. Rules, the buildings, staff, and school policies are the apparatus. Students and teachers interact together over a long period and in time social skills rub off of some and onto others. Perhaps some of a student's unsociable rough edges are smoothed out over time.

Acquiring social skills in a home environment is a distinctly different process. Think now of the skills of a gemstone cutter. This is how homeschooling parents approach teaching social skills to their children — by paying close attention to the facets and rough spots in the child's personality. In the course of choosing social activity for their child, parents guide and direct her to learn various social skills: self control, politeness, cooperation, and so on. Parents discourage asocial behaviors and encourage appropriate skills. In its simplest form, that is all there is to social learning!

Some parents wonder what the right skills are, of course, and who can say what the most important elements of social learning are? Certainly not I, and when I look into the wider world, I see that social skills have not been mastered in any society. The best we can do, I believe, is raise our children in families that live according to laws, moral codes, and values.

Some social learning issues do raise universal concern. In this chapter, we'll explore a few points of *social learning* as they relate to homeschooled students.

## Individualizing Social Experiences

How should you choose the kinds of social learning skills and guidance that your child needs? The first thing you might do is explore your child's unique social profile. Most children have some fascinating personality aspects and probably a few annoying ones. You'll want to provide social guidance that enhances the positive side of her personality while helping her redirect or control the more challenging parts.

Is he naturally self-aware and expressive? Some children move through the world at a frenzied pace. Without guidance, a quick-to-act child can become a strident bully, expecting the world always to turn his way.

Perhaps you have a child who is a quiet peace-lover, willing to wait his turn or let the world come to him. Without guidance, a reticent or shy child may harbor unexpressed emotions that can build into explosive results.

I am thrilled to report that children with all types of personalities — from those who express bullying behaviors, to those who are extremely shy, and all between — are likely to flourish in a homeschooling environment.

## Derailing Bully Behavior

Does your child show signs of being a bully? Sometimes bully behavior develops when a child is naturally rambunctious or aggressive and hasn't learned self control — a fairly easy source of bullying to identify.

Another cause of bullying is barely detectable even to the most attentive parental eyes and ears. Children whose parents are highly empathic may become bullies — without the parents noticing, simply because it is almost impossible for empathic parents to imagine. For some reason, the child does not imitate his parents' empathy by showing empathy for others. Instead, he is self-centered or requires ever increasing understanding. His parents may excuse away his poor behavior toward others which exacerbates the problem. Parents should be alert for clues that their child has trouble keeping friends. If other parents complain about your child's behavior, that may mean your child has not learned the skills of empathy and self control.

Children who bully need to learn *to feel empathy, to exhibit self control*, or both. If he learns to feel empathy, he will begin to understand what it means to be victimized. Self control will help him redirect the feelings that cause him to act against others.

Helping your child learn *self control* takes more time than skill, clever tricks, or knowledge. It demands focused parental attention. The homeschooling parent has an advantage — you can spend as much time as needed to help your child learn *self control*.

Your child will learn self control through the normal family routines of togetherness, play, and conversation. When your child plays with other children, either siblings or playmates, a parent's steady presence assures that your child will learn the skills of interaction. You can give your child nudges and subtle guidance to help her learn to play with others.

You will want to find many ways to *redirect* aggressive behavior. When your child lashes out, step in immediately. "The truck is Billy's. You cannot take it apart unless he says you can." "Pat the kitty with soft hands," you say, holding your child's hand and directing it. "The bat is for hitting balls, not children. Let's go outside and hit a ball with your bat."

As the child grows older, help her learn acceptable ways to channel rambunctious behavior. Sports are popular, and you might also offer activities such as music, art, and science. Some students enjoy the martial arts, playing drums, or building large sculptures. These activities have a wonderful physicality, yet still require self control and discipline. Outdoor activities such as diving, biking, hiking, or climbing — taught with safety precautions, of course — provide other outlets for surplus aggression or energy.

For a child to gain control of his aggressiveness, *empathy* must also be taught starting at an early age. Bullying children may act aggressively out of their own inner pain, unable to care about the pain others may feel. She must *learn* to feel true remorse for aggressive behavior that affects others.

How do parents teach a child to internalize what the other person might feel? One step at a time, you can help your child learn to focus inwardly on her own emotional state and to describe her feelings in words. Set an example of empathy for the bullying child by being sensitive to her prior pain. When you listen carefully and provide feedback to this child during her own episodes of suffering, she learns by your example how to behave when someone else is hurt.

Keep the channels of communication wide open. Spend time talking with an aggressively inclined child. Such a child needs ample time to talk about difficult social experiences or how he might act differently in the future. Parents need these conversations, too, in order to continually check in on their child's empathic understanding of others.

Remember that your aggressive child needs constant assurance from her parents that she is loved and very special to them, especially when her behaviors have gone way out of line. Unconditional love, even at her most unlovable, gives her a sound footing for correcting her poor behavior.

Unconditional love also demands that you teach your child how to make amends. If your child has stomped a buddy's sweater in a mud puddle in anger, help her to focus on the hurt her friend feels, to wash the sweater, and to return it to the friend with a verbal or written apology. This is the path to teaching your child empathy.

Be sure she knows that you know she can learn socially acceptable behavior and you will be at her side helping her learn. Unconditional acceptance, guidance, and love are the foundation.

## Drawing Out Shy Students

Is your child shy, quiet, compliant, timid, or easily embarrassed? No children have their social needs better served by homeschooling than those who are naturally quiet or observant.

Reflect on that thought for a moment. Homeschooling offers the shy child a chance to bloom in a quieter space. No more must he wait for a turn that never comes. No longer must he listen to behavioral guidance that is irrelevant, confusing, even contradictory to his personal social needs. No more must he always follow while others lead. Often, timid children merely need more time, less pressure, a more relaxed environment, equal opportunities, or perhaps a bit of coaching.

*Small group activities* are especially important for a shy child. In small groups, timid students are less likely to be left out, overlooked, or lost in the shuffle. Shy or compliant children can develop leadership skills in small interest-based groups. In large groups, compliant children have little opportunity but to work on their already excellent "following" skills. Small groups might rotate leadership activities among members, giving all students a chance to try out all roles. The leadership skills are similar except for scale.

Shy children may approach group activities with *natural reserve.* It helps if you think of that reserve as a natural and healthy response to a new situation. As soon as trust develops, the reserved attitude just melts away. Don't feel shy about accompanying your child to activities until the child feels comfortable. And to help other adults draw out your shy child in a group, encourage them to provide the entire group with common experiences upon which to build trust and friendship. Insist that the adults who work with your child use techniques that build trust.

Is your child withdrawn in groups, yet shows no shyness whatever in the home environment? Build on that courageous lack of shyness in the home first. Help him notice the different feelings he has while at home and while with strangers. Then help your child take his courage on the road, finding ways for him to interact with comfort and confidence.

Your timid child may benefit from a series of small victories. Instead of taking her to a large playgroup, let her try activities with just one or two children first. When she is comfortable with these friends, try a small club so she can experience more group activities.

You might be surprised how outgoing he can become, once he finds his safety zone.

Another strategy for helping your reluctant child try new activities is for you to join him in a partnership. You may be able to draw him further into exploring an activity of interest if you work together. Writing or telling stories, painting or drawing, participating in activities of all kinds — together — provides a bridging activity across which a shy child can pass to greater personal involvement. Your child learns so much about the world by participating at your side, so don't hesitate to provide that support if he needs it.

Alternative avenues of *self expression*, such as music, art, drama, creative writing, sports, and hobbies might be a springboard out of shyness as well. A hobby such as building a collection or bird watching can be enormously satisfying for a student, a satisfaction that can grow new skills and relationships that last a lifetime. Some shy children lose their shyness completely when in the company of adults — strangers, even — who are knowledgeable about the hobby interest! One little fellow was bashful in his Scout group until it was his turn to give a talk about a subject he loved. Who would have guessed he was shy — he spoke eagerly and well!

*Decision-making skills* may be slow to develop. Shy children often struggle mightily over minor decisions, sorely tempting parents to intervene and make the decision for them. Sometimes narrowing the choices to just two or three is helpful. Occasionally, parents should allow the time their child needs to decide if he wants pickles on his hamburger. The more opportunities he has to practice decision-making, the sooner the skill will develop. When he is old enough, teach your child to write out a "Ben Franklin balance sheet," a list of pros and cons to any decision that is troubling him.

Some shy children have a tendency to become embarrassed. That tendency is countered when children realize that *mistakes are natural*, a necessary part of learning. Sometimes children need a reminder that if one is not risking occasional errors, learning is limited. Both parents and children must allow the milk to be spilt and the words to be misspelled. Errors are remarkable teachers, and followup tips easily absorbed if offered with a light touch. "Hold the milk jug this way. Now let's clean up the spill." "That word has a silent *gh*, so we pronounce it this way." You can help your child by telling him about errors you make yourself and by demonstrating how to manage the embarrassment. If a child can learn to laugh at her own foibles, she can control the embarrassment that brings on the blush.

Parents need to be patient while that personality blossoms. A child may require long periods of quiet reflection to be able to identify unique interests and insight into himself. You may discover that your compliant child will develop a strong personality in the more intimate and attentive homeschooling environment.

## Peer Pressure

Homeschooled students may acquire a degree of resistance to the worst kinds of adolescent behaviors. Their exposure to large crowds and groups is nearly always among a widely diverse population. That is to say, homeschooling events of all sizes and kinds absolutely teem with adults and all ages of children!

Large homeschool events, such as conferences, retreats, family dances, camp-outs, graduation celebrations, and park parties are common. Whether the homeschool gatherings count attendance in tens, hundreds, or thousands, adult to child ratios are inevitably family-sized. Each parent is responsible for his own children and those borrowed for the day. Students, parents, and babies are seen everywhere. Adult presence is so pervasive that even the most rebellious youngster has little opportunity to create havoc without eventually attracting adult intervention.

Teens often enjoy participating in larger homeschool events by taking on service type activities of responsibility under friendly adult direction. Activities such as running a snack stand, offering a baby-sitting service, supervising a toddler room, or working on the clean-up committee are common. Young teens have a chance to stretch their wings of responsibility, huddle together with newfound self-importance, and spend time together with peers.

That pivotal opportunity of a teen peer group serving alongside adults for the first time helps young people move onto the bridge from childhood to adulthood.

While teens are proud to be busy with newfound responsibilities and busy with their own affairs, the entire community benefits. The teens are unwittingly laying groundwork for the "next generation of teens," those younger children who admire them. Younger children have saucer eyes as they look up to teens, former children who have finally achieved the cherished goal of "insider" in the adult world. Each succeeding group blazes a stronger and stronger path for the next group to follow.

Homeschooled students generally have less time to learn or practice dangerous behaviors because there are usually too many adults around. They are busy. They have increased their social skills from an early age. Not separated by same-age groupings, they have a chance to see where they've been and where they are headed as they continue to grow up.

Of course homeschooled children do not wear halos. Homeschooled students may indeed explore some of the dangerous behaviors and undesirable activities of their peers. However, the opportunities to practice and learn these behaviors are limited when they are busy swimming in the fish bowl of family, friends, and the community.

By the time homeschooled students have the freedom, time, and transportation to indulge in a darker side of adolescence, they have pretty much passed through the stage of interest and choose instead to occupy themselves with enjoying their todays and building their futures.

## Learning to Be Alone — Private Time

Now is a good time to talk about the relationship a person develops with his one for-sure lifetime companion — himself. Private time is when children learn to be alone with themselves, to reflect on and learn from the events of their lives, and to listen to their inner voices.

Once you take up a homeschooling lifestyle, you realize that privacy is more precious than ever. Helping your child manage private time is important in several ways: your youngster learns to be alone with himself, you can have some needed down time, and a homeschooling lifestyle generally runs more smoothly when your child can entertain himself, by himself.

Very young children generally vocalize their inner voice through play. Parents can actually hear the inner voice of the child in the chatter that is part of the play. Try eavesdropping on the joyful chatter as a kind of "checking in" to see what's going on with your child. I gleaned many insights into my children's needs and interests by keeping an ear tuned to private play time.

As children get a little older, they begin to keep their inner voice to themselves. Still, they continue to need quiet time to play, fantasize, reflect, or think. Your child's inner voice needs to be a friendly and familiar experience and should not be neglected. We as parents quickly learn that a slammed door and a sour look are richly vivid communications from the inner voice!

Inner voices can be squelched by over-scheduling. Home-schooling families easily fall into the trap of being too busy, and privacy can be lost without notice. Be sure you allow your youngster enough time that he can hear his inner voice regularly.

Consider how confused a student must feel if he hasn't heard his inner voice since early childhood. Suppose his long squelched inner voice suddenly pops up when his adolescent life is full of turmoil. The teen, now unpracticed in dealing with his inner voice, has no way to sort out the meaning or source of the inner conversation. While most young people resolve the confusion, those who misinterpret their inner thoughts may complicate their lives unnecessarily. In the most extreme cases they may even endanger themselves or others. While that extreme is unlikely, it still makes sense to assure that your youngster knows how to spend time with himself.

For some students, alone time is best spent reading, practicing a musical instrument, developing a physical skill, playing solitaire or computer games, solving puzzles, building models, exploring art, or just hanging out. What does your student love? Is she fond of watching TV, surfing the Internet, and listening to music? Handwork, such as the fiber arts, cooking, auto repair, or woodworking, is a traditional type of activity that provides private time while occupying the hands productively.

Private time may be a spiritual or searching time. Some listen to their inner voice and write their thoughts in journals. Some pray, meditate, read sacred writings or inspirational literature, write poetry, or otherwise participate in rituals that calm the mind.

Successful parents respect the unique needs for privacy of each family member, including themselves.

## Finally

Social skill is quite naturally learned by living among socially healthy people. Later, when a child practices social skills, parents and others give him feedback that guides his interaction. Step by step, the child learns the social standards of his community. This natural process is social learning.

Most homeschooling families have no trouble assuring that their children have strong social wings when they are ready to fly away into the world.

## chapter sixteen

# EXPLORING HOMESCHOOLING STYLES
*seeking a lifestyle for full family expression*

An adorable little family grouping, with smiling faces gathered around the kitchen table — isn't that what you envisioned when you first heard the term *homeschooling*? How rare that stereotypical picture is! Yes, some do fit the picture part of the time, but most homeschooling families differ sharply from that image — in style, approach, requirements, emphasis, philosophy, structure, and method, in ways both large and small.

Let's talk about what homeschooling *really is*. In most successful families, homeschooling *is* a way of life — a way of life that has grown and developed beyond the original reasons for choosing to homeschool. As soon as they develop a style that fits, families are easily able to find educational approaches for their individual children.

In this chapter, we'll explore two categories of homeschooling styles[1], and look at some of the variations of each. What homeschooling style will fit your family?

---

[1]    The associations, books, and periodicals listed in the Appendix will help you explore the various homeschooling approaches in greater depth.

## Child-Specific Developmental Styles

A developmental approach frequently unfolds as parents and families grow more confident in their ability to homeschool.

To understand the developmental style, consider a flower in your garden that is about to bloom. There are many things you can do to support that bloom. You can water, fertilize, weed, cultivate, even adjust the amount of light. When the balance is right, you have but one task remaining — patience. An amaryllis on my table takes a painstakingly long time to show its full bloom. But the flower takes as long as it takes, and I can only bide my time. If I have nurtured its development, the flower can be trusted to show its full glory in its own time.

A child too can be trusted to bloom and develop, learn and grow, each in her own time and way. Parents can encourage and nurture the biggest, best, and earliest "bloom" but they cannot mandate or command development.

Each stage of the child's development is best nurtured in different ways. What excites a very young child is dull or insulting just a few years later. What excites an older youth flies out of the reach of a younger child. Parents quickly become competent gardeners, looking to the child for clues as to the kinds of learning materials and resources to use.

Academic mileposts (reading by age eight, for example) can be ignored in lieu of attending closely to the developmental rate of individual children. Because children develop at different rates, what difference does it make if the child reads at age four or age eleven? In the long run, it won't matter. Skills, like flowers, bloom in their own time.

The most popular developmental approaches to homeschooling stem from two historical approaches to homeschooling.

### Unschooling

The seeds of the unschooling approach were planted during the 1950's and 1960's alternative school movements. A key leader, John Holt, wrote two pivotal and well-received books of that movement, *How Children Fail* and *How Children Learn*. Eventually, Holt turned his attention away from trying to help unresponsive school systems. Instead, he continued to develop his ideas about how best to meet individual children's needs. Meanwhile, daring people had begun, quietly, to remove their children from the classroom to teach them at home. By the late 1970's, Holt was publishing a newsletter, *Growing Without Schooling*, and in the 1980's wrote *Teach Your Own*, a book that continues to support families today.

Based on his clear understanding of learning — that it happens everywhere and all the time, Holt advocated for parents who chose to follow their children's interests by guiding and supporting them in their process of learning at home. Schedules and traditional curriculums take a back seat to thirsty exploration of interests. If the child is learning eagerly, what would be the point of stopping that learning according to some arbitrary timetable to learn about something that is completely unrelated? There is time enough for structured learning as the child approaches the teen years or desires more disciplined material. Children are natural lifelong learners and, if encouraged, will continue to learn enthusiastically throughout adulthood.

To introduce subjects that children might not discover otherwise, such as reading, writing, and math, parents make sure the home environment is rich in math and language opportunities, materials, activities and games, in addition to regularly engaging them in practical math and language activities.

Parents take advantage of their young children's explorations and excitement about learning and help them delve further into the subject as their interest directs. If one interest should fade, in time a new interest will arise to take its place.

Children are likely to hold many interests, and by exploring these they are generally introduced to most traditional subjects along the way. As children get older, they and their parents may discover a few holes in their interest-driven education. Eventually they choose to tackle some of those subjects they feel are crucial to getting what they want in life, sometimes opting for a textbook or class, and other times utilizing the library, Internet, a mentor, or direct exploration.

Careful observers of the unschooling process grasp the extraordinary depth and breadth of learning that erupts. Unfortunately, ignorant, careless, or unsympathetic observers sometimes dismiss unschooling harshly. Parents of unschoolers may need to educate the "unschooling-misinformed public" about the advantages and rich opportunities available through this unconventional approach.

## Study, Entrepreneurship, Service

This approach, sometimes called the "Moore homeschooling formula," was developed by Dr. Raymond Moore and his wife Dorothy. Dr. Moore had long been an educator and researcher, and in the 1950's and 1960's, advocated delayed schooling. This was about the time alternative educators (including Holt) began advocating for public school reform.

With one foot in the developmental camp and the other in the curriculum camp, this approach calls for delaying formal schooling (i.e., close book work) until age eight or so. The Moores were particularly concerned that young children have the time to build the underlying experiential base of knowledge that comes through natural physical exploration of the world. They were also concerned about potential damage to vision resulting from too much close book work too early. Close work of any kind is to be limited to brief sessions for young children, with play and large motor activity interspersed for a developmental balance.

Children begin formal instruction at age eight or so, and continue to benefit from a three-pronged approach to balancing activities. First, serious academic work is required, usually one to three hours a day, less for younger children. A second prong of the approach requires children to participate regularly in service work of some kind, perhaps through their church or a community project. Some families do their service work independently, such as providing companionship and yard work for an elderly neighbor. The final prong is entrepreneurship or work. Children may work in family businesses or set up businesses of their own, such as lemonade stands, babysitting, animal care, or other kinds of real work. Real life learning is a great benefit as the child experiences the ups and downs of even the tiniest home business.

This approach has many advocates, particularly those who want to combine religious training with a developmental approach that meets the child's needs.

## A Smidgen of This, A Dab of That

Seasoned homeschooling families are often reluctant to tuck their family in one or the other "style camps" because they find the label too restrictive. Families may find that what works for them does not fit neatly into one or another category. Many new style names have been coined, including terms such as *home-based learning* and *eclectic homeschooling.*

Regardless of the style name, parents draw from any style, approach, curriculum, or material that seems useful for an individual child. The family may include unschooling, entrepreneurship and service, school-at-home, learning cooperatives, learning clubs, educational software, apprenticeships, mentorships, test-prep courses, community classes, online work, and so forth. Balancing the child's learning needs with the family's needs and resources is the goal.

Many parents mix and match along the continuum of the child's development. A common mix-and-match is to use an unschooling approach during the early years, then move toward a Moore-type or home-based learning approach as children get a little older. Finally, a curriculum based model may be used during the high school years. For many, it makes good sense to draw from different sources as children's needs grow and change.

## Curriculum-based Styles

In this category of styles, the selected curriculum is the centerpiece. The structure of homeschooling practice revolves around the administration of and/or adherence to the curriculum program. The curriculum may be purchased or teacher/parent devised. Many parents individualize curriculum programs to meet their child's needs, although individualization can be a challenge when using a one-size-fits-most plan. Some of these models strike a resonant and familiar chord with some families, at least in the beginning of their homeschooling venture. Until parents really delve into how learning works, they tend to seek styles that reflect their own schooling experiences. With time and confidence, many families move to the individualized approaches mentioned above.

### School-at-Home

School-at-home looks just like you think it does. Gather the kids around the kitchen table every morning until noon or so, and plan another one or two hours of directed activities after a lunch break. Lay out a conventional or home-designed curriculum, stacks of textbooks, paper, pencils, maps, and a globe. Add mom or dad to the mix as explainer, question answerer, paper checker, assignment giver, and project director, and you have a day of school-at-home.

The school-at-home approach of course has its roots in traditional schooling. When it was realized that not all children could attend school — children living abroad or traveling with their families, ill children, or children living in isolated regions, correspondence curriculums were developed.

Fewer homeschoolers use this model than is popularly believed. Burnout is unfortunately a common result of imposing a classroom atmosphere in the home. A shift to one of the developmental approaches helps resolve potential burnout issues.

A pure school-at-home model seems to work best for families in which all family members thrive on a structured and predictable routine and in which the children are verbal learners.

When children do not fit this model, successful parents usually move to one of the developmental styles.

## Dual Enrollment
## Parent-Partnered or Hybrid Programs

Another curriculum-based approach is dual enrollment, a combination of public classroom-schooling and homeschooling.

Dual enrollment usually refers to an arrangement in which a child attends a regular public classroom part-time to participate in selected classes such as music, foreign language, art, or math. Additionally, sports and other interscholastic public school activities are available to homeschooled students in many regions.

Parent-partnered or hybrid programs are two of the terms used to describe special programs that have been set up by public schools to accommodate homeschool families. Besides these, you'll find a fruit salad of terms — alternative education, parent-partnered programs, charter schools, charter homeschools, independent study programs, just to name a few — describing these attempts to make public education accessible and appealing to homeschooled students.

These programs are experimental and vary widely from state to state and community to community. While many of the advantages of homeschooling are lost in hybrid programs, the benefits that remain may still be a significant improvement over many traditional public school programs, if that is your alternative.

If you seek such a hybrid or dual enrollment program for your child, remember that you won't be homeschooling in the fullest sense of the term. Public group programs are inevitably a compromise that places the administrative and logistical needs of the school above the needs of individual families. Parent control of the details of education — scheduling, curriculum, evaluation, group size, teacher choice, methods, and individualization — may be sacrificed. Family togetherness, play and exploration, and of course those all-important family conversations will take a back seat to the classroom program.

The hybrids gain a mixed review from the homeschooling population. Some families love these programs. Many believe that the hybrids muddy the accepted definition of homeschooling as a private family activity, possibly endangering a family's right to homeschool without intervention.

The great future for these public programs should not lie with the homeschooling population but with the public at large. Parent-partnered programs make at least some of the benefits of homeschooling available to all public school children.

As a taxpayer, I am bewildered when I learn that many school systems have chosen homeschoolers — widely known to be well-educated, often without spending a single dime of public money — as the sole market for tax-funded parent-partnered programs. That is unconscionable, when the vast majority of public school students do not have access to those programs. School systems break the public trust when they fail to promote quality programs to all.

## Tips for Finding Your Style

Now that we've surveyed the styles, how will you decide which style fits your family best? Will you adhere to a highly structured homeschooling program? Will you follow a developmental approach, allowing your children freedom and personal choice to learn what interests them? Or will you move between the two extremes until you find a style that feels natural? Here are some tips to help you find your path.

## Look Inward

Imagine visiting two homeschooling families as a fly on the wall, observing. The first day, you visit a family that has carefully scheduled study periods, a packaged curriculum, and a tidy and orderly study area. Do you feel comfortable and relaxed in this setting, feeling that you could do this too? Or do you feel suddenly overwhelmed by the immensity of the task of daily instruction of your children, perhaps battling to get them to do schoolwork in addition to your other daily tasks?

Suppose you visit a different family the next day, a family that has building blocks, animals, books, puzzles, microscopes, and many projects-in-progress scattered all over the house. Do you feel comfortable, knowing that you have walked into a rich learning environment, where children can easily learn all they want all day long? Or do you feel overwhelmed by the immensity of the task of keeping up with all this stuff in addition to your other daily tasks?

As you notice your reactions to each environment, you will realize that a successful homeschooling style that works well in one family can drive another family crazy. You can choose what fits your family best, because children do thrive in each homeschooling style.

## Observe Real Families

If you can, find some families through your local support group and gently finagle an invitation to someone's home. You will notice that there are as many homeschooling styles as there are home-schooling families. Learning styles, personalities, interests, and methods all affect the family style.

In addition, attending support group meetings, homeschool workshops, conferences, or field trips can help you learn about homeschooling styles in a less invasive manner. You can usually find families who are happy to tell you how they came to the lifestyle that works for them.

## Read "How-we-did-it" Books and Articles

Reading homeschooling literature is another way to explore the homeschooling life. Try books, newsletters, magazines, and personal web pages that showcase homeschooling families. How did these families handle mistakes, learn, and adapt their approach as their children grew and changed?

Try to avoid comparing your homeschooling lives with the lives of the "stars." Don't worry if your students haven't built telescopes, traveled abroad, raised sheep, played concertos, or achieved full scholarships to elite universities. Homeschooling is an option for everyday people — not just superstar families.

## Observe Your Children Realistically

If your children have differing learning styles, your family's style may need to include something different for each child. One child may require lots of attention and support when taking on a new learning project, and later may hang on to the project for a long time. Another child may rarely take an interest in anything that is easy. Instead, she thrives on challenges that push her to the limits of her capabilities. How will you meet the needs of both?

One family member may be an early reader, while another can't make sense of print until much older. Is it fair to assume that both children will learn to read in the same way? Are the same materials and schedules likely to be appropriate for both children?

If one child fights allergies and another loves and needs pets to care for, what unique solution will you develop to meet the needs of both children?

A lovely homeschool plan that fits Dad's fantasy of what homeschooling should be, but does not fit the learning styles of the children, will be endlessly frustrating. Being realistic about your children can help you avoid this mistake.

## Consider the Personal Styles of Both Parents

What do you enjoy? Which subjects do you love or hate? When do you have the most patience? Do you enjoy big messy projects, or do you prefer more structured activities? How will you make time for yourself? Which approaches seem overwhelming? Which seem possible?

Many parents take the opportunity homeschooling offers them and learn something new themselves. Your kids will love you for it if you do. You will become more understanding of the difficulties that your children encounter in their learning activities. You will gain insight into your personal learning style and how you incorporate new learning into your life.

## Take Inventory of Your Lifestyle

Individual tastes and differences, interests, values, and attitudes will influence your style. Are you urban, suburban, small town, rural, nomadic? Are you connected with other homeschooling families or are you isolated? Do you live in a neighborhood with many appropriate playmates, or will you need to drive for social opportunities? Does your family like to spend quiet time at home with good books, computers, art, music, craft and building projects, and games? Or do you prefer to get out in the community for events such as camping, socializing, taking classes together, shopping, and taking cultural trips? Will you need to budget carefully, or can you purchase resources more freely? How will each parent participate?

## Start Now, Adjust Later

Try the ideas you have, the ones you remember from teachers you loved, the ideas you always wanted to try but never had the chance. Learn French, climb a mountain, read the encyclopedia, build a waterfall. In other words, if you have ideas about how you might begin to homeschool, then begin. Begin today, and your homeschooling style will unfold along the way.

If you feel shaky about jumping in, reach out for help first and then take the plunge. Attend a conference or workshop; join a support group; or hire a veteran homeschool parent as a consultant for an hour or two. Your confidence will grow surely and steadily, as you take back personal responsibility for your children's education.

## Don't Confuse Hard Work With Drudgery

Homeschoolers — parents too — work hard at learning, often for the sheer pleasure of learning a difficult concept. Just as marathon runners suffer pain and exhaustion for the simple joy of completing the course, learners sometimes struggle valiantly to achieve their goals. Learning is often fun, and it can be very hard work. The rewards multiply if you master the challenge.

## Watch for Signs of Burnout

If you think you are facing burn out, take the time to step back and chart your course anew. If the structured curriculum you loved last fall has produced a child with dull eyes who pushes a pencil across a page without a thought, set that program aside. Use it for reference if you want, but even if you never touch the thing again, consider it a well-learned lesson for your family.

Meanwhile, use the time you have gained to rediscover the joy of learning with your children. Look at bugs and try to identify them; ooh and aah at the sights seen under a microscope or through a telescope; study fish anatomy; enjoy a read-aloud marathon; do math problems on paper napkins at dinner; make up silly poems as you ride along in the car. You will be surprised at how much they are learning.

On the other hand, if you find that your unschooling dream has become a nightmare of unfinished projects, sticky floors, and cranky children, rework your plan. Perhaps you will bring more structure into your life with a simple change, such as a regular math program, working through a reading list, publishing a newsletter, taking piano lessons, getting a pet to care for, scheduling a weekly trip to the library, doing regular household chores, or planning a fun day with friends.

More structured activities can improve life in some families, while fewer activities and better structure may be needed in others. If setting aside certain hours for particular tasks might bring peace and order to the lives of your family members, then establish a schedule and learn to stick to it.

## Finally

Evaluate regularly and change directions as needed. Your students will generally let you know if your plan is working. Are your children usually happy, busy, engaged, enthusiastic, and challenged, whether at play or at work? It's working, folks! Are they sullen, squabbling, always bored, negative, television-addicted, or combative? They might be telling you that something is amiss. Then it's time for Detective Dad or Mom to help the child find direction.

So try something new! Don't worry about disrupting the children's learning processes with a midyear change of program or curriculum. Life is full of change, and change always provides opportunities for growth and learning. They will adapt as they always do. Just keep tweaking the plan, the schedule, the style, and the materials until your students are so busily engaged learning that they forget to squabble.

When you find that the daily routine is fun and satisfying, you are there. You have found a workable homeschooling style — so relax and enjoy the ride.

## chapter seventeen

# LEARNING ACTIVITY CENTERS
*optimizing your home environment for natural learning*

Are you one of the "lucky" homeschooling families? That is, are you living in your home while it is under construction? Are you planning to remodel? Then you are lucky because you can really let the learning activities roll! Bare floors that are waiting for carpeting and tile are fine for the messiest activities. Are there walls to be ripped out? First, let your children apply the wildest murals, hand prints, and smudges, and you need only grin at their creativity. Who cares about paint spills on an underfloor or crayon on the wall studs? If you live the chaotic and dusty life of home improvement, a little more dust and mess won't matter. You may as well bring out the messiest of all possible learning activities before the new walls go in or the carpet is laid. Enjoy!

Most of us are not quite this "lucky." Most homes need maintenance. We have personal treasures to care for and personal activities besides those of homeschooling. I hope to spark some ideas of ways to use your home effectively as a learning space without turning it into a future remodeling (or demolition!) site.

Learning or activity centers can be set up in every part of the home. Every family will have a unique set of "centers" that fits the style, home setting, and individual children's needs. Have you identified the natural center of activity in your home? Large kitchens, family rooms, and living rooms are likely suspects. When you identify a space as your natural center, work with it. Improve the storage, create a work space, and be willing to adapt the room to meet the changing needs of your family. You'll have it all to yourself again in just a few years.

## Kitchen

Many homeschooling families find their life centers in the kitchen. Who knows why? Perhaps the kitchen is the ideal place to begin the nourishment of both body and mind, or maybe we just love to eat!

You may be surprised at the variety of activities you can squeeze into even the smallest kitchen. If you have a larger kitchen or a family kitchen, you might set up a child's work table and chair for drawing, coloring, or play dough. Some children love using a little washing tub or other miniature versions of kitchen activities. A reading or writing space, or the family computer, are popular options for older students.

## Dedicated Project Room

If you have a spare room, how will you use it? Don't automatically think schoolroom or you might not use the room to its best advantage. Your preconceived ideas of "schoolroom" may limit your vision of how to use the bonus room.

Think "project room" instead. Declare your spare room a project room, a space set aside for the whole family to use. Games, reading, computer, TV, music, construction sets, dress-up or doll corners, and other messy or time-consuming projects, are perfect activities to tuck away out of the main traffic path.

Drag your favorite adult projects in, too. Set up your sewing machine, a letter writing corner, your computer, your home office, a knitting corner, craft projects, or whatever you enjoy. You'll be right in the middle of things if you are needed, and you'll have something worthwhile to do when you are not needed.

Some project rooms sizzle with learning excitement. One memorable space I visited included overflowing bookshelves, a comfy couch strewn with pillows, math books and papers, a computer station, walls covered with children's art, a cupboard full of games, tables with games and puzzles in progress, an ironing board and sewing machine, an exercise bike, indoor climbing apparatus, a bunch of dolls, bedding laid out for a sleep-over, and even curtain fabric waiting to be sewn. The room was a well-used retreat for the whole family, nicely tucked away from traffic flow.

You may be able to create a project room as we did, quite inexpensively. We converted half of the garage/shop. Finally! Enough shelving for activities, games and projects! A big table dominated the space, and just like the kitchen table before it, it was always cluttered with various projects. A dress-up area, a tool area, a floppy bean bag chair, craft projects galore, a writing area — we really used that space!

---

## Messes and Clutter!  Can You Cope?

Life with children is a messy business, and learning projects may be the messiest part.  You may want "restoring order" to be a part of your daily curriculum.  Clutter can be controlled without squelching the child's need to have materials and projects available.  See if one of these ideas would work for you.

- Allow clutter and mess to accumulate for a period of time, and then have the whole family pitch in for as long as it takes to shine it up. Then choose a simple (non-messy!) treat, such as a walk to the park or a video.

- Tidy up everyday after breakfast or before dinner, everyone pitching in and doing their assigned chores.

- Schedule a moderate clean up once or twice a week, freeing some days from cleanup tasks.

- Allow messes to accumulate in certain places, such as the children's rooms, workspace, or designated project areas, but not others, such as the living or dining room.

## Laundry or Sewing Room

When you are busy in the laundry room, your young child will probably want to be there with you. Some children enjoy helping with laundry, while others just want to be near you.

Erin loved her little ironing board. Other children have enjoyed having their own washboards and tubs. Creative dramatics activities are compatible with laundry and sewing rooms. Simple sewing and stitchery projects can be worked on while you launder, sew, iron, or work on projects. Coloring, drawing, and writing may suit your space, or if your child enjoys building, set up a building block corner. Try a math exploration table where your child can measure, weigh, and count or sort beads and buttons.

## Rough Space — Garage, Basement, Shop

These spaces are perfect for large motor activities on rainy days. Riding toys, small trampolines, balls, hoops — whatever you, your budget, and the space will tolerate is fair game. Messy projects such as tie-dyeing, papier mache, clay, soap or candle making, or model building can be done anywhere, of course, but may be more relaxed in rough space if you have one.

Perhaps one parent enjoys crafts or automotive repair and has a workshop. With careful planning, your child can be safely nearby, playing or asking questions, while you saw, mold, build, sand, or solder. Buy child-sized safety equipment, such as work gloves, goggles, and ear protection. You could tape bright yellow safety lines on the floor so your child knows where the safe zone is. Get your child her own workbench, child-sized hammer, some nails and wood, and let her work nearby. So what if she ignores the tools, or prefers instead to sort her screwdrivers into little family groupings and cuddle them? Who cares if she brings out her coloring books, Cheerios, Hot Wheels, or baby dolls? What matters is the time she spends at her parent's side. She's learning more than you know.

## Outdoors

The outdoors is another important learning center. Whether you have an apartment with a deck, a nearby park, an average suburban yard, or a three hundred-acre farm, you'll want to plan regular outdoor activities. Even if you have limited access to the outdoors, get out as often as you can. Consider bringing nature into your home via terrariums, aquariums, pets, plants, rocks, sticks, and shells.

Regular contact with nature helps a child find his place in the world. How can a child study the stars and planets if he has no knowledge of sand and soil and sticks and mud? How can he appreciate the diversity of life if he hasn't watched ants, baby spiders, ladybugs, and grasshoppers? Intimate experience with wind and rain, balls and wheels, mud and sand, ramps and seesaws — your child's outdoor experiences are the essential foundation to the sciences.

## Living Room

Some families limit living room activities to quiet activities such as reading, piano practice, or quiet games. Grandma's antique secretary is safe from rambunctious activity and on display for everyone to enjoy.

If you have a small home, realize that your children may have extra energy to burn and no space to burn it in on rainy days. Consider placing some of your treasures in your bedroom or even in storage for safekeeping, particularly if your children need the living room space for indoor activity.

In our home, the living room was the center for music, such as singing, rhythm activities, piano, and recorder playing, dancing, and selected (!) gymnastic moves. Many of our two or three daily read-aloud sessions took place curled up together in big rockers, on the couch, or sprawled out on the floor. When the television overshadowed living room activities, it mysteriously broke, and we returned to our treasured learning life within days.

## Art or Music Studio

The space where you do your own creative work is important to your child's learning. You set such an important example! Bring your child into your space in ways that work for both of you.

Artists who homeschool their children easily find ways for their children to work alongside them. The principles of art, along with safety and good old "clean up after yourself" skills are well taught when parents and children work side by side.

Musicians may have scheduling challenges. It is not so easy to work on your own music while your child bangs away on his. Be

---

### Hey!  It Is Loud In Here!

Do you have noisy learners?  It is such a shame to shush the natural noisiness of enthusiastically learning children. However, if one or more family members is sensitive to noise levels, you may need to factor the noisiness into your larger plan to maintain a peaceful home and meet the needs of all.

- Consider the placement of sound-producing items of all kinds (musical instruments, radio, TV, etc.) and how will they be used.

- Schedules can help balance quiet times with noisy activities.

- Invest in quality headphones for either the noisemaker or the peace seeker.

- Is soundproofing a possibility?  One family made that choice for a [loud] musically oriented child when they remodeled.  Peace fell on the rest of the family.

---

sure to set aside time to play and explore music together. When you are working on your own music, your child may want to be with you. Lay out some reasonable guidelines and help him select quiet activities to do while you work.

## Home Office

Some home offices are fairly basic, set up in a corner of the kitchen or living room where parents use their computer, write letters, or pay bills. Other home offices are bustling businesses that take up one or more rooms and are often well-equipped with all the latest electronic gear.

Unless your home business is a dangerous one, such as sharpening knives, most hobbies and home businesses are compatible with children's learning activities. Include your child in your office when you can. Do you have a second computer that you can dedicate to children's learning software? Is this the place for that old electric typewriter or adding machine? A drawing / writing corner? Cars and blocks? Paper dolls? A toy cash register and some play money?

Teach your child various aspects of your business as she shows an interest. Even very young children can seal envelopes and apply stamps.

## Children's Rooms

How or even if you use your child's bedroom for learning activities will vary from family to family. Sometimes an older student needs a protected activity space that is safe from younger siblings. Smaller musical instruments are often played in bedrooms. Older children may enjoy working on individual projects in their bedrooms.

## Other Spaces

Do you live on a farm with a barn, a silo, or other buildings with accessible space? Do you live in a city and have access to a nearby community center, art gallery, or park? Is there a stream, a pond, or a lake nearby?

Homeschooling will help you see your environment in fresh ways. You'll find many ways to use your environment to its best learning advantage. Before long, you will discover that potential "learning centers" pop up everywhere you look.

## A Few More Hints

*Work with your space, not against it.* For example, put the art center near a water source such as laundry, bath, or kitchen. Alternatively, set the center up over a floor that is easy to clean. Perhaps you have a long range plan to replace that floor and can live with stains for now. You might lay roll plastic, vinyl tablecloths, or painting drop cloths under the art table if flooring needs protection.

*Take advantage of unique features of your home.* Do you have a bay window? What a nice reading area that could make. An oversized hall closet, a butler's pantry, an enclosed porch, or a space in an outside building can be adapted to meet your particular homeschooling needs. An infrequently used bathroom could be a darkroom, a science lab, a dressing room, or even a home for turtles. A hallway may be wide enough for a chalkboard, an art gallery, or a bookshelf. Our home featured a sliding- glass door that offered a full view of our yard, so I set up my writing area where I could keep an eye on outside activities while I worked.

*Vary the materials and projects in your centers.* The kinds of materials in my family's favorite space were mixed, according to the kinds of projects we were working on. The activities and furniture arrangement changed regularly as the kids grew and changed. About the only thing that stayed the same was the paper and craft supply (paper, paint, markers, crayons, pens, scissors, glue — that type of thing). Otherwise, the space was generally a mishmash including games of all kinds, craft projects, books, experiments-in-progress, science materials, dictionaries, an electric typewriter, a computer, pets, bulletin board, chalk board, and who knows what else.

*Keep parent and child activity centers close.* Our family kitchen was ideal when the girls were young. While preparing food or cleaning up, I was available if the girls needed me. Writing or bookkeeping projects found me at my desk or the computer table nearby. My occasional sewing projects and even my volunteer phone work centered around this area. Learning is a family activity when children are young, and they want to be with you anyway, so keep the areas close together.

Besides being practical, there is another compelling reason to work closely with your children when they are young. When students are older, they may not want or need your assistance, but you will have ample opportunity to rub shoulders with them frequently simply by the precedent of togetherness that you have set when they were younger. After all, your projects are right there beside theirs. Parents can be so sneaky!

## Finally

Remember that learning centers aren't forever. When learning seems mundane around your house, or when the kids are squabbling instead of enthusing, change the physical learning environment. As your students grow up, they outgrow a need for learning centers in the home as long as project and quiet spaces are available. And all too soon, you will have your home all to yourself.

## chapter eighteen

# A LEARNING CALENDAR
*finding the rhythm of daily living and learning*

What is a typical homeschool day? Who does what, when, and where did I leave the calendar? Am I doing enough? Am I covering the basics? Are the kids learning the *right stuff*? How can I make sure the days flow smoothly?

Do these questions echo some of *your* homeschooling anxieties? Planning ahead can relieve these fears. Even when days go very badly, you'll find reassurance by noting all you have accomplished and all that lies ahead in the plan. You will gain peace of mind when you plan ahead.

Two straightforward scheduling aids, A *Master Calendar* and a *Learning Idea List*, will help you move your ideas into action. See if these tools make your planning easier.

## The Learning Idea List

This *Learning Idea List* is exactly what you think it is — a collection of ideas and notes jotted down whenever ideas pop up. To keep the list visible and available to the entire family, try keeping your list on a sheet of butcher paper or in a handy notebook.

Anything goes on the *Learning Idea List*. You might think of your list as an ongoing brainstorming session. Include topics to study and skills to teach. Jot down: burning questions children may have asked that require research or that lead to a broader exploration; field trips to take; books to read aloud together; supplies to purchase; math concepts that need reinforcement.

Did you miss a great homeschooling field trip because your children were too young? Note the contact names and phone numbers so that you can sponsor that same trip later when your children are older. Now that is planning ahead!

Your children will give you many ideas as you listen to them play or watch them work. You can also ask them to add their own ideas whenever they think of them. They may learn to keep personal lists of their unanswered questions, an important step toward taking charge of their own learning.

You will find fantastic learning ideas everywhere once you get the hang of looking for them. Ideas can come from many sources: newspaper articles, television, books, talking with other parents, and even walking down the street can trigger a great project. Keep a notebook handy for jotting down notes when you are not at home and add them to the *Learning Idea List* later. You'll be surprised at how quickly it overflows. But later, when you are stuck for ideas the last month before the new baby is born, won't you be glad you made those notes?

You'll notice that ideas roam freely through your mind at the oddest times. For example, as you jot your son's October birthday on the list, you recall an interesting autumn greeting card, which reminds you that spatter-painting leaves is an art project you definitely want to try. Since you are a busy person, you won't want to waste these ideas! Your Idea List is a perfect catch basin for ideas to use later, any time your idea well runs dry.

Now let's look at some specific categories.

## Annual Events

Let your mind flow through your upcoming year. What is on the calendar? Think of everything from vacations and long weekend travel plans, to scheduled business or work trips, to conferences and retreats.

Will Grandma spend her usual two weeks with you in October? What kinds of activities will she enjoy with her grandchildren? Give her a call and ask for her input — maybe she'll want to take them on bird walks or speak dinner table French with your gang.

Does your extended family migrate to a warmer region and rent a condo on the beach during spring vacation? What activities will you plan in conjunction with the trip? It may be a good time to study maps, geography, sea life, and the climate of the region.

Will your family travel to a homeschooling conference or camp-out this year? (You should!) Does your support group schedule a"Not Back to School" event? Will your teen participate in a Graduation Ceremony or other rite of passage? Don't forget birthdays! You may want to allow time for preparations, such as making and addressing invitations.

## Holidays

Holidays are a terrific source of interesting curriculum ideas. What spiritual and religious events and activities does your family engage in? You may study your own belief system or include many major holidays of interest, such as Christmas, Passover, Ramadan, the New Year, or Solstice.

How will you spend Independence Day this year? Will you study and make flags? Should you delve into the Revolutionary War during June, just before the Fourth of July? What other kinds of patriotic ideas are important in your family? Where were your ancestors at the time of the Revolution? Will you trace the history and science of fireworks this year?

Think of the learning opportunities you have in various holiday-related social gatherings then plan your holiday with the whole family. Holiday programs and presentations provide a chance for music, poetry, drama, making decorations or programs — learning opportunities abound. Cookie exchanges offer baking experiences. Is this the year you plan to visit nursing homes for the holidays? Will you serve holiday meals to the homeless? Your children learn many skills through the preparations, hustle and bustle, celebration, and projects you participate in as a family.

## Scheduled Activities

Most families have plenty of scheduled activities. Include scheduled classes and activities such as piano, art, foreign language, gymnastics, softball, dance, soccer, and swimming. Any regular activity should be mined as a rich source of learning ideas.

Don't forget to include medical and dental appointments. A study of parts of the body, health, nutrition, or personal hygiene is a natural offshoot.

Does your homeschool support group offer a regular Friday field trip? If so, why not designate Friday, or alternate Fridays, as your family field trip day? Then you can either take advantage of the trip offered by the group or schedule your own Friday adventure.

Your support group is a rich source of activities, including Learning Clubs, Homeschool Park Days, Roller Skating Days, and similar events. Erin came to depend on Roller Skating Monday as an important time for physical exercise and social contact. Park time, a field trip, a play date, or overnight with a friend often followed skating — we always knew our plans for those Mondays.

Do keep an eye open for events that lend themselves to piggybacking. Your Boy Scout's annual camping trip may be a perfect time to schedule swim lessons for little sister, for example. Another strategy is to try to schedule dance or fencing classes for two kids at the same time and location.

## Family Life Events

Although it may distract from your plan, real life brings the best learning of all. Think about large singular events, such as marriage of a close relative or the birth of a baby. Your child's understanding of the world expands so much when you use once-in-a-lifetime events as curriculum springboards.

Are you or a close relative expecting a new baby? Carry bags of sugar around the house to simulate a baby's weight. Study life and biology.

Is your favorite cousin getting married soon? Find books about marriage and courtship in other cultures and times. Explore the origins of marriage customs. Design wedding gowns. Plan imaginary honeymoon trips and calculate expenses.

Some singular events are unscheduled. If the family is suddenly plunged in crisis, skip the fraction lesson. Focus instead on the nature of the event itself. Is a loved one hospitalized? Learning about anatomy, health, hospital care, microscopic life, and medical careers might be a good fit for your family. Other unscheduled events merit a change of plan as well. Did Uncle Louie just fly in from Tanzania? Focus your learning activities on Uncle's stories, gifts, and artifacts.

The schedule is disrupted anyway, so take advantage of the disruption for related learning.

## Academic Goals

Yes, there really is time in your schedule for academic work. Luckily, your family is probably so busy learning through life that you won't need to set huge amounts of time aside. Some families feel that if the children read, write, and do math every day they are generally on target with their academic goals. Others find that their students thrive when they dive into one academic topic at a time, sometimes for weeks on end. No matter what works for your family, make sure there are regular at-home times available for intellectual work.

Some other academic concerns: Are you part of a learning club that addresses some of your academic goals? Do you need to schedule time for library visits? If your children take annual tests, will you need to set aside some review time? Will your teenager be taking a college entrance exam, such as PSAT, SAT, or ACT? Will she want to visit prospective campuses? Will he need to complete portfolios, essays, or other academic work for consideration at his first choice college or university? What kind of help or support will she need, if any? Even if your teen is very self-sufficient, she may need to borrow your car, so be sure to note these events.

By now, your *Learning Idea List* is probably burgeoning with good ideas, ideas that have already spilled onto your calendar. Now you are ready to create a useful learning plan without feeling you've created an ironclad curriculum that may limit life learning.

## The Master Calendar

Let's turn to the calendar. Use any twelve-month calendar that suits your style. I like one with plenty of space for jotting notes. Some families post wall calendars in a hallway, kitchen, or near the door, bringing the family schedule to everyone's eye level. You might use a purchased daily planner system, a PDA, or a notebook. A free calendar from a local retailer may work well. Some folks like made-for-homeschooling planners. I have used yellow legal pads, a stenographer's notebook, a daily planner, recycled office stationery, backs of envelopes, and our chalkboard. One year I used a giant ink-blotter type desk calendar. For a time, I adapted an old teacher's plan book.

Will you start your calendar in January or in September at the beginning of the traditional school year? Why not start it today? No matter when you plan to begin, start by filling in the annual events, holidays, and scheduled activities from your Idea List. Don't forget to block out time, if needed, before and after the event for related activities.

## Weekly and Daily Planning

With your *Master Calendar* and *Learning Idea List* before you, you probably realize that much of the year is already planned. All that is left is to organize your daily and weekly activities. I'll tell you right now that many people are perfectly comfortable with the annual calendar alone. Daily and weekly events, even long-term plans, are sketched in, and the details are carried in their minds. Personally, I tried it both ways — "in the mind" plans and plans on paper. I often felt more confident when I planned our activities by the week in more detail. I missed fewer appointments too! Even when I didn't plan ahead, I tried to jot down what happened anyway, after the fact. In the end, it comes down to doing whatever you are comfortable with, while adhering to any record keeping requirements your state may place on you. Many people start with a written plan and work from there. Some people plan the night before, while others may plan in greater detail for a week or so at a time. Some plan on-the-fly with great success.

I usually did my planning at the breakfast table or over coffee while the kids did their morning chores. My children often made their own daily schedules while I did mine. Some children print out their daily schedules on their computers. They all learn the value of writing things down and of planning ahead.

When you have sketched out all the regular events you can think of, fill in the at-home details. If there are more than a few monthly and bimonthly activities, you may want to sketch out the full month ahead of you.

Working a week or so in advance allows time to gather needed materials. If you use a structured or packaged curriculum, schedule the most important work — the basics — first, and skip the study items that your child is learning through daily living. If it appears that every week has a similar structure, just sketch out one week in detail, and fill in the other details only when the schedule varies.

Remember to drag out your *Master Calendar* and *Learning Idea List* for stimulating reading on those days when you feel discouraged. A written daily plan builds confidence in the home-schooling process, even on the toughest days.

## Review, Revise, and Re-prioritize

Do you have a balanced schedule? You'll want to provide a pace that allows each child the amount of time he needs — time to explore ideas his own way, time for reflection and reminiscence, and time for asking those burning questions. To accomplish that balance, ask yourself questions such as these.

Is every family member represented? Is there a balance of social, sport, artistic, academic, and other endeavors? Did you forget a detail such as math or soccer? Does your family athlete have a competitive season that dominates the schedule? If one child has a

---

### A Sample Schedule at Our Home

BBW (family code for Brush hair, Brush teeth, Wash face and hands)
Feed and Pet cats (private time is included in this chore)
Play piano
Read
Write to Grandma
Piano teacher comes at 11:00
Lunch, then read with Mom
Play "Laura and Mary" with friends
Jump on the trampoline
Gymnastics
Dinner (and dinner napkin math with Dad)
Play piano
Bath, stories, bed

particularly hectic schedule, can you still meet the needs of the rest of the family? Is any child under-scheduled? If you have little ones, how much car time can they tolerate while you cart older siblings around? How much car time can *the driver* tolerate?

Over-scheduling — even the very best activities — can stress the entire family. Paring down can be a challenge if you have scheduled too much. Some families have handled this problem and have gained an exquisite home peace by reducing or eliminating television from the home. Limits can be set on other entertainment, including computer games, movies, social time. Housework can be stream-lined. Activities can be cut back.

Students who want or need a busy schedule might contribute to the functioning of the household in some other way. For example, a teen who needs to be driven to soccer practice every day can help out with chores such as cooking, cleaning, or reading to a younger child.

Under-scheduling may result in bored students with too little to occupy their time. One single working mom neatly sidestepped that danger by requiring each of her teens to participate in exactly two outside activities, not more and not less. Two activities each week still allowed enough family and individual time with her children. She had assurance that they were involved and busy in activities, and the schedule remained manageable. Her reasoning was a sound compromise: better to have a mom who is busy but not totally exhausted, than have to worry about two children who were sitting around bored while she was away at work.

## Planning Tips

- *Think of summer vacation as a model.* Some days are jammed with activities and some are lazy days spent at home. Trips, camps, reading days, swimming — there are many ways to learn any time of the year.

- *Become a Multitasking Momma or a Double Duty Daddy.* Seek ways to overlap tasks. Catch up on personal reading, pay bills, or make shopping lists while children are busy.

- *Allow for the individual styles of family members.* If one child is a lark and the other is an owl, you may need a different plan from your neighbor's family who are all up and going at the crack of day. If your family functions best on swing shift, embrace it — don't fight it. Adapt your schedule to meet idiosyncratic needs of students and parents.

- *Allow enough play time, free choice, down time — whatever you call it — every day.* Open-ended times for privacy, play, and conversation are the fertile grounds where the seeds of understanding germinate, interests grow, and creativity blossoms. Big ideas need time to simmer.

- *Allow time between activities.* Making a transition from one activity to another can be trying for young children when they are engrossed. We all need time to change focus.

- *Be prepared to abandon the plan.* When the schedule runs you ragged, the telephone rings all day, pots boil over, and dogs get sick, remind yourself to stop and focus on finding the greatest value for your family. I'm betting that on some days, being a sane parent is a better bargain than trying to help your child master long division. Long division can wait for tomorrow!

- *It doesn't matter, really, who does what when.* Math at dinner! Literature at midnight! Piano before breakfast! Our family had many late night learning sessions. Our unusual schedule hasn't affected either daughter's adult ability to get herself to appointments, classes, or to work.

## Finally

*Every homeschool day is unique.* You will find the rhythm and flow that move through each day. Your daily routines lend a basic structure around which you create the rest of the day. Always be ready to cast the schedule to the wind when something wondrous is happening. An unusual bug, a sudden hailstorm, the birth of kittens, the best game of *Monopoly* ever played: what is the best learning opportunity for your children this very day?

## Selected Resources
*if you feel a need for additional structure, try these resources*

### Homeschool Organizers
590-B Schillinger Rd. S., #104, Mobile, AL 36695      866/243.8476
www.homeschoolorganizer.com/  hso@homeschoolorganizer.com
Organize your homeschooling records with a handy notebook system.

### Homeschool Solutions
J&M Creations, PO Box 709, Minier, IL 61759
www.homeschoolsolutions.com  help@homeschoolsolutions.com
Software to help you organize your homeschooling records. Windows.

### Keepers At Home
Kunker Hill Publications, 8796 Kunker Road, Morrow, OH 45152
www.home.earthlink.net/~cmautry/keepers
A practical home organizer for the Christian homeschooling mom for all
aspects of home life from homeschooling to medical records to meal
planning. The three-ring notebook format makes it easy to toss the parts you
don't need.

## chapter nineteen

# AGAINST THE FLOW

*handling criticism of your decision to homeschool*

We often teach best by not teaching at all, but by setting a clear example. Dealing with personal challenges gives us an extraordinary opportunity to set an example for our youngsters. One such challenge is being seen as different by our own peers for choosing a homeschooling life. Is it possible to deal with this challenge effectively, set a strong example for our children, and still make a difference in the community? Yes, with a bit of effort and planning, you can gracefully handle the criticism of peers, family, and neighbors — even turn them into supporters — when you choose the less-traveled path of homeschooling.

## The Problem

Many times family and friends do not approve of your choice to homeschool. Sometimes they feel abandoned. They may think you have gone wack-o! Some may strongly criticize your choice, even to your children.

An attack on your decision to homeschool can come without warning, possibly from an individual you had considered an ally. The event itself can be emotionally charged, and can create stress or uncertainty. If you plan now for the possibility of criticism or personal attack, you are better prepared to handle it with grace. Homeschooling parents can use the incident to demonstrate the strength of their convictions to their children and show them how mature people handle problems. Granted, this may not be an easy task.

How can a family defend its choice to learn together at home, representing it as a serious and carefully considered decision, without inviting a further barrage of criticism? When the decision to homeschool is under attack, how can parents best use the moment to educate their critics? And ultimately, can our critics be turned into allies?

## Three Assumptions

To effectively respond to criticism, it helps to have our own little ducklings in a row. Make these three assumptions about the criticism and you will be far better able to speak both effectively and respectfully when attacked for your decision to homeschool.

*Assume that the people who criticize have the best interests of your children in mind.* You will generate more respect for your position by setting a tone of respect for others' ideas and opinions.

Often, critics of homeschooling don't feel qualified to teach their own children. They may easily project that perceived lack onto you and other homeschooling families. Thus, your critic may sincerely question whether you are qualified to teach your children based on *their* lacks rather than any lack they find in you.

Critics are often uneasy with the unfamiliar territory of homeschooling. They may have a vague anxiety that the children will somehow suffer an unknown and irreparable harm. Frequently they support their criticism with popular media-generated myths about homeschooling. Or they may be caught up in the pervasive intergenerational perpetuation of misinformation: classroom schooling was good enough for me and mine, so it's good enough for you and yours.

Second, you can *assume that your decision to homeschool is thought of as snobbish or elitist by some.* You may be perceived as judging other people's decisions to send their children to school. People who criticize homeschooling may feel they must defend their personal beliefs about education and schooling. They may be influenced by a pervasive and unfair myth that homeschooling undermines traditional schooling.

Third, *assume that most people see "education" and "classroom schooling" as the same thing.* The decision to keep your children out of school may be viewed, perhaps unconsciously, as a decision to deprive your children of some aspect of education or socialization. Homeschoolers therefore bear an added challenge — a challenge to educate the community that homeschooling is a reasonable alternative to public or private schooling. When they accept the challenge, homeschooling parents try to convince doubters, one at a time, that the option to homeschool is not just acceptable, it is an absolutely essential member of the broad spectrum of educational options that meet the diverse needs of children and families.

## Respond Calmly to Criticism

How, then, can you effectively communicate the strength of your decision and even begin to transform your critics into your staunch allies? Rather than arguing or debating the pros and cons of homeschooling, the best approach is, what else? Gently educate them about homeschooling.

You have a philosophy of learning that is uniquely yours. Share it! Let people know that you know what you are doing and why. Help them realize that you did not arrive at your decision to homeschool lightly.

The following points have proven helpful.

- While anyone *can* homeschool, not everyone will or should choose to homeschool. Not everyone can make that kind of commitment, nor will everyone who tries homeschooling find a successful stride. No one needs to feel guilty about choosing to send their children to classroom schools for their education.

- Speak of what you want for your children, not what you are avoiding. Almost everyone can agree that one-on-one instruction is a good thing. You can praise the advantages of one-on-one instruction, your enjoyment of the homeschool lifestyle, flexible scheduling, and so on without condemning anyone else's choices. Don't complain about public classrooms — crowding, competitiveness, program, whatever bugs you about classroom education — because these complaints may condemn the critic's choice. Taking the time to re-frame your position in terms of what you want for your child is well worth the effort.

- Speak of the personal rewards you gain from homeschooling your children. "I homeschool my children because I love to spend time with them." "I have always wanted to study science, and here is my chance!" Such comments can generate, if not acceptance or even envy, at least a resigned sigh, "Oh, well, to each his own."

- Present a positive image in the community. You don't have to go on television or send news releases to the local paper every month to show the world how great homeschooling is for your family. Simple daily interaction in the community speaks louder for most of us anyway. When shopping with the kids at 10:00 Monday morning, chat with the clerks about today's cooking project, field trip, or whatever, before they even get a chance to ask why the kids aren't in school today. If they do ask, answer, "My children learn at home, and we enjoy a flexible schedule."

- Remind your critics that homeschooling saves taxpayer dollars. The math is easy. If one million students are homeschooled every year, and one uses a modest annual per child cost, such as $5,000 ($10,000 in some regions) for public education, significant tax dollars are saved every year. School officials have in fact already adapted to the loss of those students. And no matter how much they complain and wring their hands over the homeschooling trend, school personnel shudder — they should, at least — at the thought of every homeschooled child suddenly showing up at the local school on the first day of school. Home-schooling is now a permanent part of the educational landscape.

- Be respectful of the rights of others whose opinions are different from yours. Isn't that what we want for ourselves? Homeschoolers want the right to choose their own way, without being judged, condemned, or discriminated against. Sometimes the best we can hope for is to agree to disagree.

- Avoid complaining. Save your worries, fears, and complaints about homeschooling for support group meetings. Most critics consider complaints as a sign that homeschooling does not work. Perhaps, they think, you want to be talked out of this nonsense, or why would you complain to them? Their hidden fears that you may ruin your children seem validated when you complain. Your casual complaint about a minor frustration invites an extra measure of criticism.

- Avoid argument. Listen to opposing opinion thoughtfully. Many critics of homeschooling firmly believe that the positive aspects of school socialization outweigh the negative aspects. When you have listened respectfully, you can comment that you can see where they are coming from. Then share where you are coming from. Talk about your children's friendships, their group activities through church, com-munity, homeschool groups, Scouts, or 4-H. Clarify that you have given social issues a great deal of thought. Respond to a store clerk's concern, "But what about socialization?" by simply saying, "I agree, learning social skills is very important. Homeschoolers work hard to make sure that our children have social experiences."

## Finally

If you speak kindly and respectfully to those who criticize you; become proactive when needed, choose your confidants carefully, listen to criticism respectfully, and share yourself with others by talking of the benefits of your commitment. If you do all these things, you do much more than handle criticism. You educate your children in the skills of standing strong against the odds.

The role model is a powerful force: If you handle criticism gracefully and respectfully when your children are with you, you demonstrate a groundwork of tactics your children can use later as they pursue their dreams.

## chapter twenty

# JOYFUL DISRUPTION
*guiding with kindness and gentle humor*

Ah, family togetherness. Togetherness brings with it the realization that children have needs — day and night — and those needs often interrupt parents' lives. While some interruptions will tickle you, others will frustrate you. The causes are endless: a hurting tummy, boredom, a burning question, loneliness. Parents soon learn to accept the many interruptions as part of the parenthood package.

Some interruptions are absolutely delightful — bubbling invitations to joyful celebration. What parent won't drop everything to celebrate when their child comes tearing into the kitchen screaming, "Daddy! Mommy! I can read! I can read!" The moment is captivating and contagious. We happily lay down our preoccupations and celebrate with our child.

Why not take a lesson from these spontaneous celebrations? The hint is broad if we catch the drift: We love to celebrate the small moments of life spontaneously, joyously, immediately. Joyful interruptions are practically irresistible, aren't they? While there is an obvious lesson for parents in this fact — make sure you enjoy the daily moments with your children — we'll find some other ways parents use interruptions to ease their load. We'll come back to joyful interruptions in a minute.

You and I know that sometimes, family togetherness is just plain frustrating. How do you balance it all: learning activities, discipline, meals, friends, communication, and guidance of children toward responsible use of freedom, not to mention maintaining your own equilibrium?

"Pick your battles," advice most parents are given, is a helpful strategy that successful homeschooling parents really do heed. It just makes good sense to work on one skill or behavior at a time.

But for all the wisdom of that sage advice, don't you *really* want to know what to do about some of the battles you *don't* pick? Don't you sometimes need to derail a behavior for safety or sanity (yours, if not your child's) reasons? Don't you really need a few workable strategies at your fingertips?

Enter joyful disruptions.

## The Liberating World of Joyful Disruption[2]

A few paragraphs back, I left you savoring the thought, "Joyful interruptions are practically irresistible." Here is why.

If you — a mature adult — are delighted to drop everything you are doing when your child interrupts your routine with a joyful celebration, just think how powerful an effect you have on your child when you choose to interrupt *her* (possibly annoying) activities with a joyful activity that you choose. Remember how the tears turned into giggles when you picked up your upset toddler and laughed and giggled with her?

A joyful disruption is a powerful way to redirect energy or activity that is undesirable, but for whatever reason, is not a battle you want to pick today. It is so powerful, in fact, that you may find it is a strategy you will want to choose frequently. Often, these are the moments when Mom's or Dad's creativity kicks in and delightful family activities are spontaneously initiated.

No one will remember the day everyone bickered and all were in tears before breakfast over who-knows-what and even the oatmeal was lumpy. But won't everyone smile at the memory of a candlelight breakfast of lumpy oatmeal served under the table?

---

[2]   My husband Don coined the term "joyful disruptions" and has taught this concept to hundreds of parents. His contributions to this chapter are deeply appreciated.

All you need to do is take the "tears-to-giggles" strategy you used with your infant and adapt it to your child's current age and the issues at hand. The natural skill you have in delighting your child can redirect your child's behavior in a fun and delightful way. No matter what behavior guidance system you use, having a few joyful disruptions at the ready gives you one more strategy for the days that, more than anything, you want to send yourself to your room.

Let's take a look at some ways successful parents have used this technique. Would these ideas work for your family?

## When to "Joyfully Disrupt" Misbehavior

You might try to use joyful disruptions when you know a behavior needs to stop and you are personally exasperated, days when you are desperate for a break. Rather than yelling or scolding, you turn your attention to finding a way to derail the negativity by doing something joyfully outrageous or completely off the wall.

Another effective use for joyful disruption is to deliberately and gently move your child forward and help him learn. For example, if your child has fallen into the habit of an annoying repetitive behavior (i.e., whining, pestering, nonstop talking, bugging siblings) it may be that he needs something but does not know what that thing is or perhaps he doesn't know how to ask for it. Perhaps she is bored or needs some alone time with you. You know that, in time, your child will outgrow the need for all that attention, or he will discover enough interests to keep him satisfied. Meanwhile, a joyful disruption can help you attend to the child's need without reinforcing the annoying behavior.

You might also use a joyful disruption purposefully when your child bombs out while learning a skill or concept. By using a joyful disruption, you can help her sidestep feeling stupid or ashamed. We all feel uncomfortable when we are wrong. Teaching your children tricks that help them laugh when egg drips from their chins helps them learn the graceful art of saving face.

Once you get the idea firmly planted in your mind that joyful disruption is a sound child rearing practice, you may be amazed at how easily you manage to develop ideas that suit you and your family. Meanwhile, here are a few goofy ploys to tuck in your hip pocket for those days when you can't put your finger on quite what is needed.

# How to Joyfully Disrupt

## Disruptions to Try with Young Children

- Be ridiculous or unpredictable; tuck a small child who is whiny and clingy and needing attention into the bib of your overalls while you finish your tasks; pause often to tickle and tease him while he giggles.

- Trap your child with your legs while you finish your phone calls. Tickle her with your feet.

- Haul your child around with you by your ankle. Just tell him to hop on your foot and go for a ride. Is your child too big? Have him "hook up" to your belt loop, and follow you around while you do your tasks. The child's task? Hang on. Your task? Talk wildly about the amazing growth on your foot or back that makes you limp so terribly, how you'll probably need surgery, and alas! the pain and suffering. Then brace yourself for giggle fits.

- Puff out your chest and sing in an off-key operatic voice: "I told you, I told you, I to-o-o-old you, not to tease the cat," picking up your child, marching, and singing together, adding verses and silly refrains.

## Joyfully Disrupt Academic Errors

Yes, you can be ridiculous while working on academics. Silliness can ease the struggle to understand tough concepts for many youngsters.

Suppose your child is in the early stages of learning fractions. He comes up to you beaming with satisfaction. He has done an entire page of problems without even being told how to work them. And every single problem, you notice, is wrong. Suppose he made a common beginner's error, adding numerators to numerators and denominators to denominators, with this result: $\frac{1}{2} + \frac{1}{2} = 2/4$. He has given you a key piece of information about where he is in his understanding of fractions and wholes. You might simply hand the paper back and say, "Can you figure out what you did wrong?" Or you could smile absent-mindedly and pretend that you didn't notice that the problems were wrong, knowing he'll catch on when you review next month. Or you may decide you have some re-teaching to do.

Or, you can use a joyful disruption. By doing so, you can playfully help him learn, let him down gently, and minimize frustration, feeling stupid, or being embarrassed.

Try something like this. "Very cool. You are doing Slimegonian fractions. In Slimegonia, they have a rule of adding denominators and numerators just like you did. Guess what else? Kids grow up ve-e-e-ry slowly in Slimegonia. They grow for ½ year, and then for another ½ year, and they are still only ½ year older, just like in your problem!"

If he hasn't figured out what you are getting at yet, create some more nonsense with another example. "Oh, yeah, and in Slimegonia, it is impossible to double a recipe! All Slimegonian math is done in fractions, you see, so even if they needed two cups of something, it would say 8/8 + 8/8, and guess what the answer would be?"

At whatever point your child tires of silliness or begins to see the light, move to Earth math. If he still doesn't get it, drop it and come back to the concept later.

## Create an Alter-Ego

An alter-ego character can convey messages for you in the battles you *don't* pick. Some people have a talking belly button. I once had a talking finger. Others have discovered an invisible puppy following them everywhere they go. You might create a character using a sock puppet or a favorite stuffed animal. Give your character a unique voice, an accent, whatever it takes to get your children laughing.

Have conversations with the character you've created. Young children will be engaged immediately. Keep your character talking foolishness and nonsense, and save moral or behavior lessons for another time. If your child is entranced by your alter-ego character, you might use it from time to time to encourage your child during tough academic tasks. Sometimes it is easier to learn math from a talking belly button than from dad.

## Push Into Faulty Assumptions

What do you do when your child tells you the moon is made of green cheese? Instead of saying, "No, you are wrong," try pushing into his statement. By pushing into the problem, I mean moving into the error and exploring it, encouraging the child to explore his thinking with you. Ask him to expand on the idea, tell you more, look it up, draw pictures for you, and so on. Pushing into a problem this way, when your child has shown a thinking, careless, or factual error, can keep your child on track to develop critical thinking ability.

We chuckle when our children put "logical" arguments together before the age of reason has dawned. When my daughter wanted to make mustard by blending canned corn and cottage cheese, I missed a golden learning opportunity to push into her assumption — to let her to learn a new piece of information in her own way. "Really?"I could have said, "Let's try it." I could have let her mix up a small batch, and let her taste for herself. If we were short on ingredients, shopping with her would have added depth to the learning experience. It wouldn't have mattered how it turned out. The powerful process of exploring one's own hypothesis would have been well introduced.

## Explore Literalism

Sometimes children are entranced by the literal meaning of words. Take advantage of that interest to disrupt a chatterbox. When your inner voice wants to say, "Put a sock in it," tell your child to find something to put an old sock in. When you squelch the urge to tell her to shut up, ask her to go through the house and close everything she can find that can be closed. Do you want to say, "Butt out?" Ask everyone to walk around with their rears out for a morning.

## Upside Down Day

With a grand flourish, and in silence, take the flowers and tablecloth off the table, and have the kids help you turn the table upside down. Dramatically place the tablecloth — upside down, of course — on the upturned table. When you have everyone's full attention, stuff the flowers into the vase blossoms first, stems to the ceiling, and place the vase on the upturned table. Announce, dramatically, that today is Upside Down Day. Soon you will be serving them an upside down lunch. Meanwhile they are to find five things to do that are upside down or backwards. After lunch, share everyone's five discoveries. (Sample lunch: upside down plates. Inside out sandwiches of lettuce leaves spread with mayo, stuffed with cheese, pickles, tomato, and wedges of toasted bread. Upside down ice cream cone in a bowl.)

## 10- or 100-Mile Drive

Everyone gets in the car and each takes a turn giving the driver directions until you have driven for a predetermined distance. Stop at the nearest play area.

## Precision Game

By giving your pestering child a precision task, you allow him to redirect his energy into a problem-solving task. Examples: setting all chairs in the home at forty-five degree angles; ranking all books on a shelf by size or height; creating a meal of all square food or green food or rainbow food; creating a meal in which all of the foods are precisely measured or weighed; arranging knickknacks on a shelf for the greatest symmetry.

## More Ideas for Desperation Days

Have a water fight or a snowball fight. Watch a favorite movie together. Play games. Read mysteries. Any activity that breaks up a negative pattern and reinforces a desirable pattern will do, as long as you do them together. These kinds of activities are fun anytime, but be sure to use them on desperation days when nothing else works. Try these or invent your own.

## Opening Doors for Teens

Teenagers can be disrupted with joy as well, but don't think you can get away with the same foolishness that charmed them last year! Oh, the occasional teen still responds with a giggle when given a head-ful of noogies, but most young adults respond better to a polished approach.

When teens are stuck in a negative behavior that you have not seen since they were two, you know that cajoling, lecturing, or nagging is a waste of breath. Now parents must tailor disruptions to the teen's developing personality. By responding to their per- sonalities, you acknowledge that they are indeed growing up and that you can relate to them as budding adults.

Yes, Dad, you can, but first you will have to discover what your teen cannot resist, in the same way that you know your infant cannot resist belly blows and giggles. You will need to peek into the future, the future in which you trust and respect her as an equal, a future in which he is no longer a child.

Has your teen developed a habit of obnoxious complaining about how hard life is for teenagers? Next time he starts it up, instead of launching into Lecture 101 — the one that begins, "When I was your age," — put your lips together and press, hard. Lips sealed, retire to another room to plot and plan. What can you do or say to show your teen that there are other things to think about besides the miseries of teen life?

Regardless of the type of negative behavior your teen displays, a useful strategy is to focus as much as possible on the good side of growing up and show him the way to get there. At this stage, much of your power as his parent lies in your ability to open doors for him. Choose a moment when he is not showing attitude — perhaps during dinner when his mouth is full of pizza.

Does he have a hobby? Give him an unexpected gift that takes him to an adult level of the hobby — a tool, a book, a magazine, or tickets to a hobby show.

Some gifts can focus attention on your teen's looming independence. Tools, car stuff, china or crystal, small appliances, and other household goods, all tell your teen that you know she is growing up and that you too are planning for her independence. When I gave my sixteen-year-old a beautiful bowl — not long after an independence tirade — I found that the tirades began to fade. She was not quite ready for me to be ready for her to become independent!

Consider a gift that fits the personality and sends a message. Is he a practical joker? Toss him some fake vomit the next time he tosses you a tirade. Is she fascinated with romance? Send her flowers with a note or poem about how quickly she is growing into a woman.

Another tactic is to push your student into more activities that require trustworthiness and responsibility. A gift of a driver's manual says that one day you expect her to learn to drive. An independent bank account is a must if you have not already taught him banking. Household chores — include all the shopping, meal planning and preparation, errands, and home maintenance projects — tell your teen that you appreciate his growing independence and the responsibility and freedom that goes with it.

Schedule adult outings with your teen. Consider a car show, bridal show, college fair, job fair, dinner, theater, concerts, or a sports event. Obviously, you will select activities that your teen would love. Chatter away as you create a base for your future life as two adults who enjoy one another.

## When You Are Stuck...

It is so easy to fall into old and familiar patterns — don't abandon joyful disruptions just because you've run out of ideas or because it isn't working as you hoped it would. Here are a couple of tips to help you move through typical rough patches.

First, check to see if you are feeding into the problem in some way. I bought into the whining game, for example. My child whined, I said no, she whined and cajoled, and eventually I gave in. And round we went again, equal partners in the annoying behavior that can easily spiral out of control.

The direct route out of a whining game is to say what you mean and mean what you say the first time, and ignore all else. That is a brutally hard tactic for some parents. Joyful disruptions are a gentler approach to derailing the whining habit, especially if you catch the habit before it is entrenched. You still say what you mean and mean what you say, but with a lighter touch. Use silliness or some other joyful disruption to give attention without caving to the demand of the whine. Your child will catch on, too — whining isn't very satisfying when the true need for attention has been met.

Second, make sure you use *pseudo-disruptions* only for desperation days. Pseudo-disruptions — TV, computer time, "go to your room," chores, homework, or hiding out in books — appear to work because the negative behavior ceases for the moment. And as I said, that is fine for an occasional desperation day.

However, pseudo-disruptions do not help your child deal with the issue, nor do they connect parent and child in a satisfying exchange. A true joyful disruption will keep parent and child interacting until the child decides to scoot off to play or work on his own projects, his emotional bucket brimming.

## Finally

Joyful disruptions are a satisfying and creative way to help children learn social and academic lessons, and the results can be astounding. Children learn without feeling wrong or ashamed. In addition to helping children learn and making life easier for parents, joyful disruptions also bring a precious side benefit: zany activities often make the most satisfying memories for all.

## chapter twenty-one

# A SURPLUS OF ATTENTION

*living with children who resist change*

Do any of these phrases describe your child? Focuses intensely; always busy; expresses passion about his interests; immerses easily in personal projects; shows amazing "stick-to-it-iveness" at favorite activities; craves knowledge; doggedly seeks answers to his questions.

If those describe your child, consider whether any of the following further expand the portrait. Resistant to change; emotionally oversensitive; stubborn; single-minded; unrealistic expectations; relentlessly focused on his interests, but not yours; volatile when interrupted.

If these descriptions fit your child, congratulations! You just might have a child with attention surplus!

And yes, I mean *attention surplus*, not *attention deficit*. But hold that thought for a minute because there is a connection. By the term *attention surplus*, I mean an unusual ability and desire to focus intensely on his interests. Not surprisingly, that intense ability to focus has a consequential side effect that can make such a child challenging to live with. He may have difficulty responding appropriately to interruptions both small and large, changes of routine, and any agenda other than his own.

If your child has been labeled attention deficit, he might instead have a *surplus of attention*, not a deficit or disability at all. The side effects of attention surplus — including extreme change resistance — may be identical to the behavior patterns that point to attention deficit disorder or attention deficit hyperactive disorder.

*Attention surplus* is NOT a learning disability. In fact, attention surplus is usually a gift, particularly when the child learns to manage her unique abilities.

Gifted or not, life with a child with *attention surplus* may upset the applecart of family life. In this chapter, we'll talk first of some of the ways children cope with excess attentiveness. If you know what to watch for, you can tune in to your child better. Next we'll cover a few strategies parents can use to make life with a child with *attention surplus* a joy while helping the student learn to use her unique gift.

## How Kids Cope With a Surplus of Attention

When your child is so overwhelmed that she cannot balance her personal interests and the demands of the world around her, she resists change in any way she can. Sometimes she dawdles, gives up, or withdraws. Some students may flit from activity to activity, unable to settle down.

Some of the coping strategies students develop are useful, even fulfilling, while others are detrimental. Here are a few examples.

### Multitasking

Some children are able to pay attention to many things at one time. If your child learns to attend to all her interests effectively and appropriately, she is well on her way to developing strong multitasking skills. Perhaps she can watch television, play cards with a friend, effectively keep an eye on a younger sibling, pet the cat, snack on popcorn, while in the back of her mind she is planning her next art project. This child has taken all that ability to focus — her surplus attention — and organized it. Now she can take advantage of many opportunities while staying in control of her life.

A child who creates a system of multitasking manages her surplus of attention in perhaps the most positive and useful way. Parents who have not had successful multitasking experiences themselves may wonder whether the child can really do all those things at once. Let her try it — you might discover the skill for yourself! Just remember that the ability to multitask is a highly desirable skill and she is developing it at an early age.

## The Motion Kid

This student beats an overly stimulating schedule to the punch. He avoids focusing his attention on anything for very long so that he is always ready to move on when the schedule changes. He avoids the anxiety of unpredictable change by maintaining his own pattern of steady change. He stays physically active, moving often from one activity to the next, always on the go. When the schedule changes, he is ready to roll because he is already rolling. The habit of maintaining long and deep focus diminishes and becomes hard to recapture.

While he is in apparent control from within, he has not learned to multitask in a way that works in a social environment. The student may have difficulty organizing his activities effectively or even staying with a task that actually interests him. Maintaining constant activity is exhausting and he may lose control as he tires. He often seems out of control to his companions, instigating frequent negative interactions and negative discipline.

## Deep Engrossment

Some children, when faced with a conflict between their own interests and outside demands, turn inward. Such a child develops the ability to limit her spontaneous and enthusiastic response to stimulation. Instead of pursuing all of her interests and desires, she abandons most of them. She focuses instead on mental activity such as daydreams or fantasy. Her intense focus shuts out the rest of the world. In the end, though, she may develop one interest or skill to a high degree.

## Withdrawal – Extreme Boredom or Underachievement

This student withdraws his attentions from the positive and focuses on the negative. He may consciously decide that the demands on his life are stupid or meaningless. In a classroom setting, this usually bright student may function right at the edge of acceptability — the bare minimum. He may take pride in not turning in a lick of homework but always acing tests, for example. As he gets older, he may view himself as "bad," take pride in his "badness," and seek a social group of similar characters. He usually develops an attitude designed to repel adult approval. Still, he remains highly focused and even advanced in his areas of interest.

Homeschooled students who withdraw rarely get very far before their parents find a way to disrupt the downward slide. I suspect that many parents notice the clues of withdrawal and underachievement in the earliest stages. Perhaps the tutorial atmosphere of home-schooling gives the student attention that he craves so he never even considers withdrawing.

## Procrastination and Dawdling

Does your child put everything off to the last minute, or drag his feet when faced with new circumstances? He may not be resisting the activities as much as he is resisting the method of transition. Perhaps he needs a narrower set of activities to be able to focus his attention. Delaying tactics might be a below-the-radar precursor to withdrawal and underachievement.

# Helping Your Child Adapt to Change

Your student may always want to focus intensely on his personal interests, and change may always be a challenge. Luckily, you can work effectively on both since you are learning together at home. You can help your child develop his attention surplus as a wonderful personal asset and at the same time reduce the elevated family stress level of life with this intense kid.

## Reduce the Number of Activities

If your child needs many hours to complete a project to satisfaction, try scheduling longer blocks of time. That way, you can respect his need to follow his interests and reduce the number of interruptions. You will still have plenty of time to spend with him on other topics.

Try to expose her to new topics in several different ways, including ways that connect to her own interests. If she becomes engrossed in just one part of the exploration, you have done your job well.

Don't feel you have to participate in every activity that comes along. Parents understandably want their children to be exposed to many ideas and don't want them to miss anything. However, that good intention is lost on a child who has no interest but his own project. Remember always that a broad base of knowledge can be acquired through the study of a single topic of interest, so help him explore the depths of his interest as much as possible.

## Use Transition Activities

Interruptions are so tough when a child is deeply focused! Though he would not say so, perhaps the change-resistant child experiences any change of activity at all as a long, dark, and scary hallway. If so, take many small steps to ease the move from one activity to another. Your job is to help your child take the needed steps fearlessly.

Plan segues that are joyful and sure to please. Does your child love music? March from the living room to the kitchen. Does she like poetry? Recite favorite nursery rhymes together while you get in the car. Does she love her dolls? Play a game of taking the dolls to the kitchen for lunch.

This approach is particularly helpful with young children. By making the switch from one activity to another via another familiar and separate activity, the child finds a way to navigate between events. A groundwork is being laid that the child will eventually internalize, giving him power to make transitions in his own way.

## Adjust Activity Beginnings and Endings

Your student with an attention surplus may be particularly vulnerable to transitions that are either too rigid or too relaxed. You may need to experiment to see what works. For instance, if you adhere to a fairly tight schedule, try softening your approach. Allow more time at the beginning and end of an activity. Some children need extra warning time. Others may delight in using a timer or stopwatch to track activities. Involve your child in planning the day's events so that he will know exactly what to expect. Keep your calendar handy for all. Be sure that your student has plenty of time for his own interests — chunks of time that are long enough for him to complete his natural cycle of deep focus.

On the other end of the spectrum, you may have a very relaxed lifestyle where activities always seem to overlap. Maybe you are reluctant to plan and schedule, preferring to be spontaneous. This approach may make perfect sense to you, while being completely confusing or crazy-making to your student. How does he know where to look or what to do? Clocks, stopwatches, timers, and calendars may help this student — maybe he can take on the role of family timekeeper.

Try to help your child better delineate the boundaries of his activities. Perhaps he needs a space of his own that is away from siblings. He may benefit from knowing time lines and schedules ahead of time. How long does he have to work on his project? Predictability can be a calming force.

## Provide Ample Physical Activity

The intensity of focused attention may bottle up in your child, and physical exertion is a great way to release the tension. We're talking large motor activity here — bike riding, running, jumping, throwing, gymnastics, martial arts, swimming, and horseback riding. As your child gets older, team sports such as soccer may be perfect. She may discover another strong personal interest!

## Keep Group Activities Small

Children with attention surplus often thrive in small groups, even if they fall on their faces in large groups. You may want to explore several different learning clubs and groups to find one that is compatible. Once that group is found or created, students can embark on their social learning activities in a supportive environment.

## Follow Interests and Passions

Attention surplus kids can be an absolute joy to be around when they are caught up in activities they love. It makes sense to follow that pattern and support the love of learning as a priority. As your child grows older and clarifies her goals in life, she will be able to see the need to fill in any gaps in her knowledge created by her single-minded pursuit of her interests.

Be warned, though. Students who fully immerse themselves in a topic may stay with it far longer than the parents would expect — hours at a time, days in a row, years on end. Then, when parents have resigned themselves to the fact that their child will live in her Renaissance fantasy for the rest of her life, she may drop it completely in order to study herbs, plant a garden, prepare to run a marathon, read science fiction, or giggle over boys. Her parents may yearn for the good ol' Renaissance fantasy days!

## Find a Balance

See if you can find ways to help your child understand his unique qualities and to learn to manage and balance his own life. Knowing his strengths and weaknesses will help him handle new situations. Long heart-to-heart talks may help your child balance his life. Your child can pick your brain and learn from your experiences and knowledge while you guide and ask questions that open doors to understanding.

## Finally

Children with attention surplus frequently thrive in a home-schooling atmosphere. Parents do well to keep the ultimate goal for their student — becoming a self-regulating and change-tolerant adult — well in mind. In time, your student will give up the less effective behaviors in favor of behaviors that empower their interests and learning style. Students with a surplus of attention often grow up to be remarkable adults.

## chapter twenty-two

# ELEVEN, GOING ON TWENTY-ONE

*tips for homeschooling the teen years*

A disgruntled teenager can dominate and disrupt family life as none other. While some teens ease smoothly from childhood to adulthood, others wrestle at every turn. Attitude changes and moodiness may be part of normal adolescent development. Sometimes, parents have not adjusted their expectations to meet the growth and developmental needs of their teen. Parents need to sort out all the emotions and needs as best they can. Then a plan of action that best suits the family's situation can be devised.

Just what is going on when your teen chafes and disrupts at every turn, even though other family members are happy and content? Is she asking for freedom to make decisions? Does she need more independence? More or less outside activity? How can you adapt your schedule so that all the children in your home can thrive? You may need to do some investigating and then re-prioritize. Teens are often ready for a fresh approach to their homeschooling life and schedule.

## Rethink Your Teen's Curriculum

- Would a more structured curriculum give you a chance to identify and fill holes in his knowledge base? Would he benefit from seeing how his skills stack up against others of his age group? If so consider substituting a structured curriculum for an unschooled interest-initiated approach.

- Does she chafe against her structured curriculum? Do the curriculum expectations cause conflict between parent and child? You may be in for a pleasant surprise if you allow her to substitute interest-directed learning through projects instead. Many teens have been launched past adolescent troubles and into the world of young adulthood while pursuing interests and projects.

- Does your student want to attend high school? Enrolling in a correspondence school is one popular way to work through the high school years. Round out book work with the pursuit of interests and activities: sports, volunteer experiences, work, travel, and so on.

- Does your teen seek adult level knowledge? Some teens are ready to attend college at age sixteen. Community college is a fantastic academic resource for students who are ready to learn at that level.

- Should you seek out an apprenticeship or a mentorship for your teen? Older youngsters can prove their mettle and join the real world, accept real responsibility, tackle real challenges, meet real people, and learn from their own real mistakes.

- Is your student ready to take responsibility for her own education? Students love to prove their maturity by demonstrating that they are successfully pursuing knowledge and developing skills independently. Parents can shift into a consultant or advisor role and provide guidance, support, and a listening ear.

## Increase Outside Activities

Some students need time to explore the world of work and ideas before they can choose what their next steps will be. Part-time jobs and volunteer opportunities are enriching in ways that academics cannot be. College or vocational training may follow when the student can see his goals more clearly.

If your student is interested in sports, seek out community, school-based, or homeschooling sports leagues. Larger communities have many opportunities. Don't hesitate to pitch in and help start the type of league your student needs! Your student will benefit and others will thank you.

There are many options for increasing learning opportunities. Some students take enrichment classes privately, at a high school, or enroll in community college courses. Others form study groups. Support groups may hire a teacher to offer specific classes. For many the same eclectic mix of academic studies, activities, work/volunteer, sports, fine arts, will carry a student happily through the teen years.

## Respect the Teenage Need for Privacy

Adequate privacy is important for your teen to be able to work through the moods and emotions he feels. He will need that skill as an adult and the teen years are the perfect practice ground. By asking other family members to respect the teen's need for privacy, you let the teen know that his unique needs are important. Too much privacy can lead to isolation, something you'll want to avoid, of course, but how much is too much? A sudden increase in your teen's need for privacy might be a sign of depression, or it might mean she is busy writing her autobiography. You will need to stay tuned in on the ups and downs of your teen's life, and then balance your teen's access to privacy with participation in family and outside activities.

One of my daughters had a huge need for privacy. However, that fact did not keep me from bugging her, engaging her as much as possible, making suggestions, and gently prying into her inner state of mind. Sometimes she responded with positive interactions that made me realize that she was doing okay, while other times her moods and my ineffective efforts set us both off in tears. How she responded to my attempts at interaction was not important. That regular attempt to engage with her was crucially important. She received the clear message that she was important to me and that I would never give up on her.

## Independence Projects

Give your young teen ample opportunities to practice independence. Try to find projects that both reflect your teen's natural interests and allow him to practice the role of an adult. Suppose your teen has a gift with younger children. Could he assist with a learning club for younger children that either you or someone else leads? Would she be the perfect person to read aloud with your five-year-old, or practice multiplication tables with your seven-year-old? Maybe her expertise in bird watching will lead to a volunteer opportunity as a nature guide for young homeschool groups.

Some teens will take off with an independence project and begin to create their own opportunities. Others will follow a series of opportunities you offer before initiating their own projects. Parents need to keep at it, making sure their teen has activities that build independence skills.

## Rethink Your Relationship With Your Teen

Parents are frequently lulled into a stage of comfort during the middle childhood years, thinking that they will sail through the teen years just as they are sailing through childhood years. Don't be so sure.

If your good relationship with your child begins to feels strained, you may need to take some steps to keep your relationship strong. Monitor yourself as you talk to your teen. How can you adapt your speaking to acknowledge that you are aware of next level of relationship between you and your teen — adult to young adult?

Try letting your teen have the last word in some discussions, even if you are certain he is wrong. A pattern of parents always having the last word of authority often develops without our being aware of it, and breaking that pattern can be tough. My relationship with my teens improved almost overnight when I gave up my comfortable role as all-knowing expert.

Learn to throw some decisions back to your teen, no matter how he may plead for you to help him decide. Some teens depend on their parents for final approval on major decisions. If you let your teen decide, and then help him cope with the successes and failures that result, he will begin to rely more on his own decision-making ability.

Respect your student's fickleness of decision. If he is to have a practice stage for indecision or bad decision-making, the teen years are his best chance. If he is extraordinarily fickle and seems to flit from one decision to the next weekly, think of him as a quick study. At least he doesn't waste time with activities that are not right for him. Be sure he knows that you believe he will settle his interests in time. Being fickle can be hard on one's self-image, to be sure, but if you as a parent insist on re-framing his indecisiveness as a positive choice to cover many topics quickly, his confidence will bounce back.

## Spend Time Alone with Your Teen

Some teens seek out their parents for conversation. Some parents must seek out their teens. If your teen tends to withdraw, you will need to be the aggressive partner in the parent-teen relationship. You may need to be patient and creative to find time together, especially if your teen is prone to moodiness.

Do you have to knock on your teen's bedroom door frequently to get a "state-of-the-teen" chat? Do it. Don't let her crabbiness stop you. Does he have an outdoor daily chore, such as taking care of animals? Find reasons to be out at the same time, or offer to help with his tasks in exchange for his helping you with one of your chores.

Does your teen need regular transportation to or from activities? Make some of those trips with her alone. While car pools are wonderful time savers, car time with your teen can be a priceless investment. Watch TV or movies together, even if you have to put up with shows you wouldn't choose for yourself. Select books to share. Play favorite games or learn new ones. Going out to lunch together is fun and there are no distractions.

Pay her for real work. While my daughter would not have chosen to accompanied me to some homeschooling events, she willingly joined me if I needed her help at my sales table as my paid cashier. She benefitted from the work experience and the exposure, and we enjoyed the time together.

If you have several children, take advantage of your other children's scheduled activities and spend time with your teen then, perhaps cooking a meal or working in your herb garden together.

## The Best Laid Plans...

The lives of teens may be fraught with change and upset. From upsets as simple as a missed car pool ride or lost soccer cleats, to the really scary kinds of mistakes teens sometimes make, the impact feels monumental to the youngster who knows he must accept responsibility for his behavior. Realize that your gangly teenager will soon be grown and independent and moving on to her own life. Remind yourself that your other children will not suffer lifelong damage because they missed one story time. Just take it all with a grain of salt and reschedule.

## Take Time for Yourself

You've heard it before. Teenaged angst can be exhausting to live with. Do take care of yourself. Find a friend who also has a teen to share ideas, concerns, and successes. Take stock of growth and progress regularly, and give yourself a pat on the back for a job well done. Soon enough you will celebrate the final lap.

## Keep Your Sense of Humor, and . . . Enjoy Your Teen

If your teen is gliding through adolescence, enjoying her is easy and natural. If your teen is struggling with swinging moods and adolescent confusion, keep working to find moments to appreciate. Cherish the good moments, jot notes, take pictures — for review during the tougher times and for memories and laughs later. The tough times will fade and before long, your teen will be a confident and capable young adult.

## chapter twenty-three

# A TODDLER IN THE HOMESCHOOL
*sharing the joy and surviving the intensity*

How do families meet the needs of toddlers without sacrificing the older children's education? "Runabout" babies, no longer content to sit quietly in Mom's lap while older siblings command her attention, have strong opinions and endless energy. Families are challenged to be flexible and patient if they want to continue their educational plans with as little disruption as possible.

As a parent, you know that the two-year-old will soon be a busy three, a curious and questioning four, and then an active five. Your other children see the toddler differently, though, especially when a carefully constructed project falls prey to a curious toddler, or when special time with you is interrupted again and again. Waiting for a baby to find his niche in the family structure can wreak havoc on formerly calm routines.

A toddler may seem to be pretty much in charge of the family by the simple fact that he has so little self-control. Fortunately, other family members can actually make choices — choices about how to adapt the activities of the older children to accommodate the toddler. What choices will you make to include this impish invader in your homeschooling program? Try these.

## Lose Your Lap

Toddlers loathe a lap unsat! Why else would your happily playing toddler know that you just sat down for a reading session with your older child? You might think that a toddler's ears can hear the sound of a lap forming from another room!

Try working at the kitchen counter, perhaps with your older child sitting on a kitchen stool. One mom found a safe place for card games, puzzles, and typing — on the ironing board! You may have to do something active, such as playing and enjoying music together. Put the toddler in a stroller or backpack and sing, dance, or march with your older child. Standing legs are working legs. Sitting legs say "lap."

## Make the Baby the Math Project

A toddler loves to be the center of attention! Take advantage of that fact and make a study of the baby.

Do math by weighing and measuring the baby and by charting his rapid growth; measure limb length, head circumference, and body proportions. Getting him to hold still will be a certain challenge! Weigh and measure his toys, clothes, food, diapers, or whatever catches the imagination of your older children.

A toddler's life activities can be an endless source of math problems. How fast does he crawl from point A to point B? Can she jump yet? How long will she play with one toy before moving on? Get the whole family involved in the activity. Let your older children use a stopwatch to time the baby — and themselves — in all kinds of routine activities. Measure lengths of arms, legs, noses; weigh everyone. Who can hop on one foot the longest? How far can each person throw a ball? Don't forget to measure Dad, Mom, and Grandpa!

While your toddler is still "jumping as high as he can," you and the older children can use the raw data to explore any of dozens of mathematical concepts. Use your family data to construct problems. Sums and differences; percentages; rate of speed; comparisons, charts, and graphs; grab a math book for some more ideas if you get stuck.

For example, you might find the Average Family Speed at dozens of everyday activities; explore the mean, mode, and median methods of showing averages. See if the kids can figure out how statistics can be distorted by using the different numbers. Try this activity again in a year or two when the children are older, and compare the two sets of figures.

Or, if you can't find time to explore the math concepts, save the data for later. Take the measurements periodically to see who has grown taller and faster. You'll have more data to work with when everyone is a little older.

## Baby-proofing in Reverse

You already know how to use regular "baby-proofing" — keeping your baby safe with gates, outlet covers, cabinet locks, storage of fragile items, and other creative environmental changes.

Reverse baby-proofing keeps the interests and projects of older children safe from little sister's exploring hands. Newly completed puzzles pulled from a table by baby hands devastated one twelve-year-old puzzle master! Reverse baby-proofing can prevent a similar disaster in your home.

Perhaps older children can simply keep the doors to their rooms closed. Some families install a baby gate on the project room or older children's bedrooms so that parents can maintain better visual and audio contact with all children. If a project area is off limits before the baby becomes mobile, the baby may accept the closed door as a fact of life.

## Study Language Through Baby-talk

Infant language development can be a fascinating springboard to the study of the English language and grammar. Older children might enjoy keeping a running list of the words the baby can understand or use. Track her sentence development — how she puts words together — as a grammar study. Can she put a verb and a noun together to form a simple sentence? Make up guessing games for the older children about how soon the toddler will use a pronoun, or recognize the difference between dogs and cats — both are complex bits of knowledge! Notice how she punctuates her sentences with body language or volume. Does she ask questions by pointing? Does she stomp her feet to show emphasis?

Are you working on reading skills with your older child? Use the baby's vocabulary for simple phonics instruction. Spell words with the baby's letter blocks. Write or tell stories about babies using your own baby's words. Spell those baby-talk words.

Create a family baby-talk dictionary to keep with the baby pictures. List words in correct dictionary form, listing the cute sayings, meanings, pronunciations, adorable usage, and funny constructions for all the children in the family as they learned to talk. Call the grandparents to find out some of Dad's and Mom's cute sayings.

For a different approach to language, the entire family could learn a foreign language or American Sign Language. You can learn French while the toddler learns English. Try to learn the same words the baby is learning in your target language. Prepare to be challenged! You will all learn a great deal about language development just by following the baby's clues. You will also be amazed at how easily the baby is learning her first "foreign" language, English, without an interpreter.

## Make a Special Time for Each Child

Each child needs some time alone with Mom or Dad. Schedule these sessions regularly, if not daily, and carefully honor the appointment time with each child. When you spend time with the older child, make sure that the time is especially for him. To prevent interruptions, take the phone off the hook and try to anticipate the needs of the baby and other children.

Older children might take turns playing with the baby while the other brothers and sisters take a turn having a special time with mom. Some children love a chance to teach the baby songs, games, finger-plays, art, and other activities. Others may want to try "lap-ware," computer software designed for toddlers and their older assistants. Videos, television, audiotapes, art, or special toys and games can be set aside for this time only.

## Take Advantage of Nap Time

Need I say more? Everybody needs a nap some days! Baby's nap time can be used for special times with Mom or Dad for your older child. Also available are baby's possibly earlier bedtime, his bath time with the other parent, walks, playtime, and whatever other routines your family enjoys.

## Give the Baby Her Own Parallel Curriculum

Are you doing workbook pages with the older children? Give the baby or toddler a crayon and her own page. Reading today? Bring out the cardboard books. Studying literature or drama? Make a simple costume for your little one and let him be a tree or a rabbit that hops through the story. You'll discover more of these ideas as you think about ways of including him rather than keeping him out. Your older children will get into the spirit of this if you set the tone.

Erin was just eight months old when I found three-year-old Alice racing around the house at high speed, zipping past the crawling baby again and again. Beaming and breathless, Alice paused to explain that she was the Hare racing past the Tortoise! Just-learning-to-creep Erin played her assigned role perfectly as the slow-moving Tortoise, delighting in her sister's gleeful game.

## Choose Appropriate Activities and Materials

Plan projects with the baby in mind when you can. Finger-painting today? Better use the chocolate pudding, not the starch and tempera mix. Make homemade edible play-dough, and save the toxic art projects, such as oil painting or glass etching, for next year or maybe the year after. The same with science: study plants and animals and the physics of water, air, and simple machines this year. Except for yummy kitchen chemistry, save chemistry sets and delicate experiments for later.

Do you have a chalkboard? Let the toddler scribble at the bottom, and use the top portion for the older children's work. There you are, all working together, a happy homeschooling family.

## Use the Outdoors

Being outside soothes many restless tykes. Environmental learning, nature walks, animal care, and gardening get the whole family outside. You can take academic studies to the yard or park so your toddler can play and enjoy the benefit of fresh air.

Try playing *Follow the Leader* on walks, letting your youngest lead. Mom and Dad and the rest of the kids can follow behind, studying plants, reciting poetry, telling jokes, discussing philosophy or whatever else interests them that day.

## Outings and Field Trips

Think hiking in the woods and save the art museum for another year. Think zoo and park, pool and river. Open-ended activities are ideal for meeting the needs of different ages.

When planning an activity at an unfamiliar location, call ahead to find out whether they can accommodate backpacks, wagons, strollers, diaper changing, snacks, toddler chatter, and leaving early. Finding a toddler-friendly activity improves everyone's experience.

Plan carefully and the trips you take will be enjoyable for the entire family. While your older child may not hear the symphony this year, she has the perfect excuse to see a children's play or visit a children's museum one more time, in spite of some grumbling that she is only going for the toddler's sake, because she herself is much too old. But watch her have a blast!

## Use Bite-sized Activities

If you plan ahead, you can take advantage of those unexpected moments when your toddler is completely occupied with her explorations. On three by five cards, jot down quick learning activities from your *Learning Idea List* that your older children will enjoy and keep them handy in your bag.

Examples: a quick game of *hangman*; *tic tac toe*; *Mad Libs*; mental math and mental problem solving games. Try doing just one huge math problem instead of a page of problems. Spell big words together. Read poetry and nursery rhymes. Make up limericks. Keep an ongoing game of children's *Trivial Pursuit* or checkers that you play at odd moments.

## Other

Try: recreation classes for Mom and the older kids; the older kids alone; Dad and baby; Grandma and baby. Seek combinations that suit your family dynamics and that provide special times for older kids without always having to make allowances for the toddler.

Try to find a friend to trade toddlers with. You and your spouse can trade too — perhaps one parent does science projects with the older kids while the other parent shops or cleans or naps with the baby. The benefits of seeking out trades are enormous, well worth the effort of finding a compatible family, if only for a few hours at a time.

## Planning for Next Year — The Big Picture

There will be a few projects you'll decide to put off until your toddler is older, so add those to your *Learning Idea List*. Include all the neat activities that you wish you could do with your support group. Note the ideas you glean from an e-mail group or your favorite homeschooling magazines. And one day, when you are feeling bad because your older kids have been neglected too long, pick one item from the list and make it a priority. Let your youngest have a day with Grandma or a special friend, take the older children, and go for it!

## Be Ready to Change Your Plans

When the toddler is fussy with a cold, the weather is miserable, and everyone is snapping at everyone else, reschedule that cool project for another day. Then do something wild to break the pattern of negativity. Get down on the floor with all of the kids and build a blanket fort in the living room. Have a picnic lunch there! Laugh and giggle all day long. Take pictures and make notes — make it a day neither you nor your children will forget because it was a good day!

## Take Time for Yourself

There is no time like being the parent of a toddler to make you forget that you are a separate person with actual needs of your own! Eat well and get plenty of rest. Give yourself a regular break. The family benefits most from a sane and happy parent.

## Keep Your Sense of Humor, and . . .

## Enjoy Your Toddler

Your "runabout" baby brings to his family a unique curriculum. A toddler provides a natural context for learning about love, honesty, joy, tolerance, and reality, each and every day. Lucky the family with a toddler!

## When You Are Immobilized...

Is your toddler: Ill?  Teething?  Having a cranky day?  Are your older children in desperate need of attention? Have you already read stories until your eyes cross? You need ideas for days when you are pinned to a chair with a feverish child in arms.

Simply talk to one another.  You will reinforce the pattern of learning through conversation.  Talk about big ideas. Make plans. Solve problems.  Make up stories together.  Tell stories of your childhood.  Go through family photo albums together or watch the family birthday videos.

Play thinking games or solve mental puzzles together. Have your children act out animals, fairy tales, or favorite stories.  Sing.  Have a dance contest.  Teach them foreign words or even Pig Latin.

Help children learn independence skills.  Try giving your child multiple steps of a task to remember.  Make a game of seeing how many directions he can remember before coming back for the next instructional step.  Whether teaching a child how to make a sandwich, how to find a word in a dictionary, how to write the letter 'k', or where to find a new roll of toilet paper, you can use verbal instructions to teach her even when you are too busy to participate.

# PART 4
## Growing Up

Featuring:

Keynote: Growing Up

Rites of Passage

Family-Friendly Evaluations

Avoiding Standardized Testing Traps

Ready for College and Work

## chapter twenty-four

# KEYNOTE
# GROWING UP
*how homeschooled students make their way into the world*

How quickly children grow up.

## Marking off the days of our lives is a time-honored activity.

Knotted ropes. Notches carved into sticks. Arcane markings etched in stone. Births, deaths, and marriages recorded in Family Bibles.

We save — and savor — newspaper clippings, scrapbooks, letters, photos, trophies, awards, certificates, genealogies, journals, and souvenirs that trigger memories of earlier times and prior generations. Family histories, photo albums, journals, diaries, calendars, narratives, audio- and video- tapes, and even web pages, are used to record individual and family experiences for posterity.

## Memorable events trace the paths of our lives.

Youthful celebrations of every kind — ceremonies, graduation, promotion, matriculation, banquets, dinners, and dances — emblazon vivid memories in the hearts and minds of celebrants. Whether the event is a grand soiree or a simple family trip to an ice cream shop, celebratory events mark the growth of the individual and the passage from one stage to another.

Astute parents realize that commencements and culminations are powerful teachers in their own right. Students learn *that they learned,* above and separate from *the learning being recognized* itself. Further, they realize — through these events — that they are becoming accepted members of adult society.

Successful families opt to celebrate beginnings, completions, or both. Celebrating a fresh start or a new activity offers a gradual lead into the next phase of learning. Closure activities provide time for celebrating successes, for reflecting, and for processing the past, as well as for considering what's next.

## Evidence of learning opens doors in a merit-based world.

Students grow up quickly: they learn new skills, develop talents, and acquire knowledge and understanding.

Eventually, students collect the evidence of their progress to present to prospective employers or university admissions officers. Evaluations, resumes, transcripts of topics studied, tests, portfolios, awards, honors, certificates, diplomas, productions, evidence of projects completed, events, plays, performances, concerts, recitations, and recitals given are the currency of merit.

## Finally

Most parents draw on their vast family resources and traditions to inform themselves of the best way to celebrate significant events that mark growth. The best way to celebrate is the way that puts sparkle in the eyes of the celebrants!

This part will explore some of the rites of passage that have been handed over, in large part, to schools, such as measuring progress and preparing students for the future. We'll discuss some ways that parents evaluate student progress, create academic rites of passage, help students deal with tests, and support their children's development as they prepare for their independence.

## chapter twenty-five

# RITES OF PASSAGE

*honoring maturation through celebrations, awards, and mementos*

Don't believe for one minute that homeschooled children and their families feel left out of school-based activities, wistfully watching all the fun from the sidelines. Nope, they are too busy creating new and memorable experiences of their own, activities that anchor memories for their children. Shall we take a peek?

## Kick-off Activities — Beginnings

Do you remember "September elixir" — the sensory explosion that greeted you on the first day of school? Do squeaky new shoes, brand-new lunch boxes, unbroken crayons, old friends, new teachers, noisy hallways, and the mingled smells of freshly waxed floors, new erasers, and chalk dust lull you into believing that "September elixir" really could make school magic? Do you associate those sensory memories with vague dreams of success, renewed hope, and a clean slate?

Homeschooling parents remember very well, and for that reason, they brew their own brand of "September elixir." Activities galore launch each new year. New projects, new books, or fresh study approaches with a homeschooling twist are always popular. Support groups plan activities calculated to launch the year memorably. Weigh these ideas against your own plans and memories.

## Homeschool Camps and Conferences

Attending a large gathering with other homeschooling families is a great way to launch into a new year, no matter what time of the year you happen to go. Parents refresh themselves and gather new ideas, while kids connect with old friends, make new friends, and share experiences.

Annual homeschooling conferences and camps are available in many states across the country. State and national homeschool organizations — and some homeschooling magazines — can direct you to these events if you want to take one in. If your family is adventurous, you could attend a different state conference each year while exploring the regions between. What a fun way to recharge batteries, meet people, and see new places!

## "Not-Back-to-School" Events

Support groups may sponsor these events on the first day of school in the community. Some groups schedule a special Homeschool Day at a nearby amusement park. If no such event is offered in your community, discuss the possibility with the manager of a park, pool, or bowling alley. They may be glad for the extra business and be willing to work with you to create a memorable event.

## Day Trips

Young homeschooled children sometimes yearn to explore the mysteries of school culture — riding buses, eating from lunch boxes, and purchasing new "school" clothes and supplies. August and September are a good time to explore these mysteries. Pack lunch boxes, put on your back-to-school outfits, and travel by bus to a park, museum, or other destination of choice.

## One-Room Schoolhouse for A Day

My kids also wanted to know what happened in the school buildings their friends attended, so our family explored traditional schooling in our own way.

For several years, we introduced the "school year" by setting up a one-room school in our home for just a few days, as part of a study of early America and the westward pioneers. Slates, desks, rulers, bells, grades, busywork, lunch buckets — we nibbled on the whole hush puppy. Sometimes we used modern materials like workbooks. The craving was soon satisfied and the experience was memorable.

Another approach is to visit a historically preserved one-room schoolhouse. Someone may even "teach" for a day, helping students reenact the stereotypical days of yore.

## Launch New Projects or Studies

Learning clubs or study groups quite naturally begin with a celebration of sorts. That is, parents get together to plan, maybe at a park or over a potluck, and the children play — a simple way to mark a new beginning.

Even small beginnings can be noted. Is your child getting a new math book? A brand-new curriculum? Maybe a shopping trip for supplies will mark the event, especially if you punctuate it with a special treat. New pencils, new notebooks, a new lamp, even a rearranged study area can bring the beginning into sharp focus.

## Culminating Activities

Some people remember "May madness," those frenzied days of school activity that signaled the end of another year. Memories of broken crayons, bullies, and test anxiety fade from memory as school programs, field days, parties, and other final activities hail the arrival of the last day of school.

Maybe you fondly remember culminating events from when you were an older student, such as the Prom. Such celebrations allow time to close one door before opening the next, giving students extra time to decide what follows next in their lives. Some students will need that time to consider options, while others will eagerly push to the next step, their plans already laid.

Culminating activities may straddle the fence between rites of passage and straightforward evaluation. Try to tailor these celebration activities to a level that satisfies the particular student. Some bask in celebration and being the center of attention — the bigger and grander the celebration, the better. Others are embarrassed by big affairs, better pleased with a smaller fête.

## Accomplishments

Some accomplishments should be celebrated! Noting significant learning with celebration ices the cake of success. An "I Can Read!" family party is justified — what an achievement reading skill is! Did she read her very first book all by herself? Act it out as a family. Let her direct the show as she tells or reads the story. Enlist all the stuffed animals in the house to take roles as dogs in *Go, Dog, Go*. Invite Grandma to the show.

Did a LEGO building construction dominate the living room for days? Celebrate the construction, take pictures, then enjoy a Demolition Party.

Why not celebrate the mastery of the multiplication table? Did he cook a first meal for the family? Experience new sports highlights? Enjoy a first sleep-over? There is no limit to the kinds of events that can be celebrated. Celebrate learning to write one's name in cursive, completing a 4-H project, playing in a recital, or participating in a play. Did he raise abandoned kittens, even getting up for night feedings? And they lived? Let him know what a great job he did!

Perhaps you prefer to focus celebration on learning habits — did your child make progress in that area? Perhaps she: took on a new project independently; learned to use the encyclopedia, dictionary, or Internet to get information; discovered and corrected errors independently.

Learning clubs can use culminating activities both as a way to share the group's work with friends and family and as a way to close a group or project. Plan a spaghetti dinner, put on a puppet show, or plan a sing-a-long.

You may want to focus celebration around personal growth or development issues that challenge your child. Learning anger control could be a cause for celebration. You'll discover that sometimes the simplest celebrations are the best. A shiny foil crown worn to the dinner table can bring on the big grins.

## Performances

Give your budding star an arena in which to perform her artistry. Recitals, concerts, plays, and other performances give students a chance to show their new skills and to discover whether they enjoy being in the public eye. If you set up chairs in the living room, improvise a stage, and invite the family to the show, young children are generally delighted to find themselves in the spotlight.

Older children may thrive on community experiences. Did she sing with the opera, committing months of her life to practices and rehearsals? Make an event of her performances. Take pictures or make a video. Write about the event for your local paper or home-school group's newsletter.

## Promotions

Did your youngster complete a course of study or project? Create a Certificate of Promotion and award it at dinner. Your older student might prefer to celebrate with a special reward instead — a recreational trip, a book, or a shopping excursion. Or you might drag out that shiny foil crown one more time!

## Awards Ceremonies

Some families and groups issue awards occasionally. Celebrating the completions that your child achieves along the way might make more sense than an annual grade level promotion for many families.

A celebration can be a small and private family event, but public events can also be quite meaningful. A good example is the Children's Celebration Ceremony at the Oregon Homeschool Conference every year. Prior to the ceremony, parents complete a Certificate of Achievement for the child and give it to the Event Coordinator. During the Ceremony, each child is called to the stage to receive his award individually before friends and family. Children love this popular event and it grows every year.

An annual picnic or play day for a neighborhood support group could easily provide a similar experience for your children. A potluck or formal dinner could follow the presentation of awards.

## The Prom

If dancin' is your student's thing, a formal dance or dinner/dance event can provide closure for a school year and a good formal experience in a very casual world. Plan a family dance with your support group, or — if your homeschool community is large enough — plan an event just for the teens. The only limits are the breadth of your imagination, the length of your day, and the depth of your pocketbook. Pooling resources with others makes events more manageable and more memorable.

## Graduation

Many homeschooling families get together and plan events to help students experience this traditional rite of passage into young adulthood. The event you plan could be as simple and personal as a family dinner, a Senior photo session, a trip, or other adventure that honors the student's passage.

For a formal and visible event, families may pool their resources and rent caps, gowns, and a hall. These kinds of events are easiest to coordinate through a local or statewide support group. A graduation ceremony is sometimes held in conjunction with a conference or other event. You could even include a Prom as part of the Conference festivities. Students might give speeches or performances or otherwise show that they are moving forward in their lives. Will you want a motivational speaker to give an address? You can hire a band or disc jockey, invite friends and family to dress up for the occasion, and celebrate with all of the pomp and circumstance you can muster.

If casual is more your style, skip the formalities and go straight to the post-graduation party. You can plan anything from a camp-out to a swimming party to a — well, you certainly don't need me to tell you how to have a party! Do something that will be memorable for your student and his friends, your family, and the group, and you won't go wrong. Announce your event in newsletters and local newspapers.

## Mementos

Memories are kindled by the simplest things. Ticket stubs, programs, dried flowers, autograph books, bits of wrapping paper, cards, photos, class rings, imprinted sweaters or T-shirts, and so much more. Students who tend toward the sentimental will appreciate the efforts you make today to carry their memories forward to tomorrow.

## Student Newsletters

When students publish a newsletter, they quickly learn that any glory they garner from a by-line is purchased several times over with hard work. If your student or group manages to publish even one issue, consider the effort a major success. Keep copies for the scrapbook.

## Diploma

A diploma is a formal document that your student may want to hang on the wall or include in a scrapbook or other record of his high school years. A diploma can easily be designed using a computer, or by hand, if you have a knack for beautiful handwriting.

## Yearly Student Photos

Those photos are so much fun to tuck in letters to Grandma, who can post them on the refrigerator. Annual photos also put students on an equal footing with their schooled friends when photo swapping is an important social activity.

Your homeschooling group does not need to be huge to schedule school photos taken from a professional school photographer. Check your yellow pages and see who can offer what your group wants. Or you might want to call the local school or a nearby private school and find photographers they've worked with.

## Yearbooks

Most families will be quite satisfied with their collections of scrapbooks, photo albums, and any handmade books they have acquired. If you want to take the official yearbook route, though, why not start a learning club of older students whose task is create and publish a yearbook for homeschoolers?

If your group is small, compile and print the collection with your computer. If your community is large, the world of yearbook publishing is eager to work for you. You may be able to schedule the yearbook to be published outside the regular yearbook publishing season to save money. You also might be able to collaborate and co-publish a yearbook with a local print shop. The newest generation of laser printing may help you print quality books at an affordable price. You could even recover some of your expenses by seeking sponsorship from local businesses.

## Finally

Don't let these suggestions limit your choices. Rather, use them as a springboard toward finding your own memorable items and events. Why couldn't you order a class ring or lettermen's jacket if that meets a personal need? No reason in the world. Now get out there and make memories — the homeschooled way.

## chapter twenty-six

# FAMILY FRIENDLY EVALUATION
*helping children know what they know — parents too*

My homeschooling records — occasional at best and haphazard at worst — make me hope that readers benefit from my rueful hindsight. It is not enough just to learn, and it is not enough to be told that you are learning.

"I know I know things, Mom, but I don't know what I know!" This plaintive cry was an unexpected wake-up call to me. Unaware that Erin did not realize how much she was learning, I kept up-to-date mental checklists for myself, even jotting notes in my calendar from time to time. I knew what she knew, so why didn't she?

Somehow I had left Erin out of the evaluation loop. Unaware of her level of knowledge, she had no faith in her ability to move forward in her learning process. The best evaluation processes lead to self-knowledge for the student and feedback for parents as well. Is he learning what he needs to know to be successful in the world? Is she ready to try harder material? Does she need to review her math skills? Will he be ready for college?

Let's explore a couple of simple methods of tracking what your children are learning. Then you can readily focus energy on what needs to be taught and quiet that nagging question in the back of your mind, "Am I doing enough?"

## Types of Evaluation

### Natural Daily Evaluation

Most parents evaluate student progress every day without realizing it. "You read that book without a single mistake." "You spelled 'cow' with a 'k' — the correct way is 'c-o-w.'"

In the process of guiding your child's learning, you constantly evaluate which skills your child has mastered. A small child whose first writing attempt is a phonetic spelling of *cow* is not corrected. Instead, the effort is celebrated and posted on the fridge for all to read. On the other hand, his ten-year-old sister, upon misspelling *cow,* might get a raised eyebrow, a reminder to proofread, or a quick comment about carelessness.

### Periodic Evaluation

Evaluation at regular intervals is natural. Most families track the story of their children's lives in vast collections of photographs, videos, keepsakes, and the like. You have a unique record of your children's learning experiences in that collection. You are probably already tripping over some of these items, perhaps unaware that you are stumbling through the evidence of learning.

Including academic progress in your family history system takes little additional effort. Just include the collected papers and photos of projects. Several times a year, spend a rainy afternoon looking through your children's "evidence of learning" with them. Help them think about what they learned. (Develop your own system, or use the Simple Portfolio System that follows.)

While you are reviewing and sorting, speak with your children about their strengths and needs — that is how we teach children to look honestly at themselves. Together with each child, write down goals and insights as a narrative. Make it fun and special, and, as they learn how they learn, what they know, and what they need to know, independent learners will sprout before your eyes!

### Reflection and Self-Evaluation

Help your children learn the art of self-evaluation. Use all the resources you have — photos, letters, projects, drawings, writings, collections, journals, reading lists, albums, videos, recordings, handmade books, presentations, performances, self-publications, displays, clippings, scrapbooks, awards, or web sites — to refresh your memories.

Take time to look through the materials with your child once in a while. Encourage your child to reflect on what he has learned based on the evidence — what does each item show that he knows how to do? That may not be easy for your child to verbalize, and you may have to help him. Help him really think about his work, to be specific, and to go beyond, "I like it."

If your child really struggles, demonstrate to her what you think she learned. "This paper shows that you know how to start sentences with capital letters. Just look! You remembered each capital letter." Jot both her comments and yours on a separate piece of paper and paperclip the comments to the work paper itself.

If the habit of self-evaluation is begun early, a sense of his own knowledge will blossom. You'll reap another advantage as well — students who are confident in what they know often readily grasp what they might want to work on next.

## Written Narrative Evaluation

Some parents prefer to write about what the child has learned using natural everyday language. Start by writing a paragraph or two to describe the child's abilities in selected skill areas, such as math, reading, writing. Describe the kinds of activities the student participated in, his relative skill and level of involvement. What has she written and read? What math activities have been accomplished? Note areas of rapid growth, such as suddenly mastering cursive writing or knowing the states and their capitals in a short time. You might also note areas that need work. You could include specific skills, such as math, and general study habits, neatness, or use of references. Close a narrative evaluation with a sentence or paragraph that indicates what is next — goals, projects, and future studies that may be planned.

If you intend to enroll your child in public school after extended homeschooling, consider writing a narrative evaluation to introduce your child to her new teacher. Such an evaluation will not go unnoticed, and may guide the teacher in helping your child find her niche. Just remember to be realistic and specific. I wrote a one-page narrative when each of my daughters experimented with public school. Many years later I ran into Alice's teacher, who still remembered things I had written on that narrative evaluation. (I commented that Alice had not learned to multiply or divide fractions since I saw no purpose in teaching that skill to an eleven-year-old who had no practical use for it at the time — Alice's teacher and I shared a good laugh over that!)

## A Learning Journal

Regularly jotting down your observations about how your children learn is another useful way to track their learning. As children grow, encourage them to participate in the journal with you. You could write together or take turns. Teens can keep most of the records of their learning on their own if they've had some practice.

A learning journal helps track projects, materials read, and activities for later reference. Parent or student may need to refer to a record of learning activities for the benefit of building a transcript or resume.

## Traditional Grading Systems

If you want to give traditional grades, start from the model you remember from your own school years. Textbook math, a world of right and wrong answers, is the easiest subject to grade traditionally because most answers are clearly right or wrong. A month or two of giving grades may be enough to help your child understand how grading systems work.

Another approach to grading is to issue a pair of grades, one assigned by the student and one assigned by the parent. When I tried this method, my kids were harder on themselves than I was.

By high school, some parents assign letter grades to give the student the experience. Grades and credits for studies completed may be used in order to compile a high school transcript.

Some parents use a mastery system of giving credit only for those subjects that have been mastered. With input from your student, establish a standard of grading for each subject at the beginning of the term. You might include such things as number of books read, difficulty level, error-handling, depth of explorations, and thoughtfulness of writing.

## A Simple Portfolio System

My daughters and I have lingered over photo albums, picture boxes, hand bound books, and that massive pile of school papers that I could not bear to throw away. I regret, though, that we did not spend more time developing projects to preserve those memories. Even though it seemed like a chore at the time, I can now see that, when we took the time to create some records or books that showed learning, the value grew for a long time afterward. So, while it is too late for me, I've found some portfolio ideas that I'd be using today if I still had children at home.

Here is a basic system for putting together a portfolio of your child's work for an entire year. This system works for any number of children of any age. The final portfolio includes selected and dated student work, reflection pieces for each work, a table of contents, and possibly the criterion for which the work was selected. There are three basic steps.

### Step I: Build a Work Collection

Help your children to get in the habit of dropping their work in a safe place. A box, a drawer, or a folder for each child works well. You probably already do this. Be sure they put their names and the date on each piece. Step one is done — that wasn't too hard, was it?

### Step II: "Show What You Know"

Three or four times a year, possibly waiting for a rainy day when you need a change of pace, jot in *Evaluation Afternoon* on your calendar. With your children helping, spend the afternoon building elements for the portfolio from the *Work Collections*. Allow plenty of time, unplug the phone, and really get into the process. Have fun with it. If you have several children, you may want to spread the activity over several afternoons.

Don't feel guilty that you are not getting regular work done during this time. What can be more important than spending time thinking critically about learning?

When *Evaluation Afternoon* rolls around, get out the *Work Collections* and spread them out. Help each child select a few samples of work that "show what you have learned." Help your child reflect on his learning, using the guidelines for reflection that were discussed earlier in this chapter. Jot down both your child's and your own observations and comments.

Take work samples that you and your child have selected as most representative and put them, with the *Reflection Comments* attached, in the *Working Portfolio*. The rest of the *Work Collection* can be discarded or recycled at this point.

That's it for step two. Start collecting material again! Repeat Steps I and II several more times during the year.

## Step III. The Final Portfolio

At the end of your "school" year, after several *Evaluation Afternoon*s, you'll help your child create the *Final Portfolio*. It makes sense to complete the *Final Portfolio* soon after the final *Evaluation Afternoon*. Schedule several work periods so your child can create a product that she feels proud of.

From the work that you evaluated and saved on each *Evaluation Afternoon*, select the most representative works, or the best ones, or the ones that show — well, whatever you want the portfolio to demonstrate. When the items have been chosen, help your child create a table of contents for the *Final Portfolio*. This activity will teach your child organizational skills and at the same time make the portfolio more like a book and easier to understand.

Some people include a page that lists the criteria used for selecting works. Other commentary about the nature of the portfolio may be helpful as well. For example, if your self-directed learner did nothing but read and write her own versions of Nancy Drew books, a written essay about her experience might be in order. In five or ten years, she may gain personal insights or big laughs when she reflects back on "My Year with Nancy Drew."

To get a sense of how to best organize the material, imagine that a trusted friend will visit your home and pull the portfolio from the family bookshelf. Does the *Final Portfolio* make sense if you or your child is not there to explain it?

Make a cover and bind the book so that the book is permanent and sturdy enough for your family bookshelf. (Bookbinding resources are included in "Exploring Writing," chapter 40.) Alternatively, you could save this year's collection to be bound later with several years' worth of work. You might videotape the *Final Portfolio*, or scan it to be viewed on your computer. Devise your own unique method of preserving the work. As students grow older, they too will become more sophisticated in the design of their portfolios.

## Special Collections

Once you've tried the *Simple Portfolio System*, you may decide that a specialized portfolio more accurately represents what your child is learning. See if the following ideas work or if they spark ideas for the creation of your personal and unique system.

### One Subject

Help your student put together a collection that focuses only on math, writing, skiing, geography, art, World War II, a pet, how to make a patchwork quilt, or a reading list.

### Videotapes of Projects, Plays, and the Arts

Your child can narrate or read from his work collection. If the entire year has been spent putting on plays, videotape the scenery construction, costume design, and the final production.

### Work Progression or Photo Journal

Begin with the barest of ideas and brainstorming notes about a project, then keep records, through all the rough drafts to the final publishable result. The project is recorded in photos, captions, and text. This method is great for those large projects that don't fold well — constructions, cakes, and gardens, for example.

### Genre Collections

Children may write stories of different types over a period of time. Have them select their best stories from each genre to include in the portfolio. You may prefer to include many stories of one genre.

### Showcase or Exit Portfolio

Here is that flashy, "put your best foot forward" portfolio, that has been edited and perfected to reflect what the student can do when at his best. An *Exit Portfolio* is a comprehensive portfolio that the student puts together to reflect his accumulated knowledge upon leaving a grade level or school, such as middle school or high school. The *Exit Portfolio* could be used when applying for colleges.

## Publish a 'Zine or Newsletter

Quarterly family newsletters or mini-magazines could record student progress in a fun "share it with Grandpa" style. Older students could publish the newsletter, while younger students contribute stories, reports of their progress, art work.

## Computer or Web Page Portfolios

If your student loves to use the computer or is "Web wise," this option could be a great way to demonstrate his computer skills. Computer literate students will have ideas of their own about how to make a website that shows off their knowledge to best advantage.

# Finally

Evaluation should be a straightforward homeschooling experience. Parents quite naturally check in with children to see how they are doing. Are the children usually happy, busy, engaged, enthusiastic, and challenged, whether at play or at work? It's working, folks! Are they sullen, squabbling, always bored, negative, television-addicted, or combative? They might be telling you that something is missing, that it's time for Detective Dad or Mom to help the child find direction. You know the continuum of their lives, have shared their joys and sorrows, illnesses and growth spurts, successes and failures.

Students and families gain confidence from looking back at the hard evidence of learning.

## chapter twenty-seven

# AVOIDING
# STANDARDIZED TESTING TRAPS
*ideas for minimizing the effects of tests on students*

Whaddja get? What is your SAT score? Your achievement test percentile? Your GPA? Your IQ? Important questions, these, because if a student has the right combination of numbers on the right pieces of paper, doors open to that student that will not open to other students, regardless of general merit. Human potential has been reduced to a series of numbers, based on a performance of just a few hours. Those few hours change lives.

Welcome to high stakes testing.

Standardized tests, at their best, may indicate the progress of large groups against a bell-shaped curve, information that could be helpful to school administrations. Homeschoolers, though, are more likely to experience standardized tests at their worst, required — as they are in some states — to be used as a deciding indicator of individual progress or placement. High stakes indeed.

What do standardized tests measure? Verbal ability, yes, but what else? Do you value creative thought and imagination, organizational skill, analytic ability? Sorry, those get but a nod, if that. Moral character, work ethic, compassion, tenacity and focus? Untested. What about the many kinds of nonverbal learning? Math, yes, but other areas? Sorry.

Standardized tests are minimally useful for measuring individual progress. The tests only give a mere idea of a child's general performance against predetermined standards based on a narrow range of knowledge. Even test makers agree that standardized tests are most useful for measuring student performance on — standardized tests!

Standardized tests are acknowledged by educators to be unfair and biased. Test scores and test-taking success have been shown to be best correlated to parental income or other social status indicators not related to actual learning. Tests are blatantly, or subtly, biased toward a white upper-middle-class world view.

Who decided the only worthwhile learning is learning that can be measured digitally? Is it possible that, in failing to promote "un-standardize-able" traits, society has systematically created the unexpected and enormous social dangers our children and grand-children will face? But I digress. Let's move on to the dehumanizing side effects of testing.

## Dehumanizing Side Effects of Testing

After administering standardized tests for many years, both in public classrooms and, more recently, to homeschooled students, I am acutely aware of the drawbacks of this type of testing. As a homeschooling parent, I agonized over whether to test my children. In all testing venues, no matter how kindly, I've observed that standardized tests teach significant lessons, lessons that are, if not outright dangerous, of no benefit to students whatsoever.

The following messages are the anti-learning and dehumanizing lessons that children may learn when they take standardized tests:

- My worth can be summarized by a single mark on a paper.

- Thinking is not valued; getting the 'right' answer is the only goal.

- Someone else knows what I should know better than my parents or I do.

- Learning is an absolute that can be measured.

- My interests are not important enough to be measured.

- The subject areas being evaluated on the test are the only things that are important to know.

- The answer (to any question) is readily available, indisputable, and it's one of these four or five answers here; there's no need to look deeper or dwell on the question.

- The purpose of learning is to get a high score. High test scores are the only purpose of testing.

- If I score very well, I am better than other people who do not score as well.

- Poor test scores mean that I am a failure. If I score poorly, there is nothing I can do to change it. Why try?

- I haven't learned to read yet. I am not smart.

- Since I must be tested once a year, so I can homeschool, my parents and I have to spend the rest of the year preparing.

- The test was easy [hard]. [Public] [home] [private] school kids are dumber [smarter] than I.

- The questions on the test are what is important. What I have been learning is not important.

- I have to get a higher score next year to show that I am learning.

- I am just a member of a herd that must be tested, without individual value.

Do you agree that standardized tests can be powerful teachers? If so, you must ask if these are the lessons you want your children to learn. And what will you do if you find you *must* have your child tested?

## Minimizing Negative Side Effects

Despite these many drawbacks to, and negative lessons from, testing, I find that I am a voice crying in the wilderness. Not only is a deaf ear turned to the drawbacks of testing, the stakes seem to be raised to a higher level with each passing year. Until the testing mania is reversed, many students will need to take tests in order to achieve their goals. These suggestions may help parents minimize the negative effects of standardized testing for their students.

### "Unlearn" Negative and Undesirable Attitudes

If your student has already picked up some of those negative attitudes, take some time to help her "unlearn" that effect. Talk about testing and what the testing experience has been like for her. Sharing your concerns can help your student develop a balanced perspective about testing.

## Use Alternatives to Achievement Tests

If you must test, can you use a placement or readiness test that evaluates what the student is ready to learn? These tests are somehow less terrifying than tests that measure what you may or may not have "achieved."

If possible, use a narrative evaluation, portfolio, or curriculum plan to indicate your child's abilities and knowledge. Any of these can give accurate feedback about what your child knows, his capabilities and needs.

## Prepare Gently

Teaching to the test, albeit a much maligned practice, is universally practiced in the high stakes testing game. Some preparation eases anxiety and familiarizes the students with testing procedures. Be aware, though, that too much preparation may backfire and create unneeded anxiety.

You'll want to seek a balanced approach. For example, many people schedule a general math review a few weeks before testing time as part of their normal schedule, but without emphasizing the upcoming test.

Try to moderate the amount and type of preparation to meet the individual student's needs and to avoid deepening test anxiety. Avoid scheduling tests if stress is high, such as when the student has been ill or when the family is going through major change.

Taking practice tests can be helpful. Practice tests generally focus on learning the format of the test, although the content is usually less difficult. Good practice tests include the types of items students can expect to encounter in the actual test, and offer tips and suggestions for taking the test. Some of the more common test taking tips include such strategies as: considering all of the possible answers before choosing; reading directions carefully; not spending too much time on any one problem; coming back to difficult problems later; ways to guess at answers they don't know.

Avoid too much preparation and study with young children and first time test takers. Until students have a strong sense of their abilities as test-takers, work to build confidence instead.

## Provide a Neutral Testing Environment

Consider this: Standardized tests were designed to be administered *in* the regular classroom, *by* the regular classroom teacher. For the homeschooled student, the regular classroom is the student's own home, and the regular classroom teacher is you, the parent. Your ideal neutral testing environment is right there in your home with you giving the test.

Unfortunately, it is often difficult, and sometimes against regulations, for a parent to acquire standardized tests to administer to her own children. If the ideal is simply not available, what is a parent to do?

First, try to find a test administrator who is a homeschool parent. If that is not possible, find a test administrator who is sympathetic to homeschooling and understands the importance of having educational options. If you need a sympathetic tester, your local or state homeschooling group is a good place to get a referral. You can learn from other people's experiences. Ideally, ask the tester to come to your home to administer the test.

Another possible testing environment is in the home of the tester. Find a tester who is compatible and who likes children. I have administered both private family tests and small group (up to six or eight) tests comfortably in my home. Other neutral environments might include these: a friend's home; someone's office that you can borrow for a few hours; a private study room at the library; a community room; a Sunday School room at your church.

The last resort is to have your child tested in a classroom situation, either privately or at the local public school. The occasion of taking a standardized test is not the ideal time to introduce your child to thirty strangers, even if they know some of the students or the teacher. For some homeschooled students, an unfamiliar classroom environment is stressful, detracting from their ability to focus on the test at hand.

## Delay Testing

Do what you can to avoid testing your young children. Children younger than age eight or nine are widely erratic in their response to a test anyway, and achievement tests are invalid at early ages. Older-blooming readers may suffer terribly when faced with a test that demands reading skill they don't yet have.

Some students sail through the first grade test but become a bundle of nervous anxiety by grades three or four. I've observed that, when students do not take tests in the earlier years, they seem somewhat more at ease when they do take a test when older. Avoiding early testing may lessen test anxiety.

## Test Less Often

Avoid annual testing if possible, particularly for young children. Annual (or — gasp! — more frequent) testing causes parents and teachers everywhere to teach to the test. Don't blame yourself. You can't help it! If your state law requires that you test your students annually, you may have to work to change the law, but meanwhile, you may feel a need to teach to the test.

In general, though, test less often, whatever that means to you in your situation, or not at all. Remember that academic testing is a rather young phenomenon and its worth, while highly lauded by some, is far less proven than we are asked to believe.

## Test More Often

I know, I know, I just told you to test *less* often, so chalk this advice up to a life full of contradictions.

More frequent testing is helpful in a few specific instances. For example, if your older child has extreme test anxiety AND personal goals that require high stakes testing, taking tests more frequently can be a good practice ground for him to become more comfortable.

Teens who are confident about testing tend to put the testing chore in the category of "dumb things I've got to do today." Sometimes the only way to turn the MAJOR EVENT of testing into the CHORE of testing is with practice.

## Balance Your Own Attitude

Are you — the parent — a Nervous Nelly at testing time? Parents may feel that in some ways they, not their children, are evaluated at testing time. And no matter how sure we are that tests don't mean that much, we want children to have a good testing experience. So we worry and stress out.

It's natural to feel somewhat anxious, but don't let your anxiety spill and overshadow your child's efforts. Stifle your inner Nervous Nelly. If you can't keep from obsessing, have your calmer spouse take the child for the test.

The parents who best prepare their children for test taking are the ones who are relaxed. When students are older, parents can encourage them to view the test as a game to be played, or a puzzle to be solved. Trying to figure out what the test writers had in mind intrigues many teens into putting forth their best efforts.

If you take this approach, remind your children that they are to "play the testing game" hard, doing their best, but enjoying the process as well. Then back off and let your child have her own testing experience.

Who knows? Maybe your child will join that tiny club of students who have told me, "I just love taking tests! How soon can I do this again?"

## Finally

Yes, we do live in a world that demands high stakes testing, a world that places an artificial value on test scores. In spite of the unfairness and potential harm from testing, many homeschooling families cannot sidestep achievement and other standardized tests. Parents, if they employ practical preparation and maintain an attitude that keeps negative side lessons of testing at bay, are generally effective in helping their children navigate the testing obstacle course.

## SELECTED RESOURCES

### Achievement Testing in the Early Grades:
The Games Grown-Ups Play
By Constance Kamii, Ed. National Association for the Education of Young
Children, 1509 16$^{th}$ Street, NW, Washington, DC 20036-1426
202/232.8777 800/424.2460 fax: 202/328.1846
resource_sales@naeyc.org www.naeyc.org
Read this book before you have your very young child tested. Kamii shows
that the ill effects of achievement testing in the early years far outweigh any
advantage.

### Bayside School Services
PO Box 250, Kill Devil Hills, NC 27948
800/723.3057 252/441.5351
orders@baysideschoolservices.com www.baysideschoolservices.com
Testing materials are made available, by a homeschooling family, to
homeschooling families. CAT/5.

### Family Learning Organization
Kathleen McCurdy, PO Box 7247, Spokane, WA 99207-0247
509/467.2552
homeschool@familylearning.org www.familylearning.org
Tests and scoring available, including MAT and CAT. Parent-administered
assessments available.

### Scoring Hi
SRA/McGraw-Hill, 220 East Danieldale Rd., DeSoto, TX 75115-2490
800/843.8855 888/772.4543 fax: 972/228.1982
www.sra-4kids.com
Test preparation materials for K-8. Available for CAT, CAT/5, CTBS, Terra
Nova, MAT 7, ITBS, Stanford Achievement Test, others.

### Seton Testing Services
Seton Home Study School
1350 Progress Drive, Front Royal, VA 22630
540/636.9990 fax: 540/636.1602
www.setonhome.org info@setonhome.org
Standardized tests, CAT-E Survey, for homeschooled students.

## chapter twenty-eight

# READY
# FOR COLLEGE AND WORK
*how homeschooled students enter the main stream of life*

Oh, that Big Step into the deep waters of adulthood! Will it be a flailing belly flop, a lovely swan dive, or will she quietly slip into the water without a splash and swim like a fish? You can't prevent a belly flop or two, but parents can offer the guidance that helps their student swim safely into life.

Your role as a guidance counselor — helping your child step successfully into adulthood — is both challenging and vitally important. By doing some research ahead of time, you will be prepared to help him as he begins to think about his future. And although you are not a trained guidance counselor, you have exactly what your student needs: the willingness and tenacity to work, both with him and on his behalf, for his future success and happiness.

To become independent, young adults will eventually need to convince strangers in positions of power — such as college admissions officers and potential employers — that they know what they say they know and have the skills they say they have.

Luckily, you don't need to know it all. You just need to be able to guide this particular student at this particular time. As your student's direction reveals itself, you'll want more in-depth material, such as the resources listed at the end of the chapter. We'll focus mostly on an overview of ways students show proof of who they are and what they can do. You may need to research particular points further with and for your student.

Please keep in mind, though, that all this "proof" — this jumping through hoops — while perhaps useful in attaining a goal, is certainly not an indicator of future success. Now for the nitty gritty details.

## Entrepreneurship?

Entrepreneurship may be the greatest unsung success story of the homeschooling world. Whether the student launches his own business venture or joins the family business, his commitment is the same — participating in all aspects of a business in an adult world, including the risk.

Students with an entrepreneurial bent may not need credentials, tests, or other educational currency. As in any business venture, satisfied customers or sought-after products are the best evidence of successful enterprise. However, while young entrepreneurs may not need certificates, transcripts, or awards, they may need a grubstake from their parents or other mentors. Money for materials, a computer, a place to work, free rent, and tons of advice are examples of ways parents can help students get a start.

Some students who take up entrepreneurship during the teen years may segue into the adult world without a blink. Some will use their valuable entrepreneurship experiences to tuck into resumes, interviews, and application forms as they move on.

## Off to Work?

Some students are ready to go straight to work in a field of their choice. Perhaps they love the work and are well-qualified by experience. Many students who have not chosen a career will want to try several different lines of work until they find a path that interests them.

No matter what the reason, students who want to work must prove themselves to prospective employers. There are several things parents can do to help them off to a good start. They will need interviewing skills, a resume, and perhaps a transcript or portfolio of their work.

Help your student fill out a few job applications for practice. Job applications usually ask about the applicant's high school education. Make sure your student knows how to translate his homeschooling education into the conventionally understood language of high school diplomas, transcripts, honors, colleges attended and so on. Pick up copies of applications from a few different businesses to see how they differ.

Parents can also draw on their personal contacts and resources to help the student make initial connections. Getting that first job is an important and scary first step into adulthood. With a first successful experience under his belt, the student can build confidence for future employment opportunities.

## Joining the Military?

If your student is interested in the military, you'll want to contact a recruiter as soon as possible. One thing to be aware of is that he or she may lose eligibility for Tier 1 status by taking the GED. At this writing, homeschool graduates qualify for Tier 1 status with a parent-issued diploma that is backed by adequate records. You may need to help your recruiter find the most current information regarding homeschooling. The rules in each service branch are somewhat different. It seems wise to contact a national home-schooling organization, such as National Home Education Network, for the latest information as soon as your student shows an interest in the military.

## College Bound?

For many homeschooled students, college is the next step because they know they need the certificates, degrees or knowledge to meet their chosen goals. Others find college to be the perfect intermediate step from home life to independent living.

If college is a strong possibility for your student, check with state and local homeschool support groups to find other families who are a step or two ahead of you in the process. They can provide information and insights.

Usually, an accredited diploma, a GED, or a homeschool tran-script is acceptable. The student's individual ability and aptitude are the deciding factors and those can be proven in many ways and can be matched to one of the many different colleges. Students should be prepared to offer materials — such as a portfolio, transcript, or resume — that represent the learning accomplished. Admissions officers are also interested in extracurricular activities, such as apprenticeships, volunteer work, sports, honors, and other activities.

Colleges vary widely in admission requirements. Some require a certain amount of math, a foreign language or threshold test scores, for example. Others ask for an application interview or written essay. Many colleges have developed a specific policy that applies to homeschooled students. For example, some colleges ask to see a detailed description, by the student, of the student's learning experiences. Shop around for a college that is complementary to your style of homeschooling as well as your student's strengths. Talk to the admissions office staff well in advance of application.

Some four-year colleges do not require test scores such as the SAT, ACT, SAT II subject exams, or other entrance exams. If tests are an issue for your student, you may want to seek those schools out. See *FairTest*, below. Another exception to the need to produce a test score is in the case of transfer students, such as two-year community college graduates who are only required to submit transcripts of their successful prior college work.

Parents of students who want to attend the most competitive colleges should probably start thinking and planning for that possibility as early as eighth or ninth grade. Early planning can help avoid disappointment later. Activities and academic courses can then be planned to provide the student with the type of high school experience sought by the college of interest.

Students who want to participate in college athletics or apply for athletic scholarships should also be in contact with colleges of interest early in their high school years. Contact the *NCAA* (see the listing below) to make sure your student meets eligibility rules for homeschooled student athletes.

Remember, too, that students can homeschool right on through at least some of the college years, doing a good deal of work by correspondence or Internet courses, taking *Advanced Placement* tests for credit, or attending community college while initially being supported by their parents.

## Types of Proof

Homeschooling parents have found a number of ways to help their young people demonstrate that they are qualified and capable. Examples of such evidence are listed below, in no particular order.

### College Entrance Exams such as ACT, PSAT, SAT

The ACT or SAT is taken by the majority of students bound for a four-year college experience. Colleges vary in their requirements: some accept either, some colleges require one or the other, while still other colleges do not require test scores. If you have a particular university in mind, find out what its requirements are before taking a test. The tests, including the PSAT, are given on specific days and in specific locations, usually high schools, throughout the country. Your local high school or college of interest can give you the necessary information for registering.

The PSAT is a preliminary test that gives the student practice with this type of test. If the PSAT is taken during the junior year, National Merit Scholarships may be awarded if PSAT scores soar. When signing up for the PSAT, be sure to use the "homeschool code" so the scores are sent directly to your home, not to the local school.

Students should plan to take the ACT or SAT closer to the end of their high school years, generally in the junior year. Some families plan to have students take the SAT or ACT several times, starting perhaps at tenth grade, in order to get the best score possible. Which one of these tests should your student take? Check with the colleges of interest to see which tests are desired.

Should your student prepare for the entrance test? Homeschooled students who have had little testing experience are likely to benefit from some preparation and taking practice tests. Additionally, college entrance exams have become the high stakes card to admission to select colleges. As more and more students top out with perfect scores, some evidence suggests that those who take preparation courses actually do improve their scores. Practice materials are available at bookstores, as software, online, or through local test preparation centers. If your student wants to compete for the highest scores, she may have no choice but to prepare extensively. Gaining confidence for the testing experience is another reason to prepare.

## The GED Option (General Educational Development)

Some students may prefer to take the GED at the end of their homeschooling years. For many there is no reason not to take the GED if that is what is desired. Most colleges accept the GED, and it may be a perfectly appropriate avenue to high school completion for your student.

You may be able to have your student take the GED test. Check with your local support group to find out how your school system handles these students, or contact your nearest community college.

Some colleges ask homeschooled students to get the GED Diploma. Some parents resist the GED route for their students, believing that forcing homeschooled students to take the GED is discriminatory. Instead, these parents prefer to grant homeschool diplomas and transcripts of grades, and have the student take achievement, placement, or college entrance tests to prove their readiness for college.

For many years, homeschooled students have been admitted to elite colleges without taking the GED. Don't automatically assume the student must take the GED if the college asks for it. Some students have successfully challenged the GED or diploma requirement at both state and private universities. If the Admissions office asks for a GED score, see if they will accept an alternative, such as a letter from the principal (you), SAT scores, or perhaps achievement test scores.

Typically, state universities require either a GED or a diploma from an accredited high school. In fact, some state universities ask more of homeschooled students than private universities. Just do your homework with each college of interest.

Transfer students do not need to show their high school work, only transcripts from the college from which they are transferring.

## Transcripts and Credits

Many, many colleges accept homeschool transcripts. Homeschool transcripts can be a highly refreshing variation to "English I-IV, Algebra I and II," the standard transcript reading fare of college admission officers. In addition, if your student joins the military or applies for a job, he may be required to provide a transcript from the homeschool.

Preparing a transcript will take a bit of work. Some colleges may want you to document "credits," the basis of high school graduation requirements. That is fairly easy to do if you have used a traditional curriculum, but it is not that difficult if you haven't. Creating a transcript for your student adds value and closure to the teen years.

"Distance education" and some suppliers may be able to provide the homeschooled student with credentials from accredited schools. Credit by examination may also be available. If your student enrolled in an accredited homeschooling correspondence school, the school will compile the transcript for you.

If you have created your own curriculum, or if your student has followed a thread of personal interest through the subjects, you will need to organize the evidence of all that learning in a readable format that addresses traditional subject matter. If you have kept track of your student's many and varied activities through the years, you'll find this task both enriching and enlightening. And if you must labor over a most unruly collection of data, you'll still enjoy the trip down Memory Lane.

How do you go about creating a transcript? Here is the basic approach. Assume that a typical high school credit, or "Carnegie credit" as they are often called, represents one hundred seventy to one hundred eighty or so class sessions plus one or two hours of out-of-class work for each class session. The homeschooled student's credit might represent a similar number of hours spent at a learning task.

You may want to check out your state's statutes on credit requirements for public schools and set up your program to coincide with state requirements. For example, in one school, a student must earn 22 or more credits: language arts, 3; mathematics, 2; science, 2; U. S. history, 1; global studies, 1; government, ½; health education, 1; physical education, 1; career development, ½; personal finance and economics, 1; applied arts, fine arts, or foreign language, 1. Student-selected electives round out the remaining credits. If this sample system does not meet your family's needs, redesign it to reflect your family goals, values, and activities. Better yet, check out a few colleges and see what they are looking for.

You may devise a system for awarding grades, as other schools do, such as the A-F system, and calculate a grade point average. Considering that your student is an eager and enthusiastic learner, and that he actually has mastered the material, rather than having "gone through" the material, your student's grades should be easy to determine. You might award grades based on degree of involvement in the subject, effort, extension, and of course, mastery.

Another approach is a straight mastery system, a pass/fail system in which only the course work that the student has mastered is included on the transcript. Grades are not assigned. In other words, you construct a transcript that includes only the studies your student has mastered, and without grade or comment. Attach an explanation of how mastery was determined.

You can print out a transcript using your computer or complete the transcript by hand. For an official touch, the transcript should be signed and dated by the school principal (you). In our family, we had the signatures notarized in lieu of a school stamp and to prevent the document from possibly being construed as "student generated." That extra effort may have been over the top but we felt it worthwhile.

Remember that while homeschool transcripts are useful for college entrance, they are not usually accepted for returning to high school after homeschooling for a part of the high school years. Unlike colleges that do want to see homeschool transcripts, most high schools do not have a system set up for accepting home-schooled transfer credits. As mentioned in "Teen Medley" (chapter 33), students who plan to return to high school to graduate should ask to see the school board policy on granting credit to homeschoolers.

Finally, remember that students may not need traditional diplomas and/or transcripts to achieve their goals. Some employers and educational institutions are more interested in what students know and know how to do.

## College Credit Through Testing

Advanced placement (AP) tests can help a student accrue college credit without attending classes. These tests substitute for course work, and college credit is given for knowledge demonstrated on the test. AP tests are an economical way to acquire a good deal of college credit if the student knows his subject well. College Level Examination Programs (CLEP) also allow students to get college credit by examination.

## Community College

Community college is a popular transitional approach to higher learning that is favored by many homeschooled students. Generally, students can take classes at age sixteen. As long as students are part time and have not applied for admission to a particular program, they just register, pay fees, and attend classes. They do not need to submit a high school transcript. They may be required to take a placement test so that they are appropriately placed in a class suited to their abilities. Some homeschooled students choose to start with the most basic classes for a thorough review. Others enter successfully at the level suggested by the placement test. This is very much an individual decision; remember that you do have choices.

Typically, homeschooled students begin as part time students, perhaps with only one or two classes. Some begin with classes of personal interest, while others take math, reading, writing, foreign language, or a science course.

If a student is interested in taking the GED exam, preparatory courses are available at the community college, in addition to the tests being administered there regularly.

Some students enroll full time in community college classes for either a degree or certificate program. Students who want to enter these programs will need to comply with all enrollment and admission requests and deadlines, possibly including a transcript.

Upon completion of community college programs, some students transfer to a four-year college to complete their bachelor's degree. Others complete a one- or two-year certificate program or seek a job.

## Interviews

Parents will want to help students prepare for interviews, whether for work or for college. Interview skills, practice in answering sample interview questions, and tips about appropriate dress and manners will ease the way for that first interview. Encouraging your young adult to see the interviewing process as one in a series of educational experiences helps her relax into the process.

## Resumes

A resume says one thing very clearly: I am an adult with an adult "ticket." Young people do not start out with long complex resumes and they shouldn't try to pad them with fluff. Your student's professional-looking and organized one-page resume should include personal information; educational background; skills related to the job being applied for; projects completed and what the student did on the project.

Don't forget to include employment background, including volunteer work, apprenticeships, internships, and mentorships. Be sure to help your student identify the specific responsibilities he held. A well-designed resume will tip the employer off to the student's unique talents and skills.

Help your young adult include a statement of her employment objective, notifying her potential employer of her motivation above and beyond Mall Money. The objective can vary widely. Erin included this statement in her resume: "My immediate goal is to expand career opportunities. My goal is to *do* a good job, not just *get* a good job." She got the job. Alice had a specific job in mind when she created a recent resume, so she listed as her objective the exact title of the job she was applying for. She also got the job.

List the most recent education first. Include college courses taken, and give the approximate date graduated from your home high school. If you named your homeschool, you can use that name, or you may prefer to use the name of a correspondence school that your student graduated from. Noting the years homeschooled inevitably sets your student off as unique, a valuable qualification.

Include, as references, names of adults with whom your student has worked closely. Volunteer supervisors, 4-H or Scout leaders, coaches, piano teachers, can be called upon. Of course, your student should ask these adults for permission to name them as references ahead of time. When my friend Katie took the time to write me a lovely letter asking for permission to list me as a reference, and thoughtfully included some of the activities she and I had participated in, refreshing my sagging memory, she got a prompt and very positive reference written on her behalf.

Remember to update and rework the resume specifically for each job applied for. Resumes that are generic won't work. Employers may have certain requirements for resumes, so research those ahead of time.

## College Through Work

Finally, don't forget the work route to college. Many larger companies pay educational expenses for employees and may even allow the employee to attend classes or study on company time. The usual requirement is that the courses or degree taken must be related to work. It would seem that a wide variety of classes might fit that category: math, writing, computer, finance, business, science, foreign language, engineering, depending on the company, of course. If your young adult finds work for a large corporation, even in the lowest position, make sure she researches the policies that may allow college attendance.

## Finally

This parental role of guiding youngsters toward independence — it is a tough one, isn't it? I recall a time when I felt I was pounding my head against a wall with my daughters. Finally, a friend said to me, "Just keep opening doors for them, Ann." Ahh! Forehead-slapping-simple advice, although not so easy in practice, was exactly what I needed to hear. I needed to keep on keeping on.

After all, there may be thousands of doors a youth needs to try. What if she doesn't want to walk through the first thirty or even the first hundred doors? To find the one that interests her, you might have to open the thousandth door! And what if she walks out a door and comes back again? And again? Are you like I was, tired and afraid just thinking about it?

Buck up, parents. You can do this, and you *will* do it, because you've come so far. You know by now to take care of yourselves, so be sure to take extra good care during this final push. What would I have done without the good support of family and friends?

When you get discouraged, try to remember that juicy carrot that dangles out there for you — a sweet moment when you and your grown and independent child reconnect — two adults who love and respect one another. It is there for you but for the waiting.

So guide that student lovingly and doggedly — he is worth it.

## Selected Resources
## Entrepreneurship, Careers, and Work

*Creating Portfolios for Success in School, Work, and Life*
By Martin Kimeldorf, Free Spirit Publishing Inc. 1991.
Use your portfolio to show what you have accomplished, learned, or
produced.

*DANTES — Defense Activity for Non-Traditional Education Support*
voled.doded.mil/
The Department of Defense's Volunteer Education Program. DANTES'
mission is to support the off-duty, voluntary education programs of the
Department of Defense and to conduct special projects and development
activities in support of education-related functions of the Department.

*Ferguson Publishing Company*
200 West Jackson Blvd., Chicago, IL 60606
800/306.9941 fax: 800/306.9942 www.fergpubco.com
A leading publisher in career education. Books on careers, colleges, testing,
job searching, more.

*The Independent Scholar's Handbook:*
The Indispensable Guide for the Stubborn Intelligence
By Ronald Gross, Ten Speed, 1994.
A wonderful resource. Learn how to become an expert on any subject on
your own. Also by Gross: *Peak Learning: How to Create Your Own Lifelong
Education Program for Personal Enlightenment and Professional Success.*

*Proving You're Qualified:*
Strategies for Competent People without College Degrees
By Charles D. Hayes. Autodidactic Press
PO Box 872749 - Wasilla, AK 99687     907/376.2932
info@autodidactic.com     www.autodidactic.com
The title says it all. Hayes has written a number of books that set a standard
for autodidacts, including *Self-University: The price of tuition is the desire to
learn. Your degree is a better life,* 1989; *Training Yourself: The 21st Century
Credential,* 2000.

*The Uncollege Alternative*
Danielle Wood, 2000.
Harper Collins Publishers, New York. Explores opportunities such as travel,
apprenticeships, internships, college.

*Un-jobbing: The Adult Liberation Handbook*
By Michael Fogler. Free Choice Press,
PO Box 1027, Lexington, KY 40588-1027     800/318.5725
An adult version of unschooling — toward voluntary simplicity.

## *What Color Is Your Parachute?*

A Practical Manual for Job-Hunters and Career Changers
By Richard Bolles. Berkeley, CA. Ten Speed Press. Revised 2001.
Classic book to help you find the right job by helping you discover what you
want to do and where you want to do it.

## *Wishcraft: How to Get What You Really Want*

By Barbara Sher, Ballantine/1986.
Step by step plan to help build goals out of vague dreams and then achieve
them. A worthwhile classic.

## HOMESCHOOLING AND COLLEGE

## *388 Schools That Do Not Use SAT I or ACT Scores for Admitting Substantial Numbers of Students Into Bachelor Degree Programs*

FairTest: The National Center for Fair & Open Testing
342 Broadway Cambridge, MA 02139    617/864.4810
fax: 617/497.2224  www.FairTest.org  fairtest@fairtest.org
The website (2001) includes colleges and universities that do not use the SAT
I or ACT to make admissions decisions about substantial numbers of
freshman. Check with each school's admissions office to learn more about
specific admissions requirements. Also available: *Test Scores Do Not Equal
Merit: Enhancing Equity & Excellence in College Admissions By De-
emphasizing SAT and ACT Results*. Take a look at some of their titles: *The
SAT Coaching Cover-Up*; *The Case Against the SAT*; *Sex Bias in College
Admissions Tests: Why Women Lose Out*; *The Mis-measure of Man*; and
many others.

## *And What About College?*

How Homeschooling Leads to Admissions to the Best Colleges and
Universities
By Cafi Cohen, Holt/GWS 1997.
A standard for college bound homeschooling students. One of a kind.

## *Bears' Guide to Earning College Degrees Nontraditionally*

John Bear. Ten Speed Press. Updated yearly.
The essential reference to alternative educational opportunities.

## *College Degrees by Mail & Internet:*

100 Accredited Schools That Offer Bachelor's, Master's, Doctorates, and Law
Degrees by Distance Learning
By John Bear, Mariah P. Bear. 2001, 8th ed.
Solid advice for those who want to attain degrees from the comfort of home.

### From Homeschool to College and Work:
Turning Your Homeschooled Experiences into College and Job Portfolios, by Alison McKee. Bittersweet House, PO Box 5211, Madison, WI 53705-5211. Good example of a homeschooled student accepted by the college of his choice.

### Getting a College Degree Fast:
Testing Out & Other Accredited Shortcuts
By Joanne Aber. 1996.
Help with turning your knowledge into a degree.

### The Guidance Manual for the Christian Homeschool:
A Parents' Guide to Preparing Home School Students for College or Career
By David and Laurie Callihan.
Career Press, 2000.  800/CAREER-1    www.careerpress.com
Information for students interested in pursuing military careers and much more.

### Homeschoolers' College Admissions Handbook:
preparing 12- to 18-year-olds for success in the college of their choice
By Cafi Cohen, 2000. Prima Publishing    www.primalifestyles.com
An excellent resource, full of useful ideas, information about resources, and "how we did it" stories.

### The Homeschooler's Guide to Portfolios and Transcripts
By Loretta Heuer, 2000. IDG Books Worldwide, 919 E. Hillsdale Blvd., Ste. 400, Foster City, CA 94404
A useful guide to gathering unconventional learning activities into traditional formats. Includes worksheets for organizing records.

### Karl Bunday
Karl M. Bunday, PO Box 674, Panchiao 220 Taiwan
learninfreedom.org/colleges_4_hmsc.html
Lists hundreds of colleges that have admitted homeschoolers at this website.

### NCAA
Initial Eligibility Clearinghouse
NCAA, PO Box 4044, Iowa City, IA 52243
319/337.1493   Forms 800/638.3731
www.ncaa.org/cbsa/home_school.html
Eligibility information for those who want to play college sports. For questions about homeschooling as it relates to NCAA legislation and academic eligibility, contact Membership Services Department, NCAA, PO Box 6222, Indianapolis, IN 46206 or call 317/917.6222

### Peterson's Guide to Distance Learning Programs 2002
Listing of hundreds of academic courses on the high school, college, and graduate level.

## COLLEGIATE TEST PREPARATION

### Apex Learning
110-110 Ave. NE, Bellevue, WA 98004  800/453.1454
inquiries@apexlearning.com  www.apexlearning.com
Prepare for Advanced Placement Exams. Complete online AP courses and
AP exam reviews.

### How to Prepare for the SAT I, 21ˢᵗ Ed.
By Sharon Weiner Green, Barron's.
Includes one complete diagnostic test and seven model tests, explanations,
solutions, tips. Vocabulary flash cards are included.

### Kaplan Educational Centers
888 7ᵗʰ Ave., New York, NY 10106  212/492.5800  www.kaplan.com/
Study for the SAT, ACT & PSAT. Test preparation materials and programs at
many levels. Courses, books, audiotapes, CDs, videos, online instruction.

### None of the Above, The Truth Behind the SATs
By David Owen. 1985, Revised and updated1999.
Classic expose on how the Educational Testing Service controls the gates to
higher education and success in American society. This book helps students
understand the mind of the test maker.

### Princeton Review
2315 Broadway, New York, NY 10024
212/874.8282  fax: 212/874.0775
www.review.com
Test preparation for PSAT, SAT, ACT, SAT II, GRE, more. Software, books,
online and live courses. Check out the website as a place to match students
with colleges.

### Ten Real SATs
From The College Board.
You can't beat practicing with real tests. Strategies included.

### Up Your Score 2001-2002: The Underground Guide to the SAT
Larry Berger, et al., Workman Publishing Company.
Tips from students who have hit at or near the SAT ceiling. Humorous and
helpful. Full of strategies to help you beat the SAT. Helpful for the PSAT too.

## Testing for College Credit

### Advanced Placement Program (APP)
The College Board, 45 Columbus Ave., New York, NY 10023
212/713.8000  www.collegeboard.com
Examinations that offer college credit to high school students. Fee.

### The College Board
45 Columbus Ave., New York, NY 10023
212/713.8000  www.collegeboard.com
The Board controls and administers the PSAT/NMSQT, SAT I and SAT II, CLEP, and AP tests, which are created by Educational Testing Service. Practice questions and test taking strategies can be found at the website. Information about college entrance, financial aid, scholarships, and more.

### College-Level Examination Program (CLEP)
The College Board, 45 Columbus Ave., New York, NY 10023
212/713.8000  www.collegeboard.com
These exams can be taken by people of any age and test knowledge gained through nontraditional methods. 3-12 credits may be awarded towards a college degree for each exam taken. Modest fee.

## Preparing for GED Exams

Accredited schools granting diplomas to homeschool students are listed in the Appendix. Those who prefer the GED may consider these resources to help them prepare.

### The Cambridge Pre-GED Program
Cambridge Book Co., NY.
A well-known preparation program. Be sure the material you select reflects the 2002 changes to the GED.

### GEDonline Internet Community
Diversified Computer Services, PO Box 2199, Kenosha, WI 53141
262/652.2492  www.gedonline.org
Study for your GED test online with practice tests, a sample essay graded, interactive study lessons, more.

### Passing the GED
Glenview, IL. Scott, Foresman.
Standard GED preparation materials. Watch for 2002 dates or later for materials that have been updated for the 2002 version, although older materials are probably still useful.

# PART 5

## Explorations I
## The Big Picture

Featuring:

Keynote: Creating Habits for Learning

Field Tripping

Learning Clubs

Apprenticeships and Mentorships

Teen Medley

## chapter twenty-nine

# KEYNOTE
# CREATING HABITS FOR LEARNING
*for exploring the world*

This chapter may seem familiar, for it is a synthesis of previous discussions — a melding together of themes, if you will — into a short list of *habits for learning*. I have taken some of the basic themes and habits that develop so well in homeschooled family life and summarized them for quick reference.

*Habits for learning* help your child experience the world, as some say, "up close and personal." The best habits will help youngsters figure out how they are interconnected with the earth and with other human beings. The best habits will help them explore and understand their inner lives as well as the lives of others, past and present. The best habits will help students discover how to live a meaningful and respectful life.

- *Opportunities to experience the world first-hand.* Learning comes easiest when children use hands, bodies, and all the senses, as well as the imagination, intellect and emotions. While paper-and-pencil representations of knowledge (i.e., packaged curriculums or workbooks) may be useful at times, used excessively, such materials are flavorless substitutes for fresh and personalized learning experiences.

- ***Opportunities to learn in different ways.*** If your child favors a particular learning style, such as visual, auditory/verbal, hands-on projects, or styles that involve memory, music, or mathematics, she should have many opportunities to learn in that way. However, she should also be given multiple opportunities to learn in ways that are not favored as well. You ask whether you really need to go to this extra effort? Absolutely yes — and here is why this is so important. Learning through a variety of approaches, favored by the child or not, stimulates brain activity. The brain develops synapses through use. When a variety of learning approaches is available, the ability to learn — no matter how the material is presented — is optimized, and brain function increases for life. There is a two-for-the-price-of-one special for you — how can you beat it?

- ***Opportunities to learn mental flexibility and creativity.*** Mental activities — free-ranging and divergent activities unrelated to acquiring knowledge — should be encouraged early and often. And it is so easy! Just encourage your child in the many activities that children love, including games, play, life experience, and real-life problems to solve. Students can work alone or with others.

- ***Time with actively available and caring adults.*** Children need access to adults involved in real work, running the gamut from scrubbing a floor to scrubbing a space mission. Parents, grandparents, aunts, uncles, friends and neighbors are a great start — they are already there! If you live far from family or in a remote region, join or create a group or club where children and adults can interact. The individual adult does not need to be extremely active in your youngster's life. She just needs to be visible and sometimes available. Students need one or two individuals in their lives who are sincerely interested in children, and their questions, and are willing — no, eager — to help them find answers and opportunities. Knowing that his questions and knowledge are important to a grown-up person will help your child build confidence and knowledge in the best possible way.

- ***Generous access to materials, books, and resources.*** These do not have to be expensive, just plentiful. The goal is to have resources to use or not, rather than having expensive material that you feel you must use because it cost so much. Libraries, mail order catalogs, online stores, used book stores, garage sales, secondhand stores, surplus stores, and community resources, can supply the materials you need. Could your homeschooling group have a materials swap meet?

- ***Loving guidance in developing a value system.*** Homeschooled children develop self-discipline and desirable values with gentle direction from parents. Many families develop a strong value system within the family circle. Others benefit from associations with religious or spiritual organizations, or other groups that share similar values.

- *Opportunities to take measured risks.* Risk-taking is not always thought of as a good thing, yet a life without some risk is stagnant. Knowing how to weigh whether a risk is worthwhile is a valuable life skill. Your child needs to be able to take chances and to experience the consequences. When he falls, the family safety net is there is catch him.

- *Opportunities to make learning mistakes.* We all attend The School of Hard Knocks. We learn important lessons from our mistakes, so long as we aren't hassled too much when we blow it. Children deserve many early opportunities to do the same. Provide an encouraging environment in which your child has many opportunities to learn through trial and error. He will quickly learn self-correction.

- *Opportunities to interact with a diverse and multi-aged group of people.* Children need real life opportunities to learn how to get along with all kinds of people of many ages in many different circumstances. While children's social needs vary widely, it is important to provide regular social contact for all, from the complacent loner to the socially hungry butterfly.

- *Time to play and fantasize.* Students of all ages need time to explore their inner world, both alone and with others. This habit was discussed at length in Part One, but it cannot be said too often that play is a child's work. Play is a child's *crucial* work, without which healthy development cannot take place.

- *Privacy.* Related to the need for play, time and privacy are a required condition for thinking and imagining. A highly structured life strips children of privacy. Homeschooling can allow plenty of time for "alone" opportunities. How important it is to learn to live with yourself just as you are! How important it is to learn that each moment doesn't need to be filled with activity! Give your child the freedom to discover her heart's desire in her way.

- *Opportunities to pursue interests.* Being compelled to learn a subject before readiness or interest has developed is antithetical to the efficient approach to learning that children are born with. Compelled learning before readiness or interest are developed is a prime cause of children being labeled learning-disabled. Even worse, compelled learning causes children to develop a distaste for learning. Teaching a child that learning is hard, or bad, or distasteful is a dangerous lesson indeed.

- *Varied opportunities for creative expression.* Students need a chance to explore a variety of avenues for expression, such as art, writing, poetry, music, sports, plays, or dance. Some youngsters feel a sense of creative satisfaction by learning to organize events and campaigns. How your student chooses to express himself is not the point: he just needs to be able to explore a variety of modes for expression.

- *Opportunities for physical activity.* Children need time to develop physical skills. Large-motor (sports, bike riding, hiking) and small-motor (playing a musical instrument, painting, cooking, soldering) activities should be pursued, as lifelong interests may develop.

- *Opportunities to do meaningful work.* Whether for financial gain or in service to others, students need ways to contribute to the family, community, or larger society. Real life opportunities — from setting up a lemonade stand to mowing an elderly neighbor's lawn to caring for a sick puppy — provide anchors in the real world for later abstract learning activities to build on.

- *Physical and emotional safety, and a sense of well-being.* Optimal learning cannot take place when a child is hurting, hungry, tired, ill, depressed, angry, or afraid. Wise parents make sure their child's sense of well-being has a high priority in the daily routine. They assure that the daily routines of activity are flexible enough to allow for change.

- *Absolute assurance that they are loved and trusted.* The security that develops from feeling cared for and trusted lends courage to your child while he is learning new and challenging things. Falling on your face hurts less when your loving parent is nearby to pick you up, give you a hug, and help you back into the fray.

## Finally

Students who have well-developed *habits for learning* stand to learn easily and enthusiastically about the world and themselves. The chapters that follow discuss some ways homeschooling families explore the world. Why reinvent the wheel?

## chapter thirty

# FIELD TRIPPING

*learning on the road and in your community*

Wanna study chocolate? You can read about chocolate, eat chocolate, buy chocolate, cook with chocolate, learn about growing cacao trees, watch movies about chocolate, fingerpaint with chocolate pudding, and even crave chocolate! You can learn to spell Hershey, Cadbury, Nestle, Dove, and even Ghirardelli. But until you stand in the candy factory smelling the smells, hearing the sounds of machinery, and watching the candy bunnies and sugary hearts find their way into pretty boxes, do you really know chocolate?

Field trips are an up close and personal introduction to new subjects, new connections, new ideas, and new ways of looking at the world. In addition, children learn so much that is incidental to the intent of the trip. Suppose that, on a trip to a fish hatchery, one of your children becomes fascinated as she listens to members of a visiting tour group speak Japanese among themselves. Perhaps on that same trip your youngest spends most of his time pocketing pretty bits of gravel in the parking lot. Could you have guessed that a desire to learn Japanese or to study geology could be launched at a fish hatchery?

The side-learning on field trips is so rich that it makes good learning sense to plan trips frequently. Trips can probe general or specific kinds of questions, and may deepen current studies.

Some questions to consider while you plan follow:

- Where does *x* (food, clothing, toys, cars, etc.) come from?
- How do transportation systems work?
- What was this community like in "olden times?"
- What do different people do to earn their living?
- What kinds of services and products does our community offer?
- How do different kinds of communication systems (newspapers, telephones, internet, etc.) work?
- How can we learn about subjects such as science? History? Other cultures?
- What are some natural wonders around our region?
- What kinds of animals and plants live around here?
- What are some interesting hobbies that people enjoy?

There are many more questions that could be asked and answered with a trip. After the trip, you may be amazed at the kinds of questions your child will ask, perhaps launching new explorations.

## Sample field trips

The kinds of trips you can take as a homeschooling family or group are endless. This is a small sampling of day-length trips available in my region, all of which have been tried and tested by homeschooling families and groups. I suspect not one family has visited them all!

| | |
|---|---|
| observatories | cheese factories |
| aquariums | forests |
| science museums | wildlife preserves |
| toy museums | interpretive trails |
| vacuum cleaner museums | lumber mills |
| historical centers | fishing operations |
| natural history sites and centers | fish hatcheries |
| art museums | food processors |
| rock gardens | candy factories |
| airfields and airports | foundries |
| ranches | manufacturers of all kinds |
| farms | wool processing plant |
| dairies | sewing factory |

saddle makers
hydroelectric plants
civic centers
retail stores
tourist monuments
libraries
bookstores
printers
wildlife preserves
zoos
clock makers
paper mills
mines
caves
living history programs
water and sewage plants
pet stores
post offices
universities
backstage tour at a theater
theatrical, puppetry, and musical
    productions
tree nurseries
bird and bat sanctuaries
train stations
horse drawn carriages

doll house factories
chainsaw wood carvers
fiber arts demonstrations
fire stations
police stations
courthouses
bakeries
antique hardware stores
hot air ballooning sites
grocery stores
pizza parlors
wetlands
llama farms
K-9 Units
Mt. St. Helens (choose your own
    favorite mountain)
TV and radio stations
newspapers
ship locks
sports hall of fame
herb growers
tulip farms
lilac gardens
geo-heat centers

I'll stop here, but you get the idea. You will find many wonderful opportunities in your region. Jot them in the margins as you think of them so you won't forget.

## Tips for Planning Successful Trips

Choose trips that meet your family's needs. Do you want to go to the biggest bakery in the city and see all the loaves of bread cooling overhead on the conveyor? Or would you prefer a trip to a neighborhood bagel bakery, where children can look at the steamers and talk to the actual baker who starts making bagels every day at 3:00 A.M.? Or both?

Decide whether your children will benefit more by going as a family or as part of a group. For my family, some of the best trips were just mom and the kids. There were memorable times at the science museum when we had the place pretty much to ourselves. I was amazed at how focused and involved my girls were during those trips. Other successful trips — sledding trips, for example — were more enjoyable with a group.

Schedule well in advance. Popular spots in your community are sometimes booked a year ahead. If you decide to schedule a group trip, extra time allows other group members to include the trip in their schedules.

When scheduling a group trip, be sure to set an appropriate limit on the size of the group. Check with the facility to find out their group size requirements. A smaller group size is generally optimal for learning, but size limitations may also be mandated by insurance restrictions. Please don't fudge with the site's requested age and group size limits as this kind of disrespect creates ill will toward future field-tripping homeschoolers.

When scheduling, ask for guidelines, directions, availability of restrooms, teaching materials or preparation suggestions, whatever the site may offer.

Now that the trip is on the calendar, what's next?

## Pre-trip Preparations

To decide what type of pre-trip preparation you need, consider both the type of trip and your children's level of interest. A hiking trip may require nothing more than packing lunches and drinks, dressing appropriately, and tossing a couple of plant or animal identification books in the backpack. For more formal trips, you may want to make sure your children have at least some idea of what to expect. Familiarity with musical instruments and their sounds can make a visit to a musical presentation more enjoyable. You'll want to find a balance, naturally. Too much preparation can take the excitement out of cool discoveries students may make on their own. With too little preparation, children may be unable to make sense out of the experience.

Coach your talkative and outgoing children to take turns and to listen to what others have to say during guided group tours. They may not realize that they should not dominate the tour guide's attention. Of course, the guide may be delighted to spend more time with your inquisitive child at the end of a group tour. Don't hesitate to ask.

Shy children benefit from being coached ahead of time to think of a question. If they are still too shy to ask their questions, be sure to set an example and ask a question yourself. You might even say, "Alice wants me to ask you about…"

Trips afford children a chance to meet and interact with many different people. Whether they are naturally vivacious and chatty, or shy and reserved, children will learn about relationships, meeting new people, talking to strangers, and remembering manners.

Field trips afford students an opportunity to see different kinds of jobs and to talk to people in their workplace. You might role-play with young students to help them understand what a field trip is like to the workers. Practice by giving them a guided tour of the kitchen, then let them give you a guided tour of their rooms or the back yard.

## The Day of the Trip

1. **Plan to arrive fifteen minutes or so ahead of time** so children can use the bathroom before the tour begins: allow enough time for a rest stop at a nearby park.

2. **Remind children to use their "guest manners."** It probably won't seem obvious to most children, but people's workplaces are often homes away from home, and you might review what that means. Work cubicles and items on desks are private, for example, and private property should not be touched without permission. The same principle applies to outdoor trips. When an exuberant city child turned a water hose on a haystack during a farm trip, he did not realize that he was destroying some animals' winter food!

3. **Follow the rules that are laid out for your group**, even if it is just your family. Please do not violate age restrictions. While age restrictions can pose a dilemma for homeschooling families with a wide range of ages, set an example for your children and follow the rule, unless you have called ahead and specifically asked for an exception. Rules are put in place for your safety or comfort. Respecting those guidelines will not only make your visit more productive, it will pave the path for the next family that wants to tour that location. Most locations that welcome tours will be very

clear about what they expect. Rules are usually simple, such as not touching, staying on the path, listening quietly, asking questions, taking turns, and wearing a name badge or a hat. Children need to know ahead of time that you expect them to follow the guidelines.

4. Don't forget to **ask questions, show your enthusiasm, and thank the guide.**

## After the Trip

Plan for a debriefing activity after the trip. Children develop memory, conversational, and interpretive skills through talking about their experiences. They will often debrief themselves spontaneously after highly successful trips, bubbling with questions and comments on the drive home. They may even want to take that trip again soon. An occasional trip may not go well, though, and it is worth your time to find out what went wrong. You may discover that the only problem with the trip was that everyone came down with nasty colds the next day! Other times, though, you may discover that a trip was inappropriate for the ages of the students. Or perhaps the content was good, but you got off on the wrong foot with the tour guide. Some trips may not be right for your family. The debriefing time can help children practice recall skills and help you plan future trips.

Whether it was a great trip or a bust, a written thank-you is still a good idea. A written thank-you from your children, or a drawing from the younger ones, possibly accompanied by a snapshot you may have taken, is sure to put smiles on the faces of the guides or workers you visited. The few moments your children spend in this activity is a useful completion activity as they review and recall the event. And aren't we always looking for ways to give children a real-life opportunity to practice writing skills and good manners?

Follow-up activities may deepen learning. The best follow-up activities are spontaneous, such as when children decide to build a stagecoach after a visit to the historical society. The best ideas are those that extend the enthusiasm students generated on the trip. Sometimes the materials provided by the tour guide are useful. If the field trip was a dud, that imperative thank-you note may be all the follow-up you need.

## How Often?

Limited resources should not prevent you from taking trips. In fact, a field-trip-based curriculum might be the most affordable way to homeschool, as long as trips to the library are included. Many trips or tours are free or have a minimal fee. Some of the more expensive destinations, such as art museums or zoos, may offer a regular free-admission time. Sometimes fees can be reduced or waived in exchange for volunteer work. Be sure to ask about off-peak and off-season discounts. In larger cities, public transportation can take you to many interesting sites. Riding transit is a field trip in itself! In more rural areas, visiting several locations on a single trip can help conserve resources.

How often you take a field trip is a family choice. Some families try to schedule one trip a month. Others are out exploring once or twice a week, or more often. The number and type of field trips may depend on your personal energy, and we know that just getting the family out of the house some days is a chore! To make those planned trips more fun, though, don't forget to plan the *entire* trip, including the drive.

## Are We There Yet?

Remember when getting there was half the fun? With just a bit of planning you can assure that your children arrive at field trips and activities eager and ready to go. You don't want to deliver a "homeschool bus" full of wild-eyed screamers to dumbfounded tour guides. Avoid that embarrassing scene by making the drive an integral part of the event. Planned car activities increase the enjoyment of field trips and activities for drivers and students alike.

### Match Car Activities to Individual and Family Needs

As a general rule, don't insist on lessons in the car. Consider the car or van as part of your family environment, an extension of the home. Sometimes you learn there, sometimes you play, and sometimes you just want to pass time in a pleasant way. Keep your goal in mind as you plan: arriving at the field trip destination or activity with students who are calm and ready to participate.

There are so many things you can try. You may want to ply your passengers with recordings of great music, conversations, or stories.

Some families reserve selected activities for travel time — favorite tapes, games, activity books, hand-held electronic games and the like. You might check out books-on-tape from your local library to enjoy together. Quiet individual activities such as handwork are also great in the car. A young child may prefer to have her own bag or box of car supplies — crayons, paper, markers, rulers, any materials that you are willing to have in the car. A lap tray or cookie sheet can keep supplies at hand and off the floor.

To provide a change of pace on long trips, switch between family/group activities (singing together, telling stories, playing games, conversations) and individual activities (listening to tapes, playing solitaire games, reading, drawing). And remember that we all need regular breaks, especially very active children who benefit greatly from frequent "wiggle" stops.

Children who learn to use their time in the car for active learning, quiet play, reverie, or recreation arrive refreshed and ready to go.

## Sibling Issues

Do the siblings rival in your car? Try some divide-and-conquer strategies. Provide one or two children with tapes and a tape player with a headset to occupy them while you have conversations, make plans, or play mental games with another. Then take turns being passengers and "copilot." Divide physical spaces with bags, pillows, or stuffed animals. Seating can be preassigned or rotated to afford the most affable atmosphere. (You could humorously hand out "boarding passes" with seat assignments.)

When siblings grind on each other's nerves despite all your good efforts, parents have golden teaching opportunities, with the kids still nicely buckled up! Help them learn the various skills of getting along with others — just keep your little lectures brief and to the point.

And don't forget the power of parental silence. When the family car must be parked along the side of the highway while you wait for children to settle so that you can drive safely — everyone sharply aware that you are already late to an appointment — silence sometimes makes the strongest statement of all.

## Finally

Taking field trips can be your core curriculum if you are so inclined. Never underestimate the learning offered by trips into the community for both planned learning and indirect learning. Getting there, i.e., car time, can easily be enjoyable with a bit of planning. Parents need but a light touch and a sense of humor to calm and renew cranky kids, and turn them back into curious learners. So get out there and see your world!

## chapter thirty-one

# LEARNING CLUBS
*creating successful group learning experiences*

Learning clubs are among the best kept secrets of the home-schooling world! Despite the fact that learning clubs have sprouted up everywhere homeschooling families gather, the existence of these clubs is generally unnoticed outside the homeschooling community.

Why aren't learning clubs better known? Because homeschooling learning clubs unfold and then thrive without fanfare, an inaccurate stereotype of homeschooling continues to proliferate. The prevailing picture — smiling families poring over workbooks at the kitchen table — remains the foremost image in the public eye. The kitchen table image represents but one small slice of the homeschooling pie; learning clubs represent a growing slice that deserves greater attention.

Let's drop the shroud of invisibility that has kept learning clubs from the public eye and wave a flag for the successes of these busy little gatherings! This chapter explores the workings of common learning clubs. Practical tips and suggestions for launching clubs are included, and clubs that worked for others are described.

# Characteristics of Learning Clubs

- Clubs are usually sponsored by families who want to meet unique needs.

- The desire to create clubs may arise from the children.

- Parent-formed clubs are common; many young people have formed successful clubs as well.

- Leadership is typically voluntary and unpaid.

- Clubs tend to develop around interactive and participatory activities.

- Clubs usually have no dues or cost requirements beyond expenses.

- Attendance is optional. Clubs that thrive are duplicated by other groups. Those that are poorly managed or that do not meet the learning needs of the members usually die from lack of interest.

- Clubs usually form among families who are already linked together in some way — a support group, an e-mail loop, a neighborhood, a church group, or a common interest. A newly formed club may be announced through state or local support group newsletters, e-mail loops, and church, library, or community bulletin boards.

- Clubs may limit membership in some way, such as setting a maximum number of students or a final enrollment date. A Spanish Club may want a larger group to defray the cost of paying a native-speaking teacher. A group planning to study microscopic pond life may be limited by the number of microscopes available. Limits may even be set according to the capacity of people's living rooms. Theme clubs seem to work best with about eight members. Social clubs such as Park Days, Swim Days, and Skating Days are typically open to all. The more, the merrier.

- Successful clubs usually admit participants based on interests, not age. Membership guidelines, when given, are broad categories: all, pre-school, six to ten, teens, moms, boys, girls, and so on.

- Clubs may be very casual (occasional play days, field trips, or craft projects) or quite formal (study traditional school subjects from a traditional curriculum on a regular schedule).

- Even the best clubs have a limited life. Only rarely will a group continue to function despite the coming and going of students, and even the organizers.

## Advantages of Learning Clubs

- Children who learn well in groups have an opportunity to shine.

- Shy children can learn social interaction skills in a structured and safe setting.

- Some activities are more enjoyable in a group setting; some activities require a group.

- Clubs make more knowledge accessible to more learners.

- Parents share educational responsibility with others.

- Learning clubs are affordable. Despite income disparity among group members, all members can participate on an equal footing.

- Parents who work outside the home, or who are single parents, can participate without being overwhelmed.

- Kids meet a variety of interesting adults.

- Clubs offer equal access to learning resources.

- Learning clubs provide opportunities for social learning.

- Clubs increase social opportunities for parents and students alike.

- Clubs create an opportunity for culminating learning activities, such as public speaking, projects, demonstration, performance, or simply celebration.

## Ten Easy Steps to A Smashing Learning Club

1. **Limit sessions to once a week, or less,** at least in the beginning. Student interest will remain high and parents avoid burnout. Stand firm on this point! If some members want more frequent activities for their children, someone else should start a different club on a different day.

2. **First clubs should be of short duration** — perhaps just a month or so — while you work out the logistics of planning and the work involved.

3. **Figure the costs out ahead of time** so you can be reimbursed and other families can budget for expenses.

4. **Keep your club size compatible with the type of club you want.** Theme or subject-based learning clubs should be family-sized, with six to eight students being an optimal size. Twelve might work for very compatible groups. Larger clubs can easily become classes and as such become prone to developing classroom-type behavior issues. Social clubs can be any size.

5. **Expect to spend about half a day or more each time the group meets.** The time you spend together need not be all planned activities. Include some social time. Bring lunches or potluck and gather afterwards at a nearby park. Younger children need time to run off steam, older students need to huddle, and parents need to gab and plan.

6. **Remember that homeschool students aren't preprogramed to change subjects every 45 minutes.** Sometimes they will focus on topics they enjoy for longer than you might think. On the other side of that coin, an activity that flops will last about two minutes. Let it go and move on. Divide the time and schedule several activities that explore the subject in different ways. If you finish early, they can always play! If you complete just one activity, save your unused plans for next time. In the best clubs, the children rarely want to stop or go home. The line between joyous learning and pure play is delightfully hazy.

7. **Avoid the temptation to "do school."** Clubs that are too school-ish may fizzle out fast. An exception (Isn't there is always an exception?) might be a group of older students who want to learn a subject together. Some students might even hate the subject, yet recognize that they need to learn it as a prerequisite to future studies. Studying with a group of peers may be preferable to struggling alone.

8. **Remember that successful clubs are voluntary.** Be prepared to change the focus of the group to meet the changing needs of students, or to close the club and start a new one. Expect some students and families to move on to other activities as their interests change.

9. **Be clear about the ground rules** you put in place. Let the following questions to help you set the rules.

- What is the maximum number of students the group can handle?

- Will parents drop students off or stay and participate?

- What is the age range allowed?

- Will younger siblings be allowed to attend, or will parents need to make other arrangements for them?

- Where will you meet — your home only, rotate among members' homes, rent a facility?

- Do you have a plan in place to help screen for compatible students and to help mismatched members adapt or move on?

- Do parents fully understand that voluntary means that students really can choose not to attend? A clear understanding of "voluntary" avoids problems that arise when students are bored or disinterested.

10. **Remember — not all students enjoy learning in groups**. If your child doesn't want to attend a learning club, don't despair. Try another group, let her start her own club, or try community activities.

## Types of Learning Clubs

There are surely as many types of clubs as there are imaginative club leaders. Many clubs, fall into one of these three categories.

*Theme or subject clubs* are very popular. Math, literature, writing, cooking, sewing, horses, computers, space, dogs, collections, foreign language, religious study, magazine subscriptions, science, history, geography, sports, board and card games, and community service are examples you can choose from. Pick your topic and form a club.

*Community service clubs*. These may be local or associated with national groups such as 4-H, Boy Scouts, Girl Scouts, or Campfire.

*Social clubs*. Sometimes it is fun to get together and hang out, have a dance, go skating, or otherwise celebrate the events of our lives. Roller skating parties, swim parties, age group clubs, girl clubs, Moms' (or Dads') Night Out, birthday clubs, dance clubs, and holiday preparation groups are a few examples. Social club gatherings may spawn smaller interest-based theme and service clubs.

## Examples of Clubs That Worked

Use these successful club ideas as grist for your own idea mill.

- *Roller Skating Parties, Homeschool Swim Days,* and *Park Days* are classic examples of social clubs. Many learning clubs get launched at these events. Twice-monthly roller skating parties have been scheduled in every skating rink in my city for more than eight years. Homeschool swim days and swim classes are also popular. This type of party is generally open to all homeschoolers. Exercising, meeting new friends, sharing information, and forming new groups are all part of the ambiance. Sessions are held during school hours, making them popular with pool and rink managers whose facilities are idle during the day.

- "Chow and Chekhov." For more than six years, families have gathered one Friday evening a month in each other's homes for a potluck meal. A theme for the food is picked each month by the hosting family — green food, dessert night, pizza toppings, foreign food, etc. After the meal, starting with the youngest child and moving by age to the oldest, everyone takes a turn to talk about their favorite book. Imagine a tiny child telling everyone — tots, teens, and adults — their two special sentences about *Hop on Pop!* while everyone in the room listens respectfully! When younger children are finished, they drift off to play elsewhere while the rest of the group moves to more complex literature. The founders of this popular event no longer attend. This is one club that took on a life of its own!

- *Little House on the Prairie.* This early group developed around the shared love of the Laura Ingalls Wilder books. The families read the books at home and meet for dramatic play, field trips, and activities with pioneer themes. Soap- and candle-making, watching a farrier shoe a pony, historical field trips, dramatic play, and socializing are typical activities. Other literature themes that lend themselves to similar clubs include the King Arthur legends, the *Chronicles of Narnia, Anne of Green Gables*, Jane Austen's books, the *Boxcar Children,* and the *Harry Potter* Series. Supplemental craft and resource books that accompany some popular series, if available, are a boon to your club.

- Book Clubs. A straightforward type of club, book clubs abound in the homeschooling community. They are often patterned after adult book clubs. Groups may meet monthly to talk about books they have read. Example: one group selects a genre (i.e., animal stories, mysteries) each month, then books from the genre are shared and discussed at the meeting. Afterwards, a related project or craft activity is offered to round out the meeting.

- Latin Club. This club included six families with students aged 9-17. They met twice a month. Each family purchased the same Latin textbook, as all group members were beginning students. One chapter was covered each meeting. Many fun and enriching activities were organized, such as a toga party, crossword puzzles, movies, preparing food, reading myths, and so on. All ages learned together.

- *Destination Imagination*, (formerly *Odyssey of the Mind*). This international organization offers an annual creative problem-solving competition. Teams of five to seven children select a problem in the fall and develop their solution for a presentation in the spring. Homeschooling groups have participated successfully in these competitions.

- *Youth Volunteer Corps.* This national program is sponsored by Campfire. In one community, a *YVC* staff person first attended a homeschool skating party. There, she communicated the intent of the projects with parents, and then recruited homeschooled teens. Students age twelve and up met once or twice a week. Projects, both staff and student generated, include working at a soup kitchen, cutting ivy in parks, building a worm bin, and visiting the elderly.

- Teen Activity Loop. More than twenty families participated in an e-mail loop to announce various social activities for teens. Activities were scheduled at least monthly with each family taking a turn. Typical activities include visiting a corn maze, game days, bowling, playing pool, going to the beach, going to plays. Parents who drove often stayed to visit among themselves.

- Historical Costume Design/Writing Club Exchange. Two moms sponsored these clubs to share with students the sewing and design skills of one parent and the writing skills of the other. The group was formed by invitation. No fees were charged, and non-sponsoring parents had no obligations other than driving. The clubs included four or five teenagers in each of the two separate groups that met one morning a week in the kitchen and family room of one family's home. The writing group designed its own format. It began as a combination peer writing group and teacher directed instruction. As soon as students developed their own projects, teacher-directed instruction was dropped in favor of individual editing and coaching. The costume design group spent a good deal of time researching costumes of various eras and then sketched the designs they wished to create. They then designed patterns for the costumes, shopped together for inexpensive fabrics and sewed their costumes under the guidance of a parent.

- Learning Parties. Five families planned a year's calendar of events. Each family picked a country and sponsored a monthly gathering with that country as a theme. They prepared food, games, activities, and crafts from the country. Guest speakers and field trips were sometimes scheduled. During the subsequent year, families pursued other topics, such as space or science.

- Unit Study Co-op. A group of families selected certain science and health topics, and then parents took turns teaching, bringing snacks, and babysitting younger siblings in a separate room. This more traditional school model works best with smaller groups of students of similar ages and interests.

- Hire a Teacher. A group of parents hired a Spanish teacher. The group met weekly over a period of several years. This model is more effective when everyone is at a similar level of learning, very interested in learning the subject, and when the age range is not too wide.

- Sports Leagues. Sports leagues are superior learning clubs for many students, meeting both physical and social needs for student athletes. Homeschooling numbers are great enough to justify the creation of extensive sports leagues for homeschooled students. Several have been launched in populated areas. If you can't find a homeschooling sports league in your community, why not organize one with the help of your support group? See "Teen Medley" (chapter 33) for more information.

- Classes offered to homeschoolers by community groups. In some communities, park and recreation districts may offer classes to homeschoolers during the day when facilities are otherwise unused. While these classes are usually not set up as learning clubs, some elements of learning clubs are present: they are voluntary, interest-based, and participatory; they involve small groups and have a limited life span. Spontaneous social time frequently follows each session.

## Finally

Creating and participating in learning clubs is a natural next step for many homeschooling families. Clubs make homeschooling a more viable option for many families. Learning clubs can be thought of as private cooperative learning centers, and are a sound model for developing community-based cooperative learning centers. Clubs are practical, efficient, and affordable. Learning clubs work.

## Selected Resources

### Creating A Cooperative Learning Center:

An Idea-Book for Homeschooling Families
By Katharine Houk. Longview Publishing, 29 Kinderhook Street,
Chatham, NY 12037   518/392.6900
Houk founded a very successful cooperative learning center and this book
tells how she did it. Includes philosophies, copies of bylaws, samples of
registration materials, fees, surveys, rules, and other forms. Where was this
book when I needed it?

### Creating Learning Communities:

Models, Resources, and New Ways of Thinking About Teaching and
Learning   Edited by Ron Miller, 2000. The Foundation for Educational
Renewal, PO Box 328, Brandon, VT 05733
Available free online at: www.CreatingLearningCommunities.org
A virtual book written by a diverse group who envision a world in which
community learning centers replace schools. Essays by Farenga, Dobson,
Priesnitz, Houk, and me, proud to be rubbing shoulders with educators I
greatly respect.

### Destination ImagiNation®

PO Box 547, Glassboro, NJ 08028   856/881.1603   fax: 856/881.3596
headquarters@destinationimagination.org
Based on the concept of divergent thinking. Teams of up to seven members
choose one challenge and spend several months perfecting their "solution"
for tournament day. Homeschooling teams welcome.

### Youth Service America

1101 15th St. NW, Suite 200, Washington, DC 20005
202/296.2992   fax: 202/296.4030  www.ysa.org  info@ysa.org
A resource center that helps groups of young people create service or
volunteer projects.

### Youth Volunteer Corps

www.yvca.org
In association with Campfire Girls and Boys,
4601 Madison Avenue, Kansas City, MO 64112-1278
816/756-1950   fax: 816/756-0258
info@campfire.org  www.campfire.org/campfire_nf.html
Volunteer opportunities for youth ages 11-17. Join or create a homeschool
group. Volunteer groups work twice a week on student-initiated projects.

## chapter thirty-two

# APPRENTICESHIPS AND MENTORSHIPS
*bringing community experts and students together*

Good apprenticeships are win-win-win-win arrangements: students thrive when they learn with adults; knowledgeable adults enjoy sharing knowledge and benefit from an extra pair of hands; parents know their student's learning is expanding; the community enjoys long-term benefits when young people feel like they belong.

Dentists' offices, veterinarians' offices, horse stables, and woodworking shops are examples of businesses that have created successful apprenticeships specifically for homeschooled students. Not a single one of those apprenticeships was advertised in the local newspaper or the telephone book. In fact, these apprenticeships didn't even exist until enterprising parents or students reached out and asked.

How can parents bring homeschooled students together with community mentors? Start with the suggestions below. Mentorships and apprenticeships are discussed interchangeably here, as the mechanisms for setting them up seem to be about the same.

## How to Create Apprenticeships

### Start From the Student's Interests

When deciding on the kind of apprenticeship to look for, beginning with a relationship based on your child's interests is a good step toward success. Perhaps she enjoys bicycling and is mechanically inclined. Ask at bicycle shops for opportunities. If he enjoys drawing, contact a graphic artists' association for leads.

## Look for Connections in Your Community

You might begin with friends, relatives, local businesses, and your own business associates and connections. Perhaps the retired person down the street is an accomplished gardener and would enjoy exchanging gardening tips for some heavy hauling. Perhaps you have a friend who is a gourmet cook and needs help with her weekly dinner parties. Maybe an uncle would welcome a young plumber as a helper.

Consider small apprenticeships for younger children. If Bobby wants to watch your neighbor work on her car and hand her wrenches, and your neighbor doesn't mind, why not encourage that friendship? Once he has experienced "small" apprenticeships close to home, your child may be ready for a larger adventure.

## Make the Arrangements for Your Student

Parents should do the legwork and phone calling. The helping adult will feel more comfortable and you will provide an example for your student if he decides to pursue an apprenticeship on his own.

Keep in mind that apprenticeships are out of fashion these days, and many adult experts and business people will not know what you are asking for. You may need to take some time to interview several potential experts and introduce them to the ideas of how your homeschooled children learn through their experiences.

You can plant the seeds of an enduring apprenticeship through regular tours or visits, followed by small apprenticeships of a few hours or days. Several interviews with you, your student, and the mentor, should help you determine whether you have a workable arrangement. Also, be sure to follow up regularly on how things are going, with both your child and her mentor, so you can help iron out any wrinkles in the schedule.

Although you should make the arrangements for your child, you should also include her on the "team" as she is ready and interested. By the teen years, your student may be able to do the legwork, with you as coach.

## Don't Be Afraid to Get a "No"

You are likely to get turned down a time or two. Don't let it discourage you. Apprenticeships are a new idea for many. If the individuals you contact are unable to work with your student, ask them to suggest referrals. Keep trying and you will find a fit.

## Begin Small

Start with a limited schedule and see how it goes. Mentor/student relationships may have a limited life span, depending on many factors, including your child's age and interest level, and the mentor's interest in keeping the relationship going. Apprenticeships can last for a week, can happen once a week for a month, or may be several hours a day for a year. Some experiences can continue over a period of years if everyone involved is agreeable.

## Be Prepared to Move On

Your child might experience one apprenticeship or many. Make sure that both your youngster and his mentor understand that there is enough flexibility to meet the needs of both individuals. Each should feel free to terminate the mentorship if time or other circumstances require it.

## Consider Community or Volunteer Service

Community service can provide valuable real-life experiences, and may be a springboard to further opportunities. Contact local nonprofit and service organizations of your choice and find out what they have to offer.

## More Advanced Ideas

As your youngster matures, he or she may want to consider apprenticeship ideas such as these: conservation work in Australia; apprenticing to be a master farmer in Greece; interning in a museum in Micronesia; working with a midwife in Kentucky; volunteering with disabled children in England; studying art in Italy; working as a teacher or doing construction in India; helping a team of solid-state physics researchers in Holland; or interning as a wildlife patient care assistant in New York.

## Making It Work

So now you've found the perfect apprenticeship situation for your child. The only problem is, the expert — a great guy, knowledgeable, and he likes kids — doesn't have a clue about how apprenticeships work. It is a first-time experience for both master and student. Using the following guidelines may help the expert design a successful experience.

### Time Commitment

For the first apprenticeship, avoid setting up an open-ended situation, and keep the initial arrangement to a few sessions. Is six weeks at one hour a week about right? Would your expert prefer a couple of days a week during his slowest season? Maybe he prefers an apprentice for one full week only. What about several half-day sessions? Encourage the expert to set up an arrangement that works well for his business, perhaps during seasonal slowdowns.

### Set Up an Application Process

Discuss with the expert whether there is a need to create some kind of formal application procedure. He could ask the student for something that indicates his motivation or commitment, such as a personal letter of interest or letters of recommendation from other adults. He might have the student fill out a standard job application. Students learn from this process even after the arrangements have already been set up. Other times, one day on the job is enough for the student to discover whether or not he is committed, and no formal application is needed.

### Assure Student Safety

Let the expert know that you want to be free to drop in at any time. Ask about safety instructions and guidelines. You might also ask whether insurance is provided by the expert, his business, or by you. Check with your own insurance provider ahead of time if needed.

### Be Clear About Expectations

An initial interview among the three parties — student, parent, and master — offers a chance to seek details about the actual activities the student will do. Businesses usually have a mix of exciting activities and menial tasks. If the expert wants to offer instruction in trade for chores, ask him to describe the tasks as precisely as possible, and to estimate about how long the student would be involved in each type of activity.

### Create a Simple Contract

A contract, whether written or verbal, can go a long way toward assuring a successful apprenticeship for both master and student. Include days and hours, apprenticeship duties, what the young person can expect to do and learn. Be sure that you sign it as well, indicating your support for the experience.

The contract can be renewed if things go well. If the apprenticeship is a washout for either party, a preset closing will help end it gracefully.

## The Next Step

Suppose the apprenticeship you set up is wildly successful. In time, though, your student may want to move on to something else. Does the expert express a desire to continue apprenticeships with homeschooled students? His problem is that he has no idea how to connect with the homeschooling community.

He has done so much for your student, you feel you should help him make contacts. You could suggest that he offer an introductory field trip or class. You might brainstorm with him to set up realistic activities that will excite student interest. Advertise the event in your newsletter.

## Finally

Many youngsters are eager to join the real world, accept real responsibility, tackle real challenges, and meet real people. Some mentorships and apprenticeships are available through the community, such as a Police Cadet Program. If you cannot find an opportunity that suits your student's needs, many families successfully create opportunities for their student. Homeschooled teens thrive when involved in compatible relationships and connections that place them out in the community. Do what you can to create these opportunities for your students.

## SELECTED RESOURCES

### Museums, Zoos, and Historical Societies
Many organizations will work with homeschooled students who want to volunteer. Most want students who are at least fourteen or so, but it never hurts to ask if your younger student has the desire.

### The Best 106 Internships
By Mark Oldman, Samer Hamadeh, Princeton Review, 2000.
Recommended for high school and college students.

### Center for Interim Programs
PO Box 2347, Cambridge, MA 02238
617/547.0980     fax: 617/547.0980
Info@interimprograms.net  www.interimprograms.com
This center has thousands of apprenticeship and internship options. They specialize in developing options for people who want to take a year off between high school and college.

### Maine Organic Farmers & Gardeners Association
Agricultural Education Apprentice Program
PO Box 170, Unity, ME 04988
207/568.4142  mofga@mofga.org
Helps place apprentices with master farmers and gardeners, who teach what they know and offer room and board in exchange for farm work. Age 18 up.

### The National Directory of Internships
The National Society for Experiential Education
9001 Braddock Road, Suite 380, Springfield, VA 22151
order 800/803.4170    703/933.0017    fax 703/426.8400
info@nsee.org   www.nsee.org
Thousands of opportunities in seventy-five fields for college, graduate, and high school students as well as for people who are not in school.

### Student Conservation Association, Inc.
PO Box 550, Charlestown, NH 03603
603/543.1700    fax: 603/543.1828
internships@sca-inc.org    www.sca-inc.org/
Nonprofit organization offers volunteer field experience and training in outdoor conservation projects throughout the US. Ages 16 and up.

### Internships:
On-the-Job Training Opportunities for Students and Adults
Peterson's Guides, Princeton, NJ
Annual. Explore 50,000 opportunities all over the world.

## chapter thirty-three

# TEEN MEDLEY

*options for independence-seeking older students*

Is your teen in a state of constant change? Does your teen's approach to learning seem chaotic? Does your youngster flit from activity to activity — always sampling, but never digging into a topic with gusto?

Although this approach to learning often looks and feels chaotic to parents, it is a common one for many teens. It may actually be a highly effective sampling of the world — an unbounded and enthusiastic exploration of activities and ideas. The teen years are a perfect time to explore many options.

One of my daughters picked up and then dropped pursuits many times. After much prodding on my part, and self-exploration on her part, she eventually found new interests. Today she takes her time, but she still sees herself as someone who enjoys exploring many different things along her path.

Since we know that many teens are not ready to choose their life path until late adolescence, and often much later, how can we best support them as they seek their path? Homeschooling offers unbounded flexibility for parents and students to develop highly individualized learning opportunities. Whether you are a lifelong homeschooling parent, or a parent seeking an educational alternative for a school-fatigued teen, you can create excellent opportunities that suit your teen's needs and interests.

This chapter suggests some of the paths taken by students — just a sampler of the many options available. These are here to get your creative juices flowing.

## Homeschooling As Usual

Does your teenager thrive in the family homeschooling circle? For many homeschooled teens, continuing the processes begun long ago — those processes of learning independently, seeking answers to questions, practice and study with and among the family — is the absolute best course of action. If your student has moved gracefully into the teen years, you will just keep on doing what works!

Sometimes school-fatigued students come to homeschooling looking for respite. These teens need some "down time" before diving into structured activities. Take the time to work with your teen to develop a program that meets her particular needs.

## Work/Volunteer Activities

Work is a natural approach to self-education for many young people. Encourage your student to work, not only for money, but to collect knowledge, perhaps in several distinctly different fields. In a very real way, your student's work experiences translate into bits of data for his work resume. "Apprenticeships and Mentorships" (chapter32), may give you more ideas.

Part-time jobs and volunteer opportunities can help the student see the need for academics. Whether your student takes on a paper route, works in your home office, babysits, or slings hamburgers, she will learn as she earns.

Parents can help in many ways. For a starter, you may be able to take advantage of your own connections and knowledge to help your student find and explore job opportunities. In addition, you can: help your student put together a resume; do practice interviews with your student; suggest appropriate dress; provide transportation; and most of all, provide essential encouragement and moral support!

Volunteer work is an excellent way to get experience and to benefit from adult interaction. Look around your community and see what is available. Helping to deliver *Meals on Wheels*, visiting senior citizens, or doing chores for them is one type of activity that is available in nearly every community. Local churches and nonprofit groups often have service activities. Some families work together on annual neighborhood litter pickup days.

## Self-Education — Becoming an Autodidact

By the time students reach the early teen years, many have developed strong areas of interest. Students sometimes begin to take charge of their own education. They prove their readiness to educate themselves by actively pursuing knowledge and developing skills independently, without your help.

Self-education may not lead to further formal studies. Some self-educated students become so knowledgeable about their areas of interest that they bypass traditional pathways in pursuit of that interest. Others discover a need for formal education in order to continue in their chosen field.

## Interscholastic Activities and Sports

Most homeschooling students who want to participate in competitive sports activities do so through local clubs and recreation districts. Homeschooling Sports Leagues are growing in more populated areas. Check with your local homeschooling organizations. Perhaps the next wave of parents of promising homeschooled athletes will throw their energy into building up Homeschooling Sports Leagues throughout the country.

Does your gifted athlete want to play college sports, even compete for athletic scholarships? No problem! The *NCAA* states that it "...does not have a different set of standards for home-schooled and traditionally schooled students. However, the certification process for home-schooled and traditionally schooled student-athletes is different." Parents of athletic hopefuls should read those requirements from time to time, to make academic record-keeping consistent with the requirements asked for when the student applies for certification. See "Ready for College and Work" (chapter28) for contact information.

Sports participation is available through local public school interscholastic programs in some states. Check with your local support group for this information. In some states, homeschooled athletes sometimes must jump through many hoops to win a slot on a public school team, while in other states, homeschool students are treated on an equal footing with public school students.

## Classes

Some students receive private lessons or tutoring to round out their academic studies. Others take public or private school classes through a nearby high school. Classes that are available to any adult in your community — such as music, art, aerobics, or basket weaving — are usually open to teens.

Driver training, math, art, music, foreign language or other classes of interest are typical classes that homeschool students seek out. Some students attend classes part-time, or take classes as part of their homeschooling experience, without any intention of graduating. They just want the experience and the knowledge. Check with your local support group to find out if your local school will accept your student for just one or two classes of interest.

## High School Classes through Community College

Community college classes are accessible as soon as your teen reaches age sixteen and as early as thirteen or fourteen in some areas. For many teens who are lifelong homeschoolers, taking a community college class or two is an ideal next step. Students can usually register for classes with little difficulty. Sometimes parental permission is required. Evidence of homeschooling may be requested and students generally take a placement test. Many students take classes that interest them or round out their skills.

## High School Completion/Diploma Program

To participate in a High School Completion/Diploma Program, the student may need permission from a district school superintendent. If that is the case, it is best to approach the superintendent well prepared, having already talked with officials from the program, having taken the placement tests, and perhaps with a standardized achievement test score in your pocket. Show evidence that your student has complied with homeschooling law in your state, if applicable. Bring along any other evidence you might have that demonstrates your student's ability to succeed at the college level. Arrive exuding your confidence that you are merely going through a formality. Arriving "hat in hand," however, and you may stir an uneasy feeling in the school staff that your student may not be able to make the grade.

First, though, call your community college to see if such a program is available in your area. The advantages may include school-district-paid tuition while enrolled in the Diploma program in which a student can earn both high school and college credits. Some students participate in the high school completion program in order to take advantage of the classes that interest them, and then move to another path without completing the Diploma Program.

## Transfers to Classroom Education for a Diploma

Homeschooled students may transfer to public high school for a variety of reasons. Some families plan for their students to attend high school full-time so they can take advantage of particular programs. Some always-homeschooled teens may want to try the generic high school experience of their peers. Some families want their students to have a diploma from the local school district. For other students, homeschooling was always just a stopgap measure, a temporary solution for just a year or so.

If public high school attendance is part of your plan, be very clear about whether graduation and a diploma are part of that plan. Students who want to graduate from high school with their age mates need to acquire the necessary credits. Most public high schools do not automatically accept credits awarded by parents, no matter how well deserved or rigorously earned.

However, some private schools accept the credits you award your homeschooled student. Consult with private high schools in your community and see if they are willing to work with you. If you prefer a correspondence school, The *American School* and *Clonlara Homebased Education Program* are examples of accredited programs that are successfully used by homeschooled students. See the Appendix for other choices.

The matter of whether credits will be assigned is best handled early, before time or money have been spent on a program that is not acceptable at your local school. Talk to the local school administrators about the private school, correspondence program, e-school, or distance school you want your student to attend. Make certain the program in which you plan to enroll your student will be accepted for credit *before* purchasing the program. You will avoid disappointing surprises when graduation rolls around. For your records and peace of mind, get a copy of the school's policy for admitting transfer students (including homeschool students) and the policy for granting credits for classes taken by correspondence. Even when school staff assure you the program you plan to use is fine, you'll want the peace of mind that comes with written reassurance for your files.

## Transfers From Classroom to Home

Some students who first transfer to homeschooling at the high school level may feel more comfortable if they use a traditional curriculum such as correspondence or online classes. They are conditioned to want to be like their peers and to be told what to learn. A traditional program will help them realize that they are learning, and they can always make the transition to a more natural and self-directed approach to learning if that suits them better. Families usually come to a mix of academics, work, service, and activities that satisfies their student's energy level and needs.

Other students who leave high school for homeschooling know exactly what they want to learn and do, moving quickly to a self-teaching approach to their education. These students may find books such as *The Teenage Liberation Handbook* and *Real Lives* (by Grace Llewellyn) helpful.

## Finally

Here's a word of caution for parents of school-fatigued teens. Remember that homeschooling is not a panacea that will magically resolve all the trials and problems of the teen years. A particular academic approach probably did not cause all your student's problems (though it may have contributed) and homeschooling probably won't instantly solve all of the problems, either. What it will do is give you time — time that you can spend with your teen helping her deal with her problems, in an individual and most useful way.

## SELECTED RESOURCES — GENERAL

### Hewitt Homeschooling Resources

www.hewitthomeschooling.com/o/workserve.htm
An extensive listing of work and service suggestions you can mine for ideas.

### Homeschooling through the Teen Years:

Complete Guide to Successfully Homeschooling the 13- to 18-Year-Old
By Cafi Cohen ©2000, Prima Publishing, 3000 Lava Ridge court, Roseville,
CA 95661    800/632.8676    www.primalifestyles.com
This book is jammed with practical information and ideas for parents who
homeschool teens.

### My Life as a Traveling Homeschooler

By Jennifer Goldman. Solomon Press Publishers, 417 Roslyn Road,
Roslyn Heights, NY 11577    www.educationrevolution.org/books.html
At age eleven, Jennifer relates her experiences as a homeschooler as she
travels with her uncle, alternative educator Jerry Mintz.

### Not-Back-to-School Camp

Grace Llewellyn, Box 1014, Eugene, OR 97440
541/686.2315    www.nbtsc.org
Popular annual international camp for unschoolers ages 13-18.

### The Self-Education Foundation

PO Box 30790, Philadelphia, PA 19104 215/235.4379
www.selfeducation.org  info@selfeducation.org
Young people at the forefront of the next wave of philanthropy who are
working to build and support a cohesive movement, across cultures and
disciplines, of communities initiating their own education. Small awards are
given to self-educators and education mavericks.

### A Sense of Self: Listening to Homeschooled Adolescent Girls

By Susannah Sheffer, Holt. Available from: FUN Books,
1688 Belhaven Woods Court, Pasadena, MD 21122-3727
fax/voice: 410/360.7330    toll free: 888/FUN-7020
www.fun-books.com/  FUN@FUN-Books.com
Shows that homeschooled teenage girls are a bright light of self-esteem when
compared to their schooled peers.

### The Teenage Liberation Handbook:

how to get out of school and get a real life and education
By Grace Llewellyn, expanded and revised, 1998.
Lowry House, Box 1014, Eugene, OR 97440
541/686.2315  www.LowryHousePublishers.com
An excellent resource for students (and their parents) who want to drive their
own education and pursue knowledge independently. Also by Llewellyn —

*Real Lives: Eleven teenagers who don't go to school*, a collection of compelling personal essays by teens who have educated themselves without formal schooling.

### *www.PeterKowalke.com*

Explore with a lifelong unschooler as he shares his experiences of learning, writing, college, and life through journal entries, essays, and more.

## SELECTED RESOURCES — ATHLETICS

### *The Amateur Athletic Union (AAU)*

c/o Walt Disney World Resort,
PO Box 10,000, Lake Buena Vista, FL 32830-1000
407/934.7200 or 407/363.6170  www.aausports.org/mytp/home/index.jsp
Most local amateur sports are connected with AAU if inter-club competition is involved. Homeschool sports clubs can join.

### *Homeschool Sports Network*

www.hspn.net
A network of homeschool sports teams in Virginia that may be able to connect you with teams in other regions. Christian perspective.

### *National Christian Homeschool Basketball Championship*

Attn: Jerry, 3908 N. Peniel, suite 450, Bethany, OK 73008
www.homeschoolbasknat.com
For more than ten years, a basketball tournament has been creatively combined with a Christian homeschooling conference.

# PART 6
## Exploration II
## Subjects

Featuring:

Keynote: Choosing the Right Stuff

Exploring Math

Exploring Science

Exploring Social Studies

Exploring Vocabulary and Spelling

Exploring Literature and Books

Exploring Writing

Exploring Music

Exploring Arts and Crafts

Exploring Foreign Language

Learning by Computer

Considering Textbooks?

## chapter thirty-four

# KEYNOTE
# CHOOSING THE RIGHT STUFF
*finding materials that help students explore deeply and broadly*

The question is familiar —
"How do I know if my child is learning the Right Stuff?"

The question is nearly always followed by a plaintive —
"And by the way, just what is the Right Stuff?"

The answer is just as plaintive —
Nobody knows.

No expert — not me or your mother, nor an educational expert, nor your homeschooling buddy down the block, nor your spouse, nor the greatest thinker on the planet — really knows for sure what the Right Stuff is. Identifying the Right Stuff is far tougher than most experts want to admit.

Consider this for a moment — some futurists speculate that as much as ninety percent of what a youth of today learns during the school years will be obsolete by the time he reaches adulthood. Further, ninety percent of what he will need to know as an adult will have to be learned on the job. What a staggering thought!

Even if those figures are wildly overstated, common sense tells us that much of what children learn today will be unneeded by adulthood, and much of what they will need to know as adults will be specific to future and unknown jobs.

*The Right Stuff* reveals itself best in the shadow of the learning twins, *the love of learning* and *the ability to learn*. Luckily, children are born with both *the love of learning* and *the ability to learn*. Parents can assist best by opening doors, assisting, guiding, and finally, standing aside.

One way to do this for homeschooling parents is to take a page from the unschooling approach and follow the student's natural interests. I heartily recommend that even the most structured home-schooling parents give the interest-led approach a try as often as possible.

If such an open-ended idea knots up your stomach and sends panic rushing through your veins, you may be wrought up over what is actually normal and natural parental responsibility. Isn't worry a natural part of the parenting territory? Doesn't every honest parent on the planet worry that they are not doing enough for their charges?

Your confidence will soar when you discover, as all unschooling parents discover time and again, that children love to learn and can become enormously excited about a topic. Doesn't it stand to reason that when children are learning with enthusiasm, they learn more, and the more they learn, the better their learning skills become, and the more they can learn? Enthusiastic learning becomes a deliciously vicious cycle in the very best sense!

Another fact you can take advantage of is this: knowledge really doesn't fit very well into tidy subject areas. Instead, knowledge is so completely interwoven that you can count on any topic of interest to provide a springboard into many traditional subjects. To prove this to myself, I have teased out the ways in which a single interest can lead to another, and another, until most traditional subjects have been covered, using various starting points. You might want to try that with your pet topics, too.

Here's one of my examples. Suppose a flock of blue jays crowd into your sunflower stalks to feast one autumn day. You are all end-lessly fascinated and get out the binoculars to look more closely. Your children ask questions until you have to dig out the encyclopedia for more facts. You do all the "bird" things you can think of, such as filling feeders, building a bird bath, and visiting the Audubon Society or a duck pond. You might help your children go online in search of more information. You may visit your library or bookstore for additional books to pore through.

By now you have opened doors to new knowledge. Your children may be reading about birds and, perhaps, writing about or drawing birds. If the interest continues, you will quite naturally begin to look for more "bird" doors to open. Without even thinking about it, you will find multiple ways to explore the avian world, touching on many other subjects as you do.

Try science, for example. Boil a chicken carcass down and try to reassemble the bones. Examine feathers under a microscope. Study bird flight patterns and introduce the concepts of aeronautics. Build model rockets or airplanes and see what follows.

Mathematics can be explored with younger children through counting, sorting, or grouping different kinds of birds, airplanes, or feathers. Older students might estimate the airspeed or altitude of birds in flight, for example.

Art and history can be explored through the art and life of John James Audubon. A student who becomes interested in flight opens a natural window into learning about twentieth century history. Drawing or sculpting birds helps children learn about the elements of drawing and more about distinctive qualities.

Your child who loves to read may take a different next step. Stories of birds and flight are everywhere, from mythology's Icarus and his ill-fated flight, to the story of the Phoenix, to modern science fiction. She might try her hand at writing a bird myth of her own.

Your students may seek out art, music, books, greeting cards, room decorations — whatever draws them deeper into the subject. Even weird connections can further learning experiences. If your kids discover that some rock and roll bands have bird names, and that leads them to explore early rock music, dig out your dusty collection and let them explore the history, music, musical instruments, electronics, or whatever else keeps the spark of interest glowing in their eyes.

All this — because you planted sunflowers.

Once in awhile, an enthusiastic interest fades for everyone, everyone, that is, except the parent! When that happens, just keep right on pursuing your new interest. Your children can fall back on their prior interests for a while, though of course you will drag them into your projects from time to time, just as they drag you into theirs. Your children will benefit from the example you set, as you enthusiastically launch a new interest and carry it forward. What textbook could teach them more than watching you delve into an exciting topic on your own?

## Finally

Now, having thoroughly convinced you, I hope, that subjects should not be isolated from one another, I will isolate those subjects in the rest of this section. Why? It is solely for your convenience as a resource, not for your children's learning. The categories simply make it easier to find what you are looking for. The remainder of this section will point to selected materials and practical homeschooling approaches for traditional subjects.

Most chapters focus on primary and secondary learning experiences for each subject. One chapter explores use of the computer, and another is devoted to textbook use, including tips on how to select textbooks. Those who want to use prepared curriculum materials will find a compendium of homeschooler approved curriculum suppliers and correspondence schools in the Appendix.

The curricular decisions you have to make are many, but as homeschooling parents, you can easily change your mind as your children learn and grow. Remember that it is not *what children learn* that is most important, but that the learning twins, *the love of learning* and *the ability to learn*, flourish within each child.

## chapter thirty-five

# EXPLORING MATH
*moving beyond basics*

This is the third chapter in which I've talked about math, and you may well wonder why. Would you believe that I think math is important? Children learn math concepts so readily through games, play, and conversation, that it seems a shame to deny them that opportunity. Foundational math concepts are also readily learned through daily living.

Eventually, though, the question of structured math instruction comes up. Most parents did not acquire their own math knowledge through daily living, but from textbooks. Thus we are inclined to depend on workbooks and textbooks. Unfortunately, as a teacher of elementary math, I know all too well that children burn out on too much textbook work, and that textbook math can be a poor basis of understanding for many students. Please use caution when you introduce your math-loving students to a textbook.

Now, I want to make a couple of points about teaching math that are particularly relevant when you might be using textbooks, workbooks, online classes, software programs, and other formal or direct instruction.

## Handling Errors

When your child makes an error in a math task, what should you do? In the early stages of learning, often the best strategy is to resist that overwhelming parental urge to correct an error. Immediately correcting the error may make you feel better, but think about what it teaches the child. Does it teach him to correct his own errors? To think about his work? Or does he learn to turn to you when in doubt?

Instead of rushing to correct his errors, try to figure out what is going on in his head. Sometimes the best task is to ask, right on the spot, "Hmm, how are you thinking about this problem?" While talking about his processes, he may discover his own error. Fantastic!

If he persists in repeating the error and holds to it as true, even when you ask leading questions or give hints, the best approach may be to let it go for the moment. You can revisit the problem later, perhaps simplifying it to a level that you know he understands, or perhaps taking up the concept in an entirely new venue. Meanwhile, you have done nothing to discourage his enthusiasm about math learning.

## What about Mastery?

One of the great benefits of homeschooling is this: if children develop at an uneven rate, it is no big deal. They won't get lost in the shuffle. For example, some very young children thrive on learning the concepts of Algebra or Calculus, but are unable to tell you thirteen minus six, or seven times nine. So what? Does it actually matter, in the long run, if he peeks into the exciting worlds of linear algebraic equations and basic calculus concepts before mastering subtraction? Should you hold your student back from the mathematical ideas that excite him until he memorizes a few facts?

Try another example. If your child begins to explore addition with a basket of river stones, he may discover multiplication on his own. What if, as he lays out arrays of stones, he becomes so fascinated with multiplication concepts that he abandons the addition tasks that he began with? Will you stop eager exploration of multiples and arrays until he memorizes seven plus eight? Of course not.

Even a teen who wants to study advanced math, even if he has not yet taken a course in, say, pre-algebra, should not be discouraged. You say he doesn't understand the basics? You might have him take a placement test to help him realize his skill level. If he still wants to study the subject, he will either back up to a level that he can learn from, or scramble to fill in the gaps on his own. That type of learning is the most valued of all.

Many families care little about meeting the "grade level" road signs along the way, preferring to focus on helping their child learn to love math. The best math learning takes place at the pace of the student, not the pace of an artificial road map in a math book. If needed, allow extra time for your student to master a difficult concept.

I don't mean to suggest that you enroll him in an advanced class without either prerequisite courses, or testing out of the prerequisite material. That could be a waste of money and time, and very discouraging to the student. But if he wants a trigonometry text to study on his own, maybe he will discover math his own way, and transition to conventional course work when he is ready.

You'll also need to consider your student's future plans. If a four-year college is on the horizon, remember that mastery of high school math is required by most colleges. Don't wait too long to start formal math learning or you may hamper your student's chances at admission.

If you are a parent who feels your math skills are limited, perhaps too limited, don't fret, you can still homeschool! Perhaps your child will work on math with your spouse, a grandparent, friend, or other relative. Another possibility is that, by the time you have met your personal math limit, you and your child will be able to go on learning together. Sometimes an older child is able to learn independently with the aid of a quality textbook, software, or class, perhaps taken online or at a public or private school.

## Finally

Many of the materials that follow are tools that can help further the mathematical conversations that you can have with your child, or help him carry on the conversation with the authors of quality materials. Many ideas for teaching basic concepts were discussed previously in "Early Math Conversations" and "Math Whiz Basics" (chapters 11 and 12). You'll also find a listing of games to try in "Game List" (chapter 6).

## HANDS-ON RESOURCES

### Abacus
The ancient calculator. Useful hands-on learning at many levels of math skill, including counting, multiplication, division, and learning place value.

### Cuisenaire Rods
ETA/Cuisenaire, 500 Greenview Ct., Vernon Hills, IL  60061
800/445.5985    fax: 800/875.9643    www.etacuisenaire.com
Cuisenaire manipulative math materials are rich in mathematical concepts. Teach everything from simple adding to algebraic and fractional concepts. Workbooks available.

### Learning Resources
380 N. Fairway Drive, Vernon Hills, IL 60061    847/573.8400
info@learningresources.com    www.learningresources.com
One-stop-shop for manipulative materials for all ages and subjects.  Catalog.

### Math 'n' Stuff
Gini and Tom Wingard-Phillips, 8926 Roosevelt Way NE, Seattle, WA 98115   206/522.4530    fax: 206/522.1235    www.math-n-stuff.com
Appealing tools and toys for learning. Lots of math, logic, and game resources. Homeschool-friendly, and will try to give you the best price.

### Math Learning Center — MLC Materials
PO Box 3226, Salem, OR 97302
800/575.8130  fax 503/370.7961  www.mlc.pdx.edu
K-8 math materials that emphasize sensory perception and visual reasoning. Manipulative materials, including money, clocks, intriguing counting sets, more.

## BOOKS, TEXTBOOKS AND PROGRAMS

### The Adventures of Penrose the Mathematical Cat
By Theoni Pappas.
Some children delight in the tales of Penrose as he explores math concepts through the abacus, binary system, fractals, origami, bubbles, more.

### Algebra on Videotape
Keyboard Enterprises, 5200 Heil, #32, Huntington Beach, CA 92649
714/840.8004   www.mathrelief.com
A full year of algebra tutoring.  Use as a supplement or sole curriculum.

## Algebra Survival Guide:
A Conversational Handbook for the Thoroughly Befuddled
By Josh Rappaport, Singing Turtle Press, #770, 3530 Zafarano Drive # 6,
Santa Fe, NM 87505    josh@AlgebraWizard.com    AlgebraWizard.com
505/438.3418 orders: 888/308-MATH fax: 505/438.7742
This book explains algebra in a clear question-and-answer format in a
student-friendly tone. Asks and explains real student questions.

## Algebra the Easy Way
By Douglas Downing. Barron's Educational Series.
High school algebra via an adventure story.

## Calculus By/For Young People
Don Cohen, 809 Stratford Dr., Champaign, IL 61821-4140
217/356.4555  orders:  800/356.4559  fax:  217/356.4593
mathman@shout.net    www.shout.net/~mathman
Fabulous books, workbooks and videos draw students of all ages into the
excitement of calculus. You really can learn this stuff!

## Creative Publications
Wright Group/Mc-Graw Hill
 19201 12ᵗʰ Ave. NE, Ste. 100, Bothell, WA 98011
800/648.2970    fax: 800/593.4418    www.wrightgroup.com
Many manipulative materials — Unifix cubes and tangram puzzles — and
traditional curriculum — workbooks and test prep. The Groundworks Series
offers algebraic thinking, puzzles, and workbooks for grades 1-7. Catalog.

## Dale Seymour Publications
Div. of Pearson Learning
 4350 Equity Dr., PO Box 2649, Columbus, OH 43216
800/526.9907    fax: 800/393.3156
www.pearsonlearning.com/dalesey/dalesey_default.cfm
Quality math materials. Great teaching posters. *Problem Solving in
Mathematics*, practice with word problems, is available here.

## Discovering Geometry: An Inductive Approach
By Michael Serra.
Key Curriculum Press, 1150 65ᵗʰ Street, Emeryville, CA 94608
800/995.MATH fax: 800/541.2442 Info@keypress.com
www.keypress.com
A formal high school geometry program that uses patty paper — you know,
hamburger patties? A hands-on, cooperative approach, and very practical.

## Elementary Algebra; Geometry; Mathematics: A Human Endeavor
Three superb texts by Harold Jacobs.    Available from FUN Books, 1688
Belhaven Woods Court, Pasadena MD 21122-3727    888/386.7020
MD only: 410/360.7330    FUN@FUN-Books.com    www.fun-books.com
Outstanding high school or college introductory texts. Reader friendly books
address the spirit and beauty of math as well as computation skills.

### Family Math for Middle School Years; Get It Together: Math Problems for Groups Grades 4-12

Equals/UC Berkeley, Lawrence Hall of Science, Berkeley, CA 94720
lhsstore@uc.link4.berkeley.edu    www.lhs.berkeley.edu/publications
Interesting and effective materials especially useful in families or learning clubs.

### Gnarly Math

By Monty Phister.
SMP Company, PO Box 1563, Santa Fe, NM 87504
www.gnarlymath.com
CD-ROM math software that puts the fun in math where it belongs. Eighteen hours of entertainment and instruction in algebra, geometry, trigonometry, probability, topology, and numbers.

### Hands-On Equations Learning System®

Creative Learning Press, Inc., PO Box 320, Mansfield Center, CT 06250
888/518.8004  fax: 860/429.7783  www.creativelearningpress.com
Easy algebraic linear equations that build interest in higher math skills through manipulative material. Gr. 3-6 and up. Fun to use, fun to teach.

### How Math Works

Dorling-Kindersley book Games, puzzles, and projects — great books!

### The I Hate Mathematics Book; Math for Smarty Pants; The Book of Think; This Book is About Time

Marilyn Burns Education Assn, 150 Gate 5 Road, Ste. 101,
Sausalito, CA 94965        405/332.4181
www.mathsolutions.com/mb/content/publications
Books that encourage a creative understanding of math in the real world.

### Key to... Series Concept Workbooks

Key Curriculum Press, 1150 65th Street, Emeryville, CA 94608
800/995.MATH fax: 800/541.2442  Info@keypress.com
www.keypress.com
Workbooks teach concepts, including basic operations, fractions, decimals, and algebra in a straightforward and readable format. Can be used with many ages. Hands-on materials, posters, textbooks. Miquon materials are available, including Cuisenaire® rods.

### Learn Quickly

Janet Scarpone, PO Box 336, Boulder, CO 80306-0336
888/LRN.FAST  www.learnquickly.com
Middle school and up. Math videos and workbooks can be used for test preparation or study groups.

### The Logical Journey of the Zoombinis

Broderbund Software, ages 8-12. Enjoyable math learning.

## *The Math Kit, A Three-Dimensional Tour Through Mathematics*

Ron Van Der Meer and Bob Gardner. Macmillan, 1994.
A cleverly designed pop-up math book jammed with mathematical information and models that make math understandable.

## *Math-U-See*

888/854.MATH (6284)   www.mathusee.com
Manipulative-based K-8 plus basic algebra & geometry curriculum. Multi-sensory approach to math emphasizes BUILD, WRITE, SAY.

## *Mathematics Programs Associates, Inc.*

PO Box 2118, Halesite, NY 11743   800/672.6284 fax: 516/643.9301
www.pixelperfect.org/sites/pyramid/html/_developmental_math.html
Developmental Mathematics — a self-teaching program, for both accelerated and remedial students. Math Made Simple. Free brochure.

## *Meridian Creative Group*

1762 Norcross Road, Erie, PA 16510 800/530.2355 www.meridiancg.com
Consumer Math Workbooks for high school; Leapfrog Math, K-6 CD-ROM .

## *Mighty Math – Number Heroes, Cosmic Geometry, and Astro Algebra.*

Edmark Software, popular with many families.

## *Moving With Math*

Math Teachers Press, Inc., 4850 Park Glen Road, Minneapolis, MN 55416
800/852.2435  fax: 952/546.7502   www.movingwithmath.com
Pre-K to algebra. Manipulatives and workbooks.

## *Saxon Math Books*

Saxon Publishers, Inc., John Saxon Blvd., Norman, OK 73071
800/284.7019  fax: 405/360.4205  www.saxonpublishers.com
Math texts for older students who thrive on practice and learn independently.

## *Wildridge Software, Inc.*

245 Wildridge Farm Road, Newark, Vermont 05871
888/BIGGERWORLD   888/244.4379    fax: 802/467.3442
ABIGGERWORLD@wildridge.com    www.wildridge.com
Math and Music Software. Find the math in music, an exciting approach. If your young children loved counting piano keys and figuring out the fractions in music notation, they will love this. Teens and younger strong readers.

## SELECTED DRILL RESOURCES

### Barnum Software
3450 Lakeshore Ave., Ste. 200, Oakland, CA 94610-2343
800/553.9155    fax: 800/533.9156    www.thequartermile.com
*The Quarter Mile* series math drill software allows students to compete
against themselves, both for accuracy and speed.

### Digital Media Productions, Inc.
PO Box 1925, Oakdale, CA 95361
800/533.2653    fax: 209/881.3901    www.candokids.com
Videos combine exercise with a review of math facts. Ages 4-14.

### Math Strategies
Pixelgraphics,  2459 SE TV Highway, Ste. 250, Hillsboro, OR 97123
503/693.7578    orders: 800/GAME-345    fax: 503/648.4857
learning@teleport.com  www.pixelgraphics.com
Number recognition and counting through high speed mastery of the four
basic operations. Dynamic arcade game format that can be paced for fun and
success.

### Naturalmath.com
www.naturalmath.com/mult/mult3.html
Help with multiplication facts and much more, the way kids love to learn.

## chapter thirty-six

# EXPLORING SCIENCE
*getting to know the world*

Your child is a born scientist/explorer. His mission — discover the world! Your job — mission control. Begin in the kitchen, the yard, the stream, the beach, or the sky, and then watch the fun.

As a practical scientist, your child desires to know everything she can learn about the world in which she lives. Her earliest explorations begin with her body (especially the senses), her intellect — and you, her loving guide. Since most young children are captivated with their own bodies and development, health and science are naturally learned together in the early years.

Children may take an interest in plants and animals of all kinds, kitchen chemistry experiments, natural habitats, how the body works, simple machines, technology and physics, rocks, weather, microscopic life, and electronics. Who can tell where these early explorations may go? Being involved is what is important. Who knows when a simple interest in spiders may become a lifelong fascination with entomology!

Children will naturally form many faulty hypotheses, to the great amusement of parents. You can generally let the erroneous conclusions go, knowing that the practical scientist in your child will resolve errors as intellect and knowledge grow. Alternatively, you might help her create a test experiment. And although you may be tempted to do so, resist correcting the error verbally, as your child may not yet have an understanding of the science involved. Use verbal correction of facts judiciously until the student is older. When they are older, your students may actually become annoyed with you if you don't correct their errors! "Mo-om! Why didn't you tell me?"

Natural interests continue to develop through experiments and activities, exploring with the senses, and careful observation. Occasional discussions about scientific methods can help connect their explorations to the world of working scientists.

Science is a natural introduction to other subjects. Read the biographies of scientists. Learn the connections between music and science through a study of harmonics and sound. Investigate colors, light waves, and how the eye perceives color as you work with various art media. Read the history of a major scientific discovery and explore its impact on history. Learn to spell interesting scientific words. Study scientific names of plants and animals; learn Greek and Latin. Learn how a steam locomotive works. Create unique explorations of your own.

## Family Science Notebook

If you worry that your family won't learn enough science, a *Family Science Notebook* can track the work you do. Just think — if you kept a record of just one experiment or science activity a month, your family notebook would bulge in a few years! And if your family is able to track only a couple of experiments each year, the record of questions, experiments, projects, and discoveries will be there to help you zero in on uncharted topics for next year.

You can make the entries in your notebook as elaborate or as simple as you want. Some may want to include a description of how the experiment was set up, what happened, which questions were answered, and which ones were not. Perhaps you'll just include the brochures and literature you've collected on field trips. A more involved notebook could include sections of *observations* and *questions* for each child.

You might choose to focus on including each child's contributions and interpretations. Drawings, photos, verbal descriptions of the activity, when accompanied by the parent's description, help students track the development of their scientific understanding over the years.

Beyond the early years, a *Science Notebook* for each child might work best for your family. Most experiments will generate new questions that can be a springboard for future experiments or simply left unanswered for the time being. In later years, when your students go back and read their *Science Notebooks*, they will chuckle over the misconceptions they held when they were younger. They might also be amazed at some of the hard, even unanswerable questions they asked at such a tender age.

Other sections in the science notebook could include field trip records, classes taken, books read, and videos watched. Your book should suit your family needs. Teens may use the book to help them build their portfolios and / or extend their studies.

## Basic Exploring

A few tools of exploration and observation, as well as selected resources, can build the basis of an effective science program. Allow ample time for careful observation of the natural world, and for systematic exploration of questions or hypotheses posed. A smattering of suggestions may get you started.

binoculars
telescope
sky chart
microscope
hand lenses
stethoscope
otoscope
blood pressure monitor
compass
scales
sextant
barometer
rain gauge
hygrometer
anemometer
weather vane
thermometer
measuring devices of all kinds

plant press
butterfly net
aquarium
terrarium
pet ownership
gardening and farming
nature collections
cooking
simple machines, such as lever,
    wedge, pulley, inclined plane
chemistry kit
electronic construction kit
theodolite
children's science magazines
adult science magazines
books, videos, and CDs
selected television programs
science section in the newspaper

## Books, Magazines, Kits, Curriculum, Catalogs

### Backyard Scientist
PO Box 16966, Irvine CA 92623   714/551.2392   fax: 714/552.5351
www.backyardscientist.com
Hands on science activities include experiments in physics, chemistry and the
life sciences. Several books are available for different levels.

### Biotech Publishing
PO Box 1032, Angleton, TX 77516-1032
281/369.2044   services@biotechpub.com   www.biotechpub.com
Science fair ideas and help with writing science research papers.

### Bioviva Games
c/o PFA, PO Box 2314, Orleans, MA 02653 www.biovivagames.com
Board and card educational games about people and nature.

### Elemento®
Lewis Educational Games, PO Box 727, Goddard, KS 67052
order: 800/557.8777   fax: 316/794.8239
The Periodic Table of Elements for basic chemistry. Also: Trig-O.

### The Exploratorium Museum Store
3601 Lyon St., San Francisco, CA 94123
800/359.9899   415/EXP-LORE   exploratorium.edu
Hands-on science projects. The *Snackbook* series includes projects such as
building an electroscope, a fog chamber, and pan pipes.

### Friendly Chemistry
Hideaway Ventures, RR 2 Box 96A, Berwyn, NE 68819
800/774.3447  hideaway@nctc.net  www.custercounty.com/friendlychemistry
A high school level chemistry curriculum for individuals or groups.

### Insect Lore
PO Box 1535, Shafter, CA 93263
805/746.6047 Orders: 800/LIVE.BUG  www.insectlore.com
Live insects, worms, and other nature items.

### Lyrical Life Science
800/761.0906 www.lyricallearning.com  lyricallearning@proaxis.com
Learn serious biology concepts via songs and familiar tunes.

### MicroChem Kits LLC
395 Flower Court, Platteville, WI 53818
608/348.3908  www.microchemkits.com  microchem@email.com
College prep level. Enough materials to repeat 17 experiments 5 times.

### Odyssey, Adventures in Science
Cobblestone Publishing
30 Grove Street, Ste. C, Peterborough, NH 03458

603/924.7029   order: 800/821.0115    fax: 603/924.7380
custsvc@cobblestone.mv.com   www.cobblestonepub.com
Serious topics are discussed and explained in language students can
understand, age ten and up. Teaching tips included. 9 issues/yr.

### Ranger Rick
National Wildlife Federation, POB 2049, Harlan, IA 51593
888/226.3696  www.nwf.org
Wildlife magazine for elementary age children ages 6 to 12. *Big Back Yard*
and *Animal Baby* are for younger children.

### Peterson Guides; Audubon Guides
From your favorite bookseller. First rate guides for exploring and learning
about flora and fauna.

### Pint-Size Science: Finding-Out Fun for You and Your Young Child.
Linda Allison and Martha Weston. NY: Little, Brown & Co. 1994.
Family-life-based activities that give your child a chance to explore the world
around him in a joyful way.

### Science Arts: Discovering Science Through Art Experiences
Mary Ann F. Kohl and Jean Potter, 1993.  Bright Ring Publishing, PO Box
31338, Bellingham, WA 98228.  800/480.4278  www.brightring.com
Science projects that turn out to be art projects. Easy to use. 3-9/ up.

### Robert Krampf's Science Education Company
PO Box 60982 Jacksonville, FL 32236-0982
904/388.6381  www.krampf.com  krampf@aol.com
A scientist who wants to make science affordable, understandable, and fun.
Free *Experiment of the Week* E-mail at the web site. All ages.

### Science Experiments You Can Eat; More Science Experiments You Can Eat
Vicki Cobb. Fun science projects in the kitchen — gobble the results.

### Science Kit Rental Program
Museum of Science, Science Park, Boston, MA 02214
617/723.2500   800/722.5487   www.mos.org/learn_more/ed_res
Bring a variety of science materials into your home, for your own family or for
your study group. Programs for homeschoolers. K-8.

### Science Kit & Boreal Laboratories
777 E Park Drive, PO Box 5003, Tonawanda, NY 14150
800/828.7777  www.sciencekit.com
Lab materials for elementary or secondary study groups.

### Sharing Nature With Children: Nature Awareness Guidebook
### Sharing the Joy of Nature: Nature Activities for All Ages
Joseph Cornell. 1998. Nature books that foster enthusiasm for learning.

### Stratton House
17837 1st Avenue S. #186, Seattle, WA 98148
206/242.4448    800/694.7225
www.homeschoolscience.com    hello@homeschoolscience.com
Hands-on science kits. Grades 3-8. Sample lessons at the web site.

### Tobin's Lab
PO Box 725, Culpepper, VA 22701
800/522.4776  info@tobinlab.com    www.tobinlab.com
Hands-on discovery for all ages, collected with family life in mind.

### TOPS Learning Systems
10970 South Mulino Road, Canby, OR 97013  503/266.8550   orders:
888/773.9755  fax: 503/266.5200  tops@canby.com  www.topscience.org
Bi-annual magazine/catalog of projects using inexpensive materials.
Pendulums, metric measure, machines.

### Trans Tech Creative Learning Systems
16510 Via Esprilo, San Diego, CA 92127  800/458.2880
fax: 858/592.7055    www.clsinc.com  info@clsinc.com
Technology at /home/work/play. Creativity meets hi-tech and science.

### Young Entomologists' Society
Minibeast Zooseum /Edu. Center,
6907 W. Grand River Ave., Lansing MI 48906  phone/fax: 517/886.0630
YESsales@aol.com  members.aol.com/YESbugs/bugclub.html
Everything a bug lover could possibly want or need.

## SCIENCE EQUIPMENT AND SUPPLIERS

### American Science and Surplus
3605 Howard St., Skokie, IL 60076  847/982.0870
www.sciplus.com  info@sciplus.com
Optical, electrical, mechanical, bearings, military, plumbing, industrial surplus,
and much more. Unusual and affordable resource.

### Carolina Biological Supply Company
2700 York Road, Burlington, NC 27215
800/222.7112    carolina@carolina.com    www.carolina.com
Well-regarded source for science resources for sixth grade and up.

### Edmund Scientific Company
60 Pearce Ave., Tonowanda, NY 14150
800/728.6999    716/874.9091  www.scientificsonline.com
Science materials, educational products, great stuff! A fascinating source of
real science and technical materials.

## chapter thirty-seven

# EXPLORING SOCIAL STUDIES

*bringing history and geography to life, and life to history and geography*

The easiest and most natural way to help a child develop a love of history and geography is — yes, you guessed it — to follow the child's interests. Why not? All topics have a history, and that history can be a springboard to developing a broader knowledge of the past.

Even the most history-resistant child will enjoy learning the history of his favorite topic. If he loves gymnastics or baseball, explore the history of those sports. LEGO bricks, Tinker Toys, Barbie Dolls, American Girl books and dolls, and Nintendo — each has a history you can explore. When you pull out all the stops to explore a favorite subject in depth with your child, you'll find that you have covered many subjects along the way.

Do you want to integrate social studies throughout your other studies? Notice how the explorations crisscross through many subjects in the following example.

Is your child interested in trains? Immerse yourselves in train lore and information. Go to train stations and museums. Read train books. Learn how trains were developed and how the railroad networks were built. Build a model train. Paint, draw, or sculpt a caboose. Visit a model railroader's club. Meet some engineers, conductors, and brakemen. Count train cars. Estimate freight weight or boxcar volume. Save up, and travel by train.

Ask many questions together. How have trains changed the ways people live? How did the transcontinental railroad influence the development of the West? How are trains different in other countries? Can you locate art and music about trains? If your exploration of trains leads to a further fascination in transportation, model building, art, music, math, or any other subject or interest, your train discovery days were the wildest success!

When children are very young, you'll want to emphasize experiential activities. For example, "olden days" activities stimulated my children's interest in history. We did many of the following activities: made candles, visited museums, built model stagecoaches, camped out or cooked over an open fire, sewed pioneer clothing, stitched samplers, pieced quilts, and played pioneer school. You might even try old-time human-powered carpentry or blacksmithing.

As students grow older, reading historical fiction or mythology can light a fire of interest. Does the story of King Arthur strike your child's fancy? No matter what his age, allow ample time for him to explore the Arthurian legend through activity. Make coats of mail, gowns for ladies-in-waiting, or models of Excalibur. Invent safe jousting games and learn about chivalry, manners, and castles. Explore the lives of ordinary people.

Want to bring geography and map studies to life? Make papier maché or salt clay relief maps or globes of your home, your local community, or your state. Be sure to have fun! Your child's awkward attempts to re-create a map or a globe will deepen understanding regardless of the success or failure of the project. If your youngest creates a lopsided lumpy globe named Planet Gloodge, where water is pink, mountain tops are orange, and rivers run uphill, you have a wild success, as long as your child is brimming with enthusiasm!

When you focus on the process of learning, developing imagination, and creating memorable activities, the result you seek — increased knowledge and understanding — will slip naturally into place.

## Digging Deeper

The basic tools for digging into the past and learning about geography are fairly simple: maps, a globe, an encyclopedia (books, software, or online), and generous access to books, either purchased or from your library. Many families post a blank time line and then fill in the details as different bits of history are explored.

The following resource ideas expand and deepen understanding of how people and events are connected together through time. Try:

- family trips to explore local cultures, historical sites, museums, geographic features, or climate

- biographies, autobiographies, historical fiction books or videos, magazines, selected textbooks, and software.

- cultural, historical, and geographical nonfiction books or videos

- authentic artifacts (such as ancient coins, arrowheads, cultural items, or ethnic dress)

- models of artifacts (create your own, based on real or imagined items)

- materials for play and exploration of the culture, such as dress-up clothes and models

- role-playing activities (churn butter, write with quill pens, read by candlelight, learn dances, games, and songs)

- culminating activities such as plays, speeches, and presentations

- selected computer programs and public television programming

- historical board games, geography puzzles and games

- local music, art, dance, sports, ethnic and cultural activities

- detailed road maps, aeronautical and navigation charts

## Finally

Social studies activities, undertaken together as a family, can serve as a joyous foundation of your entire curriculum if you take an immersion approach such as I've described. You will be amazed if you've never tried this approach before. Trust me.

## RESOURCES, GAMES, BOOKS, MAGAZINES

### Amazon Drygoods
411 Brady Street, Davenport, IA 52801
800/798.7979    fax: 319/322.4003
www.victoriana.com/amazon    Info@amazondrygoods.com
Study the Victorian era history through catalogs of period reproductions.
Clothing patterns, shoes, or general catalogs are available for a modest fee.

### Bluestocking Press
PO Box 2030, Shingle Springs, CA 95682-2030
530/621.1123    800/959.8586    fax: 530/642.9222
uncleric@jps.net    www.bluestockingpress.com
Many historical items, such as craft kits, books, music documents. *Little House on the Prairie* items. Constitutional studies.

### Chatham Hill Games
PO Box 253, Chatham, NY 12037
800/554.3039    fax: 518/392.3121    www.chathamhillgames.com
info@chathamhillgames.com
A unique resource for studying Colonial and Revolutionary America through event-based games and posters.

### Cobblestone Publishing Group
30 Grove St., Ste. C, Peterborough, NH 03458
603/924.7029    order: 800/821.0115    fax: 603/924.7380
custsvc@cobblestone.mv.com    www.cobblestonepub.com
Highly regarded history theme magazines for extended learning. *Cobblestone* — American History as you've never seen it before — fresh, exciting, accurate. *Calliopes* — World history for kids; includes art, photos, narratives, maps, charts, activities, all related to the topic. Resources, kids' writings, and more. *Faces* — *World Cultures* — People, places, cultures. A great companion to map, globe and atlas studies. Discover life in a region by meeting the residents. Many photos. *Footsteps* — African American history. Recommended resources, kids' writings, and more. Nine issues/yr.

### Discover America Game
Second Avenue Creations, PO Box 472, St. Nazianz, WI 54232
800/713.1105    fax: 920/773.3053    second@discoveramer.com
www.discoveramer.com
A board game to help players learn facts while having fun. History, geography, states, capitals, presidents, government, authors, songs, sports, spelling, more.

### Kaw Valley Films & Video
6532 Switzer, PO Box 3541, Shawnee, KS 66203
913/631/3040    orders: 800/332.5060    fax: 913/631.4320
www.railtravelvideos.com    wesiegel@kc.rr.com
American passenger trains, history of American Railroads. Panama Canal,
Lewis and Clark, Mississippi River — among the topics of these award
winning videos.

### Global Art:
Activities, Projects, and Inventions From Around the World
By Mary Ann F. Kohl and Jean Potter.
Gryphon House, Inc., 10726 Tucker Street, Beltsville, MD 20705. 1998.
Explore the world through art! Art projects from Europe, Asia, North
America, Antarctica, Oceania, South America, and Africa will propel learning
effortlessly.

### Greenleaf Press
3761 Hwy. 109 North, Lebanon, TN 37087
615/449.1617    800/311.1508    fax: 615/449.4018
www.greenleafpress.com   info@greenleaf.com
A resource for hands-on materials, activities, and quality books for the
chronological study of history and much more. Biblical perspective.

### Hammond World Atlas
95 Progress St., Union, NJ 07083
800/526.4953    fax: 908/206.1104
edusales@hammondmap.com   www.hammondmap.com
Print and software maps, atlases and more. Educator's discount. Free
catalog.

### Geography Matters
PO Box 92, Nancy, KY 42544    606/636.4678    fax: 606/636.4697
info@geomatters.com   www.geomatters.com
Time lines and many geography resources.

### Historic American Productions, Inc.
PO Box 763, Addison, TX 75001
800/715.6337    hap@airmail.net    web2.airmail.net/hap
American history learned through videos of essential pioneer skills and crafts.

### Kids Discover
PO Box 54206, Boulder, CO 80323    800/284.8276
Theme issues on many topics — great unit studies starters. Well planned and
informative. Ages six and up. Twelve issues per year.

### National Women's History Project
3343 Industrial Dr., Ste. 4, Santa Rosa, CA 95403
707/636.2888    fax: 707/636.2909   nwhp@aol.com   www.nwhp.org
Many materials that are not available elsewhere. Even the free catalog
includes information not commonly known about women's history.

*Pleasant Company Publications*
PO Box 620497, Middleton, WI 53562-0497
800/845.0005   www.americangirlstore.com
Learn American history with period American Girl dolls, historical fiction and History Mysteries. *American Girl Magazine* available.

*Other Lands, Inc.*
PO Box 169, Corbett, OR 97019
503/695.3210     order: 800/993.3210
www.otherlands.com   Email@otherlands.com
Friendly online catalog. Learn about other lands through flags, maps, languages, music, puzzles, and geography. Many interesting items, including geography games such as Terra Carta.

*Standard Deviants*
Cerebellum Corp., 2890 Emma Lee St., Falls Church, VA 22042
800-238-9669   www.standarddeviants.com   info@cerebellum.com
Study American government and much more with academic study guide videos. Available in bookstores.

*Skipping Stones: A Multi-cultural Children's Magazine*
PO Box 3939, Eugene, OR 97403-0939        541/342.4956
skipping@efn.org   www.treelink.com/skipping/main.htm
Award-winning multi-cultural magazine. Articles are rewarding and informative for people of all ages. Articles and art by all ages and in many languages. Six issues per year. Reduced rates for low income subscribers.

*Weekly Reader Corporation*
3001 Cindel Drive, Delran, NJ 08075
800/446.3355     fax: 856/786.3360
customerservice@weeklyreader.com   www.weeklyreader.com
Classic schoolchildren's newspaper. Current events and more, in many editions geared to your child's age and reading level, all ages through high school. Individual subscriptions available.

## chapter thirty-eight

# EXPLORING VOCABULARY AND SPELLING
*words, words, words*

## Developing Vocabulary

Vocabulary — that body of words that we understand and use — naturally develops when parents and children converse together. We talk to our children long before they can respond or fully understand. This is exactly right, as children need time and repetition to sort out the intricacies of words, sentences, and meaning.

Does your family *actively* read, listen to tapes and radio, watch TV and movies together? Do you talk about what you see and hear? Then you are engaging your child in an excellent vocabulary building program, much better than a vocabulary list or drill.

Actively listening to your child — really attending when he speaks — gives you a chance to enrich his vocabulary in the context of daily conversation. By getting into his head to really understand his question and help him find the answers he seeks, you help your child bring forth subtle meanings from words and language.

Try to pay attention to those amusing misunderstood meanings and mispronounced words so that you can take the challenge to another level. Tucked behind smiles and adoration of the clever misuse of a three-dollar word, Dad just might be planning to bring the word up in conversation at a later time, carefully used in context so that the meaning will reveal itself to the child. The child can then self-correct. Clever Dad!

If your child takes her time beginning to talk, you can relax if she responds to the conversation around her. As long as she is healthy and her hearing has been checked, just keep talking.

Wait for her input, and when she is not forthcoming, do as I did with my younger daughter. "Erin, do you want jam on your toast? You said 'uh.' I guess 'uh' means yes." Erin let me know loudly and clearly that I guessed wrong! Before long her ideas, wants, and needs grew more and more complex, and she began using words to express those complex ideas.

Some late talkers have so much to say and so many ideas that they may be at a loss for words. Be patient and give them time to sort out their thoughts. Keep exploring language — reading, talking, writing — with your child. When language does develop, watch for the flood of communications that have just been waiting to spill!

As children grow older, you may want to try some of these ideas.

## Tips for Building Vocabulary

**Leave a dictionary and a thesaurus around for easy access and discovery.** Use a children's dictionary or a picture dictionary when your child is very young. Look up words with your child together.

**Immerse yourselves in language experiences.** Read aloud, listen to audio books, and watch selected videos together, especially those in which the writing is creative and rich in imagery. Discuss. Sing songs. Attend plays. Read poems. Have conversations.

**Study words together.** Try a "word of the day" calendar and talk about the day's selection over breakfast. You can also subscribe to a "word of the day" over the Internet. Pick words from your shared reading to study together. Learn big words that you find in the dictionary. Try to stump each other with words from the dictionary. Play word games of all types. Let your child help you with your crossword puzzle. Learn the specialized words of the topic of interest you are currently exploring. (Trains: locomotive, steam engine, diesel, engineer, conductor — you get the idea.) In my family, these activities were accepted as part of their playing.

**Explore grammar and usage patterns together.** Learning some of the structural conventions of how we put words together in sentences extends vocabulary while teaching children appropriate usage. Words are used in so many different ways — some nouns can be used as verbs, and verbs are used as nouns, for example. *Mad Libs*, available from your favorite bookseller, are a favorite of children everywhere for learning parts of speech. Vocabulary, no matter how hilarious or silly, grows at the same time. Practice with a grammar book may help an older student analyze and understand the elements of sentence structure. These can be especially helpful if your child struggles with correct usage, verb tenses, or whether to use singular or plural noun forms. Many students benefit from studying Latin.

**Explore foreign languages.** For the purposes of vocabulary development, I use the idea of foreign language loosely. For example, include codes of all kinds as well as a study of word origins. Explore Greek, Latin, Anglo-Saxon, and other origins of English words. Around age eight or nine, many children love to learn American sign language, pig Latin, and other secret codes. Some will memorize the sign language alphabet or Morse Code easily at this age. Don't miss this window of opportunity. Find a couple of books in the library, teach your children your favorite version of pig Latin, and have a blast together! While you are at it, build a telegraph or a string-and-tin-can "cell phone."

## About Spelling

First I have to tell you what not to do and get it off my chest. The biggest mistake parents and teachers make when children are learning to spell is to require perfection. Demands for perfect spelling, especially at an early age, often result in an aversion to both spelling and writing. That is not what we're after, is it? There, I feel better. Now let's talk about spelling and why it is so tough for some kids to learn.

Just think about English spelling for a minute. We know the majority of English words follow rules, but it is all too easy for accomplished adult spellers to forget that the most common words, the words children are most likely to want to use or write, are irregular and defy the usual spelling rules.

Consider the child's dilemma. He really wants to write the words he actually uses, words like *the, of, love, you, night, light, from, through, who, why, one, two, guess, once upon a time, mother and mom, father and dad.* For a child who hasn't quite settled that left to right business in her mind, is it *stop* or *pots*, or *spot* or *tops*? It is no wonder that kids get confused sometimes, and these are just a small sampling of words that torment the beginning writer.

Does it make sense to thwart the budding writer and make him learn all the spelling rules first, rules that the above words break? Of course not. Nor does it make sense to make him learn a bunch of irregular spellings and obscure rules before his reading/writing vocabulary is big enough to support that list.

The simple solution is to let spelling skill grow right along with reading and writing skills. In the earliest days of your child's attempts to write, you might need to spell every single word she wants to write.

Later on, you can say, "Oh, I'm busy right now. Just spell it the way you think it should be. If you are really stuck, just put down a few letters to remind you, and I'll help you in a bit."

Do you see what a sly bit of work we are up to? First, we encourage the child to take a small step to writing independence. At the same time, we get to take a look at the choices she makes. Is she spelling phonetically? Good! Phonetic spelling gives you some clues that indicate how well she understands the sound/symbol relationship within words, the relationship that helps her read the words she doesn't yet know.

Now, before we go on, don't jump to the conclusion that I don't value accurate spelling! I am actually a spelling fanatic. What I *am* saying is that it is okay to ignore spelling and other conventions in the early stages of writing.

When she is older, you can also ignore spelling on early writing drafts while she is getting her thoughts down on paper. Help her correct the spelling on *selected* first drafts (not everything she writes) during editing sessions. Of course you will help edit letters to Grandma if Grandma does not enjoy "special" spellings. Grandma may not realize that phonetic spelling is a temporary step, so help your children please Grandma with corrected spelling.

Stories or poems to be published in a newsletter might also be corrected prior to publication. Publication can mean preparing a letter, a story, or a poem to be shared or saved in some way. A good basic rule is to always edit for publication, but don't edit everything that is written. That's how serious writers write and edit. Beginning writers are very serious writers.

## Tips for Improving Spelling Skills

**Help your child make a personal alphabetized spelling book.** Young children enjoy making and using these books. On a blank page for each letter of the alphabet, children can record words they want to be able to spell. Your child might also collect troublesome words from his written work to include in his spelling book. A personal spelling book is the most meaningful and useful early spelling tool I have ever used with children.

**Use a beginning dictionary** and help your child look up the spelling or word meaning she needs. Do keep an adult dictionary available, though, so you can help her look up word choices that are not found in the beginning dictionary.

**Study phonics together.** Some children improve their spelling when they study phonics in conjunction with spelling. Try one of the many phonics games.

**Let your young child make her own book using invented spelling.** (Invented spelling is when the child writes the word the way she thinks it might be spelled.) Stories written with invented spelling can later serve as a source of spelling words for study, particularly if your child doesn't pick up the correct spellings on her own.

**Together, you and your child can watch for word spelling patterns as you read**. Make up a rule for the patterns you notice and find words that break the rule! Read poetry and limericks, which bring together words that have similar spelling patterns, as well as words that sound the same but have different spellings.

**Engage the senses.** Practice spelling difficult words to music; words can also be spelled to the beat of a drum or metronome. Bounce a ball, jump, or clap your hands to hear the different syllables in a word. Try mirror writing. Use markers and oversized paper to write huge words. Spell words in a tray of sand. Sew or paint the words. Make the words in clay. Bake them into bread or cookies.

**Should you use a spelling book?** At some point, your child's vocabulary, spelling skill, and maturity may warrant the purchase of a spelling book. If your child enjoys the book or program, that is the book for you.

**A good dictionary and a thesaurus are essential.** A number of other tools are available that can help your child produce correctly spelled written work. An electronic speller and a computer with a spell-checker and thesaurus are useful spelling tools and great for expanding vocabulary. Spell-checking software not only helps the poor speller produce a correctly spelled document, but it forces him to consider many possible spellings for a word and to make a choice. (One adult writer of poetry and fiction, an atrocious speller, admits that his spelling actually improves as he uses his spell-checker.)

**Equip a hesitant speller with a hand-held or computer spell-checker or an adult spelling book,** and make sure he knows how to use these tools. Try the writing section at your local book store for spelling books that your teen can use. If a child continues to be a poor speller as she matures, parents may renew their anxiety. I'll say it again — try to relax. Remember that the goal for most children is not winning the spelling bee, but being able to spell correctly when necessary. If he cannot spell well naturally, that is a secondary concern. The primary concern is to make sure he has the tools to find and use correct spellings.

## SELECTED RESOURCES

### English From the Roots Up
Literacy Unlimited, PO Box 278, Medina, WA 98039
425/454.5830    www.literacyunlimited.com
Build vocabulary and spelling skill.

### Grammar Key
Video Resources Software
11767 South Dixie Highway, Miami, FL 33156
888/223.6284    fax: 305/256.0467
mailroom@tutorace.com    www.acemath.com/grammarkey/gktext.html
Catch up on the basics. PC or MAC software. Grades 4-12.

### How to Teach Any Child to Spell
By Gayle Graham.
Common Sense Press, 8786 Highway 21, Melrose, FL 32666
www.cspress.com   service@cspress.com
Basic guidelines for teaching spelling.

## Mad Libs

Available from Brook Farm Books, POB 246, Bridgewater, ME 04735
506/3785.4680   jean@brookfarmbooks.com
Joyful grammar and vocabulary development activity that will have you
rolling on the floor in giggles. Like crossword puzzles, *Mad Libs* ask players to
use divergent thinking, a skill that improves precise word choice skills.

## The Natural Speller

By Kathryn Stout.
Design-A-Study, 408 Victoria Ave., Wilmington, DE 19804
302/998.3889   www.designastudy.com
Multi-sensory program by a home educator. Word lists, Latin and Greek
roots, prefixes, suffixes. K-8.

## Rhymes & Nyms

Fireside Games
Joan C. Berry, PO Box 82995, Portland, OR 97282-0995
503/231.8990    800/414.8990
A fun card game for those who love words.

## Rummy Roots

Available from FUN Books, 1688 Belhaven Woods Court,
Pasadena MD 21122-3727     888/386.7020     MD only: 410/360.7330
FUN@FUN-Books.com  www.fun-books.com
English vocabulary-building card game.

## Schola Publications

1698 Market Street, #162, Redding, CA 96001
530/275.2064   fax: 53/275.9151   www.thelatinroad.com
*The Latin Road to English Grammar.* Textbook, vocabulary cards, audio
tape and more. Free brochure.

## Spelling Power

Castlemoyle Books
Hotel Revere Building, #520, Pomeroy, WA 99347
888/Spell86  beverly@castlemoyle.com  www.castlemoyle.com
A comprehensive and multi-sensory spelling program. Multilevel, multi-
sensory arts curricular materials are also available.

## Total Physical Fun: Strategies and Activities for Learning Language Through Cooperative Play

Jo Ann Olliphant, 11004 111th St. SW, Tacoma, WA 98498  206/584.7473
More than 100 games and activities that offer entertaining and effective ways
to support your specific teaching goals. Step-by-step instructions.

## Learn to Spell a Word
*A Multi-sensory Method*

- Look at the word. (Visual)

- Say the word aloud. (Auditory, speech)

- Close your eyes and imagine the word written on a chalkboard in your mind. (Imagery)

- Trace the letters of the word in the air with your hand. (Kinetic)

- Open your eyes, and without looking at the word, write the word on your paper. (Memory, kinetic)

- Check the word. If you make an error, repeat this process as needed. (Self Correction)

## chapter thirty-nine

## EXPLORING LITERATURE AND BOOKS
*read, read, read*

Whether you read to your child or your child reads for himself, this chapter is for you! For the how-to's of reading instruction, refer to "Early Reading and Writing" and "The Laptop Approach to Reading" (chapters 8 and 9).

There are so many kinds of books! Books are the absolute backbone of learning activities for many families. It would be hard to go wrong if you focused entirely on reading together.

Even if you love books, though, it is often hard to decide where to begin. Luckily, there are libraries, used book stores, homeschool swap meets, and garage sales. You can easily introduce your child to many different kinds of books without breaking the budget.

Investigate everything — comic books, jokes and riddles, magazines, fables and myths, poetry, information books, biographies, autobiographies, and historical fiction. Compare stories retold by different authors, or compare a novel to the movie or television counterpart. Our family enjoyed finding variations on the storyline and illustrations in different renditions of fairy tales such as *The Three Little Pigs*.

When your child begins to read fluently on her own, you should take advantage of her love of having you read aloud to introduce books she might not read herself. As your child matures in reading skills, consider point-of-view stories, historical novels, classics, science fiction and biographies. Mysteries will certainly keep the family on their toes, even trying to sneak a peek at the next chapter between readings. Your child may discover a new genre of books that is enjoyable.

Many children enjoy reading or listening to complex literature with you, material full of challenging words and ideas they don't fully understand. as long as you are available to answer their questions, they can understand it and improve their comprehension abilities. For young readers, longer picture books and short chapter books are good bets. Take turns reading sentences, pages, or chapters, or perhaps each of you can take on the role of one of the characters. Explore unison reading. Encourage a child who is an emerging reader to read aloud to younger siblings and friends.

Older readers will begin to make many of their own selections, or at least to share the selection process with you. Encourage them to explore a variety of genres. If your older students enjoy sharing literature with others, help them join, or start, a book club.

Continue to read aloud, though. You might choose classic books that have old-fashioned vocabulary to read together. Select books from your own favorite adult literature. When your students choose a book independently, you might occasionally read the same books they read, and encourage them to discuss the concepts, characters, writing styles, and themes, with you.

These tips may help in narrowing your selections.

## Try Nonfiction

For some learners, nonfiction is more satisfying than fiction. Make it a habit to include a few books that relate to current interests (baseball, dolls, butterflies, whatever) with every library visit. As a terminally sneaky mom, I often left books, opened to interesting pages, lying strategically around the house. I often found a girl or two skimming through these books or diving into one for the full experience.

## Use Book Lists

If you are looking for quality novels or picture books, try some of the books that have won annual awards. The *Caldecott* and *Newbery Award* winners are a good place to start. *Young Readers' Choice* nominations give youngsters a chance to express their opinions about what they read and to read books recommended by other youth. Libraries have lists of these books, as well as lists of books by topic and by reading levels.

## Savor Picture Books and Other Primary Books

Many picture books are for everyone, adults included. For very young readers, though, there are picture books with just a word or two; books of rhymes and jump rope chants, alphabet books, concept books (over, under), pattern stories, repeated readings, folk and fairy tales, and wordless books to help you create your own story.

When choosing books that you plan to read to very young children, try to read the entire book before purchasing it. Choose works with stories you and your child enjoy that have pleasing illustrations. Young children benefit from multiple readings of favorite books, so make sure that you can enjoy it along with him.

### Limited Vocabulary

Does your beginning-to-read child become frustrated with books that have big words she cannot yet read? Try some books with a deliberately limited vocabulary for a while.

The best bet is popular or classic literature that has stood the test of time for this type of book. Books such as Dr. Seuss' *Cat in the Hat* and P.D. Eastman's *Go, Dog, Go* are favorites for many beginner readers. If Dr. Seuss makes you cranky, try *The Bob Books* or other choices recommended by your librarian.

Be very careful when choosing this type of book, though. Some limited vocabulary books are insultingly simple-minded. Others focus so heavily on the set of sounds being taught that the stories are impossibly contrived, wrapped together with a web of tongue-twisting sentences. Many reading textbooks fall into this category. While the authors may have good intentions, the books have little literary interest or instructional value.

### Oral Literature

You might also consider storytelling and retelling, singing songs, and book/tape combinations. Some families successfully introduce literature through video or audio tapes, and later tackle reading the book itself, either individually or as a family. You can find excellent audiotapes of both classic and original tales to supplement your own reading of favorites. Some parents have recorded themselves reading a favorite story to their child. The child can turn the pages and look at pictures, or even read along, with Mom's or Dad's familiar voice telling the story in their ear.

## Write Your Own

Try making your own books with photographs from your adventures together. You can write simple captions or elaborate explanations. Alternatively, you might have your child dictate to you, then do drawings of the adventure. You may think of this as a writing activity, and it is, but you'll find the effort pays off in the reading time. How fun it is to re-read a book you have written!

## Chapter Books

Introduce the first book of a new book series by reading it together. Developing readers enjoy reading series of books such as *The Little House on the Prairie, Hardy Boys, Nancy Drew,* the *Redwall* series, *The Boxcar Children, The Chronicles of Narnia, Harry Potter,* and many others. Many a parent has read the first book or first chapter in an appealing series aloud only to discover that — guess what!— the kids sneak off to their rooms to read ahead when they think their parent isn't watching.

## Poetry

Are your children too restless to sit for long read-aloud times? Calm your tiger with the strong rhythms of poetry. Poetry, including nursery rhymes, finger plays, and children's songs, is the perfect read-aloud genre for children with short attention spans. Very active children can dance or tap out a rhythm to engage their bodies while listening.

Books with songs and music that you sing together can also captivate your child with the wonders of print. Explore the music of poetry and the poetry of music. I still remember the verses of Robert Quackenbush's *Clementine,* and I'm betting my daughters do too!

Include a few volumes of poetry in your book collection. Older children and teens enjoy the intensity of feeling that can be portrayed through the well-chosen words of good poems. They will also enjoy the immense freedom of expression that writing poetry and song lyrics can offer — there are so many ways to write poetry. A love of poetry will last a lifetime.

## Dramatics

Another outlet for children on the move is dramatics. Very young children can act out stories using a few simple props and their rich imaginations. Older children may thrive on putting on elaborate productions for family and friends. In addition to learning to enjoy literature, children learn about themselves as well, as they try out the personalities of the characters in the story.

Why not try a reader's theater? Choose a classic play, check out several copies from your library, assign roles, and read your parts — what fun! If you have more roles than family members, invite another family or two over and make the reading an event.

Don't overlook the possibilities that drama has to offer your shy child. Some children can find their own voices better when pretending to be someone else. Puppetry is an enjoyable dramatic activity for children who don't enjoy being in the spotlight themselves.

Drama, puppetry, and making plays can integrate many studies into one activity — writing, reading, arts and crafts, cooperation, social learning, organization. Older students may want to form a production company of their own or join a homeschool or community theater effort.

## SELECTED RESOURCES

### Audio Bookshelf
Heather Frederick, 174 Prescott Hill Road, Northport, ME 04849
800/234.1713 fax: 207/338.0370 audiobookshelf.com
Unabridged classic literature on tape for students of all ages. Free catalog.

### Books to Build On: A Grade by Grade Resource Guide
by E. D. Hirsch, Jr. www.coreknowledge.org
A well-respected guide for building a classic literary curriculum.

### Brook Farm Books

POB 246, Bridgewater, ME 04735
506/3785.4680    jean@brookfarmbooks.com
A very good resource for affordable books and literature. Order from their book/catalog, which is filled with commentary by down-to-earth homeschooling parents.

### Chinaberry Book Service

2780 Via Orange Way, Suite B, Spring Valley, CA 91978
619/670.5200    order: 800/776.2242    fax: 619/670.5203
customerservice@chinaberry.net
Quality books and more for the entire family.

### A Gentle Wind

Box 3103, Albany, NY 12203
518/482.9023    888/386.7664    www.gentlewind.com
Audiotapes and CDs of folk tales, songs, and stories from around the world.

### Greathall Productions

Jim Weiss, PO Box 5061, Charlottesville, VA 22905-5061
800/477.6234    fax: 804/296.4490
www.greathall.com  Greathall@greathall.com
Award-winning storytelling. Popular cassettes and CDs. Free brochure.

### The Growler Tapes Audio Adventures

Bob Sakayama, 110 West 86th Street, NYC, NY 10024
800/GROWLER    www.growler.com
Lively, un-narrated, quality audio programs. Listeners are "flies on the wall," and must make sense of the sounds they hear. Thirty tapes, ages 4-12. Free catalog.

### Some of My Best Friends Are Books: Guiding Gifted Readers

Judith Halsted. Ohio Psychology Publishing/1995.
Gifted children have different reading styles and needs. Covers preschool through high school.

### High Noon Books

20 Commercial Blvd., Novato, CA 94949
800/422.7249    fax: 888/287.9975
www.academictherapy.com  sales@academictherapy.com
Easier reading level (Gr. 1-4) mysteries, classical literature and other subjects.

### Movies Unlimited

6736 Castor Ave, Philadelphia, PA 19149        800/523.0823
www.moviesunlimited.com/musite/homepage.asp
Find favorite classics on video. Free catalog.

## *The New Read-Aloud Handbook*

Jim Trelease. Penguin Books, 1989.
Tips on reading aloud, as well as selected books to read aloud, from picture books to novels, with commentary.

## *Newport Publishers*

100 North Lake Ave. #203, Pasadena, CA 91101-1885
800/579.5532   www.newportpublishers.com/
Children's and adult classics dramatized on audio cassettes.

## *Odds Bodkin Storytelling Library*

Rivertree Productions, PO Box 410, Bradford, NH 03221
800/554.1333   fax: 603/938.5616
rivertree@conknet.com  www.oddsbodkin.com
Richly textured tapes of classical tales told by master storyteller Odds Bodkin.
Award-winning. Cassettes/CDs for three and up. Free brochure.

## *Parent's Guide to Children's Reading*

Nancy Larrick. Westminster Press/1982
Suggestions of different types of books available for enjoyable reading.

## *Playing Shakespeare*

Aristoplay, 8122 Main Street, Dexter, MI 48130
800/634.7738   fax: 734/424.0124
info@aristoplay.com   www.aristoplay.com/contactus.asp
Board game. Ages 12 and up. No prior knowledge of Shakespeare is needed.

## *Plays and Musicals for Young Actors*

I.E. Clark Publications, PO Box 246, Schulenburg, TX 78956-0246
979/743.3232   fax: 979/743.4765
ieclark@cvtv.net   www.ieclark.com
Catalog of more than 100 plays and musical productions. Children and teens. Free sampler catalog.

## *Reading Lists for College-Bound Students*

Doug Estell, et al, 2000.
A book of suggested reading for college preparation.

## *Scholastic Book Service*

2931 East McCarty Street, Jefferson City, MO 65101
800/724.6527   fax: 800/223.4011   www.scholastic.com
Inexpensive paperback book clubs and software clubs for children.

## *Treegate Publications of Wisconsin*

833 Liberty Drive, DeForest, WI 53532          608/846.8728
www.treegatepublications.com/  treegt@aol.com
Literature unit study guides for classics such as *Alice in Wonderland, The Wind in the Willows*. Free sample lessons are available.

## SELECTED CHILDREN'S MAGAZINES

*Boomerang!*
PO Box 261, La Honda, CA 94020
800/333.7858    www.boomkids.com
Award-winning children's audio magazine. 70 minutes. Back issues.

*Boys' Life*
1325 W. Walnut Hill Lane, PO Box 152079, Irving, TX 75015-2079
972/580.2366    www.scouting.org/mags/boyslife
Published by Boy Scouts of America. Twelve issues per year.

*Boys' Quest*
PO Box 227, Bluffton, OH 45817-0227
800/358.4732    www.boysquest.com
A magazine that focuses on activities that appeal to boys, without
commercialism. Includes cartoons, stories, codes, games, activities. No
teenage themes. Ages 6-13. Six issues per year.

*Cricket Magazine Group*
Carus Publishing Co., 315 Fifth Street, Peru, IL 61354
800/827.0227    www.cricketmag.com
Popular series of magazines for children 6 months to 14, including *Babybug*,
*Click*, *Ladybug*, *Spider*, and *Cricket*. Sample issues available. Also *Muse*,
ages 8-14.

*Highlights for Children*
PO Box 269, Columbus, OH 43216  800/603.0591  www.highlights.com
"Fun with a purpose." A school style magazine that emphasizes basic skills,
creativity, and activities. Ages 2 to 12. Sample issue available.

*Hopscotch: The Magazine for Girls*
PO Box 164, Bluffton, OH 45817-0164
800/358.4732    www.hopscotchmagazine.com
Focuses on activities that appeal to girls, without glitzy commercialism.
Includes book reviews and readers' poems and letters. Ages 6-13.

*Jack & Jill*
1100 Waterway Blvd., Indianapolis, IN 46202    317/634.1100
fax: 317/684.8094    customercare@cbhi.org  www.cbhi.org
Elementary stories and activities with a health focus. 8 issues per year.

*New Moon: The Magazine for Girls and Their Dreams*
New Moon Publishing, PO Box 3620, Duluth, MN 55803-5507
218/728.5507    800/381.4743    fax: 218/728.0314
newmoon@newmoon.org www.newmoon.org
Girls and women create a magazine which celebrates girls aged 8-14. Send
for information and writers' guidelines. Six issues per year.

## chapter forty

# EXPLORING WRITING
*toward becoming a writer*

How do we learn to write, *really*? My personal explorations, in my efforts to improving my writing, have led me to write, read the writing of others, write, think and reflect, and write some more. Though editing and guidance are often helpful — and absolutely essential at certain points — great progress can also be made by filling stacks and stacks of journals.

As your child matures, he may want to expand this approach to writing by studying various aspects of the craft with other writers through classes, discussion groups, courses, and reading books on writing. As skill grows, writing can be published for all the world to read. Let's consider some of these strategies separately.

## Learn Writing Skills by Reading

A writing student might pull a page from an art student's copybook. Artists learn to paint by imitating the techniques, design, and style of master works. The student of writing might try copying the style of an admired master writer, but with the student's own material. Many good writing skills are learned just this way. When very young, my children developed language skills of usage, including punctuation and spelling, skills that I had not directly taught them. When I asked where they learned these things, they told me, "I did it the way they do it in books." Well, of course!

Children just might become engaged with writing through their current reading. An idea from a book often triggers a different idea — why not try writing about it? Parents can also help students try their hand at writing in the styles they enjoy in books. Does your child love to read or listen to fairy tales? Try writing a few together just to explore the idea. Are you giggling together over limericks and jokes? Write limericks after you've read some of the classics and discovered the formula. Is your daughter writing a "girl story" loaded with conversation? Introduce her to Jane Austen's books!

## Pre-Writing — Thinking and Reflecting

Sometimes it is tough to get the *thinking* juices flowing. Pre-writing activities can help. Here are a few to try with children.

**Listen carefully to your child's ideas.** Your child has been sharing her innermost thoughts and ideas with you most of her life. Some children will naturally want to put their ideas on paper, but others will need encouragement. Who else but Mom or Dad is likely to teach the reluctant writer that her ideas are worth writing down?

**Remind your child that writing can be seen as spoken conversation**, a way of sending ideas to another across time or space. When you are talking with your child, listen for ideas that lend themselves to being recorded on paper. Did your son come home from his swimming lesson bubbling over the excitement of his experience? Write down the anecdote with him. Even the youngest child can find the beginning, the middle, and the end of a personal experience. First have your child tell you the story before he sets about writing it down. Or write it down for him. If you do that a few times, you tell him through your responses that his ideas and experiences have value and are worth preserving.

**Keep paper and pencil handy**. Everyone has moments when ideas come to them more readily — lying in bed trying to wake up, while drawing, skating, knitting, doing yard work, or playing music. Finding one's "muse" isn't as mysterious as it is practical — knowing when and how ideas come to you and making sure you have a pencil handy at that moment. The eventual goal writers seek is to have ideas immediately flow upon picking up the pencil or sitting down at the keyboard.

**Help your student develop "idea-productive" moments.** Writers use a variety of techniques, such as outlines, note cards, notebooks, doodling, lists, webs, and flow charts. For some writers, pre-writing is a completely mental activity. Encourage your child to try all the strategies and then use what works best.

**Help your student think about different kinds of writing** — after she gets her idea, not before. Will this be a short story, a poem, or an essay? A riddle, an argument, or an explanation? Stories usually appeal to children, probably because they are so familiar with "story" from read aloud time with you. However, another type of writing may be a better choice. Try opinions, arguments, ads, explanations, descriptions, jokes, or riddles.

## Learn Writing Skills by Writing

Parents can jump-start interest in writing and self-expression by helping young children take intermediate steps.

**A nice beginning for some families is shared writing**, an experience where writing as conversation becomes firmly established. Parent and child take turns writing and responding to one another's writings. Writing notes to one another, asking and answering questions on paper, making up riddles, poems, jokes, and scavenger hunts — these are good ways to engage your child in shared writing. Pen pals, e-mail pals, and letters to distant friends and family expand a child's understanding of writing as conversation. And if family members write back, all the better!

**Shared journals add a rich dimension to the parent child relationship.** Take the time to write out your ideas and thoughts, even have arguments, in the journal. Respond to one another on that topic only through the journal. Mother/daughter arguments preserved for posterity! When your relationship is smooth, try other kinds of writing, such as taking turns developing a story line or writing poems together.

**Older children usually enjoy using journals and diaries** for getting their ideas down on paper. Private journals should be just that — private. Consider the skills that your student develops while writing in his journal: self-expression with an audience of one — himself, fluency and flow of ideas, self-correction and editing (or not, it doesn't matter), handwriting practice and fine motor control. Journaling can be a deeply satisfying private experience. Set down self talk, feelings, or work through problems. Journals are a good place to jot down notes on personal goals, disappointments, successes and celebrations. A journal is a safe place for reflection.

**Young children can ease into writing by dictating stories and letters** for the parent to record. Remind your children, often, this is writing that they are doing, and you are just helping. Later they will be able to write by themselves. What a thrill it is to have one's very own ideas recorded!

**Use audio-visual approaches to launch writing activity.** Let him make audio and/ or video tapes. Give him a camera to record a story, then write captions for each photo. Let her collect a set of drawings that tell a story and then write captions, dialogue, or a summary. Does he make up plays that he acts out for you? You could videotape, transcribe, and then let him read the play he wrote. Make sure your student knows that, as long as he is expressing himself in language, he is writing, even though he is using shortcuts, aids, or transcribers, such as Mom or Dad.

## Editing — Preparing for Readers

Eventually, a writer needs to try his work out on someone else. What? Someone else will read it? Torture! Since many beginning — and not so beginning — writers have trouble separating their feelings from their work, a safe and supportive audience helps soften the blow of editing. Parents and grandparents are the usual "first public" for whom a student edits his work. A "public of one" is still public, and students can prepare their writings as if they will be read by strangers.

Particularly during the early stages of learning to write, criticism and correction are frequently a waste of time. Students learn little from the perfectly corrected paper, even though the parent has poured effort into finding every error. Worse, a paper that drips red ink is enormously discouraging.

Keep in mind that, when a *mature* writer is ready to put his best effort forward, he or she treasures the insights and corrections of a capable editor. Good editors help us find errors we cannot see and help us improve our communication. Our job as parents, though, is to help *immature* writers remain interested in writing until they mature.

Instead of striving for perfection on every paper your child may write, focus on a particular skill for each editing session. Work on punctuation one day, capitalization on another, and spelling on yet another. Some days, focus on the content of the work. Are the ideas organized so the reader can follow them easily? Are the words both accurate and interesting? Are there other or better ways to express the ideas?

Parents need to be circumspect about corrections. Too little editing leaves a work that may be either difficult to read or unappealing to the reader. But, on the other hand, excessive editing disheartens the writer. Choose wisely. You can be editor-in-chief without the grim red or blue pencil. Just sit with your child — perhaps with a reference book or two at hand — and go through the paper together. Editing is an enjoyable process if approached from a problem-solving viewpoint. You acting as a walking-talking speller /dictionary/grammar guide/idea source makes the editing task easier for the beginning writer.

Your child will usually pick up on some of her errors upon re-reading her work aloud, especially after letting it sit for a few days. She will also be better able to point out places where she is unsure and may ask for help. If you and your student disagree about a correction, use a reference tool such as a grammar book or a dictionary as a higher authority. When your child begins to answer writing questions by picking up that reference book instead of turning to you, you'll know you've done your job well!

## Learning With Other Writers

As writing confidence builds, students benefit from sharing their writing with others, while learning to critique written work. Help your student find an audience that suits his style. Writing clubs can be an enjoyable way to help students develop advanced skills. Some students enjoy corresponding with a pen pal. A writer/mentor relationship could be perfect for some budding authors. Some prefer to read how-to-write-books by well-known writers.

## Ideas for Publishing Student Writing

Make sure that, occasionally, a paper, a letter, a story — some piece of writing — is prepared for publication. Try some of the publishing ideas that follow.

## Write Letters and E-Mail

Letter writing almost goes without saying. In this day of instant messages and e-mail, one might think that computer-using children would know how to construct a basic letter. Don't be too sure. Make sure they write and receive letters once in awhile. At a bare minimum, writing thank-you notes is still considered good manners.

## Make Books

Whenever a book is made, something special happens to the writings contained therein. They become more permanent than writings left on mere on notebook paper. Making a book can be as simple as stapling a few pages together. It can be a matter of collecting writings into a notebook as a personal anthology. You can bind and decorate books that are works of art. Make sure each child makes a few handmade books during his youth, then finds a permanent place for them on your family bookshelf.

## Write and Produce Plays, Skits, Songs, Poems

Many children enjoy dramatic projects, and some even create plays and skits spontaneously. Creating scripts takes discipline and control, but may be the perfect writing project. (Groups participating in *Destination Imagination* have a rich script-writing experience.) A book or two on how to write scripts might be of help in creating a useful format. If several students collaborate, have them make enough signed copies of the script for each to have one. Photocopies or computer printouts are good enough. Will the group put on a program or show for friends and family? Programs and invitations offer another writing project. Allow plenty of time if such a rich learning activity develops in your home.

## Make Audiotapes, Videos, or Web Pages

Children design and produce the scripts, plans, and outlines. There is no need for the parent to have great expertise in creating such projects. Just be willing to work along with the children in a learn-as-we-go approach, You can learn to design a simple web page right along with the kids. If they want to make a video, perhaps you can borrow a video camera if you don't own one of your own.

Remember to have fun with the process. Don't expect perfection. I hope I am not the only person who got "on" and "off" confused when first using a video recorder, and ended up recording set up, chitchat, the floor, my feet, and even the practice scenes, but nary a second of the actual play.

## Submit Work to Contests, Magazines and Newsletters

Some students who love to write eagerly seek chances to publish their work, enter contests, and otherwise try their efforts out against the efforts of others. Some more self-conscious writers may find motivation to do their best work if they can first publish in a local newsletter or perhaps on the family web page.

Numerous opportunities exist, some of which are noted in the resources that follow. Some publications are edited by students; others are edited by adults but feature only student work. To find publications by and for homeschooling students and families, subscribe to favorite homeschooling newsletters and magazines and watch for announcements.

Homeschooled student successes are a source of constant surprise and delight. One young man's *first* writing project was a poem, which he submitted to the State Fair, and won first prize — at age eighteen!

## Publish a Magazine or Newsletter

Or why not try publishing a newsletter of student writing? Send for several sample copies of other student publications and then get to work on your premier edition. It's fun, it's hard work, and it's very satisfying. State, local, and national homeschooling magazines will happily announce your project!

### SELECTED RESOURCES

*Editor in Chief Series*
Critical Thinking Books & Software,
PO Box 448, Pacific Grove, CA 93950-0448
www.criticalthinking.com     800/458.4849
A nifty program that bridges the gap between grammar head knowledge and practical application. Books or software.

## Institute for Excellence in Writing
Andrew Pudewa, PO Box 6065A, Atascadero, CA 93423   800/856.5815
fax: 603/925.5123  ww.writing-edu.com  info@writing-edu.com
A writing program that trains parents and teachers to teach writing to students
using a prescribed syllabus.

## Speaking and Writing ~~Good~~ Well
By Kathy Alba, Ph.D. Thatch Tree Publications,
2250 N. Rock Road, Ste. 118-169, Wichita, KS 67226
thatchtreepub@aol.com
English basics self-taught with humor. Teens.

## Wordsmith Series
By Janie B. Cheaney.
Common Sense Press, PO Box 1365, Melrose, FL 32666
352/475.5757    www.commonsensepress.com
Creative writing program with student-friendly exercises. Solid writing
techniques. Grades 6 up.

## Write Away: A Friendly Guide for Teenage Writers
Peter Stillman. Available from FUN Books, 1688 Belhaven Woods Court,
Pasadena MD 21122-3727   888/386.7020    MD only: 410/360.7330
FUN@FUN-Books.com  www.fun-books.com
Humorous and practical writing help.

## Writing Because We Love To: Homeschoolers at Work
Susannah Sheffer. Available from FUN Books, 1688 Belhaven Woods
Court, Pasadena MD 21122-3727   888/386.7020  MD only: 410/360.7330
FUN@FUN-Books.com  www.fun-books.com
Ideas on how to help children and young people with their writing, based on
Sheffer's experiences working with homeschooled students.

## Writing Strands
By Dave Marks
National Writing Institute, 624 W. University #248, Denton, TX 76201
Catalog: 888/644.8686  orders: 800/688.5375  www.writingstrands.com
Straightforward writing instruction for all levels.

## SELECTED PUBLISHING RESOURCES

## BooksByChildren
PO Box 122, Argyle, TX 76226   940/241.2588
editor@myibook www.booksbychildren.com and www.myibook.org
Submit books, art stories, poems, and other written work for online
publication. 1-12. Print materials are scanned for publication and work is left
on the site for 90 days.

### Creative Kids Magazine

PO Box 8813, Waco, TX 76714-8813　800/998.2208　fax: 254/756.3339
Creative_Kids@prufrock.com www.prufrock.com
Publishes material by and for children ages 8-14. Four issues.

### Creating Books with Children

Valerie Bendt. Common Sense Press, 333 Rio Vista Court, Tampa, FL
33604. A manual for creating a bound book, with a six-week plan of action
from pre-writing to author's party.

### Dick Blick Catalog

PO Box 1267, Galesburg, IL 61402-1267　800/828.4548
fax: 800/621.8293　info@dickblick.com www.dickblick.com
A very good source of quality bookmaking ideas and fine bookbinding
materials.

### Handmade Books: An Introduction to Bookbinding

By Rob Shepard. Available from Dick Blick Catalog, above.
A good resource book to help you make your first bound book. Photos.

### Handmade Books and Cards

By Jean G. Kropper
Zephyr Press, 3316 N. Chapel Avenue, Tucson, AZ 85716
800/232.2187　fax: 520/323.9402
www.zephyrpress.com zephyrpress@zephyrpress.com
More than a how-to guide, this book offers the "why" of the various bindings
described, along with a brief historical note on each.

### KIDNEWS

www.kidnews.com
Publish student writing online.

### The Young Writer's Guide to Getting Published

By Kathy Henderson. Writer's Digest Books. www.writersdigest.com
More than 100 listings of opportunities for young writers. Includes writing tips
and student writing samples.

### Merlyn's Pen

PO Box 910, East Greenwich, RI 02818　800/247.2027　401/885.5175
fax: 401/885.5222 www.merlynspen.com merlyn@merlynspen.com
Annual national magazine that publishes the best of student writing, ages 12-
18. A useful resource for students who want to improve their writing.

### New Moon: The Magazine for Girls and Their Dreams

PO Box 3620, Duluth, MN 55803　800/381.4743 fax: 218/728.0314
newmoon@newmoon.org www.newmoon.org
Looking for many kinds of material from girls aged 8-14. Send for information
and writers' guidelines.

## Readers Speak Out

Ronald Richardson , 4003 50th Ave SW, Seattle WA 98116

Teens can send their poems, short stories, articles and other writings.

## Stone Soup

PO Box 83, Santa Cruz, CA 95063

800/447.4569   fax: 831/426.1161

www.stonesoup.com   editor@stonesoup.com

Classic magazine of children's writing and art with an international flavor. Stories, poems, book reviews, and art of children to age 13. Six issues. Helpful website.

## Teen Ink

PO Box 30, Newton, MA 02461

617/964.6800   editor@teenink.com   teenink.com

A national teen magazine, book series, and website, written by teens and for teens to read.

## Word Dance Magazine

Playful Productions, Inc., PO Box 10804, Wilmington, DE 19850

800/378.8815   302/322.6699   fax: 302/322.4531

www.worddance.com   playful@worddance.com

Quarterly magazine that publishes student art, haiku, letters, field trip stories, and more. Sample the magazine and get writing and publishing tips online.

## Young Voices

PO Box 2321, Olympia, WA 98507

360/357.4683    fax: 360/705.9669

support@youngvoicesmagazine.com    www.youngvoicesmagazine.com

Publishes stories, poems, essays, and drawings. K-12. Quarterly.

## chapter forty-one

# EXPLORING MUSIC
*Can you afford not to?*

Children naturally love music, and will frequently sing, dance, and sway to the beat before they walk! Exposure to a wide variety of music adds a rich dimension to a child's life.

Music lays a solid background for many subjects, actually crossing the lines of most disciplines. Music is a *conversation* between composers, performers, and their listeners. Music is uniquely social: we usually *play* or dance to music *together*. Students can *read* music, they can *dance* to music and they can *write* music. Study the *science* of sound and the *history* of composers, instruments, and music theory. Much classical music and most music notation exposes the student to *foreign language*. And *math*! Music notation is a great exposure to fractions. Time needs to be counted and rhythms need to be tapped out. And don't forget to learn music for music's sake alone — the great enjoyment and satisfaction music can bring to life. You will not regret the money and time involved in immersing your child in the richness of music.

Generally, music is learned in two ways: by listening to it and by performing it. Singing to, and with, your young child and listening to records and tapes that you both enjoy, may be all the music you need for a long time. Add in some fun with rhythm instruments (homemade or purchased), marching and dancing, and a more terrific music program cannot be found. A few high quality children's recordings will keep your youngster occupied for hours, and can soothe many difficult times.

As your child matures, singing in a local homeschool, church, or community choir, or learning to play an instrument, may give him a lifelong love and appreciation of music. Follow your child's interests as much as possible. Why should your child play the trumpet if he is fascinated by the clarinet or guitar? Handbell choirs are great for many ages of players!

In larger communities, you might take in local music productions such as "brown bag" concerts, the symphony, or the opera (dress rehearsals and matinees are often inexpensive). Musical productions in local communities can be just as much fun, whether the student listens or performs. If you do not have access to live performances of the type of music your family enjoys, video, audio, and televised productions are good resources.

Some homeschool support groups may have a small orchestra or band. The group doesn't need to be large, it just needs an interested individual to get you all started. Some families join with another musically inclined family for regular music-making evenings. In some areas, homeschooled students can participate in public or private school music activities, such as orchestra and band.

If your family is naturally musical, you don't need me to tell you what to do — just do it! If your family is on the tone-deaf side of music appreciation, there are still many ways to introduce music to your family. One family took lessons together from a voice teacher so they could better enjoy singing together. Try listening to many different kinds of music until you find favorite styles that you enjoy. You might want to find a teacher who will work with you as a family. Perhaps a musically inclined friend or family member can guide you. Whatever else you include in your homeschooling program, you will always be glad for the music you explore.

## SELECTED RESOURCES

*Centre for Musical Empowerment*
> Winter Harbor Haven, Route 608, Port Haywood, VA 23138
> 804/725.0355   dickbozung@guitarsimplified.com
> www.guitarsimplified.com
> The Guitar Barre® Beginners Method makes guitar playing easy for beginners and those with hand difficulties.

### Courtly Music Unlimited

Richie and Elaine, 3785 Maine St., Warrensburgh, NY 12885
800/274.2443   fax: 518/623.2869   Richie@courtlymusicunlimited.com
www.courtlymusicunlimited.com   If the recorder is your instrument of
choice, how can you beat this resource? Free expert advice and a full range of
recorders and recorder music for all levels.

### Homespun Tapes, Ltd.

PO Box 340, Woodstock, NY 12498   845/246.2550   fax: 845/246.5282
www.homespuntapes.com   Homespun@hvi.net
Instructional videos and CDs for many instruments, from beginner to
professional.

### Lark in the Morning

PO Box 799, Fort Bragg, CA 95437   707/964.5569
fax: 707/964.1979   larkinam@larkinam.com   www.larkinam.com
Musical instruments. Free 144 page catalog. Many cultural music instruments
available, as well as recordings, instruction, and videos.

### Lester Family

PO Box 203, Joshua Tree, CA 92252   760/366.1023
info@lesterfamilymusic.com   www.lesterfamilymusic.com/
Your whole family learns to harmonize and sing unaccompanied, along with
the Lester family. CD and cassettes.

### Making Music with John Langstaff

683 Santa Barbara Rd., Berkeley, CA 94707
206/756.1804   toll free: 510/452.9334   order fax: 206/756.9422
sfbayrevels@earthlink.net   revels.bizland.com/store/index.html
Highly praised video music programs. Six award-winning instructional and
sing-along videos show children ages 2 -11 the basics of joycus, excellent
music-making. Music games, songs and music experiments.

### Mrs. Stewart's Piano Lessons

FUN Books, 1688 Belhaven Woods Court, Pasadena MD 21122-3727
888/386.7020   MD only: 410/360.7330
FUN@FUN-Books.com   www.fun-books.com
Popular beginning piano lessons for preschool and up.

### New Creation Music

Bill and Alison Purdon, 800/337.4798   www.newcreationmusic.com
Orchestra and band instruments for sale or rent to own.

### Practicing for Young Musicians: You Are Your Own Teacher

by Harvy Snitkin. Order from:
Brook Farm Books, POB 246, Bridgewater, ME 04735
506/3785.4680   jean@brookfarmbooks.com
An interesting book to help you and your child's music teacher put the
student in charge of his learning.

### *Rise Up Singing: The Group Singing Songbook*

edited by Peter Blood and Annie Peterson
This songbook includes words, chords, and sources of 1200 songs, from ballads to Beatles, Bob Dylan to Broadway.

### *Rounder Kids*

800/223.6357    fax: 802/223/5303
Buy@rounderkids.com    www.rounderkids.com
Cassettes and videos, for the very young.

### *Music For Little People/Earthbeat!*

PO Box 1460, Redway, CA 95560    phone: 707/923.3991
toll free: 800/346.4445    fax: 707/923.3241
musicforlittlepeople@mflp.com    store.yahoo.com/melody/index.html
Children's and family audio recordings, instruments, toys, and more.

### *Rhythm Band Instruments Inc.*

PO Box 126, Fort Worth, TX 76101-0126    phone: 817/335.2561 or
800/424.4724    fax: 817/332.5654    800/784.9401
e-mail: RHYTHMBAND@aol.com    www.rhythmband.com
Wide selection of recorders, method books, music instruction aids and books, multi-cultural instruments, even Boomwhackers and bells. Many rhythm instruments can be purchased individually or in sets.

### *Sing 'n' Learn*

2626 Club Meadow Dr., Garland, TX 75043
800/460.1973    www.singnlearn.com
Songs and music that help you learn other subjects.

### *Song of the Sea*

47 West Street, Bar Harbor, ME 04609    207/288.5653
fax: 207/288.8136    orders: 888/SONGSEA    www.songsea.com
Bagpipes, harps, dulcimers, recorders, drums, flutes, lessons, more. Free catalog.

### *Usborne Books*

Many music course books. Piano, keyboard, flute, clarinet, recorder. Colorful and enjoyable books.

### *West Music*

1212 Fifth Street, PO Box 5521, Coralville, IA 52241
800/397.9378    fax: 888/470.3942
service@westmusic.com    www.westmusic.com
Many instruments and other materials, videos that encourage kids to make music. Call for catalog.

## chapter forty-two

# EXPLORING ARTS AND CRAFTS
*learning with the hands and heart*

You've probably noticed that, throughout this book, I refer again and again to hands on activities and crafts. There is method in my repetitious madness — ideas learned through the hands and senses do not easily slip away. Just as music can soothe our hearts and minds, arts and crafts provide a calming outlet for active hands. Successful homeschool families focus energy and resources on the whole child, not just the intellect, providing opportunities for students to express themselves in as many ways as possible. Whether students develop a career, a satisfying hobby, or just explore arts or crafts for enjoyment, is not important. The important thing is to give children many chances to learn through their senses, their hands, and their bodies. Arts and crafts are key to that developmental process.

In addition to providing the fine arts activities, techniques, and materials of painting and modeling, remember to introduce the other arts, including fiber arts such as spinning, sewing, weaving, knitting, crochet, and embroidery. Using carpentry tools in simple woodworking projects is a satisfying learning experience for many students. Paper crafts are fun to explore. Try paper airplanes, boxes, dolls, windmills, snowflakes, origami, and papier mache projects.

If you have an art interest of your own, explore it with your children. Stuck for ideas? Visit a local art or craft store. You might seek instruction from a local artist or find art classes in your community. Some art teachers make a special effort to provide instruction for homeschooled children — check with your local homeschool support group. Art museums and larger libraries are excellent resources for art prints and art history materials. Look for craft books and craft projects at your local craft store. Computer programs may add variety to your program.

## SELECTED RESOURCES

### The Annotated Mona Lisa
A Crash Course in Art History from Prehistoric to Post-modern
By Carol Strickland, PhD. Andrews and McMeel,
A Universal Press Syndicate Co., Kansas City, MO
A reader-friendly and well-organized introduction to art history.

### Architecture Everywhere: Exploring the Built Environment of Your Community
By Joseph A. Weber. Available from Brook Farm Books, POB 246,
Bridgewater, ME 04735    506/3785.4680    jean@brookfarmbooks.com
Learn about the art in architecture and more.

### Artdeck
Available from Brook Farm Books
POB 246, Bridgewater, ME 04735
506/3785.4680   jean@brookfarmbooks.com
A fun game that introduces you to thirteen of the world's the great masters.

### Art Extension Press
PO Box 389, Westport, CT 06881
203/256.9920   fax: 203/259.8160
Reproductions of world masterpieces. Free brochure.

### Back to Basics
Rt. 1, Box 297, Bagley, MN 56621
800/367.0537    218/668.2884    fax: 218/668.2334
jberntson@backtobasicscrafts.com    www.backtobasicscrafts.com
Children's art and craft supplies and idea books.

### Brandine Crafts, Inc
725 SW 16th Ave, Bay #1, Delray Beach, FL 33444
561/266.9360    fax: 561/266.9361
www.brandine.com/    craft4kids@aol.com
Wood, foam, and bead craft kits for kids. Make toys, household items, gifts.

## *Cheap Joe's Art Stuff*
374 Industrial Park Drive, Boone, NC 28607
800/227.2788   fax: 828/262.0795   www.cheapjoes.com/
Many supplies for artists. Free catalog.

## *Child Sized Masterpieces*
Parent Child Press, PO Box 675, Hollidaysburg, PA 16648
866/727.3683   fax: 814/696.7510
info@parentchildpress.com   www.parentchildpress.com
A good source for postcard-size art reproductions.

## *Draw Today Homeschool Program Set*
Art Skills, 217 Ferry Street, Easton, PA 18042
800/552.3729   fax: 610/253.0715   www.artskills.com
A series of 10 - 15 drawing lessons with video instruction, teacher manual
and toll-free help line. Ages eight up.

## *Drawing on the Right Side of the Brain*
By Betty Edwards, 2nd Ed., 1999. J.P. Tarcher, 9110 Sunset Blvd., LA, CA
90069 A course in enhancing creativity and artistic confidence. This book
helps beginners learn basic drawing, even if convinced they have little talent.

## *Drawing With Children: A Creative Method for Adult Beginners, Too*
By Mona Brookes. Revised, 1996. St. Martin's Press.
A method of teaching and learning drawing that can be used even if you
have little art experience. Learn along with your children, ages eight and up.

## *Fabric Fun for Kids: Step-by-Step Projects for Children*
By Karen Bates Willing and Julie Bates Dock.
Now & Then Publications, 725 Beach St., Ashland, OR 97520
541/482.7935   fax: 541/482.7937
quiltnow@aol.com   www.nowthen.com/main.html
Offers a variety of fabric projects. Two other books, *Quilting Now & Then*
and *Cotton Now & Then* are both geared for 6-12 year olds.

## *Flash 'N Fashion*
Media Motion Publications, PO Box 658,Cherry Hill, NJ 08003-0658
order 800/770.3878   www.media-motion.com   sales@media-motion.com
V4.0. Win 3.1 and 95. Learn sewing skills while designing outfits for dolls,
from concept to sewn product. Ages seven up.

## *Harrisville Designs*
PO Box 806, Harrisville, NH 03450
800/338.9415  603/827.3333  fax: 603/827.3335  www.harrisville.com
Award-winning weaving and fiber projects for children. Free catalog.

## *Lark Books*
67 Broadway, Asheville, NC 28801     800/284.3388
www.larkbooks.com     larkmail@elarkbooks.com
Catalog of craft books and kits.

## Miller Pads and Paper
2840 Neff Rd., Boscobel, WI 53805
608/375.2181   www.millerpadsandpaper.com
Art supplies at discount prices.

## Mudworks
By Mary Ann F. Kohl. 1993. Bright Ring Publishing, PO Box 31338,
Bellingham, WA 98228-3338.   www.bringring.com
Sculpt, model, squish. Enjoyable projects laid out in an easy-to-use format.
For younger children, try *Preschool Art*.

## National Gallery of Art
Publication Department, Sixth and Constitution Avenues,
NW Washington, DC 20565   202/737.4215   www.nga.gov
View part of the national collection online. Reproductions available.

## Natural Child Project
www.naturalchild.org/gallery
An on-line art gallery for child artists ages 1-10.

## Share-A-Care Publications
240 Mohns Hill Rd., Reinholds, PA 17569
Art with a purpose. 36 lessons for each grade K-8 — ready to go.

## Visual Manna
PO Box 553, Salem, MO 65560
888/275.7309   arthis@rollanet.org   www.rollanet.org/~arthis/
Art curriculum and supplies for grades one through twelve. Sample lessons
available online. Integrates art with other subjects. Catalog.

## You Are An Artist!
20 fun, easy exercises to help your inner artist out!
By Tej Steiner. Everyday Arts, 2002.
541/535.1859   fax: 541/535.8585   Everydayarts@aol.com
The perfect little drawing book for shy or fearful artists of any age. Whimsical
activities and encouragement gently undermine your inner critic so that you
can enjoy taking the small risks that art calls for.

## The Young Masters Home Study Art Program
Gordon School of Art, PO Box 28208, Green Bay, WI 54324
800/210.1220   920/437.2190
Gordon@netnet.net   www.newmasters.com/
A complete drawing skill development art curriculum for home learners.
Family or individual instruction, ages six and up.

## chapter forty-three

# EXPLORING FOREIGN LANGUAGES
*Et tu?*

Why study foreign language? There are two reasons — three, if you count acquiring foreign language credits that may be required for college admission. We'll discuss the other two here.

The first reason is communication. Most homeschooling families commence foreign language study to improve communication. Study of another language may also improve communication by helping your child grasp the fundamentals of English, such as grammar and vocabulary root words — it worked that way for me.

But what if there were another compelling reason? Would you work harder to study a foreign language with your children if you thought it was good for their (and your own) thinking processes?

Foreign language study has been found to enhance brain development and mental growth. Aerobics for brain cells, you might say. Older people are often encouraged to keep their minds sharp by studying another language. It seems that stimulating the language centers of the brain builds synapses, thus creating a stronger mental ability, protecting against the damage of stroke, and other age related ailments. Doesn't it seem reasonable to assume that people of any age would enjoy the same benefits?

When you think about it, it is easy to understand why taking up a foreign language is good for mental growth. Learning a second language takes focus, attention to detail, the ability to memorize, and practice. You learn to think and process information differently. In order to understand the grammatical differences among languages, the idioms, the different conventions of sentence construction, and the ever enigmatic realization that concepts can be expressed in an infinite variety of ways, flexibility of thought is essential.

When should foreign language study begin?

Perhaps you've heard the old gardener's advice upon being asked when he pruned his prize roses. He rubbed his chin, thinking, then said, "Well, I always prune when I have a sharp tool in my hand."

That is sage advice for the study of foreign language. Perhaps the best time for learning a language is when you have the time and materials. Start today! It is never too early or too late for the brain to build synapses.

If your family's study of a language bogs down, just remember that you are building mental strength, so don't abandon the project forever. Simply take a break or work on a different language for a change. You might try American Sign Language for a completely different learning experience. When you return to the original language after some time away from it, you may be surprised at how much you recall.

Young children do benefit from early exposure to a second language. Their minds are open and eager. However, don't let age deter you from starting now. People of all ages can study foreign language. My father reads and studies Greek at age eighty-three. I try to read Spanish and study German when time permits. My daughters studied French and Spanish as young children and as teens. My husband learned Chinese in mid-life.

The best time to start is — well, when you have a "sharp tool" in your hand! Here are some sharp tools that can help you learn your targeted foreign language.

## Basic Materials

- at least one dictionary in the language
- audiotapes created by and for native speakers, including nursery rhymes, children's songs, and authentic music tapes
- close-captioned TV or videotapes of shows in the target language
- instructional videos

- computer software or online courses
- a newspaper or magazine in the target language
- a cookbook or two
- popular English picture books translated into the target language
- bilingual picture books written in both the target language and English
- children's books written for native-speaking children
- flash cards, or you can make your own
- a textbook for grammar and for reference
- trips to countries where the target language is the primary language
- foreign exchange programs
- time with a native speaker
- taking a class

## Finally

Try language activities in tasty bites. Perhaps first you'll learn to count, to tell time, or to read a calendar. Next year you might work on speaking the target language at breakfast, adding other meals as you gain fluency. Learn to speak the target language in the car, or the bathroom, or even in the garden. Just pace yourselves so you have some fun while you learn.

When the family has mastered all the conversational topics they can, students may extend their studies in many ways — a learning club, a class, travel, friendships, pen pals, apprenticeships with native speakers, or independent study.

### SELECTED RESOURCES

*Artes Latinae*
Bolchazy-Carducci Publishers, Inc.,
Marie Bolchazy, Ed. D., 1000 Brown Street, Wauconda, IL 60084
847/526.4344    fax: 847/526.2867
latin@bolchazy.com    www.bolchazy.com
A programmed, self-teaching Latin series, oriented toward the older student.

*Berlitz Basic*
  800/526.8047    www.berlitz.com
  1996. Tapes with a book. Easy to understand, easy to follow. You learn as
  you listen. Berlitz has many courses in many languages. Materials may be
  purchased from your local bookstore.

*Bueno — Friendly Foreign Language Learning*
  Bueno Books, 914 Pine Drive, Caldwell, TX 77836
  979/567.6769    orders: 800/431.1579      buenobooks.tripod.com/
  Mostly Spanish, some French and Russian. 16 page newsletter/catalog. One
  year subscription for $10, or free with purchase of $20 or more. Recipes,
  idioms, everyday speech in every issue, and practical Spanish instructional
  materials. A very good resource.

*Calliope Books Foreign Language Materials*
  Route 3 Box 3395, Saylorsburg, PA 18353
  610/381.2587    fax: 610/381.2587
  Materials for all ages in many languages; a variety of approaches.

*Canon Press*
  PO Box 8729, Moscow, ID 83843
  298/882.1456    orders: 800/488.2034    fax: 208/882.1568
  canorder@moscow.com    www.canonpress.org/pages/education.asp
  Elementary Latin. Conventional text materials and videotapes.

*Cambridge Latin Course*
  by Ed Phinney, Patricia E. Bell, Barbara Romaine (Editor) Cambridge
  University Press, 3rd edition
  Excellent four-unit series for beginning the study of Latin. Engaging story line
  introduces Latin in an easy-going immersion style. Workbooks and teacher's
  manual available.

*Educational News*
  PO Box 60478, Florence, MA 01062-0478
  800/600.4494    fax: 413/586.3448    www.ednews.com
  Three magazines written in three difficulty levels to maintain and improve
  Spanish. Subscription. Other Spanish items available, including crossword
  puzzles.

*Gallaudet University*
  Laurent Clerc National Deaf Education Center, 800 Florida Ave., NE,
  Washington, DC 20002 v/tty: 202/651.5000    800/526.9105
  clerccenter.gallaudet.edu/InfoToGo/111.html#I
  A source for books and materials that teach American Sign Language and
  deaf education. Help for beginners and up.

*The Garlic Press*
  1312 Jeppesen Avenue, Eugene, OR 97401
  541/345.0063    fax: 541/683.8767    www.garlicpress.com
  Beginning Sign Language materials. Free finger alphabet poster.

## *Hey, Andrew! Teach Me Some Greek! Latin's Not So Tough!*

Greek 'n' Stuff, PO Box 882, Moline, IL 61266-0882
309/796.2707    workbooks@greeknstuff.com    www.greeknstuff.com
Introduce very young children to the basics. Traditional materials.

## *How to Learn Any Language:*

Quickly, Easily, Inexpensively, Enjoyably, and On Your Own
Barry Farber, Citadel Press, 1991.
Introduction to foreign language study. Farber is self-taught, knows twenty-five languages, including Chinese, self-taught at age fifteen. Farber offers a method by which "...you *will* learn the language of your choice *quickly, easily, inexpensively, enjoyably, and on your own.*" Don't overlook this book.

## *It's Greek to Me!*

Hart and Home Publishers, Box 807, Chesterton, IN 46304
harthome@attbi.com
Self-study of New Testament Greek. Jr. /Sr. Hi.

## *The Joy of Signing:*

The Illustrated Guide for Mastering Sign Language and the Manual Alphabet.
By Lottie L. Riekehof, 2nd edition. Gospel Publishing House.
A very useful dictionary that is conveniently organized by usage categories. Includes clear drawings and text to teach signs, as well as interesting information about the origin and usage of the sign.

## *The Learnables*

International Linguistics Corp.
3505 East Red Bridge Road, Kansas City, MO 64137
800/237.1830    fax: 816/765.2855
info@learnables.com    learnables.com/
Enjoyable learning for all ages that builds first on listening and understanding. Time-tested. Many languages.

## *MUZZY: the BBC Language Course for Children*

Early Advantage
270 Monroe Turnpike, PO Box 4063, Monroe, CT 0648-4063
orders: 888/248.0480    fax: 800/301.9268
customerservice@early-advantage.com    www.early-advantage.com
Widely acclaimed and fun materials. CD-ROM, audio and video tapes, parents' guide. Spanish, French, German, Italian. Ages 1-12.

## *Oxford Latin Course*

by James Morwood, Maurice Balme   Oxford University Press 2nd ed
Series similar to the Cambridge series. Four books.

### Penton Overseas, Inc.

2470 Impala Drive, Carlsbad, CA 92008   800/748.5804   760/431.0060
fax: 760/431.8110   www.pentonoverseas.com/   info@pentonoverseas.com
Award winning programs use multi-sensory language learning techniques.
Young children and up. Spanish, French, German, Italian. Audio/video/CD-ROM. Free catalog.

### Pimsleur Language Program

Available from Multilingual Books
Internet Language Company, 1205 E. Pike, Seattle, WA 98122
206/328.7922    fax: 206/328.7445
www.multilingualbooks.com/index.html   info@multilingualbooks.com
Audiotapes only with native speakers in adult situations. Japanese, French,
Russian, German, Italian, many more. Older students.

### Power-glide Language Courses

1682 West 820 North, Provo, UT 84601
801/596.0910    fax: 801/343.3912
info@power-glide.com    www.power-glide.com
Linguistically based foreign language courses used by many homeschoolers.
CD-Rom, cassettes, books. Fifth grade and up. Spanish, French, German,
Japanese.

### Programs Abroad Travel Alternatives, Inc.

PATA, Inc., 6200 Adel, Austin, TX 78749-1656
888/777.PATA    512/892.8608    fax: 512/892.0145
www.gopata.com/default.htm   immerse@gopata.com
Try living in a foreign country to really learn a language. Homeschool and
conventional programs available.

### Teach Me ...

Teach Me Tapes, Inc., 6016 Blue Circle Drive, Minnetonka, MN 55343-9104
800/456.4656    952/933.8086    fax: 952/933.0512
marie@teachmetapes.com    www.teachmetapes.com/
Familiar songs recorded in the target language are loosely translated in
English. Available in French, German, Japanese, Russian and a growing
number of languages. Children ages 2-12 learn language with ease and
humor using this innovative book and audio set.

### Transparent Language

9 Executive Park Drive, Merrimack, NH 03054
888/245.1829    fax: 603/262.6555    www.transparent.com
Software and Internet-based language learning for ages 6 up. Kidspeak
includes games, puzzles and songs — choose from ten languages.

### Usborne Books

Many books and tapes for all ages in several languages.

## chapter forty-four

# LEARNING BY COMPUTER
*using the electronic learning machine, using common sense*

How will *your* family use your computer, your digital Swiss army knife? Or will you use it at all? You'll discover that successful homeschooling families fall into two distinct camps — those who use computers and those who don't. Let me clarify. Computers are not essential to successful homeschooling. Many have, and many still do, homeschool successfully, with limited or no computer access.

For many others, though, a computer is a most useful tool.

If you are uncertain which camp you belong in, or if you want some more ideas about computer use, this chapter is for you. First, we'll consider the many roles a computer can have as a tool of home learning. A brief discussion on the amount of time students should spend at the computer is followed by rebuttals to several common beliefs about computer use. Finally, a few resources are included.

## Common Computer Uses

These days, most people think of the Internet when they think of the computer. And why not? What a treasure trove of information the Internet brings to our fingertips. Just type a key word or two into your favorite search engine and bingo! You have, at your fingertips, more information than you could possibly use.

The Internet is where many families turn first to answer those burning questions. Are you looking for a support group? A carpenter ant reference? Information on how to spell or pronounce a word? A math learning game? Quality reference books can be found online as can many out-of-copyright classics. Just think of the Internet as a Combination World University/Library/Postal Service/Study group/ Soapbox/Coffee Klatch/Shopping Mall/Entertainment Center, with numerous and random directories of resources, and you will see the merest tip of the Internet iceberg.

Quality software is another good use of your computer in your educational plan. You might consider a CD-ROM encyclopedia, for example — complete with sound clips, pictures, and text. Maybe a point-and-click anatomy program is the perfect supplement to your budding biologist's book collection. Dictionaries, maps, charts, and atlases are available and often free.

Besides reference software, quality software tools will help you streamline common tasks. I love my word processors and the helpful spelling and grammar checkers. Bookkeeping and accounting software, cookbooks, home improvement, art and drawing software, music construction kits, and web design software are examples that we've used. These tools are not just for adults and older students. Even young children can learn to use the simpler parts of these programs. Knowing how to use computer tools can be an important part of a student's progress toward independence.

Curriculum is widely available as either single subject or full year programs. Some content and interest areas are especially enhanced by computer capabilities. For example, foreign language is particularly attractive when accompanied by pronunciation by native speakers. Educational software is available for many subjects and levels. You can purchase CD-ROM curricula or sign up for online classes, classes that may include tutoring, support, student chats and e-mail loops.

Take advantage of so-called edu-tainment products as well as traditional games on the computer. Can children learn to type, spell, think deductively, or multiply fractions while playing computer games? You bet they can. Classic games are widely available, as are adventure and other video games. Software that turns ho-hum drill into exciting games is also widely available. Some software is effective at engaging the student in thinking and problem-solving, perhaps through games, quests, or other activities of discovery. One favorite is *Myst*, which requires reasoning and problem-solving skills while being great fun.

Many children will want to use the computer for pure entertainment. There is a ton of fun to be had online and with some of the exciting software available. Many families use their computers for games, e-mail, and surfing the Internet — all just for fun.

Exploring the technical aspects of the computer itself — such as hardware, software, or web design — can be a springboard an abiding interest for some students. Some students just have to know how the darn thing works! Perhaps your student will be the family expert.

## How Much Time at The Computer?

As you might guess, both the amount of computer use, and the ways successful homeschooling families use their computers, vary widely. With so many possible ways of using a computer, you may suddenly discover that the computer begins to dominate your life without notice. Computer dependence can really sneak up on you, for while some activities are just for fun and others are for structured learning, too much time at the computer, even for the best purposes, has drawbacks. Computer time, no matter how exciting or wonderful, still limits your child's body to one location and one position, and her mind to one type of learning.

One way you can help your child to a healthy dose of computer time is by controlling the computer environment. For example, sharing a computer with other family members necessarily limits how much time any one person can spend there. Keeping the computer near the center of family activity also helps children to be drawn into alternative activities.

Most families limit computer access for their very young children. Some early childhood experts caution that young children should have no more than one half hour of "screen time" per day — computer and television combined. Their concern is not just the risk of excessive or passive computer use, but the loss of what children would be doing otherwise — running, playing, building, conversing, imagining — just being kids. You will find your own guidelines.

When children are older, more computer time may make sense. Exciting software and interesting Internet sites offer an easy way to access information. Some families may want a computer available for a workbook-type curriculum or to be used as a tool for the student who does a great deal of writing.

Try this rule of thumb: Computer time can be one of many varied activities that your children participate in every day. As long as activities are diverse, including enthusiastic and strenuous exercise, sport, or play, time spent reading away from the computer, time at activities such as arts, music, science or crafts, computer use is just one more activity.

Some students quite naturally vary their activities without even thinking about it. Perhaps your child will learn to self-regulate her computer use. Plopping in front of the computer only lasts until the wiggles hit, and then she straps on skates or builds LEGO towers or takes the dog for a romp.

Some students, though, need parental guidance, anywhere from a gentle nudge to strict limits on hours spent at the computer. Only when student activity is not balanced — as in the case of very long hours at the keyboard every day for days on end — do you need to insist on a change of pace or priorities.

## Myths About Computer Use

As with every tool or technology, there are disadvantages and risks with computer use. Parents must balance their own enthusiasm with their good common sense when using computer technology to educate children. Here is my curmudgeonly voice for caution. While there are far greater dangers than the ones I discuss, such as predatory sociopaths who may frequent children's Internet chat rooms, I want to focus on some of the subtler myths that may impact your child's learning experience.

### Myth #1: Earlier is Better

A mad race is afoot to get very young children started using computers. Parents of children as young as one year old are regularly targeted by sales pitches, and many parents scramble to obtain these products. Promoters use clever marketing drives to empty parents' wallets, playing on parental anxiety that their children will forever be behind their peers.

Heads up, parents. Clever salesmanship is not science. Excessive computer use flies in the face of what we know about how young children learn. Interactivity claims ring hollow when compared to the richness of interactive learning through actual life experiences. No matter how gimmicky and appealing the software or Internet site may be, learning at the computer pales when compared to the sensory vividness of building with blocks, making bread with Dad, or digging in the garden with Mom.

We would scream in outrage if untested medications were being injected into infants to build a better baby. Yet computer use by young children is largely unevaluated. The impact will not be known for many years. Training put into children's minds at an early age may not have an apparent immediate danger, but who can guess what the impact might be over a child's lifetime?

More important, though, is the fact that computer use wastes precious hours of childhood. Can we really afford to park young children in front of a computer screen for hours during the years they need to be running, jumping, smelling flowers, and singing in the bathtub? Do today's children need to be proficient on today's computers, computers that will certainly be obsolete tomorrow?

## Myth #2: Workbooks on Computers Are Better

Workbook-based curricula have become widely available on the Internet or CD-ROM at an affordable price. Promoters of online or software curriculum products suggest that all you need is a computer and their software to get an excellent education. Maybe, or maybe not. Many parents have found, after an expensive curriculum purchase, that they have succumbed to the spell of clever sales pitches. Why? It was the wrong choice for their child.

Do the marketers boast of interactive software? Don't believe for one minute that a workbook with clickable answers is more interactive than fill-in-the-blank answers in paper workbooks! A traditional workbook curriculum has essentially the same advantages and disadvantages, whether on the computer or in paper format.

For children who learn easily from a traditional workbook-type curriculum, the computer program does offer a nifty choice between paper and electronic formatting, and, of course, children will enjoy having a choice. For the majority of children, computer-based workbooks are best used as occasional reinforcement rather than as primary instructional tools.

But for some children, the pre-chewed and spewed content of many workbooks, whether paper or computerized, is mind-numbing. Instead of providing an efficient learning opportunity, the carefully sieved content sticks in the throat, gagging interest and dulling the desire to learn. At least with a paper workbook, a kid can take it under the table, in the car, or up a tree.

Curriculum developers should bear in mind that children are adept at learning. The best Internet sites and software programs allow many options for children to create their own learning experiences, taking students far beyond the basic workbook.

## Myth #3: The Computer is Where Learning Happens

Don't get me wrong. I know that the computer is a powerful tool for learning. Just remember that there are collateral lessons as well. "How we learn" lessons are often more powerful than "what we learn" lessons. What a student learns while working at the computer may not be all that he takes away from the experience.

Think about this: What is the underlying message for children if parents expect them to get all their learning from the computer? It may be a lesson in distaste for both learning and computer use. I've met students who learned to hate both learning and computers, right there at the keyboard, using the loveliest software you can imagine. Those stories put my teeth right on edge. That is a lesson to skip!

If parents hold that concept — that "how we learn" is as important as "what we learn" — in mind, it is much easier to keep the computer's attractiveness in perspective.

## Myth #4: The Computer Saves Time

No matter how much time it saves, the computer, as most of us use it, is also a monumental consumer of time. My computer saves time with tasks such as bookkeeping and word processing, but that is not the only way I choose to use it. Instead of lolling in my hammock, relishing the time my computer saves me, I spend even more time answering and writing e-mail and pursuing other computer-based interests. Will student days grow longer and longer so they can sit at a computer and "save time" as we adults do?

## Finally

Keep in mind that the computers of tomorrow will scarcely resemble the computers of today. As I write, computers are obsolete almost as soon as they reach the market! There is plenty of time for a student to develop computer literacy.

To maintain perspective in the face of computer hype, though, recall that most of the adult population in this country is computer literate, and none of us had the benefit of using computers during early childhood! Has that stopped us (including our parents and grandparents) from entering the computer age? Of course not. Don't be swayed into believing your child will be left behind if you don't have the latest computer and software for your tot or your teen. Instead, make sure you offer a well-rounded education, including a reasoned approach to computer use.

### Selected Resources

*BESS*
206/971.1400    www.n2h2.com/products/g2100/index.php
An Internet service provider that blocks unwanted material for children.

*Children's Software & New Media Revue*
44 Main Street, Flemington, NJ 08822    800/993.9499
908/284.0404    fax: 908/284.0405    childrenssoftware.com/
Bi-monthly magazine publishes reviews of materials for ages 0-16.

*Choosing Children's Software Magazine*
903 Falls Bridge Lane, Great Falls, VA 22066    703/444.9005
jinny@choosingchildrenssoftware.com    www.choosingchildrenssoftware.com
Annual magazine that reviews children's software. All ages. You can also subscribe to weekly software reviews at www.computingwithkids.com .

*The Connected Family: Bridging the Digital Generation Gap*
By Seymour Papert. 1996, Longstreet Press, Inc. C/o MaMaMedia, 110 Greene St., Ste. 805, New York, NY 10011
www.ConnectedFamily.com/main.html
Begin learning about how computers work. His earlier books, *Mindstorms*, and *The Children's Machine*, especially for help with learning programing.

*Dnet*
877/601.DNET    www.dnet.net
Family oriented Internet service.

*Educational Software Institute Catalog*
   4213 South 94th Street, Omaha, NE 68127
   800/955.5570    fax: 402/592.2017    www.edsoft.com
   Educational software(including some older computer models) for many
   subjects.

*Failure to Connect:*
   How Computers Affect Our Children's Minds -- for Better and Worse
   By Jane M. Healy, Ph.D. Simon and Schuster, 1998.
   Argument for limiting the use of computers before age seven. Healy offers a
   rare and sensible voice saying, "All in good time."

*Homeschool Your Child for Free*
   By LauraMaery Gold and Joan M. Zielinski © 2000.
   Prima Publishing, 3000 Lava Ridge court, Roseville, CA 95661
   800/632.8676        www.primalifestyles.com
   Internet-based curriculum via your computer. The book lists 1200 Internet
   sites, summarized and rated.

*Nordic Software*
   PO Box 83499, Lincoln, NE 83499
   402/475.5300    800/306.6502    fax: 402/475.5310
   www.nordicsoftware.com Entertaining educational software products,
   integrating game elements and animation into learning activities.

*Personal Coach Software*
   1650 Oakwood Drive, E119, Narberth, PA 19073    800/996.2791
   sales@auntellen.com    www.auntellen.com
   A straightforward and multi-sensory approach to Windows-based computer
   learning for beginners, for children and adults alike.

## chapter forty-five

# CONSIDERING TEXTBOOKS?

*tips for choosing a textbook[1] or none at all*

Times have changed; ordinary people have real access to huge sources of information. The halls of knowledge have burst open and all people can use libraries, bookstores, retail and mail-order sources, as well as other community resources. Ordinary people have more real money with which to purchase books than ever before in all history. All this, and the Internet too! The Internet, together with personal computers, brings vast stores of information closer to all of us by at least a quantum leap, or two or three. With all this richness, why would you consider using an old-fashioned textbook? We'll get to those reasons in a bit, but first, let's consider the fact that many families don't use textbooks at all.

## Textbooks Are Not Necessary

You may well wonder what reasons parents cite for looking beyond these traditional school materials. One common reason is that textbooks are designed for same-age group or classroom use, making textbooks somewhat difficult to incorporate into home life, where children of different ages learn together. Some parents find that the tedium of a textbook leads their student to dislike a subject

---

[1]   The guidelines outlined here can help you evaluate all types of packaged curriculum, workbooks, and computer- or Internet-based curriculum. See the Appendix for listings of catalogs, schools, programs, and other textbook resources.

he previously enjoyed. Textbooks are often survey courses, jammed with facts, making it unlikely that the gripping story of, say, the Revolutionary War, can be rendered within the covers of one book that tries to cover all of United States history.

Textbook series can be repetitious and, if used for several years in a row, students can become exceedingly bored. Another problem with a series of textbooks is the challenge of maintaining a consistent quality of instruction at each level. A few texts are so full of errors they are laughable. Topics that are poorly taught in the first book of a series are generally poorly taught year after year. How I've tried to forget those ghastly "new math" books, books that went on, and on, and on, and …

Textbooks are rarely the best choice for children who are not visual learners. Even though some textbook authors try to accommodate a variety of learning styles, textbooks are still, after all, predominantly text that must be read.

Some parents are opposed to national trends in education that are reflected in "sanitized" textbooks. History is sometimes re-written and literature is censored. With national testing falling in place, you may be certain that textbooks are being rewritten as I write, rewritten to teach "to the test." Those rewrites may be good for improving test scores. But they will not be the rich information sources that excite children about learning, the resources that homeschooling families want. You can be certain that topics deemed less important will be ditched in favor of the to-be-tested topics.

## Using Textbooks

With all the reasons NOT to use textbooks, and all the wonderful non-textbook resources available, you may be surprised that textbooks are ever used at all by successful homeschooling families. You would be right, though, if you guessed that those who do use textbooks do so thoughtfully, often sparingly. The textbook or program rarely dominates the family's lifestyle. Instead, it is used as just another tool for learning. When parents take a reasoned approach, they may find there are a number of very good reasons for using textbooks. For example:

**The student surpasses the parent.** Suppose you started studying French two years ago as a family, and now that your son is planning a trip to Europe with his singing group. Suddenly he is eager to learn faster than the rest of the family, so what do you do? You might look for a textbook, for one thing. When your daughter is trying to figure out differential equations and you are still playing *21* and trying to make sense of linear equations, you might start looking for a textbook. A textbook may be combined with a tutor, a mentor, an online course, a study group, or a classroom experience.

**Students learn independence by working on their own.** Eventually the work you do to help your children become independent makes kids want to be, well, independent.

For some families, life circumstances — perhaps a family illness, or a need for parents to spend more hours at work — require that students become more independent. If the children are eight or ten or so, a textbook in one or more subjects might be a good step toward independence. Some independent students may find a complete curriculum to be a meaningful part of the year's work.

Textbooks can offer certain older children, and teens with special needs, extra practice, repetition, and greater independence, as students learn to work on their own.

**A textbook is a neutral authority when parent and children clash.** I've seen this arise with math. Suppose Dad hates math because of all the repetitiveness he remembers as a student. Maybe Mom feels stupid in math because of the humiliation she felt when, as a child, she didn't know her multiplication tables. Math Time may not be the happiest time for this family, so what might they try?

A book or program can offer a neutral learning zone for parents and children to enjoy math explorations together. Learning together is more fun when the math material provides the authority.

**Sometimes kids don't learn the way parents explain.** To work around that frustration, a well-written text "brings another voice" to the discussion, and places another explanation on the table.

**A good textbook is a useful and systematic reference book.** Textbooks in nearly every subject area can be used as a reference. A grammar book can be a useful editing tool for a student, much the same way that a mature writer might use Strunk & White's *Elements of Style* or *The Chicago Manual of Style*. A systematic approach to learning a second language can help explain the nuances of verb tenses and other grammatical challenges. It can also provide a glossary of common words and pronunciation aids. A history text may include a time line, an outline for further study, and lists of suggested readings. A literature anthology could introduce a student to writing styles and authors that he may not meet elsewhere. Science and math texts can provide an overview of specific topics, and explain methods and key terminology. Quality art or music history texts can enrich a student's applied arts studies while connecting some of the dots of history. Some math texts have dry and repetitive lessons, but the extension activities are stimulating and worth doing.

**A learning club may use a textbook as a basis for their work.** A group of teens may want the experience of working together with structured material. A writing study-group leader may use a text as a springboard for activity or discussion, or to gently instruct the group on elements of usage without pointing out mistakes directly.

**A textbook or course of study can prepare a student to enter the classroom.** If your student will leave homeschooling to enter a classroom in a public, private, or higher education setting, time spent studying with a textbook can provide the student assurance that he is able and ready. Ask for suggestions at the school he will attend.

## Tips for Selecting Textbooks

If your child is enthralled with a subject and wants to delve deeper, he can learn from the best textbook, the worst textbook, or no textbook at all. Even so, if you decide to get a textbook for this student or for any other reason, why not try to get the best textbook you can find for the wad of bills the book will cost you?

**Seek materials that are educationally balanced.** Does the text provide diverse activities that stimulate: the senses, clear thinking, the student's natural interest, and further study? Does the text balance a systematic approach with engaging ideas and activities? Does the author include drill and memory activities, either as a supplement or to balance an exploratory approach? Are plenty examples given?

Is a broad range of activities suggested, such as ones that involve physical activities, art projects, family life, social interaction? Are the activities actually doable with common household items?

**Will the text satisfy your student's learning styles?** Open the book to a random lesson and read the lesson all the way through. Do the same thing with several other lessons from different parts of the book. Are the senses engaged? Are the materials and activities appropriate for your child's developmental stage? Think about how your child might respond, remembering that what seems distasteful, dull, uninteresting to you, may actually be interesting to your child.

Does the book rely on classroom structures and group activities? It may work well for a classroom teacher, or if you are working with a group, but can you use the text effectively with just one student?

**Choose textbooks that include useful reference tools.** When a textbook is to be used as a reference, more is better. A good text can be used as a road map for study, and suggested reading lists could be used as a syllabus. Look for glossaries and other word lists, drawings and illustrations, charts, maps, tables, formulae, time lines, an extensive index, suggested reading lists, rules (in math and grammar, for example) with examples, enrichment activities, review questions, practice sets, answer keys, and the like. A good reference text won't send you off to other sources for information.

**Examine the book for appropriate vocabulary and writing style.** It drove me wild one year. With a classroom of fourth grade students, I was stuck with a math book in which the directions and explanations were written a couple of levels above the reading level of most students. How can a student become an independent learner if he cannot read the directions?

Textbook vocabulary should be accessible to your student's reading and comprehension ability. And here is another tricky part: just because your child reads at fourth grade level does not mean that his math skills are at fourth grade level. What if his math skills are at second grade level? And what do you do if your math whiz seven-year-old hasn't figured out reading yet? Usually, it is best to avoid textbooks until the skill levels merge somewhat.

Sentences should be simple, clear, and age appropriate. The author should write in an appealing style, introducing concepts in ways that make sense to the student and that build on prior knowledge.

Be wary of books that rely too much on gimmicks or popular culture to keep students' interest. These ideas might fascinate some children, but they may also tire of it quickly. It is better to capture interest with classical elements of children's culture — family, community, bikes, dolls, games, lemonade stands, classic children's literature, and other timeless ideas. You might consider using old or even antique textbooks. I have an English grammar book on my desk from 1941. It is clear, concise, and easy to use.

**Select books with a simple, pleasing layout.** Layout design preferences are highly personal. Make sure the style will work for you and your student, no matter how highly your neighbor praises the material. Open the book. Can you easily figure out how the lesson is laid out? Generally, simpler is better. Avoid books with a complex page design. Some layouts are intended to be clever, but instead they confuse the student.

**Take your student along to preview textbooks.** You can avoid making expensive errors that way. Your student will also have greater commitment to using books she helps select.

If possible, have your child do a couple of sample lessons in the book. Many textbook publishers will provide sample lessons. Perhaps you can borrow a copy of the book from a friend, or from your public library, for a few days.

**Can your student use the text independently?** If you want your student to learn independently, he'll need a textbook that is designed for independent use. Look for texts that are carefully written. The format should be generally the same for each lesson. The instructions should be clearly written and amply illustrated. Typical questions for each lesson should be explained with plenty of examples.

If a book is to be useful as an independent study text, the student should be able to work independently within a couple of weeks.

**When all else is equal, save money and buy used.** The idea that textbooks must be new is pure nonsense. So what if the books are ten years old, if they are well-written books that aren't badly damaged or marked up? Some of the best textbooks I ever used were dog-eared and worn, ancient texts that wise teachers had saved from the incinerator. See if your public library stocks textbooks. If so, you can check out and renew textbooks to cover key topics.

Except for seriously dated science or health books, up-to-date textbooks probably make little difference in a student's learning prior to the high school or college level. I can't imagine that a sixth grade book is going to have new and special information in it that is so precious it cannot be found elsewhere, or that an older text will ruin your student's future SAT scores. Use your own judgment.

## Finally

If you choose a textbook or a program that you later discover just plain doesn't work with your child or student, do what other successful homeschooling families do. Get rid of it. Dump it. Admit your mistake and abandon the material. Save it for a younger child with a different learning style, or set it aside to sell it to another family. Your child will thank you forever.

## A FINAL NOTE FROM ANN

Whew! My walk on "the wild side" of education turned into something of a hike, didn't it? I hope you paced yourself and took plenty of breaks!

In closing, I want to share one last thought. Recently a mom asked me what harm could come if she just *tried* homeschooling for a year with her school-anxious and very nervous child and then failed. I said, in effect: "If you do absolutely nothing but enjoy a delightful year of learning with your child — playing, talking, developing friendships, doing projects, asking questions, reading, and exploring the world together, but doing no structured academics at all — what is the worst that could happen? Does the potential benefit outweigh the potential risk?" To my mind, I told her, the risk pales compared to the value of a year of healing.

Later, though, I realized I had forgotten to tell the mom the most important thing I know about homeschooling, so I'll tell her here. I forgot to tell her that homeschooling — even for a short while, even when you have doubts, and even if it seems hard — embodies the most precious and heartfelt gift you can give your child, the gift of your time.

## ABOUT THE AUTHOR

My homeschooling odyssey began shortly after my children were born. As I watched my joyfully learning children discover their world, I began to question, and finally to discard, many notions I had held about learning.

Distrust in certain traditional educational ideas had gnawed at the back of my mind earlier when I taught in public and private schools. Now I discovered why: those ideas interfered with the true and natural process of learning that I daily observed with my children and with their friends. I made a one hundred eighty-degree shift in my thinking about how children learn.

I delved into the scarce homeschooling information that was available, beginning with early issues of John Holt's *Growing Without Schooling* newsletter. Relieved to find that I was not alone in my transition from teacher-centered schooling to interest-initiated learning, I began to "unschool" myself. I immersed myself in this new way of thinking and eagerly learned from the experiences of that first wave of pioneer homeschooling families and from my children.

My children's learning followed no calendar or clock. Our lives were rich with the explorations and discoveries of two busy and happy little girls. They learned what they needed to know through experience, books, games, conversations, classes, extensive play and life itself. They had ready access to their mom, and were supported by a dad who believed in what we were doing and cheerfully provided the means.

Through homeschooling, my children and I gained a precious opportunity to learn and grow together that cannot be approached in other educational models. Alice and Erin continue to learn independently and enthusiastically as adults. I am still learning, too.

— ALF —

# APPENDIX I
# LEGAL COMPLIANCE & FINDING SUPPORT

Complying with homeschooling regulations and understanding your state's law are readily accomplished by connecting with a support group.

## Compliance — Learning Your Law

While homeschooling is legal in every state, the regulations for compliance vary widely. I highly recommend a local or state support group, a community of veteran homeschoolers in your state who know the legal ropes. These folks can help you avoid tripping up on details so you can get on with the fun and serious business of homeschooling.

Grassroots homeschooling groups are important in ways you may not have thought of. Think about this. Just as you know your own family's needs and capabilities better than anyone else can, no other group is as invested in successful homeschooling in your state as your homeschooling neighbors. Your homegrown experts can help find needed resources for your particular situation.

National organizations are wonderful resources for general information and can refer you to a statewide group, copies of the law, and other general information. National organizations, though, no matter how wonderful, can rarely be true experts on the intricacies of fifty unique laws — laws that vary widely — and fifty unique state homeschooling climates. You need a local connection to guide you through the fog.

You may also find a useful summary of your state law in one of the homeschooling books on the market. Be wary, though, for even the most recently published book may have some obsolete information. That is just a fact of publishing that cannot be avoided. As I write, homeschooling regulations face challenges in several states, and that seems to be the case most of the time. Some laws have changed with little notice. Families who felt safe in their right to homeschool as they wish suddenly found their feet to the fire overnight. Do your own research to make sure you have the most current law.

You may be surprised to learn that the *least helpful* place to turn for homeschooling information is your local school. But think about it — you wouldn't choose to see a psychiatrist for a broken arm, would you? School staff are up to their eyeballs in the complicated business of public schooling — it is unreasonable to expect them to have the latest homeschooling information. The chance of being inadvertently misinformed by overworked school staff is great, so give those hard-working folks a break. Skip the trip to the local school office. Instead, drop by your library or plop down in front of your computer.

The Internet, along with a good library, can be a homeschooling parent's best friend. Spend an hour with a web site such as *Home Education Magazine*'s page (www.home-ed-magazine.com), *National Home Education Network*'s website (www.nhen.org), *or A2Z Home's Cool* (www.gomilpitas.com/homeschooling/). At sites such as these, you can do a simple search for your state's home-schooling organizations or legal information. Alternatively, do your own digging, using your favorite search engine to scan the Internet with search words such as "homeschool," "your state," "home education network," and "legal information." You will generate a surplus of sites to sort through.

However you get there, visit some state support group sites, read the mission statements, and see if the site offers information about complying with the law. Contact a local support group and attend some meetings or functions. You can then explore with members how complying with the law works on a practical day-by-day basis.

The best guidelines for navigating state laws and understanding the details of compliance are the *Probing Questions* (below) from National Home Education Network's web site, used here with permission.

## Eight Probing Questions
## To Ask about Homeschool Regulation in Your State [1]

1. *What is the compulsory attendance statute?* Between what ages do children fall under the statute? Are there certain subjects required under the statute, and do those requirements apply to

---

[1] © 2002 National Home Education Network. ALL RIGHTS RESERVED. Permission to copy and distribute this FAQ is hereby granted provided it is copied in its entirety, used for informational and non-commercial purposes, and includes the copyright notice and this permission notice on all copies. Available at www.nhen.org

homeschools? How are homeschoolers treated in relation to the statute? [Depending on the state, homeschoolers may be treated as a private school or as some other category, neither public school nor private school.]

2. *Is there a separate statute dealing precisely with homeschooling?* If so, what exactly does the statute say? Is there general agreement about what exactly the statute means, or are there controversial interpretations of the statute? Have there been any court decisions about the statute?

3. *If there is no separate statute dealing with homeschooling, under what authority are homeschools regulated?* Are there any controversies about homeschooling generally or about specific regulations? Have there been any court decisions to clarify any of these issues?

4. *What role does the state Department of Education play in regulation of homeschooling?* [In some states, education is still mainly controlled at the local school district level, while in other states, the DOE policy applies to all districts in the state.]

5. *What role has the legislature played?* Has there been any recent activity relating to homeschooling? If so, what was it and what happened?

6. *What actually happens in real life in terms of what is necessary to satisfy the school district?* [Just because a law is on the books doesn't mean that it is uniformly enforced.]

7. *What kinds of trouble, if any, have homeschoolers in the state faced in the past few years?*

8. *What current controversies, if any, are going on in the state, either on explicit homeschool issues, oncoming-down-the-pike legislation, or on any topics that might impact homeschooling in the state?*"[end of quote]

If you are satisfied with your answers to those questions, you are well on the way to understanding the regulations in your state. The time you invest in learning how your law works will draw interest for you as you delve into your life as a homeschooling family. First, you will be confident and knowledgeable about your legal position. Second, whatever you learn from digging into the facts of your state law is a resource you can use in helping your students understand laws, government, and the legislative process. When Mom and Dad are learning, everybody is learning!

## Finding Support

Once you've found a statewide group you like, you usually have access to the most common kinds of support. The same dedicated groups who offer tips and suggestions for complying with the laws in your state, and who can direct you to a copy of the law to read for yourself, are the same groups that offer the practical information and support you need to launch your successful homeschooling experience. Most state groups can help you find local groups, e-mail lists, conferences, workshops, and newsletters of interest.

Nationally-distributed print or online magazines and e-mail groups provide an avenue to connectedness with the larger homeschooling community. Write, call, or search online at any of the organizations or magazines listed in these appendixes. Ideally suited for all families — especially those who live in isolated regions or who have unique concerns — magazines and e-mail groups are widely popular. You'll find a sampling of homeschooling magazines in "Bibliography/Parents' Bookshelf" (Appendix II).

Should you participate in a national homeschooling organization? I say yes. Connecting with others across state lines can be vitally important when homeschooling rights are challenged or when new rules and laws are proposed. Chances are good that homeschoolers in another state have gone through the same challenges that face your homeschool community. For example, testimony presented recently in a challenge to homeschooling rights in an eastern state included statements almost identical to those made by an Oregon superintendent a few years ago. Many veteran homeschoolers are willing to share their experiences so that others can take advantage of all they learned.

What about homeschooling events such as conferences, workshops, camp-outs, and curriculum fairs? Many folks love to attend these. Events are an exciting way to connect with homeschooling leaders, to get the latest information, to find materials and resources, and to meet new people. You may want to seek out conferences that include children's events, or that are at least child-friendly, so you can attend as a family. Conferences are sponsored by many statewide organizations, some national organizations, and an occasional local organization. You'll find that some magazines, correspondence schools, and curriculum suppliers sponsor homeschooling conferences as well. Local groups are more likely to sponsor workshops, swap meets, retreats, "not-back-to-school" events, camp-outs and other low-key events. Check them all out.

Although I generally recommend single issue statewide groups, some families are more comfortable with a group that incorporates other issues, such as a preferred religious perspective, ethnicity, or educational approach. In some states — unfortunately, not all of them — statewide groups of every stripe work cordially and cooperatively for the benefit of all homeschooling families. Some families join several groups to get differing viewpoints.

Joining a group or two cannot be over-emphasized — take it from me and my experience with burnout. By nature I am not much of a "joiner," but I learned the hard way how important these groups are in avoiding burnout. When I recovered from burnout and continued to homeschool, there were still no compatible groups in my state, so I helped create one. If I can do it, so can you.

## SINGLE-ISSUE HOMESCHOOLING ORGANIZATIONS
*of, by, and for homeschoolers, with no other agenda*

### American Homeschool Association
PO Box 3142, Palmer, AK 99645
800/236.3278   www.americanhomeschoolassociation.org
aha@americanhomeschoolassociation.org
AHA is a service organization created to network homeschoolers on a national level. Online news and discussion list provides news, information, and resources for homeschoolers, media contacts, and education officials.

### National Home Education Network (NHEN)
PO Box 7844, Long Beach, CA 90807   fax: 413/581.1463
www.nhen.org   info@nhen.org
Supports the freedom of all individual families to choose home education and to direct such education. Provides information, fosters networking and promotes homeschooling public relations on a national level. NHEN has a huge resource in its website that includes, in part, state and national networking groups and resources, homeschooling contacts, and legal information by state.

### Statewide Homeschooling Groups

Many states, but not all of them, boast one or more single-issue (often called inclusive) homeschooling groups. A simple Internet search is an easy way to discover if your state has such an organization. You might visit HEM's site (www.home-ed-magazine.com), A2Z Home's Cool Homeschooling Web Site, (www.gomilpitas.com/homeschooling/), or NHEN's site (www.nhen.org) and search for your state's homeschooling organizations. Visit the sites, read the mission statements and FAQ's, and explore the groups for yourself.

### Coalition of Independent Homeschoolers

PO Box 246, Wauna, WA 98395
http://www.homeschoolcoalition.org    homeschoolcoalition@yahoo.com
A non-hierarchical, consensus-based, grassroots network of independent homeschoolers, present, past, and future, dedicated to:  (1) Informing and connecting individuals and organizations interested in working to preserve the rights of parents to homeschool, and the rights of their children to learn, free of invasive and burdensome oversight and regulation;  (2) Preserving a true and accurate historical record of the homeschooling movement from its earliest inceptions;  (3) Reclaiming homeschooling as the unique province of children and their parents.

## SELECTED MULTI-ISSUE NATIONAL ORGANIZATIONS
*advocates of homeschooling that may suit your needs perfectly*

### Alliance for Parental Involvement in Education, Inc. (ALLPIE)

PO Box 59, East Chatham, NY 12060
518/392.6900 allpie@taconic.net www.croton.com/allpie
Provides support for parents with respect to their children's education. Newsletter, referral service, workshops, book catalog, conferences. Publishes a newsletter, *Options in Learning*.

### Alternative Education Resource Organization (AERO)

Jerry Mintz, 417 Roslyn Road, Roslyn Heights, NY 11577
516/621.2195    800/769.4171 fax: 516/625.3257
info@educationrevolution.org www.educationrevolution.org
A non-profit organization founded in 1989 to advance "learner centered" approaches to education. A worldwide hub for educational alternatives. Publishes *Education Revolution*.

### The Foundation for Educational Renewal

Box 328, Brandon, VT 05733-0328 800/639.4122
www.great-ideas.org     info@great-ideas.org
Publishes *Paths of Learning: options for families and communities*, a quarterly journal for families and communities, exploring diverse ways of educating young people, including homeschooling.

## *Homeschool Legal Defense Association (HSLDA)*

PO Box 3000, Purcellville, VA 20134   540/338.5600   fax: 540/338.2733
www.hslda.org   info@hslda.org
A Christian, non-profit, membership organization of families who home
school their children nationwide. Membership is open to all; leadership is
exclusively Christian. This organization lobbies actively for homeschooling
issues throughout the country. Referrals are made only to selected Christian
affiliates in each state.

## *HUUmans on the Web*

www.uuhomeschool.org
For Unitarian Universalist Homeschoolers and Kindred Spirits; a voice for
alternatives to traditional public schools including homeschooling.

## *Jewish Home Educator's Network*

2122 Houser, Holly, MI 48442
jhen@snj.com
Connect with Jewish homeschooling families.

## *Muslim Home School Network and Resource*

PO Box 803, Attleboro, MA 02703
MHSNR@aol.com   www.muslimhomeschool.com
Muslim resources and support. Conference.

## *National Association of Catholic Home Educators (NACHE)*

6-102 Saints Hill Ln., Broad Run, VA 20137
540/349.4314   www.nache.org   Magazine Editor, 1payne@cts.com
Quarterly newsletter, *The Catholic Home Educator*, support, and resources.
Regional conferences.

## *National Black Home Educators Resource Association*

6943 Stoneview Ave., Baker, LA 70714      225/778.0169
fax: 225/774.4114   nbhera@internet8.net   www.nbhera.org/
Networking with national/local organizations and pairing new home school
families with veteran families; encouragement, support and fellowship.

## *National Coalition of Alternative Community Schools*

1266 Rosewood Unit 1, Ann Arbor, MI 48104   734/668.9171
888/771.9171   www.ncacs.org ncacs1@earthlink.net
International support for diverse learning environments, including
homeschooling. Mission is to unite and organize a grassroots movement of
learners and learning communities dedicated to control by participants.

## *The Native American Home School Association*

PO Box 979, Fries, VA 24330   expage.com/page/nahomeschool  and
expage.com/page/nahomeschool2   The Ani-Stohini/Unami Nation officially
supports and endorses homeschooling as a way to preserve and protect its
cultural heritage.

# APPENDIX II
# BIBLIOGRAPHY/PARENTS' BOOKSHELF
*homeschooling books and journals*

Reading one book cannot sustain a homeschooling family forever. Reading from the growing body of work on homeschooling will go far to build your homeschooling confidence and know-how. The body of homeschooling literature written for homeschooling parents is exploding. How will you choose?

The lists that follow are bibliographies of resources that I have referred to myself over many years. Some I have read word by word, lingering over ideas that inspire me, while others I have skimmed for tips of general usefulness. Some of the most popular homeschooling magazines are reviewed below. It is easy to stay current with homeschooling practice and trends when you subscribe to one or two favorite periodicals.

There are three sections: magazines and journals, general homeschooling books, and books that explore some of the rationales for the growing popularity of homeschooling.

## SELECTED PERIODICALS
*specializing in various aspects of homeschooling life*

### A2Z Home's Cool Homeschooling Web Site
By Ann Zeise. www.gomilpitas.com/homeschooling/
Not a magazine, it is true, but a rich, useful, easily navigated, and constantly updated web site that puts key homeschooling information at your fingertips.

### At Our Own Pace
Jean Kulczyk, editor. Christie Berry, publisher.
VAST Network, PO Box 8391, Huntsville, AL 35808
A newsletter, print or e-mail, for homeschooling families with special needs, edited and published by homeschooling moms with lots of personal experience with learning challenges. Resources are included.

### The Eclectic Homeschool Online
Founded by Beverly Krueger
EHO, PO Box 50188, Sparks, NV 89435-0188   www.eho.org/
Moderate Christian world view online homeschool magazine. Many resources.

## Home Education Magazine (HEM)

PO Box 1083, Tonasket, WA 98855
800/236.3278    509/486.1351 fax: 509/486.2753
HEM-Info@home-ed-magazine.com    www.home-ed-magazine.com
Bi-monthly 68 page issues. Extensive website. Founded by Mark and Helen
Hegener in 1983. Its features spotlight both everyday homeschooling
concerns and the cutting edge of homeschooling issues. *HEM* leads the way
in keen analysis of educational thought. Some of the most thoughtful writing
about homeschooling can be found here.

## Homefires® The Journal of Homeschooling

Diane Flynn Keith, editor.  180 El Camino Real, Ste. 10, Millbrae, CA 94030
415/365.9425   North. CA:  888/4HOME-ED
Editor@homesfires.com    www.Homefires.com
This online journal features thoughtful insight and California flavor. Many field
trip ideas.

## Homeschooling Parent Magazine

Cyndi Simmons, publisher.
13258 Overlook Court, Conroe, TX 77302    936/756.2226
fax: 936/756.0228   www.homeschoolingparent.com
A tabloid-style newspaper available free through support groups.

## Homeschooling Today®

PO Box 1608, Ft. Collins, CO 80522
970/493.2716     fax: 954/964.7466
service@homeschooltoday.com   www.homeschooltoday.com
Bi-monthly, 68 pages.  Christian perspective.  Regular features include Unit
Studies, Living Literature, Preschool Activities, Science Corner, Ask Dr.
Beechick, and a pull-out art lesson.  An enjoyable magazine.

## Life Learning Magazine

Wendy Priesnitz, publisher.
The International Magazine of Self-Directed Learning, Box 112, Niagara
Falls, NY 14304 or Box 340, St. George, ON N0E 1N0 Canada
www.lifelearningmagazine.com    editor@lifelearningmagazine.com
Bi-monthly published by a Canadian homeschooling author and publisher.
Dedicated to providing inspiring and intelligent discussion about self-directed
learning (unschooling), democratic alternative schools, and more.

## The Link

Mary Leppert, publisher.
587 N. Ventu Park Road, Ste. F-911, Newbury Park, CA 91320
888/470.4513    805/492.1373    fax: 805/493.9216
www.homeschoolnewslink.com    the.link@verizon.net
A free homeschool newspaper chock full of articles, information, and
advertising of all varieties of homeschooling resources. Order one or a bundle
for your support group.

### The Moore Report International (MRI)

The Moore Foundation, Box 1, Camas, WA 98607
360/835.5500    800/891.5255
generalinfo@moorefoundaton.com    www.moorefoundation.com
The Moores, called the grandparents of the modern homeschooling
movement, created the Moore Homeschooling Formula — a balance of
study, work, and service that works for many.  Christian.

### Paths of Learning: Options for Families & Communities

Richard Prystowsky, Editor. PO Box 328, Brandon, VT 05733-0328
800/639.4122   www.great-ideas.com
A useful magazine for homeschooling families who want to extend
homeschooling approaches to community learning centers.

### The Teaching Home

Pat and Sue Welch, publishers. Box 20219, Portland, OR 97294
503/253.9633   www.teachinghome.com
A forthrightly Christian magazine supporting a school-at-home approach.

## SELECTED HOMESCHOOLING BOOKS
*how to do it, lifestyle stories, resources, and more.*

### And the Skylark Sings With Me:
### Adventures in Homeschooling and Community-Based Education

By David Albert. 1999.  New Society Publishers, PO Box 189, Gabriola
Island, BC V0R 1X0 Canada www.newsociety.com    800/567.6772 in
cooperation with Holt Associates    www.holtgws.com   617/864.3100
Beautifully written, literary narrative of a family's learning venture.

### The Art of Education: Reclaiming Your Family, Community, and Self

By Linda Dobson, Holt Associates/1995.
A lively and complex discussion of both the how-to's and the power of
homeschooling. For a quick pick-me-up, open to any page!

### Awakening Your Child's Natural Genius:

Enhancing Curiosity, Creativity, and Learning Ability
By Thomas Armstrong.  Tarcher Putnam Publishing, 1991.  Ages 3-12.
Highly recommended. Includes both philosophy and suggested activities.

### The Beginner's Guide to Homeschooling:

How learning as a family is different from learning in school
By Patrick Farenga, Holt Associates.
A useful and thoughtful guide to getting started with homeschooling. Key
resources are listed. A unique resource.

## A Charlotte Mason Companion:
Personal Reflections on the Gentle Art of Learning
By Karen Andreola. Charlotte Masson Research & Supply Co.,
PO Box 758, Union, ME 04862    www.charlottemason.com
Andreola has led the way in rediscovering this approach to learning.

## Child's Work: Taking Children's Choices Seriously
By Nancy Wallace, Holt Associates, 1990.
One family's experiences discovering their unique homeschooling style, how the children grew and, in the course of pursuing their interests, developed talents in music and writing. Validates child led learning.

## Christian Home Educator's Curriculum Manual
By Cathy Duffy.
Grove Publishing, 16172 Huxley Circle, Westminster, CA 92683
714/841.1220   caduffy@aol.com
Help in choosing materials to fit the child's learning style for all levels, written by a seasoned homeschooling parent.

## The Complete Home Learning Source Book
The Essential Resource Guide for Homeschoolers, Parents, and Educators.
By Rebecca Rupp, 1998. Three Rivers Press.
Covers many subjects. This is a huge resource — 700+ pages. It is hard to imagine that any need has been overlooked. A homeschooling parent, Rupp includes anecdotes of her own family's homeschooling experiences.

## Christian Unschooling
By Teri J. Brown with Elissa M. Wahl. 2001 Champion Press, Ltd.,
13023 NE Hwy 99, Bldg. 7, Ste. 207, Vancouver, WA 98686
Encouragement, personal essays, and tips for faith-based unschoolers.

## The First Year of Homeschooling Your Child:
Your Complete Guide to Getting off to the Right Start
By Linda Dobson, 2001.
Prima Publishing, 3000 Lava Ridge court, Roseville, CA 95661.
800/632.8676       www.primalifestyles.com
A guide for the weak-kneed and the not-so-weak-kneed beginning homeschooling family that will get you safely through that first year. Dobson is a most interesting and encouraging homeschooling writer. Try *The Art of Education* and *Homeschooling Success Stories.*

## Freedom Challenge: African American homeschoolers
Editor, Grace Llewellyn, 1996.
Lowry House, Box 1014, Eugene, OR 97440
541/686.2315  www.LowryHousePublishers.com
Resource book for African-Americans considering homeschooling. Resources, personal accounts, more.

## *Growing Without Schooling: A Record of a Grassroots Movement*

Founded in 1977 by John Holt. Available from FUN Books, Dept. W, 1688 Belhaven Woods Court, Pasadena, MD 21122-3727
Fax/Voice: 410/360.7330  410/360.7330 orders:  888/FUN-7020
FUN@FUN-Books.com     www.FUN-Books.com/contact.htm
The original text of the first twelve issues (August 1977-December 1979) of the classic — and no longer published — *Growing Without Schooling Magazine* (GWS). Reformatted and indexed for easy reading and reference. First-hand accounts from early homeschooling pioneers and Holt's ruminations on homeschooling.

## *Home Learning Year by Year*

How to Design a Homeschool Curriculum from Preschool through High School, By Rebecca Rupp. 2000.
A useful book, especially for those who are just getting started with homeschooling. Grade by grade overview of curriculum with suggestions.

## *The Homeschool Reader*

Collected Articles from Home Education Magazine, 1984-1994
Edited by Mark and Helen Hegener, 1997.
Some of the truest writing about homeschooling includes the musings of the first folks on the scene. The best of the best.

## *Homeschooling Book of Answers*

Edited by Linda Dobson, revised 2002
Prima Publishing, 3000 Lava Ridge court, Roseville, CA 95661
800/632.8676    www.primalifestyles.com
Common questions about homeschooling are answered by seasoned homeschooling veterans — a classic collection of wisdom. Dobson edits a series of homeschooling books, including her own *Homeschooling the Early Years: Your Complete Guide to Successfully Homeschooling the 3- to 8-Year-Old Child*. Watch for Linda's forthcoming books, including the *Homeschooling Book of Ideas*.

## *Homeschooling for Excellence*

By David and Micki Colfax. Warner Books, 1988.
Experience of a northern California family well known for their homeschooled children who have attended Harvard. Also wrote *Hard Times In Paradise*, Published by Mountain House Press, PO Box 353, Philo, CA 94566. The second book is the story of the challenges they experienced on the forty-seven acre classroom.

## *Homeschooling Our Children, Unschooling Ourselves*

By Alison McKee
Bittersweet House, PO box 5211, Madison, WI 53705
The story of one family's journey into the unknowns of homeschooling. Offers reassurance to parents that nurturing the child's natural desire to learn can lead to a life of joyful learning.

### Homeschooling: Patchwork of Days
By Nancy Lande. 1996. Windy Creek Press,
4738 Meadow Lane, Bozeman, MT 59715    www.windycreek.com
Share a day with thirty homeschooling families.

### Homeschooling the Middle Years:
Your Complete Guide to Successfully Homeschooling the 8- to 12-Year-Old
Child, By Shari Henry, 1999.
Prima Publishing, 3000 Lava Ridge court, Roseville, CA 95661
800/632.8676    www.primalifestyles.com
Shari aptly approaches homeschooling during the elementary years as a
journey.  Shari is an ace tour guide, and makes it clear that learning through
life experiences is the richest journey of all.

### I Learn Better By Teaching Myself / Still Teaching Ourselves
By Agnes Leistico, Holt Associates, 1997.
Relates the story of a parent who first struggled, and then made the transition
from a strong belief in traditional schooling to strongly advocating for interest-
initiated learning.

### The Successful Homeschool Family Handbook
By Raymond and Dorothy Moore,
The Moore Foundation, PO Box 1, Camas WA 98607
Guidance for creating a structured homeschool setting. The Moores, the
"grandparents of homeschooling," offer a helpful formula to balance family
life and structured academics. Other Moore titles: *Better Late Than Early,*
*Home Spun Schools, School Can Wait, Home Style Learning* .

### Home School Source Book, 3rd Ed., Revised.
By Jean and Donn Reed, 1999, Brook Farm Books, PO Box 246,
Bridgewater, ME 04735   or Box 101, Glassville, NB, E7L 4T4 Canada
877/375.4680    jean@brookfarmbooks.com
How to describe this one-of-a-kind book?  It is so much more than a
resource book or catalog — it is an educational odyssey, a how-to, and a
philosophy, all rolled into one.  A liberal sprinkling of comments and essays
cover a tremendous scope of "life subjects."  When you are putting together
your curriculum, this book will ease your journey and open your eyes.

### The Unschooling Handbook:
How to Use the Whole World As Your Child's Classroom
By Mary Griffith, 1998.
 Prima Publishing, 3000 Lava Ridge court, Roseville, CA 95661.
800/632.8676    www.primalifestyles.com
A reader-friendly and informative overview of the unschooling approach.
Also by Griffith, *The Homeschooling Handbook*.

## *Learning At Home : A Mother's Guide To Homeschooling*
By Marty Layne 1998.  Sea Change Publications,
1850 San Lorenzo Ave., Victoria, BC V8N 2E9 Canada
250/477-0713    seachangepublications@home.com
Written in "mother time," this book is an encouraging book that is perfect to
read in "mother time."  Marty narrates the path of her family's homeschool,
including many games and activity ideas her family used.

## *Teach Your Own*
By John Holt, Holt/GWS, 1997, abridged edition
An essential homeschooling classic, by the first unschooling visionary. Many
timeless ideas about how to create a successful learning lifestyle.

## *The Teenage Liberation Handbook:*
how to get out of school and get a real life and education
By Grace Llewellyn, expanded and revised, 1998.
Lowry House, Box 1014, Eugene, OR 97440
541/686.2315  www.LowryHousePublishers.com
Explores ways that teens can take charge of their own learning outside of
school, from a teen's perspective. Insightful and useful.

## *Things We Wish We'd Known*
Compiled and edited by Bill & Diana Waring, 1999. Emerald Books, PO
Box 635, Lynnwood, WA 98046.
Fifty devoutly Christian homeschooling parents reflect on ways to develop a
homeschool style that meets family needs.

## *What Your [First - Sixth] Grader Needs to Know*
Edited by E. D. Hirsch
Core Knowledge Foundation,
801 East High St., Charlottesville, VA 22902
434/977.7550 or 800/238.3233    www.coreknowledge.org/
Use as basic curriculum guide as long as ideas are adequately supplemented.
Great for students who want to know if they are up with their peers.

## *You Are Your Child's First Teacher*
By Rahima Baldwin, 1989.
Celestial Arts, PO Box 7327, Berkeley, CA 94707
Recommended for parents who are drawn to the Waldorf philosophy and
want to homeschool through the early years.

## *You Can Teach Your Child Successfully*
By Ruth Beechick, Education Services,
8825 Blue Mountain Drive, Golden, CO 80403
Details on what to teach in grades four through eight. Covers basic subjects
plus Bible. Also by Beechick, *The Three R's*. Christian.

## HOMESCHOOLING RATIONALE
*exploring some of the reasons people choose homeschooling*

### 48 reasons not to go to school
By Heidi Priesnitz
The Alternate Press, PP 1, St. George, Ontario, ONE 1N0 Canada
800/215.9574   www.life.ca/books
A small artful book that touches on the heart of the homeschooling
experience from a student's perspective.

### The Book of Learning and Forgetting
By Frank Smith. Teachers College Press: 1998.
A close look at the ways schooling can interfere with the learning process.

### Challenging Assumptions in Education:
From Institutionalized Education to a Learning Society
By Wendy Priesnitz, The Alternate Press
PP 1, St. George, Ontario, ONE 1N0 Canada  www.life.ca
As the title suggests, this book exposes some of the more insidious effects that
conventional schooling has on individuals and on society as a whole.

### Deschooling Our Lives
Edited by Matt Hern, New Society, 1995.
Collection of writings favoring cooperative education and unschooling.

### Deschooling Society
By Ivan Illich, 1971. Still in print at Marion Boyers Publishers Inc. of London
or 1489 Lincoln Ave., St Paul, MN 55105 USA
philosophy.la.psu.edu/illich/deschool/intro.html
A classic which preceded the homeschooling trend by many years. Many of
John Holt's ideas originated in conversations with Illich.

### Dumbing Us Down:
The Hidden Curriculum of Compulsory Schooling
By John Taylor Gatto, 1992.
New Society Publishers, Philadelphia PA.
Hard-hitting, thought-provoking essays that often topple fence-sitters to the
homeschooling side. After 26 years of award winning teaching, Gatto now
advocates for homeschooling and educational reform. See also *The
Exhausted School* and *The Underground History of American Education*.

### Family Matters: Why Homeschooling Makes Sense
By David Guterson, Harcourt Brace, 1993.
A thought-provoking discussion. This homeschooling dad and high school
English teacher makes his case for homeschooling.

### The Genius of Play
By Sally Jenkinson. Hawthorn Press.
This book discusses the value of play and advocates for protecting children's
playtime, especially during the early years.

### The Gift of Dyslexia
By Ronald D. Davis, Ability Workshop Press/1994.
Why some of the smartest people can't read and how they can learn. Also
available on cassettes.

### Guerrilla Learning:
How to Give Your Kids a Real Education With or Without School
By Grace Llewellyn and Amy Silver, 2001. John Wiley & Sons.
An argument for incorporating child-led learning practices into family life,
regardless of schooling approach. Many suggestions, some of which are sure
to stir a hornet's nest at your local school.

### Hard Times in Paradise: American Family's Struggle to Carve Out a Homestead in California's Redwood Mountains,
By David and Micki Colfax. 1992, Warner Books.
How can families possibly homeschool, never mind thrive, when times are
tough? The Colfaxes, well-known unschoolers, take a light approach as they
tell the story of their struggles, and how the kids learned, not only in spite of
struggles, but often because of them.

### Home Education: Training and educating children under nine
By Charlotte Mason. Originally published in England in 1935, and re-issued
in 1989 by Tyndale House Publishers, Inc., Wheaton, IL.
Mason was a nineteenth century educator who saw children as "thinking,
feeling human beings … and not as vessels to be filled."

### Home Schooling Children With Special Needs
By Sharon C. Hensley, M.A.
6291 Vegas Dr., San Jose, CA 97120     408/997.0290
Children with special needs often thrive in a home learning environment.
The book lists resources for autism, slow learner, learning disabilities, others.

### Homeschooling the Child with ADD (or Other Special Needs):
Your Complete Guide to Successfully Homeschooling the Child with
Learning Differences.
by Lenore Colacion Hayes, 2002. Prima Publishing.
Helpful resource for families who want to homeschool special-needs
children—children with challenges ranging from autism and ADD to other
learning disabilities.

### Human Brain, Human Learning
By Leslie Hart. Discusses the brain, theories on how the brain works, and
applies that knowledge to how children learn. An excellent read for scientific
reassurance that experiential learning works.

### In Their Own Way:
Discovering and Encouraging Your Child's Multiple Intelligences
By Thomas Armstrong, 2000. Tarcher/Putnam.
A popular book that describes seven different personal learning styles and
ways that parents can encourage learning.  Children often thrive when
allowed to learn in their own way.

### Learning All the Time
By John Holt.  Emphasizes Holt's philosophy that children will teach
themselves what they want and need to know.  Other books by Holt include:
*Instead of Education: Ways to Help People Do Things Better, Teach Your
Own; Shared Treasures, How Children Fail, How Children Learn, Freedom
and Beyond, Instead of Education, What Do I Do Monday?*  It is no secret that
I admire much of Holt's thinking.

### The Magical Child: Rediscovering Nature's Plan for Our Children
By Joseph Chilton Pearce. 1977.  E. P. Dutton.  A classic work on the nature
of children and how they learn and grow.

### The Myth of the A.D.D. Child
50 Ways to Improve Your Child's Behavior and Attention Span Without
Drugs, Labels, or Coercion.  By Thomas Armstrong, Dutton/1995
You'll discover that Armstrong's suggestions are highly compatible with a
homeschooling approach.

### The Public Family: The Ideas That Shaped Your Child's School
By Dan Johnson, 1997.
Charlotte House Publishers, PO Box 50147, Reno, NV 98513-0147
An unconventional look at John Dewey's influence on American schools.

### Scaffolding Children's Learning:
Vygotsky and Early Childhood Education
By Laura E. Berk and Adam Winsler, 1992.
National Association for the Education of Young Children, 1509 16th Street,
NW, Washington, DC, 20036-1426.
Focuses on early language development, upon which future learning stands.
Tired of your child's never-ending questions and answers?  This book will
remind you how important those questions are.

### Separating School and State
Sheldon Richman.  The Future of Freedom Foundation, 11340 Random Hills
Rd., Ste. 800, Fairfax, VA 22030
A provocative argument against government-funded schooling.

*Taking Charge Through Homeschooling:*
Personal and Political Empowerment
By Larry and Susan Kaseman
Koshkonong Press, 2545 Koshkonong Rd., Stoughton, WI 53589
The Kasemans are pioneer homeschoolers whose insight into the principles, politics, practice and legalities of homeschooling are thoughtful and well-grounded.

*The Twelve Year Sentence: Radical Views of Compulsory Schooling*
Edited by William F. Rickenbacker ©1974
Open Court Publishing Company.
A collection of essays on the problems of compulsory schooling that still ring true at the beginning of the twenty-first century. Includes a bibliography of related writings from the nineteenth century on. Out of print, but worth finding.

*The Underground History of American Education:*
A Schoolteacher's Intimate Investigation Into The Problem of Modern Schooling, By John Taylor Gatto, 2001.
The Odysseus Group, East 8th Street, Ste. 3W, NY, NY 10009
888/211.7164    fax: 212/529.35555    www.johntaylorgatto.com
Gatto digs far beyond the conventionally accepted history of schooling to expose what he sees as an out and out conspiracy to control the populace. Agree with him or not, you will be stunned by what you learn in this fascinating history.

*Your Child's Growing Mind:*
A Parent's Guide to Learning from Birth to Adolescence
By Jane M. Healy. A classic, based on research in brain development. Suggestions for parents to provide a better environment for learning.

# APPENDIX III
# CURRICULUM RESOURCES
*correspondence schools, programs, curriculum guides, catalogs*

This Appendix is divided into two lists. The first includes correspondence schools, packaged programs, and curriculum guides that can help you plan your own program. The second list is a sampling of educational materials catalogs that are of interest to many homeschooling families. Each resource is briefly described.

## SCHOOLS, PROGRAMS, AND GUIDES

### A Beka Book Publications
Box 19100, Pensacola, FL 32523-9160
877/223.5226  fax: 800/874.3590  www.abeka.com
A Scope and Sequence for ages 2-18 and a full range of Christian curriculum materials. Homeschool packages are available.

### Alger Learning Center Independence High School
121 Alder Dr., Sedro-Woolley, WA 98284    800/595.2630
fax: 360/595.1141  orion@nas.com  www.independent-learning.com
Private K-12. Assistance, curricula, assessments, transcripts, diplomas, credit analysis. Enroll any time.

### Alpha Omega
300 N. McKemy, Chandler, AZ 85226-2618
800/622.3070  www.aop.com
Biblically-based K-12 curriculum. The unit-study-based Weaver Curriculum is available here. Educational software. Free catalog.

### Alta Vista
1719 NE 50th St., Seattle, WA 98105
206/524.2262  fax: 206/524.1837
Integrated K-9 Christian curriculum. Free brochure.

### American School
2200 E. 170th St., Lansing, IL 60438
708/418.2800    800/531.9268  www.americanschoolofcorr.com
Traditional, accredited, long-established correspondence high school program.

### Bob Jones University Press
Dept. E-22, Greenville, SC 29609
800/845.5731  www.bjup.com
Textbooks and curriculum. Tests available. Christian.

### Books to Build On
By E. D. Hirsch. Core Knowledge Foundation
801 East High St., Charlottesville, VA 22902
434/977.7550 or 800/238.3233  www.coreknowledge.org/
Resource for a curriculum based on Core Curriculum. K-8.

### Calvert School
105 Tuscany Road, Baltimore, MD 21210    888/487.4652    fax:
410/366.0674  inquiry@calvertschool.org  www.calvertschool.org
A long established and accredited correspondence program. The program is
packaged, classical, and includes books, tests, materials and supplies. K-8.

### Cambridge Academy
3300 SW 34th Ave., Ste. 102, Ocala, FL 34474
800/252.3777    www.cambridgeacademy.com
Grades 6-12, accredited diploma, toll-free tutoring. Call for free video and
catalog.

### The Center for Talent Development
Northwestern University, 617 Dartmouth Place, Evanston, IL 60208
847/491.3782  fax: 847/467.4283    www.ctd.northwestern.edu/
Resources to help gifted students grade 4 and up reach their goals.

### Christian Liberty Academy Satellite Schools
502 W. Euclid Ave., Arlington Heights, IL 60004
800/348.0899  www.homeschools.org  custserv@homeschools.org
Complete curriculum for K, 1-8, 9-12.  Diploma.

### Christian Light Education
PO Box 1212, Harrisonburg, VA 22803-1212
540/433.8896    office@clp.org
K-12 Bible-based curriculum.  Record keeping, diploma, testing. Mennonite.

### Clonlara School Home Based Education Program
Pat Montgomery, Ph.D., Director, 1289 Jewett, Ann Arbor, MI 48104
734/769.4511  fax: 734/769.9629
info@clonlara.org    www.clonlara.org
Highly regarded accredited program, contact teacher, and a private school
diploma.  Clonlara works well with an individualized or unschooling
approach.

### Compuhigh
Stan Kanner, 515 Wilson Ave., Morgantown, WV 26501
866/983.8481 or 866/291.7040 (toll free numbers)
stan@compuhigh.com    www.compuhigh.com
The world's first online high school.  Students enrolled in Clonlara can take
these online courses as part of their program. Students desiring a single high
school class may also enroll, as may students who want course materials and
credits online.

### Covenant Home Curriculum
N63 W23421 Main St, Sussex, WI 53089
800/578.2421  educate@covenanthome.com  covenanthome.com
Reformed Evangelical curriculum; classical approach.  Teacher services.

### Distance Education and Training Council

1601 18th Street, NW, Washington, DC 20009   202/234.5100
fax: 202/332.1386     detc@detc.org   www.detc.org
One stop shopping for accredited schools. A clearinghouse of information about the distance study/correspondence field and sponsor of a nationally recognized accrediting commission for distance education.

### Home Study International

PO Box 4437, Silver Spring, MD 20914
301/680.6570    fax: 301/680.5157  www.hsi.edu
Correspondence courses through college. Accredited.  Christian education.

### Keystone National High School

420 West 5th Street, Bloomsburg, PA 17815
570/784.5520  800/255.4937  fax: 570/784.2129
info@keystonehighschool.com  www.keystonehighschool.com
Licensed and accredited.  Diploma, college entrance, financial aid is available.

### KONOS

PO Box 250, Anna, TX 75409
972/924.2712  fax: 972/924.2701  info@konos.com  www.konos.com
A unit studies program in which curriculum is built around character traits. Includes drill. Free catalog. Christian.

### Laurel Springs School

302 W. Ojai Ave., Ojai, CA 93023
800/377.5890    805/646.2473 info@laurelsprings.com
www.laurelsprings.com
Accredited private school with standard, web-based, honors, and special-needs curricula that can be individualized.

### Learning is Living Curriculum Guides

FUN Books, 1688 Belhaven Woods Ct., Pasadena, MD 21122-3727
Fax/Voice: 410/360.7330  410/360.7330    orders : 888/FUN-7020
FUN@FUN-Books.com www.FUN-Books.com/contact.htm
Nancy Plent's curriculum guides are based on school curriculum, including user-friendly suggestions for guiding your child; easy checklists for record-keeping. A useful reminder of all the learning that takes place during daily life. K-12.

### The Moore Academy

Box 1, Camas, WA 98607  206/835.2736 www.moorefoundation.com
Well-regarded curriculum and programs based on the philosophy of homeschooling pioneers Dorothy and Raymond Moore.

### Mother of Divine Grace School
Laura Berquist, PO Box 1440, Ojai, CA 93024
805/646.5818   fax: 805/646.0186   www.motherofdivinegrace.org
Roman Catholic homeschooling for K-12.  By the author of *Designing Your Own Classical Curriculum*, Laura Berquist.

### Nebel's Elementary Education: Creating a tapestry of learning
By Bernard J. Nebel.  www.pressforlearning.com/index.html
200+ hands-on activities are included in this elementary curriculum guide, activities that emphasize experiential learning while remaining academically rigorous.  You will better understand the learning processes of children as you read this book.

### Oak Meadow School
PO Box 740, Putney, VT 05346  802/387.2021  fax:  802/387.5108
oms@oakmeadow.com  www.oakmeadow.com
K-12.  A well known and highly praised curriculum based on the Waldorf philosophy.  Optional teacher support.  Diploma program.

### Rod and Staff Publishers, Inc.
PO Box 3, Hwy. 172, Crockett, KY 41413-0003
606/522.4348  fax: 800/643.1244   www.anabaptists.org/ras/
Bible-based curriculum from Mennonite publisher. Free catalog.

### Sonlight Curriculum, Ltd.
8024 South Grant Way, Littleton, CO 80122
303/730.6292  fax:  303/795.8668
sonlight@crsys.com  www.crsys.com/sonlight
Christian Pre-K-9 curriculum packages based on books and literature from which parents can readily build further learning experiences.

### TRISMS (Time Related Integrated Studies for Mastering Skills)
1203 S. Delaware Pl., Tulsa, OK 74104
918/585.2778   Linda@trisms.com   www.trisms.com/index.htm
A research based integrated curriculum for Junior and Senior High School. Christian world view.

### Thomson High School Program
Education Direct, PO Box 1900, Scranton, PA 18501
800/275.4410   www.educationdirect.com/
High school diploma by correspondence.  Accredited by Distance Education and Training Council.

### Typical Courses of Study, Kindergarten through Grade 12
World Book Educational Products
233 North Michigan Ave., Ste. 2000, Chicago, IL 60601
800/967.5325   fax: 312/729.5600
www2.worldbook.com/parents/course_study_index.asp
Nominal fee or free at the web site. An overview of school subjects by grade. Useful guide for the home educator.

### Waldorf Education and Curriculum Resource Guide
Rudolf Steiner College Bookstore, 9200 Fair Oaks Blvd., Fair Oaks, CA 95628  916/961.8729  fax: 916/961.3032  www.steinercollege.org/
A free publication, categorized by subject and grade level. Also online.

### The Westbridge Academy
1610 West Highland Ave. #228, Chicago, IL 60660
773/743.3312  www.westbridgeacademy.com
westbridge@safeplace.net
A college prep school for academically accelerated homeschoolers. Christian.

### West River Academy
779 Jasmine Court, Grand Junction, CO 81506   970/241.4137
WRAcademy@aol.com  www.geocities.com/wracademy
Independent private school. Families may choose unschooling or the learning approach of their choice. Grading of students is optional. K-12 Accredited by the National Association for the Legal Support of Alternative Schools. (NALSAS)

*Many state universities offer independent learning courses at both the high school and college levels. Contact your state university or try one of the programs below.*

### Indiana University
790 East Kirkwood Ave , Bloomington, IN 47405
800/334.1011   fax: 812/855.8680
Scs@indiana.edu   www.scs.indiana.edu
Independent study high school courses, online or conventional format. Diploma.  200 accredited university-level courses are available through independent study.

### University of Nebraska Independent Study High School
Div.  of Continuing Studies, UN-Lincoln, Rm. 269, Lincoln, NE 68583
402/472.4422  fax:  402/472.4450  unlishs2@unl.edu
A correspondence school that grants a recognized diploma.

### University of Wisconsin
Learning Innovations, 505 S.  Rosa Rd., Madison, WI 53719
608/265.9379  888/414.2534   fax:  608/265.9396
info@learn.uwsa.edu  learn.wisconsin.edu/contact
Six hundred independent learning courses for high school and beyond.

## INSTRUCTIONAL MATERIALS CATALOGS

*When you need materials but aren't quite sure what you are looking for, try armchair shopping! I've tried to list a mixed selection of traditional and special interest catalogs.*

### Beautiful Feet Books
Russ and Rea Berg, 139 Main St., Sandwich, MA 02563
508/833.8626  www.bfbooks.com
Literature approach to studies of many topics. Christian.

### Birch Court Books, Inc.
N7137 County Hwy. C, Seymour, WI 54165
800/655.1811  birchcourtbooks.com  birchcourtbooks@aol.com
Homeschooling materials selected to supplement or complete your individualized curriculum.  Free catalog.

### Book Links
PO Box 65, Mt. Morris, IL 61054      888/350.0950
www.ala.org/BookLinks      Sponsored by the American Library Association, this magazine is designed for adults interested in connecting children with high quality books.  Includes bibliographies, essays linking books on a similar theme, retrospective reviews, and other features targeted at those educating young people.

### Builder Books, Inc.
PO Box 5789, Lynnwood, WA 98046 info: 425/778.4526 order: 800/260.5461
books@televar.com   www.bbhomeschoolcatalog.com
A source for Usborne books and many other materials for all subjects.

### Childcraft Education Corporation
PO Box 3239, Lancaster, PA 17604
800/631.5652  fax: 888/532.4453    www.childcraft.com
Quality educational toys and materials for young children.  A source for hard to find child-sized real woodworking tools — gloves, goggles, saws, and hammers.

### Children's Books
PO Box 239, Greer, SC 29652
864/968.0391  orders only: 800/344.3198    fax: 864/968.0393
www.childsbooks.com
Free catalog.  Christian and secular reading materials as well as other resources.

## Child's Work/Child's Play

PO Box 760, Plainview. NY 11803   800/962.1141   fax: 800/262.1886
www.childswork.com
Games, books, and other products that can help you address the social and
emotional needs of children and teens.  Catalog.

## Discount School Supply

www.earlychildhood.com
Order art supplies, sensory learning materials, and other items for use with
young children.  Many free or sample activities are available at the website.

## Creative Learning Press, Inc.

PO Box 320, Mansfield Center, CT 06250
888/518.8004   860/429.8118 fax: 860/429.7783
clp@creativelearningpress.com   www.creativelearningpress.com
Many titles and subjects, including Marilyn Burns' math books. Free catalog.

## Dover Publications

Customer Care Department, 31 East Second St., Mineola, NY 11501
fax: 516/742.6953   store.doverpublications.com
Many subjects.  A vast selection of affordable activity books. coloring books,
paper doll books, much more.  Fifteen free special interest catalogs.

## The Education Connection

Jason and Lori Schall, PO Box 910367, St. George, UT 84791
800/863.3828 www.educationconnection.com
catalog@educationconnection.com
Books, games, and manipulatives. "Giving children freedom to learn."

## Family Unschoolers Network — FUN Books

FUN Books, 1688 Belhaven Woods Court, Pasadena, MD 21122
Fax/Voice mail: 410/360.7330  410/360.7330 orders: 888/FUN-7020
FUN@FUN-Books.com www.FUN-Books.com
Many items suggested in this book can be found in this catalog.  Print or
online catalog. Great stuff that will appeal to unschoolers and
not-so-unschoolers.

## Follett Educational Services

1433 Internationale Parkway, Woodridge, IL 60517
800/621.4272  fax: 800/ 638.4424  fes.follett.com
textbooks@fes.follett.com
The world's largest provider of pre-owned textbooks and instructional
materials. Free catalog.

## Electronic Text Center

University of Virginia Alderman Library
Box 400148, Charlottesville, VA 22904
434/924.3230   fax: 434/924.1431
etext@virginia.edu   etext.lib.virginia.edu
5,000 texts publicly available, including many for young readers.

### Essential Resources for Schools & Libraries
Counnaught Education Svs.
PO Box 34069 Dept. 349, Seattle, WA 98124
604/689.1568    fax: 604/689.1767
www.connaughted.com    jclark@connaughted.com
Subscription newsletter combines print and web listings of educational
resources and reviews. Five annual issues include 70+ free items.

### Free Spirit Publishing
217 Fifth Avenue North, Ste. 200, Minneapolis, MN 55401
612/338.2068    800/735.7323    fax: 612/337.5050
help4kids@freespirit.com   www.freespirit.com
Books for creative learning, parenting, self-help for kids, and more.

### Hands-On Learning Resource Center
885 Jones Road, Vestal, NY 13850
607/785.5517    888/20.LEARN
learn@handsonandbeyond.com    www.handsonandbeyond.com
Hands-on activities for teaching traditional subjects. *Bob Books.*

### Harvest Educational Products
96 Main St., Seymour, CT 06483
203/888.0427    fax: 203/888.0413   www.HarvestEd.com
Many educational products including wooden puzzles and games, McGuffey
readers, Charlotte Mason information. Traditional materials.

### Hayes School Publishing Co., Inc.
321 Pennwood Avenue, Pittsburgh, PA 15221
800/245.6234    800/543.8771
www.hayespub.com    info@hayespub.com
Conventional workbooks, posters, and masters. Free catalog.

### Hearthsong
Processing Center, PO Box 1050, Madison, VA 22727
order: 800/325.2502    fax: 800/638.5102    service: 800/533.4397
www.hearthsong.com
Waldorf style games, playthings, quality craft kits. Natural materials.

### Home Again
4208 NE 107th St., Seattle, WA 98125    206/361.2677    888/666.0721
fax: 206/417.9710    www.home-again.com
Educational supplies, including games, handwork, literature, quality art
materials, somewhat reflective of the Waldorf approach.   Free catalog.

### Lakeshore Learning Store
2695 E. Domingez St., Carson, CA 90810
800/421.5354   fax: 310/537.5403   www.lakeshorelearning.com
Traditional school-type catalog, with many manipulative materials.

## Michael Olaf's Montessori Company
65 Ericson Court, #1, Arcata, CA 95521
888/880.9235   Fax: 800/427.8877   www.michaelolaf.net
Catalog includes an overview of the Montessori approach and 100 pages of materials, books, games, musical instruments, and more that are highly effective in a home learning environment.

## Milliken Publishing Company
11643 Lilburn Park Road, St. Louis, MO 63146
314/991.4220   800/325.4136 fax: 314/991.4807   www.millikenpub.com
Complete line of supplementary workbooks, wall charts, and much more.

## NASCO
PO Box 3837, Modesto, CA 95352-3837    fax: 209/545.1669
PO Box 901, Fort Atkinson, WI 53538-0901    fax: 920/563.8296
Order: 800/558.9595 fax: 920/563.8296
www.eNASCO.com   Custserv@eNASCO.com
Specialty education catalogs, including arts & crafts, farm and ranch, health education, To-Sew kits, and more.

## The Sycamore Tree
Sandy Gogel, 2179 Meyer Place, Costa Mesa, CA 92627
949/650.4466   800/779.6750   fax: 949/650.3647
www.sycamoretree.com
Complete Christian curricula. Books, science kits, arts and crafts kits. K-12.

## The Teaching Company
4151 Lafayette Center Drive, Ste. 100, Chantilly, VA 20151
800/832.2412    fax: 703/378.3819   www.teach.com
custserv@teachco.com  High quality audio and video lecture series and courses for high school students and adult education.

## Timberdoodle Company
E. 1510 Spencer Lake Road, Shelton, WA 98584
360/426.0672   fax: 800/478.0672
mailbag@timberdoodle.com  www.timberdoodle.com
Carefully selected items, emphasizing science and math. Christian.

# Index